FAMILIES IN CRISIS IN THE OLD SOUTH

Families in Crisis in the Old South

DIVORCE, SLAVERY, AND THE LAW

LOREN SCHWENINGER

THE UNIVERSITY OF
NORTH CAROLINA PRESS
Chapel Hill

This book was published with the assistance of the
Fred W. Morrison Fund for Southern Studies of the
University of North Carolina Press.

© 2012 The University of North Carolina Press
All rights reserved
Set in Arnhem and The Serif types
by Tseng Information Systems, Inc.

Manufactured in the United States of America

The paper in this book meets the guidelines for permanence
and durability of the Committee on Production Guidelines
for Book Longevity of the Council on Library Resources.

The University of North Carolina Press has been a member of
the Green Press Initiative since 2003.

Library of Congress Cataloging-in-Publication Data
Schweninger, Loren.
Families in crisis in the Old South : divorce, slavery, and the
law / by Loren Schweninger.
p. cm.
Includes bibliographical references and index.
ISBN 978-0-8078-3569-2 (cloth : alk. paper)
ISBN 978-1-4696-1911-8 (pbk. : alk. paper)
1. Domestic relations—United States. 2. Divorce—Law and
legislation—United States. 3. Slavery—Law and legislation—
United States. 4. Adultery—United States. 5. Wife abuse—
United States. I. Title.
KF505.S39 2012
306.890975′09034—dc23

                                         2012002040

cloth 16 15 14 13 12 5 4 3 2 1
paper 18 17 16 15 14 5 4 3 2 1

THIS BOOK WAS DIGITALLY PRINTED.

*For Guion Griffis Johnson
and
Helen Tunnicliff Catterall
Pioneer Scholars*

CONTENTS

Preface / ix

1 The Evolution of Divorce Laws / 1

2 Adultery and the Question of Race / 17

3 Insanity, Alcoholism, Abandonment, and Abuse / 32

4 Lawyers, Judges, Juries, and Decrees / 58

5 Married Women and Property / 80

6 Slaves and Owners' Domestic Conflicts / 98

Conclusion / 115

An Essay on Sources and Methodology / 119

Appendix 1 / 127

Appendix 2 / 131

Notes / 151

Bibliography / 205

Index / 229

ILLUSTRATIONS AND TABLES

Illustrations

Barren County chancery court order / 7
Tennessee statutes, 1840–1846 / 10
Court order for alimony for Sarah H. Black / 30
Talladega County Courthouse, Alabama / 34
Evelina Roane / 49
Bill in chancery of Sarah Duncan / 60
Perquimans County Courthouse, North Carolina / 95
African American nanny and her white charge / 113

Tables

1. Jurisdictions: Divorce and Separation, Southern States, 1790–1853 / 12
2. Husbands Accused of Adultery, with Sexual Partner Identified by Race and Status / 29
3. Husbands Accused of Domestic Violence / 53
4. Legislative Divorce in Maryland, Virginia, and Tennessee / 74
5. White Women in Slaveholding Families / 91
6. Average Prices of Prime Field Hands / 125
7. Complaints and Decrees in Chancery, or Equity, Court, 1779–1867 / 127
8. Decrees and Slave Ownership among Plaintiffs' Families, 1779–1867 / 129
Appendix 2. Petitioners to General Assemblies and to Chancery, or Equity, Courts, 1779–1867 / 131

PREFACE

Given current attitudes toward marriage and divorce, it is difficult from today's perspective to understand the critical societal role of marriage and the importance people attached to the family two centuries ago. Unfortunately, for the time period of this study, between the 1780s and the 1860s, there are no precise statistics for marriage and divorce in the United States, but Michael Grossberg's estimate that about 90 percent of all men and women in the country during the nineteenth century married at one time or another is probably correct. In the southern states, there is little doubt that the vast majority of the white population lived in husband-wife-children-kin households.[1]

With most of the population engaged in labor-intensive farm work, children were needed not only to assist in the fields but also to ensure the continuity of the family patrimony. In addition, ministers, politicians, jurists, authors, businessmen, elected officials, and local leaders heralded the family as the centerpiece of democracy, "the cradle of morality," and a "nursery of patriotism." In 1833, a North Carolina lawmaker declared that social relationships among family members constituted the cement that held the country together. "Indeed," he asserted, "what else is it but the social ties of family connections, when rendered happy and prosperous by their own industry that stamps a value upon society." In a similar vein, an Alabama chancery judge prefaced an 1848 decree with his belief that "the source and fountain of all social virtue is in the family union." Marriage made up "the great community of mankind," provided the bedrock for all "earthly ties," and created a "great chain that binds society together in harmony, peace, and happiness."[2]

Divorce, on the other hand, was viewed as a form of "madness," bringing disgrace and dishonor upon a couple and depriving children "of the greatest earthly advantage, the nurture and admonitions of a parent." One member of the legislature of the Territory of Orleans asserted that divorce reduced communities to the "lowest ebb of degeneracy." It undermined fundamental societal principles, violated "all the original institutions of nature," and should not be tolerated, even under the worst of circumstances. In a volume titled *Marriage Indissoluble and Divorce Unscriptural*, a Virginia Presbyterian minister added that God made Adam and Eve of one flesh and husbands and wives should remain together until death.[3]

Closely related to the idea that marriages should endure forever and that divorce was an anathema was the strong belief, found in custom and in the law, that a husband was the head of the household and his wife was *sub potestate viri*, or "under the power of her husband," whereby her legal existence was suspended when she entered the state of matrimony. The ideals of southern male honor and manhood, so often cited in the historical literature, were connected in the minds of contemporaries to the all-important concept of patriarchy. A South Carolina judge explained that "looking to the peace and happiness of families and to the best interests of society," the husband and father should serve as a benevolent sovereign, ruling his domestic realm in a mild and considerate but firm manner. Although changes occurred over time and there were differences across various households, the patriarchal structure of southern society remained strong throughout the period, among both slaveholders and nonslaveholders.[4]

Despite these attitudes and pronouncements, the number of southerners seeking to end their marriages rose steadily during the antebellum era. In the early period (1786–1829), increasing numbers petitioned their general assemblies, and during the late period (1830–67), even greater numbers, certainly in the thousands, brought their "causes," as civil suits were called, to the chancery, or equity, courts. Of course, many couples lived apart without filing formal papers, as husbands or wives abandoned their families, or spouses separated by mutual consent. This was especially true of people at the bottom of the economic spectrum who often could not afford to hire a lawyer or, perhaps distrustful of the legal system, did not wish to submit grievances to assemblies or the courts. Historians have correctly pointed out that "self-divorce" and remarriage, or bigamy, was probably one of the least prosecuted and most common crimes of the period.[5]

Neither societal taboos against broken marriages nor the unwillingness of many people to expose themselves financially or legally to the process of dissolving their unions diminishes the importance of studying divorce in the Old South. As this study will demonstrate, the decision to seek legal dissolution of one's marriage could not be made lightly; the law required that it be supported by persuasive arguments of domestic turmoil and proven by verifiable charges of violation of the marital bonds, a process that entailed a thorough and unsparing look into the domestic lives of those suing for divorce. It was an adversarial process that made it necessary to uncover the intimacy of family life and to draw in all members of the household, free and enslaved alike, in order to obtain the desired outcome. It demanded of those who decided to go forward not only that they overcome their reluctance to initiate action but that they withhold no details in prosecuting it. As a consequence, divorce offers a penetrating view of one crucial aspect of society in the Old South: families in crisis.

This study examines, analyzes, and summarizes the wealth of information about the domestic life of families in crisis found in a small but representative group of divorce, separation, and alimony cases, drawn from every southern state and most geographic regions within each state and from virtually every year during the first six decades of the nineteenth century (see Appendix 2). The collection includes cases presented by 610 white women, 123 white men, and 35 free persons of color from a total of 211 counties in the 15 slave states and the District of Columbia. In one way or another, all of the cases are connected with race and slavery. In fact, many of the cases were filed by women of the slaveholding class. Not only did these women have the financial wherewithal to hire lawyers and prosecute suits more readily than those with less means, but as members of the most prosperous group in the region, they had the most to lose if their families split apart.

In various chapters and Appendix 1, tables have been created from the selected cases. The tables answer several important questions: What laws did the southern states pass concerning divorce and separation before the Civil War, and how did they change over time? What proportion of white women who filed for divorce charged their husbands with adultery and/or domestic violence? How do the outcomes of cases submitted to general assemblies compare with those submitted to the equity, or chancery, courts? And what was the profile of wealth and slave ownership among these families?

Although there is no book-length study focusing on divorce and separation in the region, historians have touched upon the subject from a variety of perspectives: local, state, regional, and interdisciplinary as well as social, legal, economic, familial, and political history. During the 1980s and 1990s, historians analyzed a wide range of subjects relating to divorce in the United States: They compared legal codes in the different states and examined the transfer of legal authority from state legislatures to chancery courts and the advancement of married women's property rights. Pioneer legal and women's historian Jane Turner Censer, in her seminal article "'Smiling through Her Tears': Ante-bellum Southern Women and Divorce," for example, analyzed 169 cases of divorce, alimony, property, and custody that were appealed to the higher courts in the southern states, examining state laws, the grounds for divorce, and the ability of women to file suits.[6]

From the mid-1990s through the first decade of the twenty-first century, historians ventured into new frontiers and examined, in particular, the impact of the law during various periods. They argue that the law had its own distinctive institutions, language, ideology, and rituals, but that it also helped fashion and shape the values, attitudes, and mores of society. They emphasize that the law contained its own rules and customs and that legal proceedings do not necessarily provide a window into social relations, but if used carefully, with attention to the ways that legal rules and conventions shaped various issues, legal sources, including chancery court proceedings, can offer insights into various aspects of nineteenth-century households.[7]

Besides this broad interpretation of the importance of the law in American society, other historians have delved into local court records to advance new and far-reaching interpretations of the social order. Examining civil suits and criminal cases involving slaves in Adams County, Mississippi, Ariela J. Gross argues that it was difficult to silence slaves, even though they could not testify in court. She wrote about the ways "slaves' agency" infused itself into the courtroom and brought the masters' honor into question "when the words of slaves were repeated." In her prodigious study of six counties in North and South Carolina, Laura F. Edwards also broke new ground in analyzing three concepts that had generally escaped the attention of historians in their analysis of the South during the Early Republic: "localized laws," "keeping the peace," and "credit." "Localized laws" referred to ideas, customs, and practices that guided the determination of justice; "keeping the peace" referred to the set of values, attitudes, and mores considered tolerable by the community to ensure order and stability; and "credit" referred to the importance accorded character, reputation, and personality in determining the fate of those caught up in the legal system.[8]

There is also a significant literature about white women spanning the seventeenth and eighteenth centuries, overlapping with the early years of this study. Several of these studies argue that the women of that earlier era were better positioned legally than women in the nineteenth century. They note that treatises describing the common law did not represent actual situations in households. A husband and wife did not represent one person in law; her legal existence was not suspended by her husband during marriage, "under whose wing, protection, and *cover*" she performed everything. In Virginia, for example, married women went in and out of the courts, entered business partnerships with their husbands, possessed their own personal property, and if mistreated by their husbands could obtain "an action of the peace," requiring the posting of a bond. They experienced some constraints, such as not being allowed to sell property without their husbands' permission, but wives "enjoyed relative freedom from rules limiting their legal capacity, at least compared with the nineteenth century."[9]

The following chapters build on the insights of these and other historians, especially those dealing with race, class, property, and slavery in the Old South. Despite the large literature on questions surrounding this study, the pages that follow offer a different view on several issues raised by historians. In contrast to common-law courts, which relied on legal precedent, the chancery, or equity, courts examined here were bound by statute law. Even during the early period (1786–1829), the chancery, or equity, courts were less concerned about the reputations of persons involved than applying the legal codes to the arguments advanced by plaintiffs and defendants. At the same time, the suggestion in some studies that white women were virtually powerless before the bench does not match the results in these proceedings, as women secured lawyers; filed suits, sometimes without *prochein ami*, or a "next friend"; and won a significant portion of their contests. After their divorce, a number of white women became independent property owners and protected their holdings by becoming *feme sole*, or single women.

An examination of other aspects of these households in crisis suggests several other new perspectives: Most slave owners accused of adultery did not have sexual relations with slaves they owned but with white women, the relationships between slaveholding mistresses and slave women could be a contested ground where the balance of power sometimes shifted to the enslaved, and slave owners candidly expressed views that suggest they primarily considered those held in bondage first and foremost as human property.

Each chapter begins with the first part of a narrative taken from a single case. It describes the family's domestic and economic situation and provides in some detail the charges made by the complainant. The chosen cases are those of Harriet Laspeyre of North Carolina, Sarah Black of Texas, Lydia Rawdon of Alabama, Sarah Duncan of Missouri, Louisiana Banks of Tennessee, and Eliza Ransom of South Carolina. Each chapter concludes with the second half of the same family narrative; it provides the case outcome, when available, and follows the domestic and economic situation of the complainant and members of her family in subsequent years. The purpose of these family histories is to highlight the personal background of those involved in the case, information that would otherwise be lost in analysis. The six selected narratives offer stories that are replicated many

Preface | xiii

times over in the cases under study, with variations on the same themes regarding how and why families broke apart.

Various chapters then examine the evolution of state laws; how, when and why complainants decided to file for divorce, separation, or alimony; how successful their suits were in the general assemblies and in the superior, district, and circuit courts, where the equity, or chancery, causes were adjudicated; and the socioeconomic distribution of complainants across the spectrum of southern society. Were most of the complainants male or female? Were they mostly small farmers with only a few slaves or members of the planter class? How often did nonslaveholders seek to end their marriages because of interracial sexual relations? How did the laws work in practice, and how did those who sought to end their marriages fare in the legal system? Lastly, how often did slaves become involved, and when they did, what part did they play and what was the impact on their lives?

The marital problems uncovered in the cases of this study are universal—infidelity, excessive use of alcohol, abandonment, and domestic violence—but they are of particular interest to the study of southern antebellum society because, at that particular time and place, they could not be separated from the reality of life in a slave society: the vulnerability of black women to the advances of white men, the reach of race and slavery issues into the marital conflicts of nonslaveholding families, and the precarious position of slave families drawn into the marital discord within white families and their struggles to protect themselves from the consequences. In fact, in every section of the South, racial issues often lurked under the surface or rose to become the primary cause of divorce or separation.

In many respects this analysis is a dreary tale, bringing to light the hidden anger and hostility within many white families and the fears and anxieties within many black families. Viewing the underside of the South's peculiar institution from this vantage point, although dark and sad, is also illuminating. It can be fairly assumed that there were others who similarly violated their marital vows but did not petition assemblies or file equity court papers seeking to rectify their situations. Indeed, the infidelity, abuse, family breakups and social disruption that became public in divorce and alimony conflicts mirrored what occurred in many other families who chose to keep their personal lives out of the public eye or did not have the financial ability to seek legal redress.

The genesis of this book occurred in August 1991, in Hinesville, Georgia, at the Liberty County courthouse, where the author, at the beginning of the Race and Slavery Petitions Project, came across an eight- or tenpage petition for divorce by a slaveholder who told about his marriage and marital woes in remarkable detail. That petition never made it into the project's collection, but after leaving Hinesville the author decided to include similar chancery cases because of their unique richness as historical records. Over the years, several research assistants, including Kellie Wilson Buford and my son Michael Ivan Schweninger, compiled data from the U.S. census returns and investigated various state laws on the subject. The project's assistant editor for seven years, Nicole Mazgaj, provided information about the unique laws in Louisiana and read two drafts of the manuscript, offering many insightful and useful suggestions. The project's associate editor for eleven years, Marguerite Howell, went through the final draft of the manuscript with an unfailing eye for redundancy, omissions, and inconsistencies. Various aspects of the issues examined in this study were given in the form of papers and presentations during a Fulbright Fellowship at the University of Uppsala, Sweden, in 2007, including lectures at the University of Oslo, Norway; the Renvall Institute of North American Studies, School of Law, University of Helsinki, Finland; and the University of Uppsala. In 2008, antebellum divorce was the subject of the author's presidential address to the Historical Society of North Carolina, published in 2009 in the *North Carolina History Review* as "'To the Honorable': Divorce, Alimony, Slavery, and the Law in Antebellum North Carolina." The questions from audiences and fellow scholars on these occasions were most helpful. Especially beneficial were the detailed and lengthy critiques provided by Victoria Bynum and Bertram Wyatt-Brown and an anonymous reviewer for the University of North Carolina Press.

FAMILIES IN CRISIS IN THE OLD SOUTH

THE EVOLUTION OF DIVORCE LAWS

1

A week before Christmas in 1816, Harriet Laspeyre, the daughter of a prominent political and slaveholding family, submitted a petition to the North Carolina General Assembly. She asked for a separation of bed and board from her husband, Bernard Laspeyre, a French-born émigré from the island of Hispaniola, and requested that she be able to retain what remained of the property she had brought to their marriage and any property she might acquire in the future. She claimed that she lived in "hourly expectation of violence to her person" and feared for her life. Her husband was profane, vulgar, menacing, and tyrannical; the only reason he had married her was to secure her property, including twenty-odd slaves, and despite a prenuptial agreement, he forced her to sell several black people and ordered those who remained to ignore her instructions. Not only was she "divested of her keys" and "stripped of the right that every woman claims" to managing her slave property, but her husband had eventually taken most of the slaves and moved into the town of Wilmington, where he lived "in open adultery with a negro wench" and permitted her "to exercise all the rights and authorities of a Wife."[1]

In both substance and style, Harriet Laspeyre's plea for separation was similar to many others presented to general assemblies and, in subsequent years, to chancery, or equity, courts of the southern states during the late eighteenth century and the first six decades of the nineteenth century. Her case offers insight into the various issues confronted by southern women and men who sought to end their marriages as well as the laws pertaining to marriage, divorce, alimony, and women's property. Over those decades, not only did the venue where petitioners could seek redress change, but the grounds for obtaining a remedy greatly expanded. By the last few decades before the Civil War, most pleas were no longer submitted to state legislatures but to the equity, or chancery, courts, where plaintiffs, defendants, lawyers, and witnesses offered arguments and testimonials, and judges and sometimes juries issued decrees and verdicts. Why and how this occurred is the subject of what follows.

■ During the colonial era most American colonies did not grant absolute divorce, meaning divorce with the right to remarry. Only Massachusetts and Connecticut enacted statutes providing for divorce in instances of adultery or extreme cruelty by the husband, or instances of adultery by the wife. The Puritans believed that marriage was a civil matter and should be treated in the same manner as other civil contracts. The Massachusetts General Court decided on a number of divorce cases during the eighteenth century in which women and men complained to the court about "marital travesties," including "desertion, adultery, or neglect." These were brought to the court as civil matters, and there was no lack of enthusiasm on the part of neighbors, lodgers, servants, hired laborers, nurses, and relatives to testify about them on moral and religious grounds. "I ought not to Suffer Sin in My Fellow Creature or Neighbor," Nathan Haskell said after observing an adulterous affair. Breaches in the marriage contract, he believed, were also sins against God and reprehensible.[2]

Although absolute divorce was rarely granted, separation of bed and board was available. This could be accomplished through the chancery courts, where a judge would decide the case on fairness and justice. If separation was granted, neither spouse could remarry. Women had greater incentives than men to separate themselves from untenable marital situations largely because of economic issues. With property in the hands of the men, women sought to protect themselves and their children from the financial consequences of living with abusive, unfaithful, and sometimes profligate husbands. The early cases, like those in later years, were adversarial, with each spouse presenting arguments through their solicitor. In 1707, Maryland resident Margaret Macnamarra, for example, filed suit in the equity court for separation. She complained that her husband threatened her life and that she lived in constant fear. The husband countered by arguing that the chancery court did not have jurisdiction in such personal matters. In England, he contended, ecclesiastical courts made such decisions, and there were no church courts in the colonies. But the Maryland court ruled in Margaret's favor; nothing "in the present Constitution of this province" prohibited a court from deciding on a separation of bed and board, the chancellor, or judge in the case, explained. He ordered the husband to provide Margaret with clothing, personal items, and maintenance of 15 pounds per year.[3]

The argument put forth by Margaret Macnamarra's husband concerning the courts of the mother country, however, was valid. In England, the ecclesiastical courts, run by a chancellor appointed by a bishop, decided marital disputes. English common law, the body of law derived from judicial decisions rather than from statutes and constitutions, did allow divorce *a mensa et thoro* (from bed and board) for adultery or cruelty, and it did permit that alimony be awarded to the wife, but only if the case was presented to a "spiritual court." Absolute divorce, however, was almost never granted in England. "For the canon law, which the common law follows in this case," William Blackstone explained in his famous *Commentaries on the Laws of England (1765–1769)*, "deems so highly and with such mysterious reverence of the nuptial tie, that it will not allow it to be unloosed for any cause whatsoever, that arises after the union is made." In short, absolute divorce could be granted only in such cases where the marriage was invalid at its inception: if a husband or wife was already married, insane at the time of the marriage, or under the age of twelve for girls and fourteen for boys; if the marriage of a minor was made without the consent of a parent or guardian; if the partners were related by blood or by marriage; or if one of them possessed "particular corporal infirmities [impotency]." Barring these conditions, the only way to secure an absolute divorce with the right to remarry in England was to petition the parliament for a special act, a costly and time-consuming undertaking open only to the very rich.[4]

But, as legal historians have pointed out, Blackstone's treatise describing the English common law did not fit the conditions in colonial America. Common-law courts, with their slow and complicated process, strict rules of evidence, and failure to provide satisfactory remedies, proved to be inadequate, especially with regard to resolving marital conflicts. As a consequence, chancery, or equity, courts evolved in most colonies to deal with these problems. Chancellors did not act "to destroy the law but to fulfill it," one observer said, seeking to right wrongs for which no common-law remedy existed. The equity courts permitted petitioners to initiate an action by a "bill of complaint" rather than an original writ, issued subpoenas requiring appearance in court, and could attach property if necessary.[5]

However, laws created by the colonial assemblies were not uniform across the colonies; those passed in the southern colonies differed from those passed in New England and the middle colonies. In Virginia, for example, the common-law right of a widow to a life estate in one-third of her late husband's real property and a portion of his chattels, called the right of dower, differed from that of a widow in the colonies to the north. A husband in Virginia was prohibited from transferring or conveying any real property owned during a marriage. He was required to obtain his wife's permission to sell any land, and the wife's permission could not be coerced; she had to testify to that fact before a magistrate. Such practices as were found in Virginia were also found with far greater frequency in the southern colonies than in the middle colonies or New England. In addition, the strong aversion to allowing absolute divorce in Virginia and Maryland gave equity courts the authority to enforce separate maintenance agreements unavailable under common law. In such agreements, a husband and wife were no longer considered as a single person in law; the wife's existence, which had until then been one with that of her husband, "under whose wing, protection, and *cover*" she performed everything, was restored. Such authority was not conferred on equity courts in the North. Southern states established equity courts, whereas New England shunned them, "giving only piecemeal equitable authority to common law courts." A Boston visitor to Williamsburg, Virginia's capital, in 1773 was stunned when he learned that judges of the superior court constituted a court of equity (sitting without a jury), "very frequently" reversing decisions of the "Court of Law," the name given to the common-law court.[6]

Despite the development of chancery courts in the colonial period, during and following the American Revolution delegates at the first state constitutional conventions as well as lawmakers at the first state assemblies in the southern states remained silent on the question of divorce. It appears that the common-law tradition regarding absolute divorce continued to hold sway among most state leaders throughout the new Republic. As a consequence, those seeking to dissolve their marriages were forced to petition general assemblies for private acts. Only South Carolina rejected such pleas and subsequently neither amended its constitution nor passed any law on the subject, becoming the only state in the union that refused to permit divorce under any circumstances. South Carolina did, however, permit married women, by a "next friend," to sue for alimony in the equity courts and did uphold pre- or postmarital contracts. Many of these suits contained accusations similar to those presented in other states for divorce or separation.[7]

Most wives and husbands who approached southern legislatures during the late eighteenth and early nineteenth centuries charged their spouses with serious breaches of the marriage contract. Wives accused husbands of adultery and extreme violence; husbands accused wives of infidelity and giving birth to mixed-race children. As early as 1786, the General Assembly of Delaware passed a private act granting a divorce; in subsequent years, Maryland, North Carolina, and Virginia passed similar acts granting divorce and/or separation. The lawmakers also passed special acts to protect property that separating women might accumulate in the future, by purchase or otherwise.[8]

After a relatively slow beginning during the 1790s and the first few years of the nineteenth century, the number of divorce and separation petitions to state assemblies sharply increased. The difficulties legislators faced in dealing with domestic problems were obvious: How could they determine if the petitioner was telling the truth? How much time and effort should be spent trying to sort through the charges presented by one spouse? Lawmakers complained that they were at times inundated with these requests. In Maryland, between 1805 and 1815, the Assembly not only received substantial numbers of requests but often debated each private bill. A near-majority of the acts passed only after a discussion of each bill and a roll call. In Maryland as well as other states, including Virginia, North Carolina, and Tennessee, lawmakers considered various plans to streamline the process or turn over part of the responsibility to the judiciary, but they failed to pass any meaningful reforms. In 1808, North Carolina assemblymen debated a proposal to improve the process, but the opposition from ministers and religious leaders silenced the debate. Any proposal that might encourage separation, the ministers argued, would "loosen the bands of Society and turn mankind upon each other like brutes."[9]

Most of the proposals during these debates concerned the role of the judiciary. But even after the chancery courts were given some jurisdiction over the process during the 1810s and 1820s—submitting trial transcripts or summaries of arguments—members of legislative committees still objected to the amount of time they spent discussing the accusations. It did not matter whether the evidence was strong in one direction or the other, the members said, the discussions inevitably drew on their time and took attention away from important public issues, including internal improvements, taxation, crime, judicial and political reform, education, control of slaves, regulation of free blacks, patrols, militias, and various other civic, economic, and political problems facing the states. In the preamble of "AN ACT to alter and amend the ninth section of the third article of the constitution of the state of Georgia," members of the General Assembly noted that the discussions required by the "frequent, numerous and repeated applications" for divorce were a "great annoyance." Evaluating each application and publishing the results were not only time-consuming but expensive.[10]

■ As time passed, there was a growing sentiment that the legislative branch was not the place to settle marital disputes. With the western expansion and creation of new states, many politicians believed that the judiciary should either share or become the sole arbitrator of divorce applications. In general the states along the east coast, the original colonies, remained more resistant to change than the newer states in the West and Southwest. In 1799, Tennessee enacted the first state divorce law in the South. It cited impotence, bigamy, desertion for at least two years, and adultery as the four permissible causes and granted the superior chancery courts the authority to decide each case. The law stated that the husband, "in his own proper person," or the wife, by her next friend, could present a bill of complaint to the chancery court after affirming before a judge or a justice of the peace that to the best of his or her knowledge and belief the charges were not made "out of levity, or by collusion between husband and wife, and for the mere purpose of being freed and separated from each other." Despite this law, wives and husbands continued to petition the General Assembly to end their marriages.[11]

In subsequent years, other southern states enacted similar statutes. In 1809, Kentucky passed a two-page, eight-section, "ACT regulating Divorces," citing the same causes as did Tennessee but adding abandonment by a wife for three years or a husband for two years, and a felony conviction. In 1814, North Carolina lawmakers, after several unsuccessful attempts, passed a statute turning initial jurisdiction over to the superior courts and requiring a trial by jury. In 1827, Virginia passed a similar law turning over jurisdiction in the initial stages of the process to the superior chancery courts. The acceptable causes for divorce *a mensa et thoro* stipulated by the law were the same as in Tennessee but also included extreme cruelty and fear of bodily harm. The court could grant alimony to the wife without a contract for separation if the husband had forced the wife to flee from their home or threatened her life.[12]

During the 1820s and 1830s, a number of states passed laws citing many of the same reasons as grounds for divorce and/or separation found in early Tennessee. The statutes also outlined how the cases should proceed through the chancery courts. Following the filing of a bill of complaint, the court would issue subpoenas requiring the defendant to appear; if the defendant could not be found, a proclamation should be made publicly by the sheriff during the court term, and if necessary, the proclamation should be published in an area newspaper for a number of weeks. Then, if the defendant still failed to appear, the case could be brought *ex parte*, that is, without arguments from the other side. If the defendant appeared and

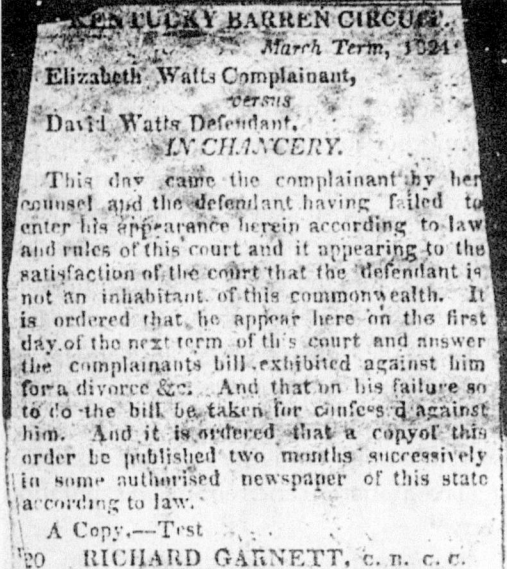

Barren County chancery court order. Typical of many similar notices, this Barren County chancery court order appeared in the Green River Correspondent of Bowling Green, Kentucky, over a period of two months during the spring of 1824, following a divorce suit brought by Elizabeth Watts. (Clipping from Green River Correspondent, ca. April and May 1824, in Records of the Circuit Court of Barren County, Equity Judgments, Betsy Watts v. David Watts, Case #245, KDLA.)

answered the complaint, in at least six states—Virginia, North Carolina, Georgia, Tennessee, Louisiana, and Texas—either or both parties could request a trial by jury. Both parties were required to provide evidence in addition to their own testimony. If the divorce was granted, the parties could remarry, but in some states only if the plaintiff had not committed adultery or admitted the defendant "into conjugal society and embraces after he or she knew of the criminal fact."

In addition, laws permitted a wife to seek separation from bed and board if her husband had abandoned her, forced her out of their home, treated her in a "cruel or barbarous" manner, or committed "such indignities to her person as to render her condition intolerable." In cases of separation of bed and board, the wife could request alimony consisting of a portion of her husband's estate, as her husband's circumstances allowed but not exceeding one-third of his annual profit or income. Although these procedures, including residency requirements and custody conditions, differed slightly among the different states, during this transition period the courts uniformly acquired increasing authority in determining questions of divorce, separation, and alimony. Even so, residents continued to file their requests with general assemblies.[13]

As with various other aspects of its history, Louisiana was unique among the early southern states with regard to its legal traditions, which were the result of a mixture of Roman law, the Spanish *Las Siete Partidas* (*The Seven-Part Code*), and the French legal system. In an attempt to organize the territory's laws into a coherent code, the *Digest of 1808* included six chapters on the separation of bed and board, forming a statute that would remain in effect in one form or another for many years. The causes for separation included adultery by the wife or by the husband when he kept his concubine in their common dwelling, cruel treatment that rendered living together impossible, public defamation, abandonment, and any attempt on the life of a spouse. The suits were to be tried before competent courts of justice. During the proceedings, the children would be entrusted to the husband, the judge would assign the wife a dwelling place and establish maintenance, the wife could demand an inventory of property, and the husband was prohibited from disposing of the immovable property or slaves. Although it did not dissolve the bond of matrimony, separation of bed and board ended the conjugal combination and required a separation of the couple's goods and property.[14]

Although divorce *a vinculo matrimonii* (absolute divorce "from the chains of marriage") was initially left in the hands of the General Assembly, this changed with the publication of the 1825 *Civil Code of Louisiana*, which repealed foreign laws that were in force at the time of cession. The *Civil Code* dealt with a host of personal matters, including the fact that divorce and/or separation from bed and board could only be obtained by civil suits in the district courts. In 1827, Louisiana passed a detailed divorce law that included, among other permissible causes, abandonment for five years, habitual intemperance, excessively cruel treatment, ignominious punishments, and felony convictions. Thus, Louisiana became the only state in the South to permit separation for defamation of character, to allow concubines to live in another dwelling, and to require a separation of property. In many ways, especially with regard to property, Louisiana provided practical and equitable solutions to couples seeking to dissolve their marriages.[15]

By the time Louisiana passed its 1827 divorce law, there was growing sentiment in many southern states that divorce and separation should be completely under the purview of the judiciary. In the same year that the Louisiana law was passed, North Carolina enacted a statute designating the superior courts as the final arbiters in such cases. In 1832, the Delaware Assembly also passed a divorce law giving the superior courts sole cognizance for granting divorces in cases of bigamy, abandonment (for three years), impotency, extreme cruelty, and adultery. The courts could also grant decrees for separation of bed and board when the evidence justified such a decree. If husbands were at fault, the court could grant wives the whole or part of "the lands, tenements, and hereditaments" as seemed equitable as well as a share of the husband's personal property. In 1830, Maryland required that the judiciary be involved in the initial stages of the process but left the final decision to the General Assembly. In 1842, the state turned the entire process over to the judiciary and established the same allowable grounds as those established by other states for granting separation or divorce: adultery, desertion (for three years), cruel treatment, impotency, bigamy, and being under age. Maryland added two more causes: the discovery that a white spouse had a black ancestor and that a wife had engaged in sex with another man before marriage.[16]

Other states passed similar statutes, while yet a number of others added amendments to their constitutions similar to the one in Tennessee in 1834: "The legislature shall have no power to grant divorces, but may authorize the court of justice to grant time for such causes as may be specified by law: *Provided*, That such laws be general and uniform in their operation throughout the State." States that amended their constitutions in a similar fashion included Georgia (1833), North Carolina (1835), Louisiana (1845), Virginia (1850), and Missouri (1853). In an amendment to its constitution, ratified in 1852–53, Missouri repeated verbatim the words of the Tennessee amendment. The three southern states entering the union during the late antebellum period—Arkansas (1836), Florida (1838), and Texas (1845)—adopted similar constitutional prohibitions.[17]

Despite laws directing marital partners to file suits in the circuit, district, or superior courts as well as constitutional prohibitions against the legislatures taking up the issue, a few wives and husbands continued to petition their general assemblies. By the 1830s and 1840s, however, the great majority of men and women seeking a divorce and/or separation filed their "causes" in the chancery courts. By 1842, all of the southern states except Alabama, Missouri, and Virginia had transferred final authority to the judiciary. Having already granted jurisdiction to the circuit courts in the initial stages of the process, Missouri passed a law in 1852 giving final jurisdiction to the judiciary. In 1850, the revised Virginia constitution prohibited the legislature from enacting private divorce acts and instructed the Assembly to pass a law conferring authority in such cases to the circuit chancery courts (which had both equity and criminal powers) (see Table 1).

Thus, by the late antebellum era, most states granted divorces for similar reasons. Not only did they continue the common-law practice of voiding marriages *ab initio* because of impotency, consanguinity, bigamy, an

DIVORCES.

CHAPTER 54.

An Act for the relief of females, and to authorize the granting of divorces in certain cases. [Passed January 6, 1840.]

SEC. 1. That hereafter in all cases where any female may have removed to this State, or may hereafter remove to this State, and shall be of good character, and shall have resided in this State for two years next before filing her petition, and where such female shall have been abandoned for two whole years next before filing her petition, maliciously and without any reasonable cause, or her husband shall have been guilty of any of the acts constituting a good cause for a divorce by the laws of this State, it shall be the duty of the judge to grant such petitioner a divorce, notwithstanding such causes for a divorce may have occured in another State. *Divorce.*

CHAPTER 133.

An act to amend the laws regulating divorces. (Passed February 4, 1842.)

SEC. 1. That in all cases, where by the laws now in force, a person is authorized to obtain a divorce from bed and board, the court shall hereafter be authorized to dissolve the bonds of matrimony, or to grant a divorce from the bonds of matrimony. *Divorce*

SEC. 2. That in all cases where a divorce shall be granted, it shall be lawful for the court to decree to the wife so divorced, such part of the real and personal property of the husband as they shall think proper, consistent with the nature of the case; and in doing which, the court shall be authorized to have reference to the property which the husband received by his wife at the time of the marriage, or at any time afterwards, as well as to any seperate property owned by the wife, and secured to her by marriage contract or otherwise. *Divorce granted.*

SEC. 3. That if any person, being husband or wife, has been or shall be convicted of any crime, which by the laws of this State is declared to be a felony, and sentenced to confinement in the Penitentiary, the same shall be a good cause of divorce from the bonds of matrimony: and if such convict shall, at the time of the exhibition of a bill for divorce under this section, be confined in the Penitentiary, the complainant may make publication, and bring the cause to trial as in cases of non-residents: *Provided*, That the proof of such conviction and sentence shall be the record of the court in which the proceedings were had: *And provided further*, That in all other cases of divorce, where petition shall be preferred and *subpœna* issued and served upon the adverse party, it shall be lawful to set the cause for hearing, and to have it tried at the first term of the court thereafter. *Cause for divorce.*

CHAPTER 176.

An act giving further relief to married people in obtaining divorces. [Passed January 27, 1844.]

SEC. 1. That hereafter, if any married man or woman shall have been guilty of an attempt upon the life of the other, either by attempting to poison the other or by any other means, showing malice, the husband or wife, as the case may be, may file his or her Bill under the rules of practice heretofore prescribed for obtaining divorces, and if upon the trial of said cause, he or she shall sustain the charge, then the court may grant the petitioner a divorce from the bonds of matrimony. *Cause for divorce.*

SEC. 2. That this act shall apply as well to attempts to take life by poisoning or otherwise, which took place before the passage of this act, as to attempts to kill after its passage.

Tennessee statutes, 1840–1846. During the 1840s, as the cases were turned over to the chancery, or equity, courts, a number of southern states, with the exception of South Carolina, passed laws dealing with various aspects of divorce. In Tennessee, three separate laws granted special relief to wives, declared that divorce from bed and board become absolute divorce, and added that attempted murder was grounds for divorce. (Statute Laws of the State of Tennessee, of a General Character, 149–50.)

underage partner, insanity, and lack of parental consent for minors; they also added divorce *a vinculo matrimonii* and *a mensa et thoro* for adultery, desertion for a number of years, cruel and barbarous treatment, and indignities rendering living together intolerable. Those who were granted a divorce *a mensa et thoro* could not remarry. Several states cited other causes, including interracial marriage, habitual drunkenness, improvidence, and the discovery that a woman had engaged in sex with another man before marriage.

Most of these laws were augmented, revised, and refined over time. Some states entering the union during the late antebellum era sometimes enacted into law a long list of reasons why a person was permitted to file for divorce. Arkansas, for example, enacted an 1839 statute that cited "personal indignities," including rudeness, vulgarity, unmerited reproach, contumely, studied neglect, intentional incivility, injury, manifest disdain, abusive language, malignant ridicule, and other manifestations of hatred, such as alienation and estrangement, that were proven to be habitual, continuous, and permanent. In Arkansas and other states, whatever the statute requirements, proving the allegations with testimony from witnesses was necessary. As had been the case in the courts during the early years, neither the plaintiff's accusations nor the defendant's responses, in and of themselves, were enough to prove a cause and trigger a favorable verdict. By the 1850s, only Alabama maintained legislative divorce as a matter of law and only South Carolina refused to grant divorces under any circumstances. In all of the other slaveholding states and the District of Columbia, final decisions fell to the judiciary, and state laws had expanded greatly the list of permissible causes for bringing such legal action. By then, the procedures and policies concerning divorce and separation in most of the southern states were not far different from those in other parts of the country.[18]

■ Besides laws relating directly to divorce and/or separation and alimony, various other statutes could be brought to bear in divorce cases, including those concerning marriage and cohabitation between whites and blacks. Some states did not change their colonial statutes prohibiting interracial cohabitation, whereas others either revised their old laws or created new ones. During the colonial period Maryland and Virginia made interracial marriage and interracial sexual relations criminal offenses, and in 1792 Virginia imposed a jail sentence of six months and a fine of $30 for any white person who married a black person or a mulatto.[19] In 1808, Louisiana declared null and void any marriage between a white person and a

TABLE 1 Jurisdictions: Divorce and Separation, Southern States, 1790–1853

Year	AL	AR	DE	DC	FL	GA	KY	LA	MD	MI	MO	NC	SC	TN	TX	VA
1790			Ge													
1796														Ge		
1798						Su								Su		
1799						Ge								Ge		
1801				Ci												
1803																Ge
1807														Ge		
1809							Ci							Ci		
1812							Ge	Ge						Ge		
1814												Su				
1817										Ch / Ge	Su	Ge				
1820	Ci / Ge										Ge					
1827								Di				Su				Ch / Ge

12 | *The Evolution of Divorce Laws*

Year	Courts
1830	CC, Ge
1832	Su
1833	Su, SJ, Ch
1835	Ci, Ci, Ch
1838	Ci, Su
1842	Ch, Ci, Ge
1845	Ci, Ge, Di
1848	Ch
1853	Ci

Sources: Derived from state constitutions, state constitutional amendments, and state laws concerning divorce, separation, and alimony; U.S. Congress *Federal and State Constitutions*; Howard, *History of Matrimonial Institutions*, 3:31–96.

Notes: Ch = Chancery Courts; Ci = Circuit Courts; Di = District Courts; Ge = General Assembly; Su = Superior Courts; CC = County Courts; SJ = Special Juries

Ratification years are cited. The courts involved were the equity, or chancery, courts. In different states, chancery cases were decided in district, circuit, and superior courts.

The Evolution of Divorce Laws | 13

free person of color. Other states during the antebellum period also prohibited interracial marriage or cohabitation. In 1822, Tennessee subjected a white person living with "any negro, mustee or mulatto man or woman, as man and wife" to a fine of $500. In 1830, North Carolina prohibited marriage between whites and slaves or free blacks, stipulating that any minister or official performing such a marriage would be subject to imprisonment. Florida and Texas passed similar statutes in 1832 and 1837, respectively, while Georgia stipulated that any white man living in adultery with a colored woman would be subject to a fine and imprisonment. In 1839, North Carolina declared that marriages between whites and free persons of color were void, in effect making both parties liable to prosecution for cohabitation or fornication.[20]

In three southern states, including Mississippi, Alabama, and South Carolina, lawmakers failed to enact such laws. In fact, in South Carolina it was *legal* for whites to marry free blacks. As a consequence, judges were bound by common law regulating nuptial rights and refused to impose any restrictions without legislative initiative. In one case that came before the South Carolina Supreme Court, the justices wrestled with the question of whether they could annul, as prayed for by the plaintiff, an inheritance provided to children born of a marriage between a white man and a free black woman. Agreeing with the defendant's lawyer, the court opined that, although such marriages were "revolting and justly regarded as offensive to public decency," they were not contrary to law.[21]

Other states passed laws that might be termed ancillary statutes concerning separation and divorce. In Louisiana, from the early years after statehood in 1812 through subsequent decades, a woman seeking separation of bed and board or divorce could claim the property she had brought to the marriage or possessed over and beyond a dower or jointure (i.e., over and beyond what she could expect at the time of her husband's death). This property, including, among other things, livestock, furniture, crops, machinery, land, and slaves, was called extra-dotal, or paraphernal, meaning that it was not part of her dowry. Furthermore, a wife could sell or convey her property through a court order; she could also sue her husband if he improperly sold her holdings as well as claim her share of the community property.[22]

Married women's property acts were also passed by the Florida and Arkansas territorial legislatures and, in 1839, by the General Assembly of Mississippi. The Mississippi statute, the first in the United States, protected a wife's slaves, including those she possessed prior to marriage or acquired by gift or inheritance from her husband's creditors. In 1846, the act was amended to put real estate owned by a wife at the time of her marriage under her "sole and separate use and benefit." The hiring and labor of the wife's slaves would inure to her sole benefit, and she would be competent to make a contract with her husband for their sale or hire. Prompted by a severe economic depression and designed to protect family estates, the law permitted women to acquire separate holdings by gift, bequest, purchase, demise, or distribution. Although the husband would be allowed to manage the slaves, he could neither file a civil suit citing them as the subject of dispute nor sell them without his wife's permission. In a number of states, especially along the eastern seaboard, politicians feared giving married women such rights. Yet, as legal historian Norma Basch points out, in many other states married women's property laws transformed separate equitable estates into separate legal estates.[23]

■ The evolution of laws concerning divorce, separation, alimony, interracial matters, and women's property created a framework for the narratives presented by plaintiffs and defendants as well as the arguments made by their lawyers. The pleas presented to state assemblies in the early years and equity courts during and after the 1820s often responded specifically to state statutes. The participants created narratives that were structured in such a way as to gain the sympathy of judges and juries. There is little doubt that some plaintiffs and defendants as well as witnesses fabricated or embellished their stories. Others justified the extreme action in seeking to end or alter their marital status by emphasizing only certain aspects of their married lives that related to specific laws, focusing on adultery, abuse, or abandonment, and by ignoring other aspects of their lives. In so doing they were silent on or minimized the aspects of their marriage and households that were positive, or nonconfrontational, although some did note that they had lived in harmony with their spouses for many years before the husband or the wife had entered into an adulterous relationship.

In short, the statutes and legal rules provided the basic structure for complaints. In pleading their causes, some lawyers cited the same specific laws from one case to the next, using the same words or phrases to convince their audience of the justness of their cause, a justness that was supposed to emerge from the storyline as self-evident. The law itself structured the sequence of events to fit legal categories. To elicit sympathy, some lawyers played on gender or racial predilections of judges and juries with regard to white women, or highlighted interracial mixing by husbands, or expanded on the fall from grace of white women. There can be little doubt about the importance of the evolution of the law in structuring and presenting arguments. Even so, the narratives of those seeking to end their marriages presented a view from inside these households of slaveholders and nonslaveholders alike that is at once captivating and revealing.

■ On 11 December 1817, nearly a full year after Harriet Laspeyre submitted her petition, her husband, Bernard, who by then lived in nearby Sampson County, presented his own petition to the North Carolina General Assembly. Most husbands accused in a similar manner did not respond to legislatures, but Bernard felt compelled to offer an explanation. Harriet, he asserted, was a "Virulent and Infamous" liar; her petition was an "obscene Instrument," written by an unnamed friend, a "Well Known Blasphemous abettor of Loose morals and Vulgar Intrigue" whose "vices and immorality" were proverbial. Furthermore, the act passed by the Assembly in his wife's behalf had caused him great hardship. According to their marriage agreement, their slaves were to remain under his control, but the sheriff had confiscated them by virtue of the act of separation, ordered by the Assembly, which had granted his wife the rights and privileges to buy, sell, and possess property as if she had never been married. In addition, Bernard continued, Harriet had sent several of their children out of the state in "flagrant Violation of all civil and divine Laws." She was, he claimed, the "Proudest, haughtiest, the most Suspicious and tyrannical woman existing." He asked the Assembly, in conformity with the spirit of a law passed in 1814 conferring on the superior courts "the right of Granting Divorces, Alimony &c," to repeal the private act passed in Harriet's favor; it was, he asserted, "Subversive of the most Sacred Institutions of Society." Despite his vituperative denunciations, and despite his efforts to play on the sensibilities of assemblymen concerning the divine laws of marriage, the Assembly rejected Bernard's petition.

Some of what Bernard Laspeyre said may have been true, as it appears that Harriet's petition contained inaccuracies. Nonetheless, after twenty-three years of marriage, Harriet had obtained her desired separation. Like other older women in similar circumstances, she never remarried. In 1830, she was listed in the census as heading a household in Brunswick County with two men and two women in the age groups of her children. She possessed six slaves. In 1840, she headed a similar household and owned seven slaves. In 1850, at age eighty-one, she lived with her forty-two-year-old son, William H. Laspeyre, an inspector in Wilmington who owned thirteen slaves. Harriet died in 1853.[24]

2

ADULTERY AND
THE QUESTION OF RACE

In 1855, Sarah H. Black, wife of Brazoria County, Texas, planter and slave owner James E. Black, filed suit in the First District Court for a divorce, alimony, child custody, and a portion of the marital community property, charging her husband with adultery. She had married James, who was twelve years her senior and a migrant from South Carolina, in her hometown of Paris, Henry County, Tennessee, in 1837, and they had two children, Alonzo and William, ages nine and eleven. Like many other white women in the South, Sarah brought suit in her own behalf, without a male "next friend," but accompanied by her lawyer. In the suit, she explained that on 15 August 1854 she had caught her husband in the act of having illicit intercourse with a mulatto woman named Susan, one of his slaves, and on 28 September 1854 with a "Negro Woman named Ann or Annie," again one of his slaves.

Because of her husband's infidelity, Sarah became a pariah on the plantation. The slaves "frequently used threatening language towards her," she explained, and her husband did nothing to prevent it. In one incident a black woman raised a stick and threatened to hit her, and Captain Black, as her husband was called, witnessed the incident but only laughed and refused to have the black woman whipped as Sarah requested. On another occasion, a slave called her a liar. She instructed the overseer, who was standing nearby, to punish the girl. He replied that Captain Black had given him strict instructions not to discipline any of the slaves at her request. For some time, Sarah claimed, her husband had treated her with great disrespect; whenever she spoke to him or asked him a question or entreated him, he told her to "go to Hell you God Damned old bitch. I don't want to talk to you."[1]

When Sarah Black filed for divorce, her husband was one of the wealthiest slave owners in Texas. In 1850, at age 49, Black owned a plantation stretching some 1,800 acres along the Bernard River in historic Brazoria County; he possessed a total of 50 slaves, including 27 children under age 13 (5 of them listed as mulattoes), 13 in their teens and twenties, 7 in their thirties, and 3 over age 40. His slaveholdings placed him among the top 1.2 percentile of Texas slave owners. Despite the large number of slave children on the plantation, he harvested 90 bales of cotton (400 pounds each) and boasted 150 head of cattle, 300 swine, 20 mules, 30 milch cows, 24 oxen, and 6 horses. He also produced 200 bushels of Indian corn, 50 bushels of Irish potatoes, 1,000 bushels of sweet potatoes, 400 pounds of butter, and 3 tons of hay. In her suit Sarah Black called these high yields and extensive holdings—the land alone was valued at $20,000—"community property."[2]

■ Most historical studies of interracial sexual relations and the law in the South focus on state statutes: how they were passed, when they were passed, and their evolution over time. An examination of the specific laws against fornication and interracial marriage reveals the attitudes of the ruling class and how these attitudes influenced the debates that took place in general assemblies and state governments. They point to the politics of race and how it changed during the late eighteenth and nineteenth centuries. In addition to looking at state statutes and racial politics, historians have examined interracial sexual relations in specific locations as well as in well-known and well-documented appellate cases.[3]

None of these studies, however, analyzes the racial dynamics that occurred within households on the brink of breaking apart—such as Sarah Black's household of Brazoria County, Texas, in 1855—or scrutinizes the nature of interracial sexual activities that caused the dissolution of marriages. Although the narratives of divorce and separation tell us only one side of the story, they do connect the law with what was actually occurring in a variety of households, those of both slave owners and non–slave owners. In doing so, they offer a unique and surprising profile of adultery in a slave society, at least when compared with many contemporary accounts. Among the grounds offered by white women who filed for divorce, infidelity was not the primary cause but one of several, and when it was cited, the plaintiffs were less likely to accuse their husbands of sexual relations with their own slaves than with white women. At the same time, adultery was also used by white men suing their wives for divorce. In fact, among the grounds offered by white men who filed for divorce, infidelity was by far *the major cause*, and the men overwhelmingly accused their wives of sexual encounters with black men.[4]

The white women who accused their husbands of infidelity with other white women were, with few exceptions, members of slaveholding families (66 of 69, or 96 percent). They were often in their forties and fifties, had been married for many years, and had raised a number of children. Whereas all women who filed for divorce in this study did so, on average, after about 12 years of marriage, the women in this subgroup filed papers after about 17.5 years; the median of 16 years of marriage at the time of the suit for this subgroup was nearly twice the median for all white women filing for divorce. Some described how their husbands left home for extended periods of time, ignored family and friends, and had lost interest in having sexual relations. Others said their husbands became cold, distant, aloof, moody, and preoccupied. Most claimed their husbands left them for younger women. Such was the case for Nancy Summers of Barren County, Kentucky, who, after twenty-six years of marriage and six children, including two of "unsound mind," lost her husband to a young neighbor's wife named Winni Tudor.[5]

■ Although it is not possible to know how often slaveholding husbands engaged in sexual relations with one or more of their slaves, we know from various sources that it was not unusual. Even so, only 54 of the 233 women who filed for divorce charging infidelity asserted that their husbands took up with their own slaves. These relationships ranged from casual liaisons to associations lasting several months or years to, occasionally, long-term partnerships. Some wives went to great lengths to uncover such infidelities. They entered plantation kitchens in the middle of the night, followed their husbands into the slave quarters, ventured into various outbuildings on the plantation, and listened outside doors of rooms in their own homes. A few witnessed their husbands in the act or caught them in compromising situations. Others questioned slaves about the whereabouts of their husbands or enlisted friends and relatives to tell them about their spouses' possible sexual encounters.[6]

In Louisiana it was not uncommon for large slave owners to have slave mistresses who lived either at the same residence or in close proximity. Some wives acquiesced to these arrangements for lengthy periods or at least until they became untenable. Although marriage between whites and blacks was illegal in the state, mixed-race couples became so common that an institution called *plaçage*—white men contracting to live with black women and providing them with financial support—became widespread. The *Civil Code* recognized "open concubinage" as legal and stipulated that white men could give their black or mulatto concubines up to 10 percent of their "moveable property" but not their "immoveable property" (slaves were considered immovable property in Louisiana).[7]

Although Louisiana was unique, in terms of both the number of those who lived in interracial unions and the wealth and prominence of the men involved, a few women in other slaveholding states, especially in the Lower South, did file suits against their husbands for having taken up residence with slaves, both their own and those belonging to their wives. In Alabama, Mississippi, South Carolina, and Georgia, wives of planters complained that their husbands lived with black or mulatto women, fathered slave children, and treated the women as de facto wives. Several witnesses testified in a Mississippi case that the children of one such union were "as white as any white children, with straight hair."[8]

A few wives charged that their husbands purchased young female slaves for the purpose of having sexual relations with them. They described husbands in their forties and fifties who, after a decade or more of marriage, purchased slave girls in their teens or slave women in their twenties, often of mixed racial origin, for sexual pleasure. It was well known that purchasers in New Orleans could acquire young mulatto girls, called "fancy girls," during the antebellum era. Buyers and sellers in other parts of the South bought and sold "fancy girls." Among the buyers was Alabama planter John Smith, who after thirty years of marriage purchased "a bright mulatto negro girl just grown" and brought her onto his plantation. It was clear, his wife said, that he had come under a spell of "strange and unaccountable infatuation." Later, the unnamed "mulatto negro girl" gave birth to the husband's child.[9]

Although most husbands sought out black women solely for sexual pleasure, a few white men deserted their wives to live with their slaves. Some of these relationships were long-term and marked by genuine love and affection. Slave owners left their wives to be with slave mistresses or brought black women into their homes and forced their wives and children to live elsewhere. Despite public sentiment against such interracial unions between white men and black women, the laws dealing with interracial marriage, passed during the colonial era and later, were created primarily for the purpose of protecting white women against black men. The judicial process remained silent on the issue of white men, especially white men with property, who maintained relationships with black women.[10]

Even when genuine affection had developed between a white man and his slave, it was sometimes difficult for owners to ignore the reality that their de facto wives were also valuable property. After "cohabiting" for months, even years, and after the birth of a child or children, a slave master could be forced to sell his female companion if financial difficulties arose or if he came under pressure from friends and family members. Both reasons were at work when John Allen, a South Carolina farmer and gristmill owner, put his slave mistress up for sale after living with her for nearly eight years.[11]

■ Some women charged their husbands with having sexual relations with slaves belonging to neighbors, friends, business partners, and relatives. This group was probably about the same size as the wives who filed against husbands who engaged in sexual relations with their own slaves, but they were often wives of small slaveholders or nonslaveholders—small farmers, artisans, laborers, and town folk. The wives of these men acknowledged that their husbands were greatly attracted to black women. They testified that their husbands often sought out slave women in towns and cities, left their beds to be with slaves belonging to neighbors, or in the words of one wife, became "notorious in the neighborhood" for seducing black women and fathering mulatto children.[12]

The behavior of members of this group of male seducers is perhaps nowhere better illustrated than by the case of North Carolina farmer and slave owner William D. Robinson. In 1818, after two years of marriage, his wife filed for divorce, charging him, as her lawyer wrote, with "promiscuous cohabitation with various women." A number of witnesses confirmed these accusations. A neighbor testified that Robinson had acted in an improper manner toward one of his slaves, offering her $2.00 for sex and tearing at her clothes. Another witness, a hired hand, said that Robinson bragged to him that he could have carnal knowledge of a young black girl walking along the road near the farmhouse. He approached her, propositioned her, and when she refused, he pressed her to the ground and "entered her" but did not "accomplish his purpose" because her owner's daughter came upon them unexpectedly.

Although Robinson was certainly more promiscuous than most slave owners, he was not alone in thinking that the ownership of human property gave him license to do as he pleased with black women without fear of punishment. He boasted about his conquests, using the term "rape" not to incriminate himself but only to suggest that the black girl he molested should have consented. Robinson's case is also typical in that, although many neighbors, friends, family members, visitors, and slaves knew about his predilections, most looked the other way and said nothing until some were compelled to testify when his actions became so blatant that his wife filed court papers.[13]

The resistance offered by the unnamed slave girl to Robinson's advances suggests that black women fought back against the advances of white men. Unfortunately, the testimonies and depositions offered in such cases do not reveal the depth of their anger, defiance, bitterness, and hostility or the hatred this must have engendered with slave husbands. It is clear that some black women screamed, struggled, and fought against the white men who sought to violate them. But if they fought too hard, they could put themselves or their children or their husbands at risk. They could also be flogged, put in irons or in stocks, beaten, sent to remote encampments, or forced to watch as their children or husbands were sold, or they themselves were put on the auction block.[14]

The fact that some of the men, both slaveholders and nonslaveholders, boasted of their sexual prowess and appeared to care little about what others thought of their bragging about their "conquests" not only reveals their own confidence that nothing could or would be done to punish such conduct but also suggests that their neighbors accepted such behavior as a normal by-product of the slave system. Despite public professions of outrage and pronouncements about morality and decency, there were no criminal penalties against white men, slave owners or non-slave owners, who forced themselves upon slave women. In fact, white men could be charged with rape only if the victim was a free black or white woman. As property, slave women had no recourse to protect themselves from either the lust of their owners or sexual advances by outsiders. The only legal recourse an owner possessed when his or her slave was accosted by a white man, antebellum legal authority Thomas R. R. Cobb explained, was to seek compensation through the law courts for "trespass" upon the owner's property.[15]

■ In addition to their study of adultery committed by white men with black women, historians have also examined the reverse: illicit relations between white women and black men. Most scholars are quick to point out the difficulty of analyzing the question as a separate subject, not only because of the clandestine nature of the relationships but also because those brought to public attention often entered the judicial record in association with a variety of related issues. These issues include criminal indictments for rape, interracial marriage, fornication, and if children were involved, bastardy, as well as prosecutions for "criminal conversation," a euphemism used for engaging in a sexual act outside socially sanctioned norms, a charge that was filed as a "tort action" under the ancient theory of trespass. Historians have also argued that it was often "poor white girls" who had affairs with black lovers. The punishments for black men involved in such cases, even when the act was consensual, could be extreme, including castration, deportation, and death.[16]

Although the wives who had extramarital affairs with black men were not necessarily from poor families, they were much different, in profile, than the husbands who committed adultery. Whereas only 38 percent of suing white women in this study cited their spouse's infidelity as grounds for divorce, a high 75 percent of suing white men (92 of 123) did so. In addition, the great majority of these men charged that the men with whom their wives had engaged in "illicit sexual relations" were black (68 of 92, or 74 percent). Just as striking was the dissimilarity in terms of slave ownership between men and women who made the charge of adultery. The overwhelming majority of the white women charging their husbands with adultery lived in slaveholding families (193 of 233, or 83 percent); exactly the reverse was true for the men who charged their wives with the same offense. Among them, 76 of 92, or 83 percent, were non–slave owners. In addition, a substantial proportion of these men did not own land. In Virginia, one-third of the white men who accused their wives of having affairs with black men owned no real estate. In short, most of these white men were landless or owned small farms, and an overwhelming majority owned no slaves; these same men alleged that their wives had illicit sexual relations with blacks, slave and free.[17]

With the exception of impotency, perhaps no other situation could be more devastating to a white southern husband's notion of manhood and honor than discovering that his wife slept with a slave. Most husbands did not want to believe that such a thing could be possible. Indeed, about 25 percent of the men who charged their wives with infidelity with black men did not discover the fact until after their wives had given birth to a mixed-race child. For some, the birth occurred a few weeks or a few months after they took their marital vows. A Virginia farmer expressed anguish and humiliation shortly after his wedding when his wife was "deliver'd of a Mulatto Child . . . begotten by a negro man slave in the Neighborhood." It was equally painful and demeaning for a Tennessee man to ask for a divorce because his wife, who came from a respectable family and was thought to be an honorable woman, gave birth to a child of mixed ancestry only four months after their marriage.[18]

Other men made similar complaints, often sending their petitions to general assemblies, even in South Carolina, describing their wives who had had clandestine relationships with slaves or free men of color prior to marriage. They often discovered the betrayal only after the birth of a "Mulatto Child." Marmaduke Jones of South Carolina, described as a respectable young man, petitioned the General Assembly to have his marriage annulled. Seven months after their nuptials his wife "was brought to bed," her husband testified, "and then and there delivered of a mulatto child." To prove his case he provided a statement signed under oath by a number of his neighbors, as well as an affidavit from the midwife, who agreed that the child was "a very dark mulatto." Despite the evidence, the Assembly refused to grant the annulment.[19]

Although white men felt humiliated when they discovered their wife's infidelity shortly after their marriage, for others it was even more agonizing when they discovered the infidelity after many years of marriage and the birth of a number of legitimate children. Describing himself as a "plain labouring man seeking his subsistence by honest industry," Ayres Tatham of Accomack County, Virginia, said in 1805 that he had been married twelve years with two children when his wife gave birth to a child who was "obviously the issue of an illicit intercourse with a black man." He found it difficult, he said, to describe his feelings of confusion, distress, shame, betrayal, and dishonor. Robert Chiles of Missouri, after nearly eight years of marriage, said his wife, Celia, was "guilty of the crime of adultery with certain & divers persons," including a Negro man who had fathered her child. At the divorce trial, another midwife testified that the baby was a dark mulatto and that she believed a black man named Abram, who belonged to a local widow, was the father.[20]

In most cases the name of the slave father could not be determined. Indeed, as the complaints of betrayed husbands reveal, in some instances it was not even clear whether or not the father was black. Some babies described as "white" were indeed fathered by black men, while others described as dark or swarthy were believed not to be the offspring of a person of color. When husbands became suspicious about the color of a child, they asked friends, neighbors, physicians, midwives, and family members to render a judgment. These observers commented on the facial features, limb structure, hair texture, and skin coloring.[21]

Some husbands refused to believe that their wives might have had sexual relations with black men. If a child looked different or seemed darker than normal, a husband might not even consider at first the possibility of such a betrayal. After twenty-two years of marriage and six children, Henry Shouse's wife gave birth to a baby who "showed no particular mark" as to color. But after a few months the child's skin grew darker. Shouse thought the child might have some type of skin disease. Soon, however, even the neighbors began to whisper about the baby's color. Although Henry still could not believe that his wife had been unfaithful, he decided nonetheless to call in a physician, "a Medical Gentleman of high reputation," who pronounced the baby "to be of negro blood." Shouse immediately forced his wife and the child "to be removed from his house."[22]

Perhaps the most poignant, yet painful, response to having been placed in such a circumstance was expressed by Thomas Flowers of Nash County, North Carolina. He sought a divorce from his wife, Temperance, who had left him to live with a group of free people of color. She stayed away for a lengthy period of time and gave birth to an illegitimate child. "This wife of his bosom this friend of his soul," he wrote, with whom he had lived in "love & confidence" for nine years, had left him for a black man. He begged her to desist, but all his efforts "proved abortive." He was "stabbed to the heart, cut to the brains."[23]

Other men seeking a divorce were similarly "stabbed to the heart, cut to the brains." They were shamed, humiliated, disgraced, and embarrassed when they learned that their wives sneaked out of the house for rendezvous with black lovers, had sex with slaves in the kitchen, engaged in adultery in the quarters, or went to live with free blacks. "She has at late hours of the night long after all the family had gone to bed and after she herself had gone to bed," a North Carolina man who owned a single male slave testified concerning his young wife, "got up went to the kitchen where this fellow [Peter] staid, has remained with him for hours together no person being present except, her & the negro." It was well known in the neighborhood that she slept with slaves, one of her friends explained; in fact, late one night the friend came across the owner's wife walking along a deserted road some distance from the farm and asked her what she was doing. "She was hunting the Bull," she said.[24]

In the minds of husbands, such conduct was indeed the height of infamy and dishonor. They spoke of their wives "equalizing themselves with Negroes," abandoning themselves to "vile prostitution and debauchery," and giving birth to bastard children of "various colours and complexions." They and their lawyers termed such conduct "lewd and lascivious" and charged their wives with "the greatest luridness, immorality and vice." For many white men, it seemed incomprehensible that their partners might engage in adultery with black men, seek out "Coloured paramours," and desert them and their children to live with slaves.[25]

To make any definitive statement about the extent and frequency of sexual relationships between white women and black men is, of course, not possible, but as the statistical evidence of even the small selection of cases in this study suggests, they were not uncommon in the southern states. The record shows that, although white men may have presumed at times that they possessed a license to take advantage of slave women, deeming it neither disgraceful nor a danger to society, these same men considered the behavior of white women who accepted the advances of black men as the height of infamy, undermining the very fabric of southern civilization.[26]

This view was articulated by a group of South Carolina farmers and planters who petitioned the General Assembly in 1812 about the growing problem of black men propositioning white women, "some of them with success." Nor was this interracial sexual activity, so degrading to the women and dangerous to society, reserved to women "of the lower classes," the "dregs of society," they asserted, but indeed, some young women from very respectable families accepted the advances of slaves and free men of color. The petitioners asked that a new law be passed to curtail this "growing disgrace."[27]

About one of five white men filing for divorce in this study did so because their wives had affairs with other white men. In their petitions to the state legislatures and equity, or chancery, courts, they told of wives who sneaked out of their homes to be with their lovers, left for weeks or months at a time, or deserted their families and children entirely. A few women, probably representing many others whose husbands in such circumstances did not file divorce suits, abandoned their homes and their children, moved to another county or state, and started new families while still married. More than half of the white men who charged their wives with unfaithfulness with white men were slaveholders, whereas the reverse was true for men who charged their wives with having sexual relations with slaves or free blacks; the majority of this latter group were nonslaveholders.[28]

A few husbands informed the legislatures and chancery courts that their wives not only engaged in "carnal intercourse" with a variety of white men but accepted payment for their services. James Puckett, a slave owner in Mobile, Alabama, said that his wife, Elizabeth, met a number of different men, including persons of high standing, at a house a few blocks from their residence. Discovered and pressed to tell about her secret life, Elizabeth confessed that the owner or renter of the house, a free black woman, helped her make arrangements with clients who came to engage in "a criminal & adulterous connection." Other men divulged that their wives had become public and notorious prostitutes, engaging in "unreserved and promiscuous intercourse with men of every color, age, class, and description" and gratifying their "lust and desire for variety" with numerous assignations. A businessman in Petersburg, Virginia, discovered that his wife "was not only guilty of adultery of the most Shameless kind" but in the habit of visiting brothels, receiving "the most Lewd and dissolute men," and attempting to steal customers away from two black prostitutes. His wife spent entire nights at a brothel owned by Eliza Gallee, a free black woman, where she permitted men to take liberties with her "such as no chaste and decent woman would take or allow to have been taken."[29]

■ Despite the lack of specific information, in some cases, regarding sexual partners, a general profile of adultery can be constructed. About two of five white women who filed for divorce and/or separation (233 of 610, or 38 percent) charged their husbands with infidelity. In this group, only 54 knew for a fact that the liaisons occurred with their husband's slaves, 33 with slaves whose owners were not identified, 27 with "black women," and 8 with free women of color. Thus, slightly more than half of the white women (122 of 233, or 52 percent) identified their husbands as having sexual associations with black women. In addition, 42 wives charged that their husbands had engaged in illicit relations with either black and/or white women, and 69 charged that their husbands had relations with white women. Even if we assume that a substantial number in the category "black and/or white" were African Americans, it is fair to say that more than a third of the men were accused of infidelity with white women, and only about one of four were accused of consorting with their own slaves (54 of 233, or 23 percent). There were, of course, cases of promiscuous husbands who had numerous liaisons with both black and white women, in which cases their wives generally offered information of a general rather than specific character.

Among the white women who petitioned general assemblies and the circuit, district, or superior courts for divorce, separation, and/or alimony on the grounds of adultery, 83 percent were members of slaveholding families (193 of 233). Moreover these women were distributed within the slaveholding class, in terms of the number of slaves owned, in rough correlation with such distribution among slave owners in the South as a whole. Of the 175 cases where the number of slaves could be ascertained, 65 percent featured women in households that possessed between 1 and 9 slaves; 20 percent, between 10 and 19; and 15 percent, 20 or more. In the South, at least at midcentury, for which the first good statistics are available, 73 percent of slaveholding families owned between 1 and 9 slaves; 16 percent, between 10 and 19; and 11 percent, 20 or more.[30]

Despite the imperfect nature of the statistical evidence, several generalizations can be offered indicating that adultery among the southern slaveholding class was racially diversified and not restricted to the sexual exploitation of the slaves that they owned. The evidence found in divorce, separation, and alimony cases suggests that visitors to the South and perhaps some later historians may have overstated the extent to which illicit relationships were primarily between white men and their slaves. The cases included in this study show that slaveholders charged with having sexual relations with slaves they owned, other slaves, or blacks of unknown status represented less than half of the total (85 of 193); slave owners who engaged in relationships with white women or black and/or white women comprised more than half of the relationships (103 of 193). The racial diversity of adultery can be more specifically observed among the 26 wealthiest slave-owning families, those with 20 or more slaves. Nearly one-half of the wives in these families accused their husbands of illicit liaisons with white women (12 of 26), and 3 lodged accusations involving white and/or black women. In short, the observations by antebellum travelers and others concerning white men and slave women captured only a portion of the picture of male adultery among slaveholders.[31]

It is, of course, difficult to assess the significance of the correlation, established by the statistics provided above, between the higher incidence of divorce initiated by white men on grounds of their wives' adultery with black men and the lower incidence of property ownership and slaveholding among those men. It would appear that the more prosperous members of society who confronted issues of female infidelity were unwilling to bring their wives' fall from grace to the attention of the public by filing divorce suits. For these men, just as for their wives, divorce would mean the public exposure of family secrets, a threat to their standing in the community, possible ridicule or opprobrium, and a loss of honor. In addition, the punishments inflicted on white women found guilty of adultery were more severe than those inflicted on white men. Women could be deprived of their property and their children. Finally, the kinship ties that joined affluent members of the planter class together as well as the financial consequences associated with divorce or separation caused members of this group to remain silent about their wives' infidelity.[32]

■ Sarah H. Black's lawyer listened as she recounted to him the facts in her case, and he then presented a petition to the Brazoria County District Court. From their conversation, the lawyer fashioned a set of questions, called interrogatories, to be presented at trial concerning James Black's conduct toward his slave women over a two-year period. The lawyer pointed out to the court that his client was without family or kin other than her two children and had left the plantation to stay in a neighbor's

TABLE 2 Husbands Accused of Adultery, with Sexual Partner Identified by Race and Status

	Total divorce cases	With slave(s)	With husband's slave(s)	With FWOC*	With black	With black and/or white	With white	Total	Percent	SLAVE-OWNING FAMILIES Total	SLAVE-OWNING FAMILIES Percent
Alabama	60	4 4**	11	1 1	2 1		7 7	25	42	24	96
Arkansas	1										
Delaware											
District of Columbia	9							2	22	0	
Florida	12	1 1	2	1 1			1 1	5	42	5	100
Georgia	11		1			3 3	1 1	5	45	5	100
Kentucky	54	1			1 1		5 5	7	13	6	86
Louisiana	52	2 2	3			5 4		10	19	9	90
Maryland	20				4 1		2 2	6	30	3	50
Mississippi	22	7 5	8		1 1	1 1		17	77	15	88
Missouri	6					1 1	1 1	2	33	2	100
North Carolina	138	11 3	5	3 2	6 2	12 9	26 24	63	46	45	71
South Carolina	76	2 2	8		2 1	3 3	10 10	25	33	24	96
Tennessee	71	2 2	3		5 1	9 8	6 6	25	35	20	80
Texas	11	1 1	1			2 2		4	36	4	100
Virginia	67	2 1	12	3 1	4 2	6 6	10 9	37	55	31	84
TOTALS	610	33 21	54	8 5	27 10	42 37	69 66	233	38	193	83

Source: Compiled from Divorce and Alimony Excel File Database; includes data from both legislative and chancery court records.

*FWOC = free women of color
**slaveholders in bold

1855

Sarah H. Black
vs
James E. Black

This day the motion of the plaintiff asking the Court to grant her alimony for her support and maintenance during the pendency of this suit, coming on to be heard, the parties appeared by their attorneys, and the Court having heard the testimony, and being satisfied that she has no separate property of her own, and that she has no means of support, except such as may be derived from the community property of the said Sarah H. Black and James E. Black, or the separate property of the said James E. Black, it is ordered, adjudged, and decreed by the Court, that the said James E. Black pay to the said Sarah H. Black, for her support and maintenance, during the pendency of this suit, the sum of six hundred dollars annually, the same to be paid in quarterly installments. And it appearing to the Court that this suit was commenced on the 26th day of March 1855, and that the said Sarah H. and James E. Black have been living separate and apart since the commencement of this suit, and that during this time the said Sarah H. Black has had no means of obtaining a support, It is ordered that the said James E. Black pay the said Sarah H. Black the sum of one hundred and

1663.

Wednesday May 23rd 1855

fifty dollars on the 26th day of June 1855, and the further sum of one hundred and fifty dollars on the 26th day of September 1855, and the further sum of one hundred and fifty dollars three months from the last mentioned date, and the same sum at the end of each succeeding three months until this suit is finally disposed of. —

1855

Sarah H. Black
vs
James E. Black

And now on this day come the parties by their counsel and by consent this case is dismissed at the cost of the defendant — It is therefore considered by the Court that this case be and the same is hereby dismissed and that the plaintiff recover of the defendant all costs in this behalf expended and that execution issue for the same home on the day she commenced her suit. Since Texas was only one of two southern states (the other being Louisiana) that considered the property accumulated during a marriage as community property, he would be seeking a division of the estate in his client's behalf as well as alimony of $600 a year for maintenance. On 23 May 1855, both parties appeared in court with their attorneys. After hearing testimony from both sides, the judge granted the request for alimony. What occurred during the next few weeks and the reasons for the final outcome are not part of the court record, but the resolution of the case suggests that James H. Black decided he did not want to risk losing a large portion of his estate and made a direct plea to his wife to return, on the promise that he would change his wayward ways. It appears she agreed, as the suit, by mutual consent and with the defendant paying the costs, was dismissed.[33]

The struggle of Sarah Black was not unusual among those who sought to demand their rights in court because of their husband's infidelity. Sarah found a lawyer, explained her circumstances, and in essence won her cause, although returning to live with her husband after the breakup must have been very difficult. Typical of petitions in which the plaintiffs claimed adultery, the facts put into evidence were in the form of overlapping narratives (family background, acts of infidelity, husband's attitudes, economic situation, and slave ownership), and considering that the assertions could be challenged, most narratives, like Sarah's, were probably fairly accurate. As it turned out, however, the case outcome made little difference in the long term in Sarah's life, as her husband had only a few short years to live. In 1858, at age fifty-seven, James E. Black died, and the next year their two sons, Joseph Alonzo Black and William Black, appeared in the probate court as minors to claim their future inheritance. In 1860, Sarah Black, age forty-seven, headed the plantation household. She owned $51,000 worth of real estate and personal property worth $56,875, making her one of the richest widows in Texas. Her two boys were listed as attending school, and other people in the household included a white overseer, a white plantation hand, and fifty-three slaves. As was the case with her husband, however, she, too, had only a few years to live. As the Civil War drew to a close in 1864, Sarah H. Black, widow, slaveholder, mother, and wealthy landowner, died.[34]

(opposite)
Court order for alimony for Sarah H. Black. Judges and juries were often sympathetic toward women in slaveholding families suing for divorce. In this instance, Sarah H. Black and her lawyers obtained a comfortable alimony after she fled from her plantation. (Order for Alimony, 25 May 1855, in Records of the District Court, Sarah H. Black v. James E. Black, Case #1835, CCH, Angleton, Tex.)

3

INSANITY, ALCOHOLISM, ABANDONMENT, AND ABUSE

In 1854, following a "fit of derangement," Isaac Rawdon, father, husband, planter, and Alabama slave owner, was confined to Talladega County jail, where he remained for several months. A few days after his release, he rose from the breakfast table, took his adult son by the hand, and led him into the yard. The boy was "not endowed by nature with a Strong mind," Rawdon's wife, Lydia, explained, and as a consequence, she had instructed him always to obey his father's wishes. Knowing her husband's history of unpredictable and violent behavior, Lydia Rawdon was apprehensive that morning, but before she could do anything, she saw her son, half bent, with his hands on his knees and blood spurting from a deep gash across his throat. His father, holding a large knife, stood nearby staring at the boy. Lydia screamed in horror and ran off down a road toward the plantation of Isaac's brother. So, too, did a number of the plantation slaves who had witnessed the gruesome murder.

After his son had slumped to the ground, Isaac fetched a sledgehammer, knocked down a fence, constructed a scaffold some distance from the plantation house, and stacked kindling underneath. He then dragged his son's lifeless body onto the makeshift bier and set it ablaze. As the flames leaped skyward, Rawdon exclaimed that he "offered his son [as] a sacrifice to God, as Abraham had offered his son Isaac."[1]

With the assistance of Isaac's brother, John Rawdon, Lydia had her husband declared insane and arranged for him to be transported to the Georgia state mental institution in Milledgeville, as far away from her as possible. In June 1854, she filed for divorce. In her petition and in subsequent court testimony, a picture of Isaac Rawdon emerged that was both frightening and ominous. Isaac's brother testified that Isaac's erratic behavior had begun more than twenty-eight years before, prior to his marriage, when he started exhibiting unpredictable mood swings. One minute he would be calm, mild, and friendly; the next he would become agitated, hostile, and angry. As time passed, these "mental alterations," as they were called, occurred more and more frequently. In addition, he would walk about mumbling and chanting and would lock himself in his room for days at a time, "enraged about the subject of Religion." Following one illness, he became uncontrollably violent, whipping slaves indiscriminately, including his personal nurse. Having lost all hope of her husband's recovery, Lydia asked the court to grant her a divorce, divide the marital property, provide her with alimony, and put her husband's holdings in the hands of a guardian.[2]

During a period of lucidity before being taken away to Georgia, Isaac vowed to return and reap vengeance on his wife and his brother. The threat reminded Lydia that her husband could appear completely rational and intelligent one moment and then suddenly transform into a raving maniac. What if he escaped from the asylum and returned? What if he came in the night and cut her throat as he had cut the throat of their only son? It seemed as if her future, like her past, would be filled with fear and anxiety.

■ The case of Isaac and Lydia Rawdon illustrates, in one of its most horrific forms, the fate awaiting a family when the head of the household suffered from mental illness and engaged in insane acts, and the remedies sought by wives to alleviate the consequences for themselves and their children. This chapter will focus primarily on complaints filed by white women concerning the four grounds for divorce and separation besides adultery: insanity, alcoholism, abandonment, and domestic abuse. In all of these areas, women were more vulnerable than men, who usually controlled the family property. The chapter also examines other grounds for divorce as provided in law in the various states, including impotency, bigamy, slander, mental abuse, and profligacy. As indicated in Chapter 1, the grounds for divorce and/or separation expanded significantly during the antebellum period. Sometimes white women offered two or more causes as to why they were giving up on their marriages, but among all of the reasons presented over time, physical violence and abuse was the single most important. The need for men to discipline family members was, of course, part of the culture of the era, but the extent of physical discipline and retribution in divorce cases often went far beyond the norm. In addition, what follows reveals how female plaintiffs who filed suits for divorce and separation were able to push the boundaries of the law. They were responsible,

Talladega County Courthouse, Alabama. Built in 1836, the Talladega County Courthouse is the oldest working courthouse in Alabama and among the oldest in the southern states. It was through its doors on 6 June 1854 that Lydia Rawdon entered with her two lawyers and her next friend, slave owner William McPherson, to file a chancery suit declaring her husband insane. (USMSPC, Talladega County, Ala., Talladega, 1850, p. 391; USMSSC, Talladega County, Ala., 1850, p. 483; courtesy of the Alabama Department of Archives and History, Montgomery.)

at least in part, for new statutes designed to meet the needs of those who found themselves in unsustainable marriages.[3]

The extent of the brutal treatment of slaves on the Rawdon plantation, the murder of a slow-witted man-child, and the obvious mental problems of a slave master were unusual, but the strange behavior of other slave owners as described in divorce and alimony cases was probably also the result of various forms of "mental alienation," as mental illness was then called. Such forms of mental illness, in today's terms, include psychosis, schizophrenia, paranoia, depression, dementia, anxiety disorder, and bipolar disorder, among others—mental or behavioral problems that modern psychiatry now usually links to chemical imbalances in the brain and/or emotional and psychological disorders. Nineteenth-century physicians called these illnesses melancholia, mania, monomania, dementia, and idiocy; contemporaries called them "lunacy," "derangement," or "insanity." In the judicial system, insanity meant mental incompetence, *non compos mentis*, "not master of one's mind."[4]

Whatever the terms used to describe its various forms, the methods for detecting mental illness during the slavery era were at best crude and unsophisticated. Some of those who were judged insane were probably merely eccentrics. Slaveholders who lived alone with their slaves in remote areas or who freed their slaves and provided them with money and property, for example, were sometimes accused by family members of being imbalanced, especially by heirs who sought a portion of their estates. Others used charges of "insanity" as a convenient ploy to end their marriages. A few months after his marriage, Thomas Rowe, a Tennessee slaveholder, filed for divorce on the grounds of his wife's "natural imbecility." Not only did the wife deny the charges, but she won her own divorce suit, claiming that her husband's children by another marriage had put him up to making the accusation.[5]

There were, however, slave owners and family members who suffered from severe mental illness, a fact that was not only attested to during the course of trials by the descriptions of their volatile, mercurial, erratic, and at times sadistic behavior but also identified as such in court judgments. They were unpredictable, displayed obsessive and paranoid jealousies, failed to comprehend financial matters, and sometimes disciplined members of their families and slaves with wanton cruelty. Although mental illness did not discriminate with regard to gender, the divorce and separation petitions filed against insane spouses were presented primarily by women who sought to remove their husbands as heads of household. This was due in large measure to the fact that, since men usually controlled the family estates, those men who were not capable of managing their affairs placed the economic survival of their families in jeopardy.

Nevertheless, many women whose husbands became mentally unbalanced—they used such terms as "mentally unsound," "mentally ill," "mentally unsettled," "demented," "deranged," "idiotic," and "insane"—took care of their husbands for lengthy periods of time, sometimes many years, before filing for divorce or seeking to have their husbands institutionalized. Nancy Taylor, who had been married for thirteen years, said in her answer to her husband's divorce petition that her husband believed he was surrounded by enemies, refused to leave their home, talked to himself, and was often "quite irrational." He suffered, she believed, from hypochondria and melancholia. It was only when she feared he might sell their house as well as their female slave that she sought and obtained a court order declaring him of unsound mind.[6]

Other wives also remained with their husbands over lengthy periods of time even though the men, as one wife said, were incapable of understanding what was going on around them. Usually it was not until things appeared to be getting out of hand that a wife took action. She would do so, for example, if she feared that her husband might injure himself, members of the family, or others; if she was afraid that he might wander off and not know where he was or how to return home; or if he attempted to sell his property for a fraction of its value. After eight years of marriage, a South Carolina woman informed the Charleston Equity Court that her husband had been for some time "incapable of using his personal liberty with safety to his family." Although he had been arrested on a number of occasions and incarcerated in either Charleston's Guard House or the city's Poor House, she had not filed papers until she became frightened at the possibility of his selling their house and slaves. A Kentucky wife faced the same predicament. In 1812, she petitioned the Fayette County Circuit Court for alimony and requested that her husband's property, including slaves, be put under the control of a group of trustees or commissioners. Her husband did not have the mental capacity to head his household, she reported, and a neighbor confirmed this, saying the man's mind was "strongly diseased."[7]

The many harrowing descriptions of the ravaging effects of insanity offered by wives petitioning for divorce suggest how painful it must have been to watch loved ones become disoriented, roam about the countryside, forget where they lived, or fail to remember their own names. Some of the husbands mumbled and chanted to themselves, heard voices, hid in outbuildings, and became obsessed with devils and demons. The wife of a Tennessee man explained that her husband lived in an "invisible world," received "revelations" from spirits, and heard "invisible correspondents." Besides receiving a divorce and alimony, she obtained an injunction prohibiting her husband from selling their property, which included a thirty-year-old slave named Eliza worth about $800.[8]

The line between sanity and insanity could sometimes be blurred. Some women obtained divorces and separations by securing testimony from witnesses who described the husbands' strange behavior, including obsessions, fixations, passions, or uncontrolled jealousies. Neighbors and friends told how some husbands forbade their wives to speak with other men, erupted into tantrums after the most seemingly innocent incidents, or prevented their wives from leaving the house for extended periods. Witnesses corroborated the stories of the women who said their husbands forced them to follow strange rituals, constantly threatened them with bodily harm, or railed against them constantly and without cause. The wife of a slave-owning Alabama farmer, for example, said that each time another man passed their farm on a nearby road, her husband brought out his Bible and searched the pages until he found the name of God. He then demanded that she swear on the Bible that she had never wronged him "or been guilty of adultery with any person" and kiss a page of the Bible as a promise of her fidelity. This ritual occurred almost daily. A Virginia wife whose husband owned ten slaves said she was forbidden to speak to any other man. When she did, her husband would "mould bullets, load his pistol before her & declare that he meant to shoot someone whose name he would not give." Before retiring each night, he locked all the doors, took out his pistol and his Bowie knife, put them in their bed, and compelled her to lie down next to him, placing chairs around the bed "so that anyone moving in the room would move against them."[9]

Other wives described similar episodes involving husbands who were delusional, irrational, light-headed, obsessed, and incapable of "mental restoration." In most cases the women asked to be released from their marital vows because of the dangers their husbands posed to themselves and their children as well as to their wives and others in the community. In the early years of the nineteenth century, state legislatures were often sympathetic to these situations and granted the petitioners divorces *a vinculo matrimonii*. The Maryland Assembly passed a number of acts releasing women from their marriages owing to their spouses' unbalanced minds or obvious delusions. In later years, the courts were equally receptive to women who charged husbands with insanity.[10]

The women who resorted to having their husbands jailed or committed to insane asylums did so with the knowledge that there was probably little hope for restoration. If declared insane, the husbands might be jailed for lengthy periods of time, even if they were members of the slaveholding class. Chained, living in filth and squalor, often sharing cells with others who were mentally ill, they often grew worse rather than better. Those who were committed to institutions for the insane were subjected to treatments that made any type of recovery virtually impossible. Such treatments included "drastic depleting" therapies such as bleeding, blistering, and hot mustard footbaths, as well as the employment of calomel, cold showers, and opiates. Most southerners cared little about the condition or needs of the insane, believing that the suffering of the mentally ill was a natural consequence of "unbending Providence, meting out judgment to the wicked and innately inferior."[11]

When wealthy slaveholders were declared *non compos mentis*, the courts often put the family holdings—land, slaves, bonds, cash, and even livestock and crops—into a trust estate under the control of a guardian, or a trustee or group of trustees. In some cases, this worked well because the wife was able to discuss various financial matters with a trustee or trustees who listened and responded to her needs and desires. But in other cases, the opposite occurred, especially when a large amount of property was involved. In such cases, family members and others bickered, disagreed, fought, sued, countersued, and demanded a larger portion of the estate. Many of the cases reveal that there was much more conflict within southern families than has been portrayed by scholars who argue that white women could rely on family and kinship networks during times of crisis. No sooner had a husband been declared insane than, like a swarm of locusts, various relations—adult children, in-laws, guardians of minors, adult children by previous marriages, brothers, sisters, uncles, and trustees—descended on the family property and filed various court motions.[12]

For some women the best recourse was to file divorce or separation papers citing reasons other than insanity, including excessive use of alcohol or cruelty to those around them, rather than describing the severe mood swings, obsessive jealousies, and erratic behavior displayed by their husbands. They would thus say that their husbands constantly taunted, humiliated, belittled, and demeaned them, were verbally abusive, and treated the children and slaves in an arbitrary, capricious, and irrational manner. In a cross bill, one Tennessee wife observed that her husband threatened to cut out the heart of her favorite slave, that he did not sleep at night and wandered about the countryside, and that he was frequently "on the wing." Women living with men "on the wing" feared not only for themselves and their children but for their slaves and others around them. Although some of these slaveholding men were passive and harmless, others took their frustrations out on their own families and their human property. The very nature of their often random and unprovoked attacks revealed an unstable state of mind.[13]

Some of the threats and violence against wives, children, and slaves might be considered extreme by the judicial authorities but not sufficiently so as to induce them to declare a husband insane. Indeed, the legal ownership of human property and the social and cultural acceptance of its consequences created an environment where it was understood that the need to exert power and authority over slaves as well as family members sometimes prompted some men to do strange things. Nevertheless, many of the episodes described by wives and witnesses in the divorce and separation petitions were so pronounced that they went beyond the accepted norms and left little doubt as to the existence of mental imbalance.[14]

As illustrated by these and other cases, insanity among slave owners revealed itself in a number of ways, including unpredictable behavior toward neighbors and friends, obsessive and paranoid jealousies, failure to comprehend financial matters, and acts of violence and cruelty toward members of their own families and their slaves. Most white southerners cared for mentally ill family members at home; in some cases, however, wives, like Lydia Rawdon, found it necessary to have their husbands declared *non compos mentis* and incarcerated in an asylum, but they did so only after it had become clear that the men posed a threat.

■ As did mental illness, alcoholism included a range of behavioral symptoms. Among the women who sued for divorce or separation, about one of four (146 of 610, or 24 percent) pointed to the excessive use of spirits as one of the reasons for doing so. Excessive use of spirits ranged from engaging in recurrent drinking binges to remaining intoxicated for days and weeks. Again, a few men in their divorce petitions accused wives of drinking to excess, but the accusation was overwhelmingly made by women against male household heads.

During the early decades of the nineteenth century, southerners consumed huge amounts of alcohol per capita, probably more than at any time before or since. Much of it was purchased at modest prices (25 to 40 cents per gallon) at the country store or town grocery, although some of it, especially whiskey, was distilled by farmers in their home-built stills. They fermented and distilled oats, wheat, barley, rye, and corn; they also used potatoes for whiskey and apples, peaches, and other fruits for brandy. Hard liquor was thus widely available and often cheaper than wine. Antebellum southerners consumed more than seven gallons of alcohol per capita annually, including more than four gallons of hard liquor. It was not uncommon for a man to drink a glass of whiskey or other spirits before breakfast, to have a few shots in the afternoon, and to down a glass or tumbler before or after supper. What caused such high consumption is a matter of speculation, but certainly important factors were its easy availability, low prices, cultural acceptance, and the belief that it relieved anxiety.[15]

There were efforts in the South to curtail the high consumption of alcohol. Religious groups and temperance societies spoke out against the evils of drink and the problems it caused in the domestic sphere. In 1818, in a petition to the North Carolina General Assembly, the members of the Beneficent Society of New Providence asserted that one of the most pressing needs in the area was to halt the "intemperate use which is daily made of Ardent spirits." In 1840, Mississippi and Arkansas passed nearly identical acts to suppress "the Vice of Drunkenness." In 1849, a group of Tennessee residents asked their General Assembly "to eradicate the evil" by repealing all laws legalizing "the sale of ardent spirits in tippling houses, or elsewhere." Not only were whites drinking too much, the petitioners asserted, but many slaves were also able to obtain "spirituous and vinous liquors." A few years later, a group of Virginians in Westmoreland County, including a number of slave owners, argued that the liquor trade accounted for two-thirds of the crime and two-thirds of the pauperism in their county. In addition, they said, drinking took a toll "in the domestic circle." "Its tendency is to manufacture undutiful children and tyrannical parents, harsh husbands and oppressed wives, bad masters and dishonest servants, useless citizens and inefficient public officers." To halt the retail whiskey trade, they urged local authorities to deny liquor licenses to anyone who might apply for one.[16]

The argument that excessive drinking created "tyrannical parents, harsh husbands and oppressed wives" was not altogether fanciful. A number of wives of slave owners filing for divorce complained that their husbands imbibed various forms of drink on a daily basis, sometimes to the point of intoxication. They described men who became addicted to "habits of intemperance," grew familiar with "intoxication and other accompanying vices," and were almost continually under the influence. They also explained how the excessive use of alcohol exacerbated marital difficulties. In North Carolina, Penelope Smith, the wife of a farmer who owned four slaves, said that her husband of twenty-two years was "constantly under the influence of liquor, & [spends] more than half his time drunk." He remained away for days at a time and returned home only to change clothes or recuperate when "broken down by excess." A South Carolina wife related that her slaveholding husband drank "until sickness ensued from the quantity of liquor consumed, when he would refrain for the space of two weeks or more" before returning to his old ways.[17]

Some women lamented that the evils of drink came over their husbands gradually. At the time of their marriages, the men were hardworking and industrious farmers and planters who rarely drank hard liquor, but gradually a transformation occurred. They began to drink too much on special occasions while remaining sober for weeks and months at a time; but then they began to drink more frequently, until after some time their periods of sobriety became less frequent and finally they were drinking heavily over long periods of time. A Tennessee wife echoed the complaints of other women when she said her husband "became habitually addicted to the use of intoxicating drinks & was not infrequently very drunk—that said habit of drinking has steadily increased upon him until he is now and for some time has been a hopeless sot."[18]

There were other women, however, who should have known from the outset that their husbands were too fond of liquor. In 1852, an Alabama woman said that her husband, a planter who owned twenty-five slaves, drank heavily throughout the five years of their marriage, sometimes going on sprees that lasted a week or more. Indeed, on their wedding day, he was "in one of the worst of his paroxysms of intoxication of about a week's standing," being so much under the influence that he could scarcely stand up and take his vows. Describing her husband as a "habitual drunkard," she fled from their plantation, taking with her their son. Six years later, she won temporary custody of the boy after the state supreme court ruled that her husband, during his frequent fits of intoxication, became a "boisterous madman."[19]

It was nearly impossible for wives to control excessive drinking by their husbands who were able to acquire liquor at low prices or spent time in tippling houses, saloons, and country stores indulging in whiskey, beer, and wine. The women testified that their husbands' passion for drink outweighed concerns about their families, children, livelihood, and even reputation and property. Judith Word, the wife of a Tennessee farmer, obtained a divorce by arguing that her husband, who was almost "continually intoxicated," had squandered much of their property and "brought poverty & misery upon your petitioner and her children." Similarly, Ann West, the wife of a North Carolina slave owner, obtained a divorce because her husband was "almost continually drunk" and wasting their property. At one point, to support his habit, he had sold the eldest son of one of their female slaves. For the previous five years, she testified, her husband had been "addicted to the excessive use of ardent spirits, and the habit has grown upon him so that he has for several years become an habitual drunkard and spendthrift." He also made new friends, drinking partners described by Ann as "dissipated and lewd companions." Eleanor Morgan, the wife of a Kentucky planter who owned fifteen slaves, said that her husband's drinking habits had placed her and their six children on the brink of economic disaster. While under the influence, her husband would be cheated and defrauded out of his holdings and had already lost "a large portion of his estate," land and slaves they had accumulated over their twelve-year marriage. Eleanor asserted that her husband's "intemperance is the cause of all the difficulties which have occurred in their domestic affairs." Although some wives, as a result of divorce or separation, were able to preserve a portion of the family holdings or were granted alimony and child support by the courts, others were left to fend for themselves.[20]

A man who was "habitually drunk," "in the habit of drunkenness," "addicted to habits of intemperance," and "Settled in his beastly habits" not only put his family's wealth in jeopardy but often tore his family apart. Despite family conclaves, advice from friends, threats of imprisonment, and even arrests and incarcerations, nothing seemed to work to rid some husbands of their dependency on alcohol. Some wives of slaveholding men were forced to take on extra work to make ends meet; they even worked in the fields with slaves to harvest the crop because their husbands went to the grog shop or lay around the house drinking. Relatives and friends lamented the way certain slave owners who drank to excess became "petulant & disagreeable" with everyone around them while under the influence. The more they drank, the more abusive and profane they became. According to one Alabama wife, during a drunken spree her husband committed the ultimate outrage: He "Shamelessly & indecently exposed his naked person" to her eleven-year-old daughter by a previous marriage and "by persuasive language & conduct" attempted to "corrupt and debase the morals and chastity of the child." She took her daughter and fled from the plantation.[21]

Prior to 1829, before the enactment or the implementation of laws specifically establishing excessive drinking as a cause for divorce or separation, twenty-nine cases filed by white women cited alcoholism as a primary reason for filing petitions. In succeeding decades, as some states included drunkenness as grounds for divorce in their statutes, the percentage in relation to the other cited causes remained roughly the same. During the early period (1786–1829), 21 percent of the women who filed for divorce cited this as one of the causes for doing so (29 of 137); in the later period (1830–67), the percentage was 25 (117 of 473). In addition, although only six states—Arkansas, Florida, Georgia, Louisiana, Mississippi, and Missouri—passed laws making alcoholism a cause for divorce or separation, the charges of excessive drinking in divorce petitions were distributed across states throughout the South. In this instance, the legal requirements had little to do with what was happening "on the ground" and did not influence or constrain the charges that were being put forth; rather, the legislative petitions and chancery court suits reflected what was occurring in households that were on the verge of splitting apart.[22]

■ During the late eighteenth century and the first six decades of the nineteenth, the number of migrants moving from one section of the South to another increased with each passing decade. In the early period after the American Revolution, many residents moved from the coastal plains to the piedmont region in the same state or traveled along interior valleys and waterways from one state to the next; they often found, after arriving at their destinations, that new horizons beckoned. By the 1820s, in wagons and carts, on steamboats and sailing ships, and astride horses and on foot, migrants journeyed from Maryland, Virginia, and the Carolinas to the Cumberland and Tennessee River valleys and farther west to the Mississippi River and beyond.

Among them were slave owners leading coffles of slaves, and nonslaveholders seeking new lands and new riches. It seemed as if a whole people were on the move. "The Alabama Fever rages here with great violence and has carried off vast numbers of our citizens," a North Carolina resident complained during the mid-1830s, speaking of the migration to new cotton lands in the Black Belt of Alabama and the Lower Mississippi River Valley. "I am apprehensive if it continues to spread as it has done, it will almost depopulate the country." Towns in Kentucky, Tennessee, Mississippi, Arkansas, and Louisiana witnessed the same changes that Henry Watson observed in Greensborough, Alabama, in 1836: "Nobody seems to consider himself settled, they remain one, two, three or four years & must move to some other spot." It was not long after Watson arrived in Greensborough that he noticed that "the entire population of this town, with a dozen or two exceptions, has changed." It was notorious that "if a man is away six months & returns he must expect to find himself among strangers." Watson's comments were backed up by statistics recorded in the U.S. census. Not only was there rapid turnover among the people arriving in the West, but many communities in the East were experiencing a significant exodus of their populations.[23]

Some of those who joined the migration from one section to another were husbands who deserted their wives. They "eloped to the Louisiana country," taking along their female slaves who were the "objects of their illicit love"; they journeyed to the "western country" with other white women; or they simply found the lure of the West and the possibility of wealth too strong to resist. Indeed, the "Alabama Fever," the "Mississippi

Fever," and later, the "California Fever" made migration a normal way of life, often straining and even destroying marital relations. Besides the attraction of new frontiers and going off with another woman, wives cited other reasons for their husbands' desertion, including the desire to avoid creditors, evade arrest, get away from in-laws, and escape family responsibilities.[24]

Among the wives who filed for divorce, more than one of four (173 of 610, or about 28 percent) cited desertion, or "abandonment" as it was most often called in law, as one of the causes for doing so. The state and territorial laws prescribing the length of time required after the desertion of a spouse before a suit for divorce or separation could be filed varied considerably from one state or territory to another and changed over time. In Alabama and Missouri it was two years; in Maryland and Kentucky, three years; and in Virginia, five years. Over time, states reduced the number of years plaintiffs were required to wait. The Arkansas Territory reduced its requirement from two years to one year in 1832; the Florida Territory, from three years to one year in 1835; the state of Mississippi, from five years to three years in 1840.[25]

Even though staying alone after their husbands had deserted them created many difficulties for them, some abandoned wives chose not to file for divorce, often waiting for many years. For some women it was easier not to file for divorce, either because of the stigma attached to it or simply to avoid the problems of hiring a lawyer and submitting court papers. Some had not heard from their spouses in several years and presumed they must be dead; others were getting along well without a male household head; some found a new life with relatives and friends; still others did not wish to relive the pain of their past relationships. A number of the abandoned women started new lives and acquired property. They were sometimes assisted by relatives and friends, especially in the older and more settled areas along the east coast, but often they did so through the dint of their own efforts. During these years, however, the absent husband remained legally the head of household and guardian of the children. He could return at any time and reclaim his rights.[26]

The women left behind assumed many burdens, especially if they had no kin or neighbors and friends to provide assistance. They were anguished by questions about their future and that of their family. How would they provide for themselves and their children, and where would they live if they were forced to move out of their homes? Wives described how their husbands, having sold the family property and departed for "parts unknown," left them with very little to live on. Some men secretly disposed of their plantations and took their slaves when they left. After fifteen years of marriage, Misella Ann Henry, a Mississippi slave owner, obtained a divorce after the court heard how, while she was visiting kin, her husband rounded up the livestock, packed the furniture in a wagon, gathered the slaves, and departed. Others said that their husbands, either clandestinely or openly, sold farm acreage, horses, cows, cattle, farm machinery, furniture, slaves, and even crops in the field before going away. In addition, the men often left the younger children at home and only took with them children old enough to work, or they retuned after several years to retrieve children who had reached working age.[27]

Despite many difficulties, the women were by no means helpless in responding to their husbands' actions. A number uncovered their husbands' plots to sell their estates and obtained injunctions against the men, preventing them from removing or disposing of the family property. When Richard Moore attempted a "pretended" sale of the family farm and slaves, Mary Moore of Nash County, North Carolina, obtained a court order instructing the sheriff to "seize receive and sequester" sixty-six acres, horses, buggy, wagon, carts, stock, crops of corn and cotton, and "eight negroes, to wit, Luke, Julia, Lenora, John, Allen, Bob Lucien and Isadore." The sheriff was also ordered to collect "the rents and profits" thereof. Others asked for and received court orders for maintenance and alimony, which, although payments were most often not forthcoming, could be enforced if the husband ever returned to the court's jurisdiction. At times, the women obtained legislative acts and court rulings to protect the property they might acquire in the future. On occasion they went to a justice of the peace and swore out arrest warrants. In 1811, a North Carolina wife whose husband had left the state not only claimed "a likely negro girl," a horse saddle, a horse bridle, and "a considerable quantity" of furniture—property that she owned at the time of her marriage—but filed a lawsuit against her brother-in-law who lived in the same county and owed her husband $1,000. Divorced women also sought and obtained *feme sole* status.[28]

A few women attempted to follow their husbands, either to have them arrested and brought back or in the hope that there might be a reconciliation. Most often this only required traveling to an adjacent county, but it could also mean going to another state. Such trips were especially arduous for a woman traveling without a male escort, even more so with children, and tracking down someone was a time-consuming and often futile task. In addition, most southern states refused to recognize the divorce laws from neighboring states, and filing suits as a nonresident was an extremely difficult undertaking, especially for women. Typical of the futility of such searches was the one conducted by Sarah Johnson, who petitioned the North Carolina General Assembly for divorce in 1805 charging that her husband squandered her considerable property, including nine slaves, and then abandoned her. She traveled from Fayetteville, North Carolina, to Camden and Columbia, South Carolina; Augusta, Georgia; and Charleston, South Carolina, before learning that her husband had recently boarded a ship for Ireland, his native country.[29]

There can be little doubt that abandoned wives felt a certain amount of shame and faced economic challenges to maintain their families. Yet, many women built new lives following their husband's departure and filed suits to protect themselves and their families. When they discovered that their husbands were still within the court's jurisdiction and still owned land, slaves, and other property, they sued them for "such sum by way of Alimony as may seem just & equitable." Even in South Carolina, where no divorce or separation laws existed, abandoned wives won equity suits that allowed them to retain the property they owned at the time of their marriage. Others who had been separated for many years described how they had built up their personal holdings, although they started with very little.[30]

■ The history of violence in the South has been the subject of numerous books and articles during the past two generations. Describing a "culture of violence," early writers pointed to frontier influences, excessive use of alcohol, failure of the courts to punish wrongdoers, a hierarchal and localized society, the institution of slavery, and the self-perception of the vast majority of white men, slaveholders and nonslaveholders, as being quick to fight for their principles and to defend their honor. The early authors discussed what might be termed the "southern tumult" among white males in the region, both against one another and with regard to punishment of slaves. In more recent years some historians have turned to the subject of domestic violence, but even the extensive literature on white southern women provides only glimpses into the havoc it wreaked on southern families. Most recently, scholars have studied local courts and argue that many people in the region believed that the law played a role in mediating violent acts. Although some of these studies provide examples of the violent behavior of husbands against their wives, neither the pervasiveness nor the brutality of abuse within southern households has received the attention it deserves. For, ironically, the systematic uncovering of domestic acts of cruelty is found not in criminal prosecutions but in chancery court suits for divorce and alimony.[31]

An analysis of the legislative petitions and chancery court suits in this study reveals that by a wide margin the most prevalent complaint made by white women who filed for divorce, separation, and alimony concerned the violent behavior of their husbands. Namely, two-thirds of the cases (398 of 610, or 65 percent) cited physical abuse, ranging from hitting and punching to bludgeoning and attempted murder, as grounds for seeking divorce. Most acts of violence were described as outbursts of extreme physical abuse: severe beatings, whippings, attempted poisonings, and assaults (239 of 398, or 60 percent), which by law constituted "cruel and barbarous treatment" in divorce and separation laws. Other wives described being subjected to less severe physical chastisement: hitting, punching, slapping, twisting, pinching, and striking with a switch (159 of 398, or 40 percent).

Of course, it is difficult to assess the part subjectivity and exaggeration played in the descriptions offered by wives and their lawyers suing for divorce or separation. It is clear, however, from the phrases that recur, sometimes word for word, in many of the complaints that lawyers had a hand in crafting the language of the petitions. Terms such as "cruel treatment," "cruel and inhuman treatment," "cruel and barbarous treatment," "brutal treatment," and "uniform conduct of cruelty and barbarity" were linguistic staples of divorce petitions that were undoubtedly used to depict specific events of violence in the language of the laws defining acceptable grounds for divorce and thus were thought to enhance the chances to win cases. In various states, separation petitions contained the exact same wording, accusing husbands of harsh treatment, outrages, and brutality that "rendered living together insupportable," or used the phrase "endangered her life by cruel and barbarous treatment."[32]

It was also clear that most judges and juries viewed extreme violence as valid grounds for divorce or separation, but they did not, until the 1830s, consider less severe types of abuse as such. In 1829, an appeals court judge in Kentucky said that no amount of neglect, coldness, indifference, and unmerited reproach constituted cruelty and, consequently, did not warrant divorce. "On the contrary," the justice wrote, "we conceive it must be some injury to the body, intended or inflicted, which will endanger life, to justify a divorce." In short, cruelty meant actual or apprehended physical suffering, not merely misery, unhappiness, or absence of affection. But even after 1829, when the state laws began to expand the definition of cruelty and in some states even included "mental cruelty" as grounds for divorce, the petitions' narratives describing instances of extreme violence continued. There was a relatively small decline in the cited instances of brutal spousal abuse, from 45 percent of the cases detailing extreme abuse during the early period (62 of 137) to 37 percent during the later period (177 of 473).[33]

The level of detail provided to support the accusations made by many women, as well as the corroborating testimony of witnesses and the language that transpired in the rulings of the courts, suggests not only that most of the charges were probably true but that extreme physical violence was pervasive in many of these households. The narratives also suggest that the onset of violence might erupt at any time during a marriage, from the first years to after many years. It could occur in any locale and be perpetrated by husbands who drank to excess as well as by some who were sober and God-fearing churchgoers. It could arise in families who owned only one or two slaves as well as in families who were among the largest slave owners in their communities. The same types of violent behavior could be observed from decade to decade. Indeed, domestic violence remained a constant in the South throughout the study period, transcending the multiplicity of values, societal attitudes, economic systems, and forms of bondage present throughout the region as well as over time.

Most of the women who filed for divorce and separation said their husbands struck, hit, punched, and assaulted them. As one woman said, her husband hit her with his fists a half dozen "severe & heavy blows, over the shoulders and arms to the manifest danger of her limbs & life." Wives claimed that their husbands also used a "cowhide or horse whip" as a means of punishment, in much the same manner as they punished their slaves. Mary Davis, the wife of a Georgia farmer who owned ten slaves, revealed that her husband of eighteen years beat her with his "hands feet rods and waggon whips." She was driven "from his bed & house to seek shelter for herself & children with her neighbors or in his barns and negro kitchens." She grieved that her husband had relinquished any sense of duty or obligation toward her and their children.[34]

Some wives and witnesses recorded gruesome details of marital conflicts, depicting how husbands caught women by the throat and delivered violent blows, swore they would kill them, and threatened them with guns. A Tennessee woman said that her husband was a man of enormous physical prowess who drank to excess and, when drunk, became "very violent in his passions, & sanguinary in his disposition." She refused to go back to him because he was so cruel that it was "impossible for her to live with him." The wife of a Mississippi planter testified that her husband repeatedly whipped her "in a most brutal manner, at one time with a sword cane, at another time he Knocked her down & beat her with his fist untill she

Evelina Roane. In 1824, after eighteen months of marriage, Evelina Roane petitioned the Virginia General Assembly for divorce. The twenty-year-old daughter from a prominent slaveholding family, Evelina declared that her husband treated her and her slaves with great cruelty. In one fit of rage he beat her with a stick, knocking her to the ground as she clung to her infant child. "His actions," she claimed, "offered a scene of unbounded rage and awful violence." Evelina was granted a divorce. (Petition of Evelina Roane to the Virginia General Assembly, King William County, 2 December 1824, Legislative Petitions, Library of Virginia, PAR #11682408; Buckley, "'Placed in the Power of Violence.'")

was almost deprived of life, & until the blood was caused to flow from her ears, & on six or seven other occasions he whipped her with a cowhide, cutting & lacerating her skin to such an extent that her clothes frequently stuck to the blood & wounds upon her person." She believed that such "cruelty, violence & outrages ought not to be tolerated, & that their endurance is not required at her hands, either by the laws of her country, or the precept of Christianity." Other wives described similar cruelty that occurred during their marriages. They charged that their husbands threatened them with guns and knives, cut and struck them because they spoke out, or dragged them by the hair about the house and threatened to take their lives.[35]

The fear and anxiety expressed by women asking to be divorced or separated from their husbands was borne out by the evidence. The testimony from neighbors, friends, acquaintances, family members, relatives, and others revealed that many women had reason to fear for their lives and that something horrible might happen to their children. The witnesses confirmed many of the complaints that wives made concerning husbands who inflicted severe corporal punishment upon them and their children, making their lives, as one South Carolina wife claimed, "a constant scene of misery and distress." A witness to domestic violence on a farm in Louisiana said he saw a husband bludgeon his wife with "a stick as thick as one's wrist." The witness said that blood flowed down the woman's cheeks. Elizabeth Wilkinson, who had been married for a number of years in Virginia, stated that her husband violated every conjugal duty and obligation and was a man of enormous cruelty. In her 1796 alimony suit she said that he struck her and threatened her life on numerous occasions and possessed a "turbulent disposition and inflammable temper." A witness added that she saw Elizabeth after one assault and described her as "much beaten and Bruised."[36]

The women who filed these petitions produced a long list of brutal acts that they said they endured during their marriages, incidents often corroborated in court by witnesses and mentioned in final decrees. The incidents included not only extreme physical chastisement but public humiliation. Whether they were the victims of physical punishment or public humiliation, the women either directly or indirectly equated their condition with that of those who were held in bondage. Some women said their husbands wielded a "cowhide or horsewhip" to "correct" them and their children in much the same manner as they corrected their slaves. Others said that their husbands demanded strict obedience, and if they or their children failed to deliver it, they could expect a whipping. The specifics offered by the wife of a South Carolina slave owner are so grim that they strain credulity. In her petition for alimony, Augusta Jeter cataloged for the court the wantonness of her slave-owning husband: He often beat her and whipped her; sometimes he tied her hands "like a slave"; he also ordered his slaves to tie her up "and inflict lashes upon her, like one of themselves"; he forced her to drink "nauseous and unhealthful potations"; bound her and left her in the woods; and placed her in "iron clogs and fetters, and kept her for days."[37]

The commonplace episodes of extreme violence against women and children described in divorce, separation, and alimony suits sometimes prompted wives to flee from their homes. Although some states made flight mandatory within the law to obtain a divorce, others did not, and the instances of fleeing were common in states where statutes did not require flight to obtain a divorce, separation, or alimony. Some women found refuge with relatives and friends, but others left without such support and found their way to the nearest neighbor. Sarah Womack, a Virginia woman from a respected and wealthy family, told a story repeated by others. Her husband often whipped her and beat her and threatened to take her life. She fled from their plantation and wandered from place to place, staying with anyone who would take her in and making out as best she could. She finally found a home on the plantation of Isaac Medley, a close friend of her deceased father. Medley, testifying on her behalf, described her, when she arrived at his plantation in Halifax County, as being "in a delicate state of health and destitute of almost every comfort."[38]

Children often suffered the most when wives abandoned their homesteads. Even in Louisiana, where district courts provided relief for women who sought to reclaim their property and sought custody of their children, the period following a flight until the case could be adjudicated could extend for many months, sometimes years. In other states, wives who fled from their husbands' violence might lose their property as well as their children. Leaving also meant abandoning the past, turning one's back on societal norms, and jeopardizing the economic well-being of oneself as well as one's children. As a result, for women the decision to abandon their homes and sometimes their children was agonizing and often came only when there seemed to be no other choice.[39]

There were, of course, legal actions that could be taken by wives against husbands who treated them in such a manner. They could and did swear out arrest warrants. However, such action was most often taken as a last resort. Although some neighbors, friends, and relations knew of the penchant for violence of some husbands, for women to take legal action was in a sense announcing to the community what many families wished to keep at least partially hidden. In addition, the consequences of contacting authorities could make things even worse. Wives realized that when a husband found out his wife had sworn out a complaint or even contacted a sheriff or magistrate, he might become even more violent. Moreover, once a husband had been arrested and jailed, his wife became responsible for managing the farm or plantation; supervising the slave labor force; instructing overseers in those cases where there were large numbers of slaves; planting, harvesting, and selling the crops; and conducting financial matters. Following an arrest, husbands were required to post a good-behavior bond. Default on such a bond, the value of which was usually equal to a significant portion of a family's estate, could result in devastating consequences for the entire family. For all of these reasons, wives rarely approached authorities to solve even the most egregious domestic difficulties.[40]

Many husbands who disciplined their wives and children with a whipping or beating believed that it was not only their right but their duty. When asked about taking a cowhide to his wife's back, South Carolina slave owner Leroy Mattison said that he "whipped her and he thought it was his duty—it, was his God's duty—it was the best thing he ever did for her." This deeply held belief—that it was a husband's responsibility, even obligation, as directed by God, to correct his wife with corporal punishment—was shared by many southerners, both slaveholders and nonslaveholders. The men also advanced a variety of other reasons why domestic violence was necessary, including challenges to male authority, assertions of independence, refusal to submit sexually, drinking to excess, displaying a bad temper, using indecent language, becoming too familiar with slaves, and inciting black people against the master. One slave-owning widower in Virginia said his young wife "cast off all pretension to affection or submission." She also refused "motherly kindness" toward his children by a former marriage. As a result, he whipped her several times with a "small switch" and then cut her clothes off with his knife, exposing her naked body "to the observation of his slaves and the family."[41]

The detailed and graphic depictions of specific acts illustrate the prevalence of domestic violence in the Old South and how white southern males were quick to resort to it in order to resolve marital conflicts. Certainly, as many have suggested, the patriarchal nature of the social structure that placed the male at the head of the household offered men naturally inclined to violence opportunities to unleash it under the sanction of societal norms. There were also any number of economic problems and cultural behaviors at that time and place that probably exacerbated the everyday difficulties encountered in raising a family and negotiating domestic relations with immediate as well as extended kin, and these acted as triggers for the eruption of unbridled anger.

Yet the fact that some married women compared their plight to that of slaves suggests a more prescient reason. Slaveholders had virtually unlimited authority to discipline their slaves and to control their fate through sale, trade, and family separation, powers that imbued owners with a sense of omnipotence over all in their households. Under certain circumstances and given certain natural propensities, the responsibilities of the patriarch could easily be transformed into abuse and violence. To be sure, there were many nonviolent slaveholders who treated their families with love and affection and exercised the socially expected balance between authority and responsibility, but there were also many men who harshly disciplined their wives and children. The domestic violence cited by women seeking a divorce reveals how deeply, in the words of Alexis de Tocqueville, slavery penetrated the souls of slave owners.[42]

■ Besides adultery, insanity, alcoholism, desertion, and domestic violence, women cited other grievances that caused them to file papers for separation or divorce. Among them were impotency, incest, bigamy, mixed racial ancestry, cruelty without violence, mental abuse, public defama-

TABLE 3 **Husbands Accused of Domestic Violence**

	Divorce/ alimony cases	Extreme violence*		Physical abuse**		Totals		Percent of cases	Percent slave owners
Alabama	60	28	**25*****	10	**9**	38	**34**	63	89
Arkansas	1								
Delaware									
District of Columbia	9	4	**4**	1	**1**	5	**5**	55	100
Florida	12	4	**4**	3	**3**	7	**7**	58	100
Georgia	11	6	**6**	2	**2**	8	**8**	73	100
Kentucky	54	19	**18**	12	**12**	31	**30**	57	97
Louisiana	52	24	**24**	19	**18**	43	**42**	83	98
Maryland	20	8	**7**	4	**3**	12	**10**	60	83
Mississippi	22	8	**8**	3	**2**	11	**10**	50	91
Missouri	6	2	**2**	1	**1**	3	**3**	50	100
North Carolina	138	52	**42**	22	**20**	74	**62**	54	84
South Carolina	76	38	**38**	22	**21**	60	**59**	79	98
Tennessee	71	16	**13**	34	**33**	50	**46**	70	92
Texas	11	3	**3**	6	**5**	9	**8**	82	89
Virginia	67	27	**24**	20	**19**	47	**43**	70	91
TOTALS	610	239	**218**	159	**149**	398	**367**	65	92

Source: Compiled from Divorce and Alimony Excel File Database.

*Extreme violence included beating, whipping, assault, bludgeoning, poisoning, stabbing, shooting, and threat of murder.
**Physical abuse included hitting, punching, kicking, shoving, twisting, pinching, and whipping with switches.
***slaveholders in bold

tion, and felony conviction. The charges that perhaps brought the greatest humiliation to the men involved included impotency and incest. Both were extremely rare. The mere suggestion of a man's inability to perform the sexual act or that he sexually assaulted an underage girl in the family brought into question a slave owner's manhood and honor. In addition, the accusations were difficult to prove and embarrassing for everyone concerned. When they were offered, the women and their lawyers, as well as witnesses, described in graphic language the intimate details of a marriage. Most of the impotency cases were similar to the one presented by Cassandra Houston, a North Carolina slave owner who, after eleven months of marriage, declared that her husband was not able to perform

Insanity, Alcoholism, Abandonment, and Abuse

his duties "as a man in procreating his species." Although she was not granted a divorce, a number of her friends, neighbors, and family members supported her application. The husband, they asserted, "was not as complete as to genitals as other men" and attempted to "ride" other men "as man would with a Woman." Equally painful was the admission by a South Carolina slaveholding widow, Eliza Byrnes, who in the midst of a property dispute charged that her husband had seduced her young daughter by her previous marriage and "now cohabits with the unfortunate victim of his incestuous lust."[43]

Like impotency and incest, the charge of bigamy was extremely rare in the Old South. As previously indicated, with the ebb and flow of populations in the antebellum era, many instances of bigamy never reached the courts by way of divorce suits. It was relatively easy for a married man to start a new life in a nearby county under a new identity, or even while maintaining an old one, given that the slow communications and life in rural communities offered a measure of anonymity. In these cases, the women could file suits charging adultery and/or desertion or instigate criminal charges of cohabitation, fornication, and bastardy. Even if a wife was able to bring evidence of bigamy before the court, witnesses were often hard to subpoena and cases were difficult to prosecute, to say nothing of the time and effort involved. Because bigamy was a crime in law and before God, it appears that most men who established second, sometimes third, families did so without obtaining marriage licenses.[44]

In a number of states, there were laws against interracial marriage, but if the partners involved were nearly white or presumed to be white, charges were sometimes difficult to prove. Occasionally, however, this type of situation found its way into the divorce courts. Baltimore slaveholder Elizabeth Tinges, for instance, claimed that she was "made the victim of the most outrageous fraud." After more than a dozen years of marriage, she learned that her husband, "instead of being a white man is a mulatto and in reality had been born a slave." In his answer, William Tinges asserted that his wife knew all along that he was a person of mixed racial ancestry; in fact, prior to their marriage she told him that he was "White enough for her."[45]

Far more common than divorce suits on the grounds of impotency, incest, bigamy, or interracial mixing were those that charged cruelty *without* violence, mental abuse, or public defamation. In fact, during the 1840s and 1850s, women began increasingly to say that their life had become "unbearable" because they experienced cruelty but not physical abuse. Divorce laws in North Carolina, Tennessee, Arkansas, Louisiana, and Texas mentioned "personal indignities" that rendered cohabitation "intolerable." By the end of the antebellum era, these same states, except Louisiana, granted divorce and separation on grounds of cruelty without physical violence. This was broadly defined as neglect, disdain, and "every other plain manifestation of settled hate, alienation and estrangement, both of word and action." Such insults and affronts needed to be "habitual, continuous and permanent."[46]

Thus, in Arkansas, Nancy Rose sued for divorce because her husband encouraged his slaves to disobey her orders and to insult her by calling her a liar and a "lazy white woman." In addition, he forced her to sleep in an outbuilding for five months. She was granted a divorce. So, too, was Susan Littleton, a Tennessee woman who said that her husband made "every false accusation that he could imagine, of various and repeated acts of adultery with diverse persons indeed with every person that his jealous imagination could depict." Over the years, she continued, he used the "most foul and horrible oaths that the human tongue can utter, calling her all the base names that belong to the English language," humiliating her before her friends, neighbors, and members of her congregation. Another wife explained that she left her husband because his language contained words "such As a Gentleman would not employ to his Slave Much less his wife."[47]

Even in states where there were no specific statutes concerning mental abuse or personal indignities, wives filed for divorce charging nonphysical cruelty. They said that their husbands harassed them with foul and unseemly language, questioned their moral character, and accused them of the grossest types of misconduct. Dorcas Lacy of Sumter County, Alabama, obtained a divorce because her husband tried to force her to wear men's clothing and ride a horse through the neighborhood. When she refused, he attempted to humiliate, demean, and degrade her before family and friends.[48]

As these cases suggest, a close connection was established between mental abuse and character defamation. In Louisiana, from a very early period, women could obtain a separation of bed and board by arguing that their husbands debased their reputations. In 1817, Celeste Collins secured a separation because her husband endeavored to "defame and injure" her "good name fame & reputation" by spreading "false & malicious reports" about her character. Elizabeth Overbay of West Feliciana Parish, Louisiana, won a separation of bed and board in 1834 charging her husband with mental abuse over a six-month period during which he constantly used the most "foul and indecent language." Rebecca Harvey obtained a separation because on many occasions her husband had defamed her "fair character in the presence & hearing of diverse citizens in the Parish and state." Although some of the so-called fair-character suits included other types of accusations, many focused on charges of public insult and humiliation, such as calling a wife, for instance, a "damned whore and drunken bitch."[49]

The charges of mental abuse and public defamation were sometimes coupled with accusations of excessive use of alcohol and physical abuse, but the act of humiliating women in the presence of others carried special weight with judges and juries in a society where it was important to uphold the sanctity of the ideal southern white woman. Also carrying weight was proof that a husband had been convicted of a felony, which also was grounds for divorce in a number of states, including Arkansas, Georgia, Kentucky, Louisiana, Mississippi, Missouri, Tennessee, and Virginia. Wives suing for divorce on grounds of felony conviction charged that their husbands had been tried and convicted of robbery, rape, theft, burglary, assault, larceny, forgery, or murder. Even in states where there were no specific statutes on the books regarding felonies and divorce, women could call such convictions to the attention of the courts.[50]

It is clear that not only did increasing numbers of female plaintiffs bring their cases for divorce and separation to the legislatures and equity, or chancery, courts, but that as time passed they did so by arguing their cases on the basis of a broader range of complaints sanctioned by law. The laws in some sense were influenced by these arguments as the legal system adapted and adjusted to the changing times. Thus, not only did women mold their arguments to the existing state statutes, but by challenging public opinion and airing their painful experiences before state legislatures and chancery courts, they were at least partly responsible for the expansion and broadening of separation and divorce laws in the Old South.

■ Following her husband's confinement in the Georgia State Asylum for the Insane in Milledgeville, Lydia Rawdon struggled to put her life back together. She had suffered greatly over the years, giving birth to one stillborn child, losing two others to scarlet fever, and now grieving the brutal death of her slow-witted son. Long before Isaac Rawdon was taken away, however, she had been involved in the management of their plantation, setting work routines for the slaves; supervising the planting, cultivation, and harvesting of the cotton; and ordering provisions and supplies. With a court-appointed guardian to oversee her husband's interests, Lydia became the proprietor of a thriving cotton plantation, which she managed with the help of a trustee, also appointed by the court. The land alone was worth $8,000, and she possessed mules, horses, cattle, hogs, sheep, furniture, tools, a wagon and a buggy, and more than twenty slaves. Several of them, including Jim and Nance, were quite old, over the age of seventy, but most of the others were "prime hands" in their teens, twenties, and thirties. The slave property was worth several times the estimated value of her real estate and other holdings. In addition, the plantation was located in the Coosa River Valley near the foothills of the Blue Ridge Mountains, an area of rich loamy soils, free from fever and chills, and boasting pure spring water. The cotton crop grew year-round, and planters in the area sent several million pounds of the staple to market each year.[51]

After the divorce, Lydia's anxiety about her husband gradually subsided, as she turned her attention to managing her plantation and her slave labor force. By 1860, she had invited three white men to come and live with her on the plantation, including a physician, a schoolteacher, and an overseer who brought along his two teenage daughters. By that year, she had increased the value of her farm to $12,000, boasting 340 acres of improved land and more than 1,000 additional acres. She now owned twenty-five slaves, including Josh and Fanna, given to her by her father two decades before and who now had four adult children. She also possessed horses, mules, milk cows, oxen, twenty-one head of cattle, thirty-one head of sheep, and sixty swine. During the year ending 1 June 1860, she produced 60 bushels of wheat, 1,500 bushels of Indian corn, and 50 bales of ginned cotton. Thus, five years after her divorce, she could find a large measure of comfort in the fact that she owned a thriving plantation, a loyal and productive labor force, and a total estate worth an estimated $50,000; indeed, she had become one of the most prosperous planters in the Coosa Valley.[52]

LAWYERS, JUDGES, JURIES, AND DECREES

In 1838, Sarah Ratliff, at age fifty-six, married slaveowning Missouri farmer William Duncan, who was in his late forties and headed a family of four boys from a previous marriage. She soon discovered that they had very little in common. The older boys disliked their new stepmother and expressed their antipathy in a number of ways. The couple bickered and fought constantly, often over trivial matters, and at times their arguments erupted into violence. Sarah, who had not been married before, said that William called her an "old bitch" and an "old Whore," slapped her in the face, punched her with his fist, struck her with a large club, and threatened to "wash his hands in her hearts blood"; William asserted that Sarah was never an affectionate wife and, on one occasion, hit him as he lay in his sickbed. There was also the question of the six slaves Sarah had brought to their union and her resentment that they had become his property. After six years of marriage, Sarah moved out and went to live with a family friend, John Reed, a farmer and slave owner in nearby Clinton County.[1]

Sarah Duncan waited twenty-six months before filing for divorce. Being illiterate, she was unaware of her new rights under the law. In fact, only after she consulted the law office of Gardenhire, Vories & Routt did she discover the possible benefits of seeking a divorce. In 1845, one year before Sarah filed for divorce, the Missouri General Assembly had passed a law stipulating that all property "which came to a husband by means of marriage" reverted back to the wife if she obtained a divorce. She also discovered that a statute passed by the Assembly in 1817 and amended in 1833 permitted divorce on grounds of extreme cruelty.[2]

On 28 July 1846, accompanied by her lawyers, Sarah Duncan filed a suit in the Fifth Judicial District Circuit Court. Because of the indignities she had suffered and the treatment she had endured, she requested an absolute divorce, a divorce *a vinculo matrimonii*. She asked presiding judge Austin A. King to issue a subpoena forcing her husband to answer the charges and an injunction restraining him from selling the slaves mentioned in her bill of complaint. She also requested alimony, a cash payment until her case could be decided, and the immediate return by her husband of the six slaves she owned at the time of their marriage and a black child named David born since then.[3]

What happened in the succeeding months illustrates the legal process in divorce cases within slaveholding families. It also reveals the crucial role played by lawyers and judges, who drafted arguments, interpreted the law, filed motions, and issued decrees. In July 1846, the judge ordered an injunction to prohibit the husband from selling the slaves. Sarah Duncan and John Reed then posted a security bond of $1,000 to pay any damages and costs in the event that Sarah lost her suit. The clerk of court ordered the sheriff to deliver a summons and a copy of the complaint to William Duncan, but in October 1846, at the fall term of the Court, Duncan, through his lawyers, asked for and obtained a continuance. At the same session, the judge issued an order for William Duncan to pay alimony of $80 per month for the next six months.

In February 1847, William Duncan, accompanied by his lawyers, answered the charges. He denied his wife's accusations and asserted that he had always treated her well and he had not forced her out of the house, as she claimed; rather, she voluntarily left the farm in May 1844 and never returned. With regard to the slaves who had passed into his possession, he hired them out and turned their wages over to her, even though she was given many comforts during their time together and had no need of the money. He felt so strongly about the injustice of the charges that his lawyers filed a cross bill, arguing that his wife, not he, was at fault. In response, Sarah's lawyers filed a replication, replying to the cross bill. Meanwhile, the judge ordered the extension of the wife's maintenance allowance. Finally, in February 1848, seventeen months after the filing of Sarah's petition and nearly four years after she had moved out of her husband's house, Judge King issued a decree granting her an absolute divorce and requiring her husband to turn over eight slaves, including a second child named Cyrus, "born of the said Negro slave Jenny since the commencement of this Suit." The judge did grant the defendant permission to remarry within one year, as opposed to the statutory two years.[4]

The suit of Sarah Duncan raises a number of questions about the process of filing divorce and alimony cases in the Old South, the role of lawyers and judges in interpreting the evolving statutes, and the shrewd use

State of Missouri } Sct
County of Clay }
                        at a Circuit Court of
the fifth Judicial district of the State of
Missouri begun and held at the Court house
in the Town of Liberty County of Clay and
State of Missouri on the 4th Monday of
February AD 1848
            Present
The Honorable Austin A King Judge
        Samuel Hadley Esqr Sheriff
            Samuel Tilley Clerk

Sarah Duncan
    vs   } Bill in Chancery
William Duncan
                    Be it Remembered that
heretofore to wit on the ___ day of
___ AD 1846 Sarah Duncan filed in the office of
the Clerk of the Clay Circuit Court a Bill in
Chancery and order for Injunction against
the defendant William Duncan in the words
and figures following to wit
    To the Honorable Austin A King Judge
of the fifth Judicial Circuit in the State
of Missouri in Chancery
    Your Complainant Sarah Duncan would
respectfully represent unto your honor that
on the 5th Day of August 1838 your Complainant
a[nd] ___ William Duncan intermarried
to[geth]er as Man and Wife in the County of
Cl[int]on in the State of Missouri and have
lived in the County of Clay from that

Bill in chancery of Sarah Duncan. Most bills in chancery, or petitions, were not transcribed from the original by a scribe, as seen here when illiterate plaintiff Sarah Duncan and her lawyers filed for divorce in 1846. The copy was made when the husband appealed to the Missouri Supreme Court. Other bills of complaint, however, contained similar language and accusations as well as similar emphases on the importance of slaves as property.

by petitioners of remedies offered by the law, questions that have not to date been fully answered by historians. This chapter examines how those who filed petitions for divorce, separation, and alimony, primarily women, fared in their efforts and how lawyers, judges, and juries responded to those applications. Did the wealthiest have an advantage over those of more modest means? Did men have an advantage over women? What differences existed between the legislative acts and chancery court decrees? Did results change over time?[5]

■ The passage of laws and constitutional amendments concerning divorce and separation during the early decades of the nineteenth century had a profound effect on lawyers and judges. The shift from private legislation to specific laws governing how, when, and why individuals could seek to end their marriages coincided with the enactment of regulatory laws regarding incorporation, banking, bankruptcy, and married women's property. Although in the early years many members of the bench and bar believed that statute law merely "patched up common law," as time passed, not only did they recognize statutes as the governing medium but they realized that they needed to become familiar with state codes. At the same time, there was continued support for the idea of "equity," especially with respect to women, and some cases, as Associate Justice of the U.S. Supreme Court Joseph Story said, needed to be made by construing the words found in the codes in their "mildest not their harshest sense, it being open to adopt either." An examination of the arguments of the members of the bar and bench involved in divorce cases and of the outcomes of those cases provides a window into the societal attitudes that were shared by the various participants in the process, not only judges, juries, and lawyers—the last group variously called counsel, attorneys, and solicitors—but litigants and defendants as well.[6]

The lawyers who argued in equity courts on behalf of female clients realized that merely to describe the suffering that wives experienced was not enough to secure a favorable ruling. It was necessary to obtain evidence in a client's behalf, especially testimony from eyewitnesses, and to fashion this evidence into a clear and compelling narrative, articulating the relevant laws and legal precedents. Those who accepted women as clients were certainly cognizant of the fact that the courtrooms of the Old South were the domain of males. Indeed, during the early period, it was not unusual for courtrooms—even in the superior, circuit, and district courts—to smell of tobacco juice and whiskey. The attorneys were also aware that the appearance in the courtroom of a female plaintiff, especially if the woman were from an aristocratic slaveholding family, would create a sensation, attracting crowds of onlookers, young and old, rich and poor, slave and free.[7]

The responsibilities of legal counsel seemed to be never-ending. Lawyers constructed complaints, contacted witnesses, and obtained summonses for defendants to appear in court. They accompanied their clients into court, read depositions, called witnesses to the stand, asked for subpoenas, sought injunctions, submitted motions, requested continuances, and argued their clients' "cause" before judges and juries. They realized that they needed to present firsthand accounts of the marital conflicts, witnesses who had observed events, both to prove the allegations and, in the case of lawyers representing defendants, fashion denials. Thus, at most trials they presented depositions or testimony from relatives, friends, neighbors, visitors, bystanders, townspeople, and others who could verify the charges made by the plaintiffs or the rebuttals made on behalf of defendants. Even though many members of the bar, like other southerners, believed marriage was a sacred institution, they effectively argued in behalf of female plaintiffs, winning the great majority of their cases. Thus there is little doubt that over the years the women filing divorce, separation, and alimony suits as well as their lawyers advanced the rights of married women before the law.

Often the most difficult charge to prove or rebut was that of adultery with slaves or free people of color, as the testimony of blacks was not permitted in court except in cases where both parties were black. As might be expected, most adultery cases hinged on circumstantial evidence. Though a few observers testified in court, or in a deposition, that they actually had seen a husband engage in sexual intercourse with a slave or free black woman, most witnesses only described suspicious circumstances and left it to the judge or jury to decide guilt or innocence. There were numerous cases similar to the one brought in 1836 by three Tennessee lawyers, G. W. Campbell, Thomas H. Fletcher, and David Scott, who took depositions from no fewer than eleven Nashville residents in the case of *Winnefrid Richmond v. Braddock Richmond*. The witnesses agreed that the slave Polly worked as a cook and laundress at her owner's house on Broad Street in Nashville. They also agreed that she was attractive, self-assured, and strong-willed; that she ordered other slaves about the house, especially field hands who came to town from the owner's plantation; and that when the master stayed overnight in the city, she slept near him in the front room of the ground floor, ostensibly to be near the fire on cold winter nights.

Although no one testified that they had actually seen Polly and her master having sexual relations, several witnesses said they had seen the two of them in various stages of undress. As a result, the jury found for the aggrieved wife and "ordered, adjudged, and decreed that the bonds of matrimony, heretofore subsisting, between the petitioner and said defendant, be henceforth dissolved, annulled and for naught held." The defendant appealed to the state supreme court, which three years later upheld the lower court's decree. A man who slept near his slave and was observed in compromising positions, the higher court ruled, must have been guilty of adultery.[8]

Evidence of domestic violence was more direct, and witnesses often told of what they actually saw, either during or after the incidents, not just what they could deduce. Judges and juries were sympathetic toward women who claimed that their husbands whipped, choked, beat, and attacked them on numerous occasions. Although the laws of most states included the infliction of brutal and life-threatening violence as grounds for granting a divorce, the definition of what constituted extreme abuse was open to interpretation. Solicitors realized that most of the men who were judges and members of juries believed that corporal punishment of a wife by her husband was not only a private affair but that, when carried out in moderation, it was in fact legal and did not necessarily qualify as domestic violence. In some states, during the early period, it was necessary by law to prove that the violence was life-threatening, or that the wife was forced to flee from her home, or that the abuse was sustained, oppressive, and made living together "unbearable."

Lawyers, in conformance with the law, called witnesses who described in vivid detail how the plaintiffs had been attacked and beaten. In 1809, Kentucky lawyer James D. Breckinridge, who later became a member of Congress, took depositions from two witnesses who described Eliza Bainbridge after she had been battered by her husband. Eliza was "much beat," with "her head cut & her eyes & Breast very Black," and she had been forced to flee to save her life. Lawyers in other cases were similarly successful by calling witnesses to corroborate wives' charges of extreme physical abuse. In depositions and on the witness stand, they described how husbands whipped, beat, bludgeoned, and threatened their wives on numerous occasions. The testimony was so consistent and compelling that it was rarely successfully challenged by opposing counsel.[9]

Even during the early years, before state laws redefined abuse to include nonviolent behavior on the part of the husband, judges had the option to accept fear and intimidation as grounds for divorce and separation. In

South Carolina, lawyers used arguments in alimony proceedings about wives feeling threatened and being forced to leave their homes and about children being caught in the middle. Judge Henry William DeSaussure, a large slave owner and well known for codifying the state's equity laws, permitted abused wives, who by law could not get a divorce, to live separate and apart from their husbands when they felt threatened; forbade the men from disturbing them; and gave the plaintiffs custody of the children.[10]

Although lawyers who filed suits charging adultery or abuse or both needed the testimony of witnesses to prove their cases, those who pled cases involving desertion needed less direct evidence. These suits were most often brought by wives whose husbands had left them and either moved to another state or "parts unknown" or had gone to live with another woman in the same county or state. The law required lengthy periods of separation, at least one year and as many as five years, depending on the state, before divorce or separation could be granted. A judge in Mississippi paraphrased the language of the state law when he granted a divorce to a wife because her husband was guilty of "willful obstinate and continued desertion for more than three years."[11]

To make sure defendants had every opportunity to answer the charges, lawyers arranged for the publication of court orders in local newspapers and the posting of the orders in a public location, usually near the courthouse door. This was especially important in cases of abandonment when a husband had been absent for any length of time. How such posting was to be done and how long the notices must run varied from state to state, but the required period was usually between four and six weeks. In general, however, the chancery rules governing court proceedings in desertion cases were straightforward. In fact, they were so basic that a few women opted to file their own pleas without the assistance of counsel.[12]

Lawyers pled cases before judges based on one other major cause of women seeking a divorce or separation: the excessive use of alcohol. Wives often cited a husband's drunkenness as one of the reasons for seeking to dissolve their marriages; they did so even during the early period when there were no specific laws citing it as a singular ground for divorce or separation. Before and after the enactment of laws permitting a wife to file suit because of her husband's excessive drinking, lawyers used such behavior as a foundation in their arguments. Counsel for Melinda W. Poston, the wife of a Kentucky farmer who owned a single slave, produced witnesses to verify Melinda's charge that her husband had a great "fondness for drink" and her assertion that, when he was drunk, he was oppressive, telling her he wished she were "dead in hell" and that their only child "had as well die, as be so expensive."[13]

Of course, solicitors representing women seeking divorce or separation presented a range of other reasons for filing divorce and alimony suits. They variously charged husbands with being *non compos mentis*, improvident, or impotent; inflicting mental abuse and "personal indignities" upon their wives; threatening them with bodily harm; having been charged with crimes that led to confinement in a penitentiary; engaging in interracial mixing; or being related to their wives by lines of consanguinity. But they usually included in their pleas one or two of the most common charges leveled by complainants against their spouses: adultery, extreme abuse, desertion, and alcoholism.

Whatever the accusation, lawyers were remarkably successful in obtaining favorable decrees for their clients in the circuit, district, and superior chancery courts. The data shows, when cases with unusual outcomes and cases with no decrees are excluded, that lawyers for female plaintiffs secured favorable rulings (granted, partially granted, or granted *pro confesso*) in 81 percent of the cases (353 of 437). Another 10 percent (45 of 437) either dismissed their own suits or reached an agreement or settlement, and only 9 percent (39 of 437) saw their suits dismissed or denied. When the same data exclusions are applied, female plaintiffs charging infidelity obtained favorable rulings in 82 percent of the cases (127 of 155); they reached agreements or settlements, or dismissed their own suits, in 10 percent of the cases (16 of 155), and 8 percent (12 of 155) saw their cases dismissed or denied. In cases where the charge was extreme abuse, plaintiffs obtained favorable rulings in 78 percent of the cases (140 of 180), reached compromises or dismissed their own suits in 12 percent of the cases (21 of 180), and only about 10 percent (19 of 180) saw their suits dismissed or denied. When charging desertion, they obtained favorable rulings (granted, partially granted, or granted *pro confesso*) in 88 percent of the cases (106 of 120). They reached settlements or dismissed their own suits in only 3 percent of the cases (4 of 120), and 8 percent (10 of 120) saw their suits dismissed or denied. Lastly, when charging drunkenness, they obtained favorable rulings in 82 percent of the cases (110 of 134), reached compromises or dismissed their own suits in 11 percent of the cases (15 of 134), and only 7 percent (9 of 134) saw their cases dismissed or denied. In short, four of five female plaintiffs obtained favorable outcomes (see Table 7 in Appendix 1 and "An Essay on Sources and Methodology").

Some of the lawyers or lead counsel cited two of the major causes in their pleas to the court. Among counsel for the 211 women accusing their husbands of infidelity, 71 coupled this charge with extreme violence, 45 coupled it with excessive use of alcohol, and 64 coupled it with desertion. Among counsel for the 228 women accusing their husbands of extreme abuse, 89 coupled this charge with drunkenness and 26 coupled it with desertion. Very few lawyers combined more than two of the most common charges in one civil suit. For example, among the 211 women who accused their husbands of infidelity, only 9 cited excessive violence *and* desertion, and only 8 cited excessive drunkenness *and* desertion. Only one lawyer, John H. Bryan, representing Margaret Kornegay in Wayne County, North Carolina, accused a husband of adultery, violence, desertion, and alcoholism.

For a variety of reasons white women often waited a long time before filing suits against their husbands, and when they did, they often did so *without* a *prochein ami*, or next friend—that is, without a father, brother, male family member, or male friend acting for the benefit of a woman who could not file a suit in her own right. The next friend was neither a party to the suit nor acted as a legal guardian but, in practice, served both functions. The fact that many women seeking divorce did not have next friends suggests not only that they were not considered as "covered" by their husbands in the law, but also that immediate family, extended kin, or friends were not always available to offer support.

Among the women who went to court seeking to end their marriages or separate from their husbands, three of five did so with their lawyers as lone petitioners. Nor were those who filed without a male next friend—slaveholders and nonslaveholders alike—clustered in the period after 1830, when the laws concerning divorce and separation were expanding in the southern states. In the early period, a majority of the suits filed by women in the district, circuit, or superior courts were filed without a male counterpart (62 of 114, or 54 percent); in the later period, an even larger majority were filed in the same manner (279 of 459, or 61 percent).

With regard to results, women and their lawyers who filed without a next friend fared slightly better than those who sued with one, although both groups obtained a high proportion of favorable decrees. Cases filed by women without next friends, where the results could be determined, received favorable decrees (granted, partially granted, or granted *pro confesso*) 82 percent of the time (206 of 252); in 9 percent of the cases, the plaintiffs fashioned an agreement or compromise with their husbands, and another 9 percent had their suits dismissed or rejected. In cases with next friends, where the results could be determined, favorable decrees were delivered 79 percent of the time (147 of 185); in 12 percent of the cases, the plaintiffs fashioned some type of compromise, and in 9 percent of the cases they had their suits dismissed or rejected. In short, it mattered little whether female plaintiffs found a person to petition with them when it came to results, but most of them, along with their counsel, decided that unless required to do so by state law, they preferred to launch an independent response to their marital troubles.

■ Lawyers representing husbands in divorce proceedings charged wives with alcoholism, insanity, violence, attempted poisoning, contracting a venereal disease, fraud, and other misdeeds, but these were rare exceptions; in the main, they only used two accusations, either adultery or desertion. As did the cases filed by female complainants, most adultery cases filed by male complainants rested on circumstantial evidence. Most witnesses could point only to situations that seemed strange or out of place, such as wives entertaining single men with no other person present, inviting male friends to visit when their husbands were gone, or seeking the company of black men. Few of those who gave depositions in these cases could provide more than part of the puzzle.

Perhaps one of the best examples of the weight of evidence against a wife can be found in a suit filed by a group of Alabama lawyers led by Alphonso A. Sterrett, who alleged that their client, William Brewer, a slaveholding overseer and farmer, was deceived by his wife, Jane. The lawyers called a number of witnesses who testified that the wife's conduct toward Isaiah Phillips, a boarder, was at best imprudent. In his decision, chancery judge James Clark asked what, exactly, constituted imprudence. Was it, as some said, that she looked at Phillips in a certain way, smiled at him, walked, talked, sang, and drank with him? Was it that the pair entered private residences at night together, spent evenings in the woods, tenderly washed each other's faces, sat up together all night at the bedside of a dead child, playfully wrestled with "their knees to each other and their bodies in almost every position"? Was it, as one witness said, that Jane fondled Phillips? Clark concluded that, taken together, the evidence was overwhelming that the wife was guilty of infidelity, despite the fact that no one except the husband had actually caught them in the act. He granted the divorce.[14]

Other lawyers cited the desertion of husbands by their wives as the cause for their clients seeking a divorce. Counsel for these men made many of the same charges as did counsel for female plaintiffs: Wives had abandoned their homes and families, moved to another county or state, run away with a lover, or gone to live with another man.[15] In Kentucky, the lawyer for Robert Lewis said that Lewis's wife, "without any good cause or provocation," had deserted her husband's "house and home." Lewis had made repeated efforts to induce her to return home and live with him, but she steadfastly refused to do so. When it was clear his wife would not come back, Lewis turned over five slaves to her as well as "other property" she had inherited following the death of her father. The court granted a divorce *a vinculo matrimonii*.[16]

Lawyers representing husbands as complainants were nearly as successful as those representing wives. The major difference in the relatively small number of equity contests initiated by men was that the men were generally unwilling to dismiss their own suit or reach a compromise. As a result the percentage of those who received unfavorable decrees was more than twice that of women. The data shows, when cases with unusual outcomes and cases with no final decrees are excluded, that male plaintiffs obtained favorable rulings (granted, partially granted, or granted *pro confesso*) in 77 percent of the cases (43 of 56). In only about 3 percent of the cases (2 of 56) did the parties reach some sort of settlement, and 20 percent of the suits (11 of 56) were dismissed or denied.

The success rate achieved by lawyers who brought adultery charges against wives was about the same as that achieved by those bringing the same charge against husbands (80 percent compared with 82 percent), but this was not the case when the charge was desertion. The data shows, when the same case exclusions are applied as above, that male plaintiffs charging desertion by their wives obtained favorable rulings in 73 percent of the cases (19 of 26) as compared with 88 percent for female plaintiffs making the same charge against their husbands. Male plaintiffs reached a settlement with their wives in 4 percent of the cases (1 of 26), and 23 percent saw their cases dismissed or denied (6 of 26). Drawing conclusions from such a relatively small number of cases is difficult, but it is clear that husbands were less likely to settle or compromise in cases of desertion by their wives. And judges were less sympathetic toward husbands who were abandoned by their wives than the reverse, which can be in large measure attributed to the fact that men controlled the family wealth and were thus less likely to be economically affected than were women in such situations.

■ Although the great majority of cases were decided in the plaintiff's favor, whether the plaintiff was male or female, some of the chancery complaints were dismissed for lack of evidence or were made moot following a compromise agreement between the spouses or if a defendant had left the district and was unable to answer the charges. Some, however, were argued effectively by the defendant's counsel, with a decree going against the party seeking redress, and still others were appealed and decided in favor of the respondent. Some suits were discharged following a *pro confesso* decree. In a few instances, cases were dismissed when the petitioner failed to appear or, as one judge said, were dismissed "for want of prosecution." A dismissal, however, did not necessarily mean the plaintiff lost the case; circumstances external to the case could intervene and change the marital situation, warranting a dismissal. In Escambia County, Florida, in 1838, B. D. Wright, as counsel, filed a divorce suit on behalf of his illiterate client, Margaret Garner, charging her husband with physical abuse and plans to leave the state with their slaves. There was no decree attached to the original petition, but a supplemental petition seeking to prevent the husband from leaving the state is shown as having been dismissed. The dismissal, however, came after the husband, who owned eleven slaves and a house in Mobile, Alabama, was arrested and jailed and forced to post a $2,000 bond. Apparently, Wright discussed the matter with his client, and she accepted the bond requirement as a reason for dropping her supplemental suit.[17]

For the most part, however, the dismissal of a case usually meant that the plaintiff's counsel had failed to convince a judge or jury that his client deserved a divorce or separation. In most states a wife's single extramarital encounter was grounds for divorce, whereas a husband's adultery was more broadly defined, especially in cases where the men were accused of illicit sexual relations with women of color, slave or free. Most judges and lawyers viewed consensual or forced sex between white men and black enslaved women as outside the purview of the law, but at the same time, they harshly judged and punished white women who engaged in illicit sex with black men. When Tabitha Pope's lawyer petitioned for divorce because Tabitha's husband had carnal connections with two black women, one owned by her father, the other owned by her husband, the Alabama judge, Joseph Lesesne, dismissed the case on the grounds that the evidence did not meet the burden established by law. It was not a single act of adultery, or even repeated acts, that the statute contemplated, the chancellor wrote, but a habitual and continued adulterous connection, "so habitual and continued that the parties may be said to be domesticated together" or, in the language of the statute, "living together in adultery."[18]

Alabama lawyers and judges were not alone in applying a double standard in the interpretation of what legally constituted adultery. One of the leading equity jurists in the antebellum United States, James Kent, author of four volumes titled *Commentaries on American Law* (1826–30), pointed out how some judges and jurists believed that adultery by the husband "ought not to be noticed, or made the subject to the same animadversion as that of the wife." Infidelity by a husband was not evidence of the same depravity as that committed by the wife, nor was it "equally injurious in its effects upon the morals, and good order, and happiness of domestic life." In many states, a woman who transgressed with another man on a single occasion might prompt a husband to secure a divorce or separation, whereas men who had long-lasting affairs or kept mistresses, especially in certain locales of the Lower South, did so with impunity. Most of the cases of interracial sex in those locations never made it to the courts, and among the few that did, the men had a distinct advantage.[19]

In addition to dismissals for lack of evidence, marital compromise, or societal bias, some adultery cases were also dismissed when the male defendants' attorneys were able to convince judges that the female plaintiffs had been guilty of breaking the marriage covenant. When the wife of Kentucky farmer Leonard Fleming accused him of "notorious, open & avowed adultery" with a woman living on their land, Fleming's lawyer countered that his wife had "deserted his house" even though he always "ever since (and he trusts in all time)" wanted her to live with him. The fact was, the defense lawyer explained, that she preferred to live with her mother. The judge dismissed the suit.[20]

It was also difficult sometimes to prove accusations of domestic violence. In some southern states, the law stipulated that divorce could be granted only if the violent acts were proven to be cruel, barbarous, inhuman, and sustained, causing wives and children to fear for their lives or flee from their homes. One judge contended that the statutes regarding domestic violence in his state were aimed mainly at husbands who were depraved, that is, in today's terms, psychotic. The language used by most lawyers bringing divorce suits on grounds of violence closely followed the terminology of state laws on the subject—the husband was said to be brutal, inhuman, and barbaric; however some lawyers chose to describe husbands, often to their clients' detriment, as harsh, unkind, belligerent, abrasive, profane, ill-tempered, neglectful, dismissive, and hostile, that is, using terms that failed to meet the legal burden. The crucial role of the terminology used by lawyers in determining the outcome of such cases can be attributed to the difficulty of defining what constituted acceptable and unacceptable degrees of violence in a society where wide latitude was afforded family patriarchs in the enforcement of order in their households. In 1845, defense attorney James Baker in Maury County, Tennessee, effectively rebutted the argument that "brutal" and "inhumane" included such things as insults, threats, indignities, aspersions, and indecencies that would shock "any reflecting moral or religious individual." He also rebutted the allegation that his client treated his wife in every respect as if she were "one of his slaves." Even if this could be proven, Baker contended, that was not grounds for divorce. The court ruled in the defendant's favor.[21]

A significant number of the cases that were dismissed were done so when the plaintiffs withdrew their suits, sometimes due to a change of heart and sometimes because the parties had reached some sort of compromise. Among a total of sixty-four divorce or separation suits that were dismissed, twenty-five, or 39 percent, were done so at the request of the plaintiffs. The accusations made in these cases, primarily by women, differed little from the charges brought in successful litigation: The men had committed adultery, treated wives cruelly, abandoned their families, and attempted to confiscate their property. Their husbands, some wives charged, lived with other women for a considerable length of time; others drank to excess and became violent. Yet, even in the midst of contentious trials, with charges and recriminations going back and forth, with angry participants refusing to concede any ground, some women withdrew their complaints and ordered their attorneys to seek a dismissal of the charges. Husbands, on the other hand, rarely asked to have their cases dismissed.[22]

■ The great majority of white women who filed the 573 chancery court suits for divorce, separation, and alimony were from slave-owning families (521 of 573, or 91 percent). Within this group, the number of slaves could be determined in all but a few cases (482 of 521, or 93 percent). Despite some limitations, the data from these court actions can provide, at least in rough summary form, answers to important questions about the legal process involving domestic cases in the southern equity courts, especially answers to the question of whether or not, as some scholars have argued, the wealthy had a distinct advantage over middling and nonslaveholding groups. In short, did women from small slaveholding or nonslaveholding families fare worse in their civil suits, compared with women from larger slaveholding families?

Excluding unusual outcomes and cases with no final decrees, the data shows that female plaintiffs living in families with no slaves or with between one and four slaves obtained favorable rulings (granted, partially granted, or granted *pro confesso*) in 84 percent of the cases (166 of 197); they either withdrew their own suits or reached agreements or settlements in about 8 percent of the cases (17 of 197); and 8 percent (16 of 197) saw their suits dismissed or denied. When the same case exclusions are applied, the data shows that female plaintiffs living in families with between five and nine slaves obtained favorable rulings in 78 percent of the cases (71 of 91); they withdrew their suits or reached settlements in 14 percent of the cases (13 of 91); and 8 percent (7 of 91) had their suits dismissed or denied. Under the same criteria, female plaintiffs living in families with between ten and nineteen slaves obtained favorable rulings in 75 percent of the cases (52 of 69); they reached agreements in 13 percent of the cases (9 of 69); and 12 percent (8 of 69) had their suits dismissed or denied. Women in the wealthiest families with twenty or more slaves secured favorable rulings in 78 percent of the cases (38 of 49); they reached compromises in 10 percent of the cases (5 of 49); and 12 percent (6 of 49) saw their cases dismissed or denied (see Table 8 in Appendix 1).

These results suggest the opposite of what one might have expected. Female plaintiffs from nonslaveholding families or small property owning families, mostly yeoman farmers who possessed a few slaves, actually fared better than those who were more prosperous as well as those at the top of the economic spectrum. Why did this occur? The answer lies with the remarkable workings of the legal process whereby judges and juries in equity courts were required to listen to complaints, sort out arguments by defendants and witnesses, and make judgments according to the statute law in a given state. In short, the process demanded that the men entrusted to make decisions—men who were, for the most part, neither in favor of divorce nor predisposed to undermine the authority of household heads—set aside their private beliefs and follow the law.

The results reveal that as time passed during the nineteenth century, localized law became less important in these cases than statute law, and the "credit" of some of the wealthiest members of the communities became less influential than the arguments presented in court. Good legal counsel was important, but those who could afford the most expensive and experienced legal representation did not fare any better than those who had much less means. With regard to married white women and the law, it is also important to note, as pointed out earlier, that a majority of female complainants hired their own lawyers and filed their own suits without a male next friend. In addition, a small number of the next friends in four states, including Virginia, South Carolina, Alabama, and Mississippi, were female.

The contrast between women and men who filed for divorce and separation is stark with regard to slave ownership. Because the number of males who filed petitions for divorce and separation in the district, circuit, and superior chancery courts is small, it is difficult to make meaningful comparisons, but it must nevertheless be noted that among the 83 men who filed court papers, only slightly more than half were slave owners (46 of 83, or 55 percent). When cases with unusual outcomes and cases with no final decrees are excluded, that data shows that male plaintiffs who owned no slaves or between one and four slaves won a large majority of their suits, receiving decrees of granted, partially granted, or granted *pro confesso* (31 of 36, or 86 percent). As was the case with female complainants, this group was more successful in receiving favorable decrees than those who were more prosperous. Among the larger slave owners, only twelve were granted favorable decrees, and six saw their suits denied or dismissed, including some who were very prosperous. Among the men, both slaveholders and non-slave owners, about four of five won their suits, approximately the same proportion as that of female litigants who received favorable decrees or verdicts. Again, it is clear that, for male plaintiffs as it was for female litigants, both slave owners and non-slave owners, the effectiveness of lawyers in presenting convincing evidence, including testimony from credible witnesses, and the serious consideration with which judges and juries weighed the evidence were determining factors in winning cases.

The data provided by the few historians who have examined court outcomes in divorce cases, although not focused on slave ownership, tends to corroborate the evidence presented in this study. Over a fifty-year period in Davidson County, Tennessee, a state described by three scholars as "liberal" when it came to divorce proceedings, female petitioners outnumbered their male counterparts. By the 1850s, these scholars reported, many white women were filing suits citing "intolerable conditions," including offensive language and excessive drinking. During the antebellum era, women gained divorces at a rate of 80 percent (118 divorces out of 147 petitions), compared with 66 percent for men (48 of 73), evidence that contradicts the assumption, the historians argue, that divorces were "rare and hard to get, especially for women, in the South."[23]

■ During the early decades of the nineteenth century, a number of applicants for divorce submitted petitions to state legislatures. Unfortunately, even if the complaining parties were successful with their pleas, the private acts contained very little information about why they sought to end their marriages. The typical private acts said only that the "bonds of matrimony, heretofore solemnized and subsisting" between the parties, "are hereby, annulled and made void," or "from and after the passing of this

TABLE 4 Legislative Divorce in Maryland, Virginia, and Tennessee

	Petitioners total	Wives	Husbands	GRANTED		No data	Years
				Wives	Husbands		
Maryland	1,386	796	448	348	146	142	1782–1850
Virginia	583	292	286	81	72	5	1786–1850
Tennessee	260	171	89	125	66		1797–1855
	2,229	1,259	823	554	284	147	

Sources: Chused, *Private Acts in Public Places*, tables 5, 8; Buckley, *Great Catastrophe of My Life*, tables A1, A2, A4; Goodheart, Hanks, and Johnson, "'Act for the Relief of Females,'" pt. 2, table 4.

act," the parties are divorced from the bonds of matrimony, as if the marriage had never been solemnized, "any law to the contrary notwithstanding." In some instances, fifteen or twenty petitioners were awarded divorces in the same act, which consisted of wording similar to that cited above followed by the individual names. With few exceptions, the text of the acts passed by general assemblies made no mention of issues relating to either race or slavery, even though both sets of issues may have been at the core of why the mentioned couples were divorcing.[24]

A statistical analysis of the divorce cases in this study suggests that, in addition to the differences noted earlier between the legislative and the judicial processes, there were also important differences between the legislative and the judiciary settings in terms of the gender distribution of those who filed for divorce and their rates of success. For the legislative process, the data, presented in Table 4, has been analyzed for three states—Maryland, Virginia, and Tennessee; for the judicial process, the data covers all fifteen states and the District of Columbia.

In Maryland, 1,386 petitions for divorce or separation were sent to the Maryland General Assembly between 1782 and 1849, only 552 of which, or 40 percent, were enacted into law. The gender of the petitioner was ascertained for 1,244 of the 1,386 filed petitions and for 494 of the 552 that were enacted into law. Women filed nearly twice as many requests as men (796 compared with 448) and obtained a substantially greater number of both absolute divorces and separations from bed and board than did husbands (for wives 185 absolute divorces and 163 separations from bed and board, a total of 348 of 552, or 63 percent; for husbands 117 absolute divorces and 29 separations from bed and board, a total of 146 of 552, or about 26 percent). In Virginia, 583 petitions for divorce were enacted into law by the legislature between 1786 and 1850, for 578 of which the gender of the petitioner was determined; of those 578, about half were filed by women (292 for women, 286 for men). The Virginia General Assembly granted 62 absolute divorces, 15 separations, and 4 conditional divorces to women; to men it granted 69 absolute divorces and 3 conditional divorces (this was 33 percent of those who submitted applications in each case). In Tennessee, of the 260 petitions for absolute divorce and separation from bed and board that were acted upon by the General Assembly, 171 were filed by women and 89 by men. Among the women, 125 (45 absolute divorces and 80 separations from bed and board) were granted, or 73 percent; among the men, 66, or 74 percent, were granted.[25]

Thus, the statistical analysis shows that for the three states in the aggregate, women filed one-third more petitions and were 50 percent more likely to receive a favorable decision. For both women and men, about 43 percent of those who submitted petitions seeking absolute divorce or separation from bed and board (896 of 2,082) were successful. As indicated above and represented in Table 4, there were 147 petitions (142 in Maryland and 5 in Virginia) for which no information is available as to the gender of the person filing suit; they have been excluded from the percentages provided above.

■ The results from the circuit, district, and superior court decisions reveal a different picture. The judicial process required a greater exposure of the details informing divorce cases—often laying bare in gruesome detail the pain, anguish, and embarrassment of unhappy marital life—than did the legislative proceedings. The judicial process also very likely offered many women a more familiar and thus more comfortable venue—a factor perhaps of greater importance to women than to men and one that may have played a part in the rate of success met by women who filed suits in the court systems. Filing suit in their home counties rather than at the state level allowed women to contact lawyers they knew or had heard of through people they knew. Women could work with them, in presenting their arguments, in a local setting where they could rely on friends, neighbors, relatives, and others to testify in their behalf. They also may have more readily trusted local lawyers to connect their particular case with state statutes and to keep abreast of the laws as they changed over time. Indeed, whatever the reasons, in the end, from the early years of the century through the Civil War, women and their lawyers who brought divorce complaints in the court systems were extraordinarily successful in obtaining favorable decrees and verdicts. Four of five cases were decided in their favor; moreover, if the 10 percent that were settled in some fashion, often with the couple reuniting, is included in the statistics, then the ratio of women who either secured judgments in their favor in the courts or returned, of their own volition, to live with their husbands was nine out of ten. In short, women in this study who petitioned the courts were nearly twice as likely to obtain a divorce as those who petitioned general assemblies. This high rate of success in the courts was met by women from nonslaveholding as well as from slaveholding families.

How can one explain this discrepancy between the legislatures and the courts in their willingness to grant women a divorce, separation, or alimony? One explanation can be found in the process itself. As pointed out above, the burden of proof required by the judicial process led to a greater and more detailed exposure of marital conflict than did the legislative process. Plaintiffs and lawyers detailed betrayals, gratuitous violence, and the arbitrary abuse of authority that occurred over many months, even years, before women filed for divorce or separation. Calling on witnesses—neighbors, friends, relatives, and others—lawyers in the courts could present a penetrating view into the lives of their clients, a view that was most often not available to legislators when they decided a case. Confronted with the painful specifics of marital conflict and the sometimes desperate economic situations facing female petitioners following their filing of legal papers, judges and juries were inclined to sympathize with the plight of women and children and grant divorces, separations, and alimony. We can also surmise that the more intimate involvement in cases on the part of judges and witnesses required by the court process contributed, in some instances, to a reassessment by petitioners of their marital problems and the acceptance of compromises leading to reconciliation between spouses.

The discrepancy can also be explained by the fact that the process itself evolved over time and the transfer of responsibilities from the legislative to the judicial corresponded to an evolution in the cultural values and accepted mores surrounding marriage and domestic life. As previously indicated, the legislative and the judicial processes did not operate exactly in parallel at the same time. In most states during the early years, divorces went through the legislatures exclusively, but as legislatures were overwhelmed by the amount of time required to handle such cases, they required chancery courts to conduct trials, while for a time retaining the final say. Eventually, in most states divorce became strictly a judicial matter rather than a legislative issue. So by the time the courts were fully in control of the process, familiarity with the issue of divorce and separation had set in, and people's views on the subject had matured. It was no longer exclusively viewed as an unfortunate anomaly, something one should avoid no matter the circumstances, but rather as something that most people, especially women, were still reluctant to resort to but did so when confronted by compelling circumstances. The institution of marriage was still held as sacrosanct by many southerners, but as the laws and the process evolved, there was a growing acceptance that remaining in a desperate marital situation at all costs was not always the best option.

As for men, they were overall less likely to seek a divorce than were women, and they were also far less likely to do so in the court systems than they were in the legislatures. The reason for the discrepancy between men and women in the number of cases settled between the spouses is obvious: Since the male heads of households controlled most, if not all, of the family estate, men had far fewer financial incentives to accept a settlement than did women. In contrast to women filing for divorce or separation, who, for the most part, were members of slaveholding families, a large proportion of the men were non-slave owners. White men often filed for divorce because, they charged, their wives had engaged in "illicit sexual relations" with black men, slave and free; not only did they view themselves as humiliated and disgraced in the eyes of the public, but they believed that their manhood and honor had been threatened. Under such circumstances, reaching a compromise was not an option. Thus, although white men were slightly less likely than white women to obtain a divorce, the economic structure of the antebellum family and the grounds on which men, as opposed to women, filed for divorce meant that issues of financial settlement did not play as large a role for men as for women. Men did not seek to be just merely separated but wanted to be absolutely divorced, and they almost never compromised.

Although this study does include a few cases of divorce presented by free people of color to the courts, their number is so small that it is difficult to generalize about free blacks and divorce. The rarity of free blacks filing divorce or separation petitions was no doubt a consequence, in large measure, of the difficult economic circumstances they confronted, their problems in hiring lawyers, and their precarious position in a slaveholding society. Many among them struggled merely to survive and had little or no property to protect. Despite the fact that the economic and social circumstances of free blacks were different from those of whites, free persons of color who filed for divorce were also likely to receive favorable decrees. Free black women petitioners received a higher percentage of favorable to unfavorable decrees than did white women (13 of 14, or 93 percent), whereas free black men received the same percentage as white men (7 of 9, or 78 percent). The numbers are so small that about the only conclusion that can be drawn is that most of the free blacks who filed petitions for divorce were property owners who could afford a competent lawyer and that most of the complainants presented compelling arguments, as did their white counterparts, of betrayal, infidelity, and violence.

Over the years, the lawyers and judges evolved, as did the state laws with regard to divorce, separation, and alimony suits. The lawyers became more adept at presenting their arguments, responding to answers from defendants, and seeking court orders for maintenance and support during the duration of the suits, which could and often did last for many months, sometimes several years. The judges likewise became more familiar with state statutes concerning marital dissolution and rendered opinions that were balanced and often sympathetic to the plight of the wife and children. Judges and juries valued greatly direct testimony from eyewitnesses, whether in the form of depositions, as was most common, or testimony in the courtroom; they often rejected testimony from those who had only second- or third-hand knowledge of events. The increase of the amount of evidence presented in chancery courts was palpable, especially compared with what was sent to legislatures. The fact that the evidence and state laws guided the court decisions could be seen in the fact that the wealthiest slave owners, whether men or women, fared no better and sometimes worse than those with only a few slaves or yeoman farmers, and women fared better than men.

■ In the case of *Duncan v. Duncan* introducing this chapter, the trial in Clay County was only the beginning of a lengthy process. Following the decree, the husband filed a "bill of exceptions," an appeal to the Missouri Supreme Court, for which he was required to post a security bond of $5,000, secured with a large portion of his goods, chattels, lands, and tenements. If he lost the appeal, he would have to pay the costs incurred to prosecute it, and the judgment against him or the bond would be forfeited and his property seized. During the appeal, the court ordered the county sheriff to hire out the slaves in dispute and pay Sarah Duncan $12 per month; the remainder of the hiring fees was kept with the sheriff "subject to the order of this court."

On 19 June 1848, William Duncan's lawyer filed his appeal, and six months later, on 21 December 1848, the high court ruled that the case came "within the principle decided in the case of *Nagel v. Nagel*." In that case the husband and the wife were both guilty of wrongdoing, the husband treating his wife in a cruel manner and the wife committing adultery. The supreme court noted that over the years, the General Assembly had created nine causes for divorce, including, among others, adultery, desertion, inhuman treatment, impotency, bigamy, and habitual drunkenness, but explained that if both parties were guilty of one or another of these causes, including conspiracy to end the marriage, the court should not grant a divorce. "Thus it is seen that a party applying for a divorce must show that he or she is the innocent and injured party," the opinion said. Since William Duncan had been found guilty of cruel treatment and Sarah Duncan of moving away and deserting her husband, both were at fault. The judgment of the circuit court was reversed, and the bill was dismissed.[26]

After hiring new lawyers and defending her case before the state supreme court, Sarah Duncan remained married to William Duncan, even though she had not lived with him for more than four years. A major source of the conflict was the control and ownership of a group of slaves who remained as the husband's property despite the fact that the wife had brought them to the marriage. In 1850, sixty-year-old William Duncan, a farmer with $3,114 worth of land, still possessed the slaves. His estranged wife, Sarah Duncan, age sixty-eight, lived with John Reed and Reed's wife and family in nearby Clinton County. Despite a district court decree in her favor and the fact that she had been separated from her husband for six years, she was still legally married.[27]

MARRIED WOMEN AND PROPERTY

5

Stretching across the rolling hills of middle Tennessee, nine miles south of the town of Franklin along the main road to Columbia, the cotton plantation of James M. Banks was among the most prosperous in Williamson County. By the mid-1830s, it contained several hundred acres cleared and under cultivation as well as forests of ash, oak, hickory, "Sugar trees," and poplar. The estate included cotton fields and a splendid mansion surrounded by a kitchen, barn, corncribs, stables, gin house, smokehouse, and springhouse. It boasted livestock of all types, including horses, mules, cattle, and hogs, as well as housing for more than forty slaves. The rich soil was extremely valuable, worth between $20 and $25 per acre, and Banks's slave labor force was large and productive. Frugal and hardworking, an excellent planter and money manager, Banks not only harvested profitable crops of cotton, corn, oats, and fodder but loaned various sums to his neighbors at a good rate of interest. Even in a county containing a number of wealthy slaveholding families, Banks stood at the top of the economic ladder. He also was the proud head of a handsome family, which was comprised of his wife of thirteen years, Louisiana, in her early thirties, and their five children, four boys and a girl.[1]

But in the early summer of 1835, James Banks unexpectedly died. At the time of his death, Louisiana, who was pregnant with her seventh child (one had died), stood to inherit a dower (one-third) of the great estate. She was therefore not only surprised but shocked when she heard her husband's will read in the probate court. "It is my will that my wife and children remain at the house where I now reside and have the necessary slaves to enable them to live decently and comfortably until my debts shall be paid," Banks wrote, adding that the acreage formerly belonging to his father-in-law, Thomas Cash, and held by him "in right of my said wife . . . her heirs and assigns forever," be turned over to her and the children. But he bequeathed her only one-seventh of his personal estate, with the other six-sevenths going to his children; he said nothing about the eleven slaves given to her in a trust estate by her father in 1822, nor did he bequeath her land other than that which she was entitled to receive from her father's assignment. In January 1836, after several men mentioned in the will as possible executors had declined the responsibility, David Campbell accepted "the burthen of execution" and took possession of the property. Not only did Louisiana have reservations about Campbell's stewardship, but she believed that her husband's will was "partial and unjust towards her" and bequeathed her "less by far than she would be entitled to by law."[2]

Despite her inexperience in managing a plantation and the demands of motherhood following the birth of her sixth son, Louisiana organized the labor force and supervised the harvesting and sale of the cotton crop. During this period, as she took over the responsibilities previously assumed by her late husband, cared for her family, and remained frustrated by what she considered a "partial and unjust" will, she met Thomas McDaniel Reid, a young man who had recently arrived from North Carolina. Charming, well-mannered, well-dressed, and professing to be a man of some means, Reid began to court her almost immediately. Although cautious by nature, Louisiana soon succumbed to his persistent overtures. In March 1837, nineteen months after the death of her first husband and only a few months after meeting Reid, Louisiana accepted the latter's proposal of marriage. Certainly part of the reason she did so was her fondness for Reid, but important also was her belief that she was marrying a man of wealth who could secure her economic future. Indeed, many antebellum marriages among members of the slaveholding aristocracy occurred for economic as well as social and societal reasons. Before the ceremony, however, she insisted that he sign a "marriage contract" giving her and her children control of the property of her first husband.

Within weeks, however, she realized she had made a grievous mistake. Three months after the wedding, Louisiana filed a petition for divorce, in which she asked for a ruling that would protect "her property for the use of herself and her children." She charged that Reid had "formed the wicked design of cheating and defrauding her" out of her estate by falsely representing himself to be a man of great wealth. He had taken the identity of his cousin in North Carolina, a person of means, and was, in fact, a convicted forger. She explained that she had trusted him to register their marriage contract at the courthouse but that he had "suppressed the same with the intention of wickedly destroying it." Reid's principal object in marrying her, she asserted, was "to procure her fortune."[3]

■ The study of southern women's history has undergone remarkable transformation during the past generation. Few subjects in this area, including politics, ideology, religion, plantation management, marriage, property ownership, widowhood, and interracial sexual relations, have escaped the close scrutiny of historians. Some historians have examined divorce, separation, and alimony. When marriages began to fall apart, one author notes, one of the most important issues of dispute involved the division of property, especially among the slaveholding class. "Property was both necessary and symbolic," she writes. It was essential for economic support but also symbolized what many wives had contributed to their marriages. Yet, few historians have followed up on this insight to analyze how southern white married women dealt with the question of property when faced with the disintegration of their marriages. True, when this crisis occurred, many wives faced a period of economic uncertainty and hardship, but it is also clear that many, who had played an increasingly active role in accumulating and managing property during their marriages, vigorously and often successfully employed the law to retain as much of it as possible. These aspects of married southern women's history seem all the more remarkable given the limitations placed on women in their status as *femes covert*.[4]

In southern states during the antebellum era, a single woman could own property in her own name, convey it by will or deed, and in most jurisdictions prosecute and defend lawsuits, although some states required that she secure a "next friend," or *prochein ami*, to conduct legal business or sue in a court of law. A married woman, on the other hand, according to the common-law concept of coverture, was subordinate to her husband in her person and property. A married woman was therefore called, in legal parlance, a *feme covert*. As a result of this absorption of the legal entity of a wife into that of her husband, wives could not, until the late antebellum era, except in Louisiana or when protected under marital agreements, use state laws to claim as their separate property either what they possessed before their marriages or what they had received afterward through bequests or gifts. Only widows could claim and exercise separate ownership of property during their lifetimes or until they married again, in the form of dower or jointure (i.e., that portion of their late husbands' estates to which they were legally entitled, usually one-third). In Louisiana, and later in Texas, divorcing wives could claim a share of the community property, as well as the entire portion of their individual property, which was called extra-dotal or paraphernal property, terms used to denote the property wives had brought to or received during the marriage over and beyond the dowry. In 1839, beginning with the enactment of the Mississippi married women's property law, this began to change, and other states passed laws to protect married women's property.[5]

During the early years, Louisiana law stood alone with regard to laws governing the property of married women. When filing suits for separation of bed and board, Louisiana women often asked that the property they had brought to their marriages, over and beyond their dowries, as well as property they had acquired during the marriage through gift, inheritance or natural increase, be confirmed as their separate property. They cited as precedent the Napoleonic codes and Spanish legal traditions rather than English common law. They also cited the *Digest of 1808*, which prohibited husbands from disposing of a wife's immovable property or her slaves. After 1825, they relied on the *Civil Code* of the state, which permitted married women to administer paraphernal property without the assistance of their husbands.[6]

The enactment of laws to protect married women's property in other southern states evolved many years later. Indeed, five southern states along the eastern seaboard—Delaware, Virginia, North Carolina, South Carolina, and Georgia—failed to pass any legislation on the issue until after the Civil War. Yet, both before and after the passage of protective laws, women seeking divorce, separation, or alimony petitioned state assemblies and chancery courts to retain property as a matter of fairness and equity and to ensure they could support themselves and their children. To bolster their claims, they produced witnesses as well as a number of legal documents (wills, inventories, deeds, mortgages, indentures, receipts, and pre- and postnuptial agreements) to prove that they were entitled to tracts of land, livestock, carriages, wagons, horses, furniture, crops, machinery, promissory notes, bonds, and slaves. They also asked the courts to issue restraining orders against their husbands to prevent them from molesting or disturbing their person or property.[7]

In the early years, such suits were brought in chancery courts as a matter of equity, but in later years, divorcing or separating women could cite statute law when they sought to retain the same types of property. In 1846, Elizabeth Hamilton, a Tennessee wife charging her husband with adultery, sought the return of the slaves she had brought to her marriage, namely George, Henry, Isaac, Stephen, Mourning, Letitia, and Dick. Even though her husband defended himself by citing a court order directing the couple to hold the slaves jointly during their lives and blamed the "unkind feeling" between him and his wife on the "untimely & unholy interference of her father brother & other members of her family," the court ruled in

Elizabeth's favor. She also won after her husband appealed the verdict. Indeed, the judge proceeded on the authority of statute law. In 1842, Tennessee had amended its divorce law to permit chancery courts to grant a wife property that a husband had received from her at the time of their marriage or afterward, as well as the separate property that had been "secured to her by marriage contract or otherwise."[8]

Part of the estate women fought to retain was the property they had inherited or stood to inherit during coverture. As with premarital holdings, prior to the enactment of state protective laws, such property automatically reverted to a woman's husband unless a deed of gift or last will and testament or indenture stipulated that it should be established as a separate estate. Sometimes, even when trust estates were created specifically to set aside such property for the wives' benefit, husbands confiscated their wives' inherited property as they did their premarital property. The women who filed suits to protect their inheritances or other holdings described many of the stratagems their husbands used to secure the property for themselves. In 1833, for instance, Mary Miller of Kentucky sued her husband on charges of adultery and desertion. She explained to the court that, after the desertion, she had inherited a "considerable estate" following her brother's death, and she feared her husband might return and demand either part or all of her inheritance, including land and slaves worth between $6,000 and $8,000. She obtained an injunction prohibiting the executors of her brother's estate from conveying any property to her husband and a court order saying that she should be "permitted to receive what is coming to her under said will." Mary Miller was typical of other women who filed suits to protect themselves and their property, brought legal action without next friends, and won favorable verdicts in the chancery courts.[9]

Far more difficult for women than securing the right of ownership to premarital or inherited property was protecting a portion of the wealth they had earned individually or jointly with their husbands during their marriage. Despite the fact that women often played a crucial role in increasing their husbands' estates—as attested by the words of a South Carolina woman who said that "her care industry and economy hath greatly increased his means of comfortable subsistence"—in most jurisdictions the only way they might receive a share of this joint property in cases of divorce or separation was to sue for alimony. The great majority of such cases were contentious. Even when courts awarded women a maintenance allowance or a portion of an estate as alimony, many husbands maneuvered to hide assets, transfer property, dispose of real estate, and sell off slaves in order to avoid complying with court orders.[10]

In response, wives obtained sequester orders to prevent the sale of the accumulated family holdings: farm acreage, homes, livestock, furniture, bonds, slaves, and crops in the field. They also asked that the property be protected until alimony could be determined by the court. During the six years of their marriage, Margaret Garner of Alabama explained, she was largely responsible for her husband's financial success and the family's acquisition of seventeen slaves. Shortly after she filed for divorce and alimony, her husband began selling off the slave property and transferring and hiding his real estate holdings "to make it uncertain & hazardous whether a Decree in her favour for allimony would ever reach any part of it." Other wives made the same complaint. Shortly after they had filed for alimony, they said, their husbands converted the family holdings into cash, hid assets from the court, and in some cases, emigrated to another county or state.[11]

As a result, most women who filed for divorce or separation experienced economic hardship. Even if they were awarded a portion of the property or alimony or both, they could not count on securing either for any length of time. In many cases alimony payments depended on the husband's willingness to provide for his wife and children following a divorce or separation. One South Carolina wife said that her husband owned two tracts of land, a very valuable mill, horses, cattle, hogs, household and kitchen furniture, and a number of slaves, including Milly, the slave she had brought to their marriage, and Milly's six living children, but he refused to provide adequate support for his family. A Tennessee woman said that her husband had promised to give her a number of slaves "for her sole use and benefit during her natural life, to be disposed of by her last will and testament," but he had reneged on his promise. In many other cases, the women involved were similarly deprived of alimony or of a maintenance allowance despite decrees in their favor.[12]

Perhaps just as frustrating to women were husbands who contributed little to the common weal. Married women and their lawyers described men who were shiftless and lazy, improvident and dissolute, addicted to alcohol and incapable of providing for their families. They, too, sued their husbands seeking the "right, title, and interest" to their mutual property, both farms and slaves. The courts were sympathetic to women like the one who declared that "by dint of the greatest industry and economy" she had put together "some little property, viz a negro, a small piece of land containing between fifty and one hundred acres and a small sum of money also a small annuity bequeathed her by her uncle." In this particular case the Superior Court of Halifax County, Virginia, not only granted the wife a divorce but also said she had an "independent right" to control the property she had worked so hard to acquire.[13]

■ To protect their holdings, slaveholding women, sometimes at the insistence of parents or family members, placed their property in separate trust estates. All of the southern states permitted these marital property arrangements long before the passage of married women's property laws during the 1840s and 1850s. The separate estates took several forms, including trusts overseen by a trustee or group of trustees, marriage contracts that promised a wife access to her property, and prenuptial agreements that barred a husband from taking possession of his wife's separate estate. Occasionally such agreements were created after the consecration of marriage, but most often they were signed a few days before the wedding. In either case, the women's objective was the same: They sought to protect their land, slaves, and other property from their husbands' debts, either past, present, or future, and from their husbands' ability to sell, trade, mortgage, or transfer their separate estates, at least not without their or their trustees' permission.[14]

To be legal and binding, these agreements needed to be signed, witnessed, and notarized. Most jurisdictions also required that they be registered in the deeds office of the county courthouse, but in some locales the documents could remain unregistered, in the possession of the parties, as could last wills and testaments and bills of sale. When an estate was placed in a trust, a chancery court appointed a trustee or trustees, who became responsible for managing it, protecting the woman's property and her right to it, responding to her instructions, and as one contract stated, managing, receiving, and distributing "the rents hires and profits thereof."[15]

Not many such agreements were found in the documentation of divorce, separation, and alimony cases, and when they were found, they pertained exclusively to cases involving members of the slaveholding class. Although the language in the agreements varied, and certainly did not always determine the outcomes in divorce or alimony proceedings, the husbands agreed that their wives would possess the property for their own "benefit and behoof," "sole and separate use," and "absolutely and forever." One contract said that after her marriage the wife would possess "property rights or credits she has or may have before or after our said intended marriage." During the early decades of the nineteenth century, such legal contracts were the only means by which married women could avoid being "covered" by their husbands when it came to property.[16]

Asking a future husband to sign an agreement to relinquish his rights of coverture as well as give up some of his authority as head of the household was a delicate matter. Signing such agreements could well prove awkward for couples who professed to be deeply in love or who claimed they cared less about their property than about their future together. At the very least, the signing of such documents suggested the existence of a measure of suspicion and distrust between the parties. In some cases, the bride's parents demanded that their future son-in-law relinquish any claim on the property brought to the union by their daughter, doing so even when, as one mother said, the man was considered by everyone who knew him to be a perfect gentleman. Some grooms found such demands insulting and refused to enter such contracts, but in most cases those who were asked to do so acceded to the wishes of the bride and her family. There were a few cases of brides from wealthy families who refused to enter such agreements because they said they did not wish to insult their future husbands or make the size and value of their estates public.[17]

When their marriages were rent asunder, married women who had signed prenuptial agreements used the equity courts to assert their "rights titled interests and profits" in and from their separate estates. The courts on the "law side," or the common-law courts, as with other family matters were unable to provide such equity relief. It was in the chancery courts that the women secured injunctions to prevent the sale or confiscation of their separate property, claimed life estates should be protected, and petitioned for the removal of trustees who failed to serve their best interest. When they feared that their estranged husbands might ignore both the marriage contracts and court orders, they requested that their separate property be sequestered until their marital dispute could be resolved. In their pleas for divorce and alimony they described specific properties that were reserved for their sole and separate use.[18]

However, some women suing for divorce or alimony did not act quickly enough to protect their separate estates. They could not prevent their husbands, as heads of households, from claiming the property as their own, working in collusion with trustees to deprive them of their estates, and defying administrators' requests and court orders pertaining to prenuptial agreements. In South Carolina, a state with a long chancery tradition, Margaret Vause brought a considerable estate to her marriage in 1816 and subsequently created a trust to protect her holdings. In her petition for alimony, supported by her son and "next friend" John Peters, her lawyer told the judge that her husband had taken possession of her property, collected rents and profits, hired out her slave Elsey, and spent the proceeds, leaving her with very little means for support.[19]

Moreover, pre- or postnuptial agreements did not prevent creditors from seeking to confiscate wives' separate property as payment for their husbands' debts. Although creditors were often on shaky grounds legally, they often pressed for the payment of debts by going after wives' estates, even after the passage of the married women's property laws. In those instances when husbands had mortgaged a portion or all of their wives' trust estates to secure their own debts, creditors had legally defensible cases. In fact, some states passed laws that favored creditors over the protection of wives' separate estates, laws that applied especially in such cases when husbands had incurred substantial debts that could not be repaid without using wives' separate property. Even when the courts were inclined to decide in a wife's favor, creditors could and did place a lien on her trust property to pay her husband's debts. In 1846, Alabama slaveholder Maria Betts filed for divorce, requesting that the conveyances made by her husband to creditors, using her trust property as collateral, be "set aside" and that his creditors be perpetually enjoined from seizing any of her trust estate. Her separate estate was "free from the marital right of her then present or any future husband." The chancery court ruled in her favor on both issues.[20]

The twelve years that elapsed, in Maria Betts's case, from the time of her marriage to the filing of divorce papers was not unusual. During a marriage, women who possessed separate estates sometimes gradually lost control over their property, even when those estates were protected by premarital contracts. As time passed, an agreement stipulating that the property should be for the wife's "separate use, maintenance & support," as if she were an unmarried woman, a *feme sole*, became less immediate. The wife's separate property, including town lots, tracts of farmland, farm machinery, silverware, furniture, livestock, crops, banknotes, cash, and slaves, physically merged with the holdings of her husband. But in their suits for divorce and alimony, married women argued that their separate estates, despite the passage of many years, should remain free from their husbands' control.[21]

A few of the most public marital conflicts occurred when couples fought over the wives' trust estates. Indeed, when women accused their husbands of refusing to abide by the terms of various property arrangements and demanded that they do so, they brought into question male honor. In some instances wives filed charges against their husbands to protect their separate property. In one instance, a couple signed a prenuptial agreement stipulating that the wife would have "full sole and exclusive use" of her property but her husband reneged on the agreement almost from the beginning. As in other similar instances it was clear that the wife sought to manage her own financial affairs despite coverture.[22]

Married women recognized the importance of separate holdings, especially if their husbands proved to be inept in business matters. Those who filed for separation realized that their premarital agreements allowed them to provide for their children and sustain their families. The chancery courts either ruled in their favor or permitted them a venue where some sort of compromise could be reached with regard to their premarital separate estates. Thus, they were successful not only in obtaining divorces, separations, and alimony but also in seeking to protect the land, slaves, and other property listed in their prenuptial agreements.[23]

■ Among the various types of property that wives and husbands struggled over during marital conflicts, none was more important than slaves. Both parties described those held in bondage in economic terms. They used such terms as "likely," "very likely," "valuable," "valuable negro," "good hand," "likely young women," and "good breeder." As the term "good breeder" suggests, owners would assess the value of females in terms of how many children they had borne. They also indicated whether or not the black children were healthy or sickly or remained under their mothers' care, and sometimes they gave their ages. Tennessee slave owner Mary M. Clarke, who petitioned to end her fourteen-year marriage, explained that when she married at age seventeen, she brought with her an inheritance from her father and brother consisting of a large amount of cash as well as eleven "likely negroes." Over the years, the number of slaves had increased, and although her husband had sold a number of those "likely negroes" before deserting her, she still possessed a number of black people. Like many other white women in a similar situation, she asked that the slaves in her possession be handed over to her and that she be restored to all the rights and privileges of a *feme sole*.[24]

Nor was any other type of property more vulnerable to being sold, traded, hidden, or taken off by husbands. As movable property, slaves could quickly be converted to cash, from a few hundred to more than a thousand dollars per "head of negro," as one Tennessee farmer wrote; they were a source of immediate profits, "valuable assets" that could be hidden and kept away from authorities. In their divorce and alimony pleas, women often offered a count of the human chattel that remained on the farm or plantation and its estimated worth. A South Carolina woman seeking alimony from her husband said her four blacks, valued at $2,500 in 1851, were all "young and likely negroes." An Alabama woman seeking a divorce made a similar comment. Her husband possessed four Negroes, "most of which are valuable." These and other women asked for court orders to prevent husbands from removing their slave property, to shield forthcoming inheritances, and if necessary, to sequester the African Americans until the court could decide on maintenance and alimony.[25]

Perhaps it should not be unexpected, although it is revealing, that slaves who were the subjects of disputes in divorce settlements were described in court records in such a manner. What is surprising is that in the 8,000 pages of documentary evidence offered, there are virtually no personal comments about individual slaves except those that note that some of the female slaves had children. The white women presenting the petitions for divorce, separation, and alimony almost never noted the slaves' personal traits, talents, occupations, moral values, feelings, intellectual abilities, or even family ties. Nor did they offer any discussion of how it pained them to sell black people, including children, nor did they wonder about the fate of those being sold. They rarely, if ever, described those held in bondage in terms of affection or endearment. It did not seem to make a difference whether the slaves had been acquired in recent years or had served the same family for more than a generation. Allowance can be made for the fact that these women faced crises in their own families and were often distraught by their own predicaments. By the same token, it can be argued that such wrenching events are often conducive to deep feelings about the breakup of a family and of a household, and about the consequences for all members of that family and household. Yet these women's pleas to the legislatures and chancery courts reveal that such feelings were rarely if ever extended to enslaved members of the household, who, in the petitions, are almost always defined in purely economic terms. In short, there were very few indications that the women seeking a divorce considered their slaves, or the slaves of their husbands, as anything more than human chattel.

A statistical analysis of the 610 white women seeking divorce, separation, or alimony in this study shows that at least 550 (or 90 percent) came from slaveholding families, for the majority of whom (503 of 550, or 91 percent) the number of slaves could be determined. Table 5 provides a picture of slave ownership and its distribution across the families of these 503 women. Slave ownership is presented in terms of the number of slaves owned, with each of the 503 families falling into one of four groups based on the number of slaves owned within a range. The extent of slave owner-

TABLE 5 White Women in Slaveholding Families

Number of slaves	Number of women	Percent of women	Slaves' total value ($)	Slaves' average value ($)	TE* total value ($)	TE average value ($)
1–4	218	43	202,765	930	569,733	2,613
5–9	119	24	363,145	3,052	842,440	7,079
10–19	102	20	604,420	5,926	1,142,177	11,198
20+	64	13	1,163,124	18,174	2,248,699	35,136
TOTALS	503	100	2,333,454	4,639	4,803,049	9,549
No data	47**					
TOTAL	550					

Source: Compiled from Divorce and Alimony Excel File Database; includes data from legislative and chancery court records.

*TE = total estate
**Noted as a slave owner, but the number of slaves is not indicated.

ship is examined in terms of the total value of slaves owned by all families within a specific group and the group's average value, per family, of slave property. Table 5 also offers a comparison between the value of a family's total estate and the value of its holdings in human chattel. The total estate includes the estimated total value of all property in the hands of families within a specific group and the group's average value, per family, including the holdings in slaves. Although the statistical evidence presented in this table has been gathered from cases filed at different periods within the study's time span—and thus allowance must be made for variations in currency value, purchasing power, location, and changes in the economy—it does support the broad conclusion that women from slaveholding families stood to lose a good deal at the hands of irresponsible or malevolent husbands.

The profile of slave ownership among divorcing families was very similar to the profile of slavery ownership among all slaveholders in the South. One of the best available profiles of slave ownership showing its distribution across the slaveholding class in terms of the number of slaves owned can be found in the *Statistical View of the United States*, compiled from the 1850 census by J. D. B. DeBow. It shows that 50 percent of slave owners in the South possessed between 1 and 4 slaves; 23 percent, between 5 and 9; 16 percent, between 10 and 19; and 11 percent, 20 or more. Of the slaveholding families shown in Table 5, 43 percent owned between 1 and 4 slaves (218 of 503); 24 percent, between 5 and 9; 20 percent, between 10 and 19;

Married Women and Property | 91

and 13 percent, 20 or more. On average, they owned 10 slaves, slightly more than the 9-slave average in the region in 1850 reported by the *Statistical View of the United States*. Despite the changes over time and location in the slave population, DeBow's report showed a general picture for the antebellum period: The average slaveholder possessed a modest number of slaves, the largest group in the slaveholding class owned between 1 and 4 black people, and the smallest group—perhaps one in ten—owned 20 or more slaves. Thus, the women in this study reflected the diversity within the slaveholding class, even though their families belonged in slightly greater proportion to the group of larger and more prosperous slave owners than the population of slave owners as a whole (see "An Essay on Sources and Methodology").[26]

■ As a consequence of the legal concept of coverture, widows who remarried found it difficult to protect their estates. Yet the societal pressures to remarry were substantial. It was deemed proper, following the mourning period, that widows should remarry; it was also considered appropriate that men should head households. Widows found themselves managing their late husbands' land and slaves while dealing with mortgages and debts left behind, as well as negotiating with creditors, commission merchants, grocers, store owners, and others. Whereas some widows remained single for many years or remarried and outlived their second and even third husbands, others, like Louisiana Reid, remarried in haste and made poor choices with regard to their new partners. In most cases, once the marriage had taken place, a new husband could buy, sell, mortgage, trade, or sign away any portion of a widow's estate. In some instances, even a signed prenuptial or postnuptial trust agreement stipulating that the land, slaves, and other specified holdings were to remain under a wife's "sole and separate control" did not protect a wife's property, as most purchasers of land, slaves, and other property assumed that the property was held by the male head of the household, who most often controlled the family fortune.[27]

Most southerners believed that women living by themselves, alone or with their children, needed male protection. When a widow took over the responsibilities previously held by a deceased husband, such as supervising slaves, giving orders to black drivers, managing the sale of a crop, buying supplies and machinery, and negotiating with creditors, she was often criticized by relatives and friends, who urged her to remarry. The widow Natalie DeLage Sumter, for example, managed a plantation in South Carolina for a year and a half after her husband's death. She made the daily rounds, checking the progress of the crops, and refused to hire a white overseer as required by state law. She replaced a slave driver because he "disobeyed me having made the Negroes work in the heat of the day though I had told him it was his master's last orders they should not work when it was hot." Despite her exceptional administrative and managerial abilities, Sumter's neighbors believed these were improper activities for a woman living alone. Many observers considered widows like Sumter as performing work that only men should undertake. They predicted that if she and others continued to do such work, they would inevitably fail or, as one put it, be "borne down by the unrelenting hand of Fate." The ideal household, most southerners believed, included an intelligent and upstanding patriarch, a number of loyal slaves, and a refined, dignified plantation mistress.[28]

Such pressures from the surrounding community and society at large, combined with the need to compensate for the loss of loved ones, prompted some widows to remarry, although the rate of second marriages after widowhood declined during the antebellum era from the colonial period. Widowhood was a time of personal anguish, grief, and distress lived by many white women in the southern states. Indeed, married white women, especially those who as young women had married older men, as was often the case, stood a nearly even chance of widowhood. Writing to her sister about 1811, a Virginia woman expressed the grief she felt at the time of her husband's death, voicing what was probably felt by many others in such circumstances: "You can form no adequate idea of the anguish, of feelings produced by a loss like mine. . . . I feel that this awful event which has been so destructive to my peace of mind, has also been more than my constitution, though firm, could wholly resist."[29]

During this period of anxiety and sadness, widows were vulnerable to overtures by suitors. This was especially true for those who possessed substantial amounts of property. Most widows waited a period of time before they considered remarriage, and if they lived in neighborhoods with kin nearby, they could rely on their extended families for moral and financial support. But others, even those who were independent-minded and who had extended families, were not immune to the advances of men, usually younger than themselves, who showered them with attention, kindness, and affection. Indeed, a number of widows who remarried and later sued for divorce or separation described young men who courted them, sometimes for many months, in this fashion. During courtship such men portrayed themselves as honest, sober, industrious, and honorable—indeed, as perfect gentlemen. But some widows discovered, as did

Louisiana Banks, that the suitors had misrepresented themselves and, in fact, wished to marry them primarily for their wealth. Once the marriage had taken place, the widow's property was transferred to the new husband unless the wife had obtained a prenuptial agreement or the former husband had created a trust for his widow and children. Sometimes even with a prenuptial agreement a remarried widow found it difficult to hold on to her land and slaves. Others who brought their holdings, including land, horses, cattle, hogs, sheep, wagons, buggies, furniture, and slaves, to their second marriage lost substantial portions of their estate within a few years. Typical in this regard was Rachel Miller, a North Carolina widow who had brought livestock, wagons, and eight slaves to her second marriage. She had believed that the marriage would be a perfect match, as her suitor was a widower with seven children and she was the mother of five children. After their wedding, however, her new husband seized control of the property, forced her to labor in the fields, and threatened her to such an extent—once with a ball and chain—that she fled from her farm with her children. In doing so, she abandoned her first husband's estate.[30]

The widows who remarried too soon or chose the wrong partners were not without remedy to protect their holdings, however. In the chancery courts, not only could they file for divorce and separation, but they could also request the issuance of various orders, such as orders to protect their trust estates and for the establishment of alimony and maintenance agreements; they were in some cases successful in these "causes." In their pleas, they explained that the property they had inherited from their late husbands—land, farm machinery, crops, kitchen utensils, furniture, and slaves—had been in the family for many years and that their new husbands had ignored contracts, indentures, and marital agreements. Especially from the late 1830s forward, remarried widows could obtain property sequestration orders and injunctions to halt sales, and they could pursue other legal means to secure at least a portion of their estates during a breakup.[31]

Besides such measures, some remarried widows seeking a divorce announced to the public, often through newspaper advertisements, that they would not be responsible for any purchases their husband might make or any debts he might incur. Maryland slave owner Harriett Anne Beard's dower included sixty-five acres of fertile land. She also owned livestock and three slaves. After marrying William Watkins, she discovered that he drank to excess and failed to cultivate their wheat, corn, and tobacco crops, and she filed a complaint seeking divorce. Before the divorce was granted, she announced in a local newspaper that she would not pay for anything her

Perquimans County Courthouse, North Carolina. Built in 1823–25, the main building of this courthouse is virtually unchanged from the time of its original construction. It is still in use today, one of only three functioning Federal-era courthouses among the state's 100 counties. Excluding the furniture and chandeliers, the courtroom—including the jury box, judge's bench, witness stand, and bar—is the same as it was in 1857 when the slaveholding widow Matilda Everton filed for divorce. (Photo of exterior by Matisha Wiggs. Photo of interior by John Matthews.)

husband ordered without her written permission. Other remarried widows blocked the sale of slaves and other property by announcing in public that their new husbands did not hold title to their wives' holdings, or they obtained "writs of seizure" of their estates to stave off the sale of portions of their personal property. Widows who owned slaves and land as their separate property in the form of "life estates" of which they were the "life tenants," as such type of ownership and such owners were termed, charged husbands seeking to dispose of this property as acting against the law. Such public proclamations and legal actions were not only painful to the women involved but humiliating and demeaning to their husbands, especially so in a society that placed such a high value on male honor.[32]

Remarried women struggled to protect their separate and communal property during divorce or separation proceedings and afterward. A number took over the management of their farms and plantations, oversaw the planting and harvesting of crops, and sustained themselves and their children despite the gossip of neighbors that such activities were not proper for women. They also brought their cases to court, sometimes without the assistance of family members. The women asserted themselves in a number of ways in the male-dominated society and, more often than not, could rely on the chancery courts for judgments in their favor. The independence and strivings of these women to protect their property was in many ways remarkable, given the belief of most southerners that marriage was the most "important institution of human society."

■ Louisiana Reid of Williamson County, Tennessee, faced many financial difficulties after her second marriage to Thomas Reid in 1837, including the discovery that, according to the provisions of her first husband's will, she stood to receive substantially less than what she would be entitled to if she exercised her right of dower as provided by law. Only a few months into her ill-fated second marriage, Louisiana filed for divorce. She asked that the executor of her first husband's estate "be perpetually enjoined" from turning over to her second husband "any part of her said property." She also requested a fair share of the estate according to the rule of law rather than what was stipulated in her first husband's will. The court ruled in her favor on both counts. It noted in the last instance that because there was no provision in James Banks's will "inconsistent with the claim of Dower," Louisiana was entitled to one-third of the plantation lands (rather than the one-seventh bequeathed in the will), of which her first husband died "seized and possessed," as well as one-half of the realty formerly belonging to her father, Thomas Cash; the other half went to her children. The court ordered that the 512 acres that descended from Cash to Louisiana and her heirs be divided into two parcels of equal value, one for her and the other for her children.

In mid-December 1838, a court-appointed commission divided the land, giving Louisiana 273 acres, including the mansion house, and granting the children a tract of equal value but slightly smaller in size. Though no specific mention was made of the slaves given to Louisiana in 1822 by her father, the commissioners divided the forty-five slaves into seven groups of equal value. Louisiana received eight slaves as her share. The commissioners observed that twenty-two-year-old Emeline, valued at $700, had recently delivered stillborn twins and was in "a very dangerous and precarious situation." If she died, it would be necessary to redistribute her value.[33]

Following her divorce, Louisiana took back the name of her first husband. In subsequent years, Louisiana Banks never remarried, finding comfort and solace by expanding her wealth and observing the success of her children. In 1840, she managed the plantation and owned fifteen slaves. Ten years later, then in her mid-forties, she owned 120 acres of improved land and 130 acres of unimproved land, valued at $7,000. She directed the slaves as they planted and harvested crops of wheat, Indian corn, oats, Irish potatoes, and ten bales of cotton. On her plantation were horses, oxen, asses, milch cows, cattle, sheep, and swine. She lived next door to her son Thomas Banks, who, at age twenty-two, headed a household that included his wife Elizabeth and their one-year-old boy. Thomas was listed as owning 200 acres of improved and 300 acres of unimproved land, valued at $13,000, and fourteen slaves; he produced eighteen bales of cotton.

During the 1850s, Louisiana and her son added tobacco to their list of crops, producing more than 24,500 pounds along with 50 bales of cotton. In 1860, Louisiana's son Thomas Banks owned 21 slaves, 1,275 acres of land, 595 of which were "improved," much of it under cultivation. The agricultural census taker listed the total value of the land owned by mother and son at $40,000, placing them among the wealthiest landowning families in the county. While the Civil War swept away their slave labor force, Louisiana Banks continued to live on the land she had inherited from her father and her first husband, surrounded by her children and grandchildren. The death of her first husband, her disastrous remarriage, and her struggle to secure her father's legacy were now only dim memories of a bygone era.[34]

# SLAVES AND OWNERS' DOMESTIC CONFLICTS

In her petition for separation and alimony in Barnwell District, South Carolina, Eliza Taylor Ransom accused her husband, Dr. Thomas S. Ransom, of many misdeeds: He ignored their marriage agreement and mismanaged their finances; he slandered her good name by alleging she was an alcoholic; he had sexual relations with female slaves on the plantation; and he wielded his whip indiscriminately, not only to discipline slaves but to correct his wife. Married as a widow for only three years, she also described two incidents that revealed how slaves on the plantation became involved in her domestic difficulties.

Eliza's favorite among the forty-two slaves on the plantation was Sally, a highly intelligent, personable, and gregarious companion. She and Sally spent hours discussing domestic matters, sharing confidences, divulging secrets, gossiping about neighbors, and discussing acquaintances; in the evenings they sat together in the upstairs front room of the mansion house sewing and knitting. On one occasion, while the two women were walking through the garden talking, Dr. Ransom overheard Sally say "something about making pickles for one Mrs. Ayer a neighbor." He became incensed and immediately after breakfast, as his wife testified, he "commenced whipping the girl." Eliza intervened and asked him to stop, but he pushed her aside; as she was falling, she grabbed and tore his shirt. He then hit Eliza in the face with his fist, delivering a blow that drew blood. After he had ceased whipping Sally, he followed Eliza into the house and administered "as many as thirteen blows over the shoulders, with the whip which he had been beating the servant."

On another occasion, one evening during the summer of 1839, Eliza and Sally were sitting upstairs sewing when Eliza heard her husband order a small black girl named Margaret to fetch him some water from the well. "Sally, you had better go down and draw the water, for as Margaret (who was scarcely able to draw the water if perfectly awake) has been asleep she may fall into the well." Sally obeyed her mistress, went down to the front yard, and began drawing the water. Seeing this, Ransom stepped out of the house and began to hit and beat her. Eliza ran down the stairs and told her husband that she had given Sally the command to draw the water, upon which he turned around and without saying a word inflicted a severe blow which "felled her to the ground."[1]

■ Divorce and separation petitions suggest that, as was the case on the Ransom plantation, slaves in many slaveholding families torn apart by domestic conflict suffered more often from the consequences of being caught in the middle than they did from punishment inflicted because they disobeyed orders, slacked off on their work, or in the words of owners, became "refractory and troublesome." As they did on the Ransom plantation, slaves often bore witness to domestic difficulties or learned about them firsthand from fellow slaves. On large plantations, the word of marital discord spread rapidly through the quarters, while on smaller units, as well as in towns and cities, bondmen and bondwomen witnessed the arguments, anger, hostility, violence, and distress that existed between masters and mistresses. They saw wives being mistreated, husbands drinking to excess, and male owners displaying favoritism toward certain female slaves. They knew when their owners engaged in adultery with both black and white women; they sometimes grew up with children of mixed racial origin, the offspring of their owners. They heard obscene language, slanderous denunciations, recrimination, quarreling, bickering, and arguing. They also observed the harsh treatment of white children, separations and reconciliations between wives and husbands, and flights of white women and children after bitter disputes and threats. Slaves knew when owners remained absent for extended periods, deserted their wives and children, or got into trouble with the law.[2]

Viewing divorce and separation among the slaveholding class through the prism of those held in bondage presents special problems, as do other aspects of the African American experience, because most of the testimony comes from whites. Despite this limitation, the presence of bondmen and bondwomen in households torn apart by domestic conflict is palpable in many of the divorce and separation petitions. A clear picture emerges, albeit indirectly through the words of owners or the testimony of neighbors, of the fears, anxieties, and trepidations of enslaved people as well as of their responses to their owners' domestic strife. Not even the anonymity of black people who are mentioned in divorce proceedings—the "negroe woman," "negroe Girl," "Negro wench," "black mistress," "negro man slave," "Negro Boy," or "house servant," among other appellations—obscures what must have been their dread, not only for themselves but for their families and children, in the midst of their owners' marital problems. In some respects, divorce in a slave-owning family could have consequences similar to those caused by the death of an owner, in that it often resulted in the distribution of slave property among various heirs and the breakup of black families. But the prelude to divorce could be even worse for slaves who found themselves caught in the middle of a disagreement and forced to choose sides.[3]

It is difficult to know how slaves felt in such situations, but it stands to reason that they would try to avoid becoming involved in clashes between white family members. If they chose one spouse over another, they could easily put their own families in jeopardy. If they attempted to intervene and protect an abused wife, they could incite the wrath of the master. If they accompanied an owner's wife fleeing her home, they might be forced to leave their own children behind. If they informed neighbors or family members about personal matters relating to their owners' families, they could experience the anger of their owners as well as that of their owners' friends and acquaintances. Also, if they supported the "wrong" spouse, they might alienate fellow bondmen and bondwomen.

Thus, slaves were forced to ask themselves a number of questions in the face of their masters' domestic conflicts: Should they express sympathy or provide protection for either spouse? Should they follow orders from the mistress or from the master when the orders contradicted one another? Should they inform a member of the white family about an infidelity or cover up the adulterous affair? What should they do when they believed that following certain commands might bring harm to themselves or their loved ones?

Often they were wise to remain silent. When they knew about clandestine relationships between the master and female slaves or saw white women taking up with other men, they often looked the other way or kept quiet unless questioned and forced to reveal such matters. In some ways, what occurred on the farms and plantations in this regard was what might be termed the politics of life in a community where blacks and whites, slaves and owners, lived side by side. Many slaves probably felt that trying to remain uninvolved in such matters was the best means of protection. Such was certainly the case on the farm of William McClure in Montgomery County, Tennessee, in 1822, when the slaves observed McClure's wife, Rebecca, having an affair with a black man named Taff, formerly owned by her husband. Over a six-month period, during the husband's absences, Taff entered the McClure farmhouse in the middle of the day in full view of the other slaves. How the husband discovered the betrayal is not revealed, but it is clear that the slaves on the farm had known about the affair for many months. In his petition for divorce, William McClure said, "Your petitioner would represent that for six months last past the said Rebecca has been Indulging at all times of the absence of her husband from home with said negro slave, that she took him to your petitioners house and did so openly, with her negroes about his farm house." The slaves as well as several white workers on the small plantation of Abner Pyles in Laurens District, South Carolina, also knew about a secret love affair between Frances Pyles, Abner's wife, and a slave-owning neighbor named Alexander Winn. In fact, Frances Pyles enlisted the assistance of a female house servant, promising the latter her freedom if she accompanied her and her lover to Virginia. As the departure date approached, however, the black woman wavered and told her mistress that she would not leave the plantation. The wife then made the same offer to a "negro boy." In the end, the house servant informed the husband of the plot. The slaveholder later confessed that it was "striking" how everyone knew about the infidelity except himself. One can only imagine the whispers and innuendos circulating on these and other farms and plantations among groups of slaves as they contemplated how to maneuver within the system. In this instance, choosing one side over the other seemed like the least risky alternative among a number of difficult options.[4]

Slave women who sided with their mistresses often found themselves in potentially harmful situations. They could be punished, sent away, or sold; they could be separated from their children at the whim of their owners; they could be threatened by the master if he perceived any involvement with the mistress during a domestic conflict. If they stood up for the mistress in the midst of confrontations between husband and wife, they could experience the owner's wrath, the same "vexations, excesses, cruel treatments, [and] outrages" that wives seeking a divorce or separation complained about. One Louisiana slaveholding farmer told his wife's favorite slave, Caroline, that if she did not cease supporting her mistress during family fights, he would seek vengeance on her as well as his wife. When four slaves on Jonathan Bryan's farm in North Carolina mounted, in Bryan's words, an "Insurrection" against him, he accused his wife of instigating the revolt. It was the slaves who suffered, however. One of them, a large black woman siding with the mistress, pushed Bryan against a bench, causing a severe wound. Bryan had the slave arrested and taken to jail.[5]

Black children found themselves, as did black women, witnesses of white family intrigues and domestic difficulties. The youngsters were usually used as go-betweens, passing notes or letters between lovers, or as pawns in games that might result in the embarrassment or debasement of a white family member. Slave youngsters could move from one cabin to another in the quarters or from one house to another in towns and cities without causing much suspicion. Sometimes they were not owned by either party in a domestic dispute but served as a go-between for a person seeking to keep a relationship secret. At other times, they traveled with their mistresses when the latter consulted lawyers about drawing up papers for divorce or when they were returning after such meetings. On still other occasions, husbands used slave children to belittle and demean their wives in front of white family members. The wife of a Kentucky slave owner, who had filed for divorce charging that her husband had rendered her life miserable by his "ungentlemanly conduct," called on a friend and neighbor to provide a deposition to be read in court. The neighbor, John Doyle, said that as he was sitting at the dinner table with the husband, the husband's two sons by a prior marriage, and the wife, he heard the husband whisper to "a little negro girl," about five or six, to go around the table and tell his wife to "Kiss his arse." Although such events were amusing to the men present, there were other instances when slave children were severely punished for such impudence or when owners suspected that the black children knew about their wives' activities and kept them secret.[6]

■ Despite its seemingly benign and almost humorous nature, the incident described above exposes how the almost constant back and forth of family exchanges, which could and sometimes did escalate into anger, hostility, and even bloodshed, drew slaves into a web from which they often were unable to extricate themselves. When it was clear that there would be no possibility of compromise and the man and wife would be separating, slaves became fearful. They knew that their owners' personal problems, should they result in divorce or separation, would almost certainly have an impact on their lives. But how? they asked. Would they be sold, traded, conveyed, or taken away by one or the other involved in divorce proceedings, or would they be levied upon by creditors and taken into protective custody by the sheriff? Would they be hired out, forced to relocate to some distant county, and be uprooted and torn from their wives, husbands, children, kin, and loved ones? Their fears were more than justified, as slaves were often taken away by slaveholding husbands who abandoned their wives, hired out many miles away from their farms or plantations, and offered up in private and public sales. Indeed, it was not uncommon in cases of divorce for human property to be sold and the proceeds of the sale divided between the parties. In some cases, slaves were sold as a result of court proceedings to provide wives and children with maintenance; in other cases, husbands took the slaves away and sold them without their wives' permission, before the courts could decide how the human property should be distributed. Some of the slaves thus sold belonged to wives through either inheritance, premarital agreements, or trust estates.[7] Especially vulnerable to being sold or hired out were those with skills as blacksmiths, brick masons, carpenters, caulkers, coopers, cooks, nurses, house servants, and "mechanics," who brought very good wages as well as high prices at private or public sales. Such was the case in 1847 in Kentucky for Susan A. Brown's slave, a black carpenter "worth twenty dollars per month as hire and very valuable worth one thousand dollars or upwards." The unnamed slave was sold at a private sale by Susan's husband just before the latter abandoned his wife and was never heard from again, although it was reported that he later remarried. Susan had received the black man many years before as a gift from her father. Most skilled slaves, such as Susan Brown's carpenter, could be readily sold, as demand for such workers steadily increased and rarely declined during the antebellum era.[8]

Slaves were especially in danger during bitter fights over alimony. A number of cases show they were sometimes sold or traded or hidden from wives. They were turned over to dealers, factors, and commission merchants; conveyed to relatives; or transported out of the county. Once such a sale or transfer had taken place, even the most diligent wives had difficulty securing slave property as alimony. As previously indicated, some wives filed injunctions, sought restraining orders, or asked the county court to sequester certain slave property, but these efforts were not always successful. Indeed, in order to forestall such situations, wives demanded that their husbands appear and answer the charges levied against them and asked the courts to order them to remain within the court's jurisdiction. They pointed out that "family slaves"—those designated for their "sole and separate use" or bequeathed to their family by their kin—were sometimes the best means for them to secure maintenance and alimony as well as child support.[9]

The black people thus involved had little, if any, choice as they were sold or taken away, hired out in distant locations, or treated harshly by owners and overseers. Or they watched as loved ones were sent to slave-trading centers such as New Orleans, Mobile, Natchez, Charleston, Richmond, the District of Columbia, or Baltimore, among others. At times they became the objects of the husband's anger and were sold or taken away merely out of spite. Such was the fate of the District of Columbia slave Rose, the personal servant of Jane Mackall who was advertised for sale by Mackall's husband in a local newspaper. When Rose disappeared before she could be sold, friends and neighbors assumed that she had run away. In fact, Jane had hidden Rose in her own chambers for nearly two months before she was discovered by the husband and sold to a slave trader heading to the "southern markets." A similar fate awaited a Kentucky slave, one of the daughters of a slave woman named Turner, who, in 1806, had been given as a wedding present to Matilda Payne. During the quarter-century following the wedding gift, Turner gave birth to six children, three daughters (Dinah, Ester, and Maria) and three sons (Lewis, Simon, and Tom). When Matilda Payne filed for divorce in 1830, her husband quickly sold one of Turner's daughters to a slave trader. Only through the intervention of Matilda's brother, who followed the trader, was the girl retrieved and saved from being sold away from her family.[10]

As suggested by the sale of Turner's daughter, divorce or separation among owners often had an immediate impact on black families. Children were taken from their mothers, hired out during court proceedings, and sold for payment of alimony. Young men and women living as husband and wife were separated from their children and/or each other. Slave aunts, uncles, cousins, and other kin were distributed to various family members following the dissolution of a marriage, as were, at times, elderly couples who had spent many years together. It is ironic and tragic that the pressures of dislocation experienced by white families torn apart by divorce or separation were transferred to the black families whom they owned. Young boys and girls were hired out in adjacent counties long distances from their mothers. Occasionally, husbands sold their wives' favorite slaves, including children, before the courts could take action to halt the sale. In 1850, twelve slaves owned by Joshua Holly of Barnwell District, South Carolina—namely, a man and woman, both about sixty; three men and a woman between ages twenty and thirty-one; a girl thirteen; and five children ages one to six (two boys and three girls)—were divided when Joshua abandoned his wife. He took "all his grown negroes" and left behind "four young negroes" who were either too young or too small to work in the fields.[11]

Even when black family members were kept together, divorce and separation of the owners caused fear, consternation, disruption, and distress. The slave Sally, who had been conveyed to her mistress many years before as a gift, had given birth to seven children by the time her owner's husband began, as the mistress said, "wandering about through the county." The black mother and children, having lived in Sumner County, Tennessee, most of their lives, remained together until the husband deserted his wife for good and took up with another woman. Sally and her children were then secretly transferred to a woman who lived in Cumberland County, Kentucky, about sixty miles from their former home and out of the reach of the authorities in Sumner County.[12]

■ Children as well as mothers with children found it extremely difficult to offer resistance to such relocations, even when it meant that loved ones would be lost forever. Yet, slaves did respond to strife within their owners' families in a variety of ways. A few used their owners' preoccupations with personal matters to attempt an escape. Described as a "yellowish" woman about twenty-five, the Alabama slave Dinah had been given by the father of a bride to his daughter as a wedding gift. When the newly wedded wife gave birth to a mulatto child six months later, the husband sent his wife back to her father but kept the slave. Dinah fled into the woods, fearing what might happen not only to her but also to her child and slave husband, who, as it turned out, was the father of the white woman's baby. Dinah remained on the run for several weeks, but the new bridegroom found her and "carried her off" to Texas. Three other slaves—forty-three-year-old Chaney, eighteen-year-old Richmond, and fifteen-year-old Lucy—fled from a Louisiana farm during a suit brought by the farmer's wife for "separation of Bed, board & property." They, too, were quickly apprehended, jailed, and sequestered by the parish sheriff "for safe keeping during the pendency of said suit."[13]

Although the fate of Dinah and the three Louisiana runaways who were apprehended was typical, a few slaves did manage to escape and evade local authorities. Often they were skilled slaves such as house servants, nurses, laundresses, and artisans, or they were slaves of mixed racial ancestry—that is, slaves who possessed advantages when seeking to take on a new identity, maneuvering past slave patrols, or feigning to be free persons of color. They took advantage of their privileged position as well as their owners' preoccupations with marital problems. Indeed, in one instance an owner was so distracted by his wife's infidelity that an entire group of slaves escaped. The slaves were owned by Stephen L. Lee, a planter on the South River in Anne Arundel County, Maryland. When he discovered that his wife was having an affair with a young schoolteacher, Lee became so obsessed with his wife's infidelity—following her when she left the house, employing a private investigator to track her movements, and searching through her private belongings and uncovering a letter from the teacher so "lustful and Sensual such as not but an adulterer could write to an adulteress"—that six of his twenty-four slaves took advantage of the situation and absconded. When the census marshal arrived at the Lee plantation some time later, he cited this group of mulatto adults and children as "Fugitives from the State."[14]

There were other instances of slaves trying to escape after husbands had abandoned their wives or during violent domestic confrontations or when a spouse was planning to leave. The flights were rarely successful, but a few of the fugitives were not heard from again. Those who made successful breaks for freedom were most often men running away alone, and most often they were successful when wives were left to fend for themselves after their husbands had abandoned them. The Missouri slave Thomas saw such an opportunity in 1848 when Martha Huskey's husband left "for parts unknown" with a white woman. Thomas struck out across the hilly terrain of Jefferson County and was never seen or heard from again. A South Carolina slave named Hager did the same when his owner left his wife, although the circumstances were quite different. In the midst of the confusion that occurred during the white husband's attempt to steal Hager and Hager's wife, named Ann, and Ann's screaming and running back to the farmhouse to fetch her baby, Hager fled into the night. Such were the difficult situations that slaves had to face if they chose to abscond. The chances of success were not good, and if they chose to flee, they were sometimes forced to leave members of their own families behind.[15]

■ Another rare response to domestic conflicts was the attempt on the part of slaves to protect mistresses from abusive husbands. Such intervention, especially by male slaves, would almost certainly arouse the vengeance of the owner and precipitate severe punishments ranging from whipping and shackling to incarcerations in the plantation jail, the county workhouse, or the county jail. They could be sold or traded, whipped and beaten, or turned over to a slaveholder like Covey, the man who attempted to break Frederick Douglass's spirit. "During the first six months, of that year [1833]," Douglass wrote, "scarce a week passed without his whipping me." In addition, they could be forced to do dangerous work or be placed under the constant scrutiny of a harsh overseer or slave driver.[16]

Despite such danger, a few African American men put their own safety in jeopardy to protect white women. They confronted husbands who were threatening their wives, intervened to stop an attack or a beating, and on occasion even grappled with an owner. They also hid mistresses in outbuildings on the plantation, refused to obey orders from their masters when they believed the white women were in danger, or assisted wives when they fled from their farms and plantations. It took a remarkable amount of courage to stand up to owners in such a manner, and at times the black men who dared to do so were attacked and put their lives at risk. On a plantation in East Baton Rouge Parish, Louisiana, in 1840, an unnamed black man ignored his owner's command to go after his wife, who had fled from the plantation. The owner thrust a gun into the black man's face and threatened to shoot him if he did not bring the wife back, but the black man refused. The outraged owner cursed him and threatened to kill him but did not carry out his threat. The incident and others similar to it occurred after a buildup of violence had taken place over many weeks and months, and wives on occasion expressed appreciation for the assistance offered.[17]

A few black women also intervened to protect their mistresses. In most cases, they did so by simply disobeying orders or verbally confronting husbands or placing themselves between husbands and wives during altercations. Engaging in such acts of resistance toward men who were not used to seeing their authority challenged, especially by a black woman, could be extremely dangerous. Such interventions occurred infrequently, usually when a strong bond had developed between a female slave and her mistress. In each case, the slave risked her own safety and the safety of her family and children. A slave woman in Kentucky stood next to her mistress during a marital confrontation, and when the husband ordered her to bring him his knife, she refused to do so. The husband had a history of violence, but the two women remained motionless and the crisis passed. A visitor on a plantation in the same state recounted that the head of the household, who owned twenty-six slaves, called his wife a dammed bitch, a whore, and a liar. "I heard him threaten to give her a Cowhide and order a negro woman to bring him the Cowhide to whip her with," a visitor to the plantation testified; "the negro went after the Cowhide but did not return and I heard no more of it that night." Female slaves were perhaps most helpful in assisting wives who fled. They hid their mistresses in plantation kitchens, outbuildings, and slave dwellings, at times for many days. It is easy to understand how some slave women who observed owners punishing their wives might empathize with the women or feel sorry for their children.[18]

The reverse also occurred, that is, mistresses offering protection to female slaves. Although the literature on this subject has probably overemphasized the harmonious and affectionate relationships between the two groups of women, such feelings did exist, as evidenced by Eliza Ransom's defense of Sally in South Carolina. Wives of slave owners sometimes intervened when they deemed punishments administered by their husbands too harsh or when owners planned to break up slave families. When they intervened during a slave punishment such as a whipping, wives took the greatest risk. North Carolina farmer Wright Brannock complained that the "negro girl" on loan from his father-in-law flouted authority and was arrogant and insolent. His wife protected the girl despite her disobedience, he said. He became "determined to flog the negro & did so," but while he was whipping the slave, Martha Brannock "took a Switch & cut in upon him, & gave it to him soundly, until he got out of her way." Though successful in preventing further violence in this instance, Martha Brannock failed to prevent the sale of an "audacious" fellow, despite her pleadings to the contrary. A few other similar interventions occurred when wives confronted their husbands in defense of black women during the administration of punishments, including that of the Mississippi woman who jumped on the back of her husband as he was flogging a female slave. But in these rare instances, wives were often as likely to receive punishments themselves as to protect the slave women.[19]

■ The interracial dynamics created as a result of marital discord in slave-owning families are both complex and revealing. Especially intriguing is the fact that by far the most common response of slaves to the climate of chaos and violence created by the marital woes of the slaveholding class was neither to run away nor to try to protect the mistress but, in the case of female slaves, to reverse roles and assume that of quasi plantation mistress. Most often opportunities arose through sexual relationships with the master of the household, relationships that were sometimes of long duration and resulted in the birth of slave children; but at other times, they were short lived. In either case, these women, referred to in the divorce petitions as "de facto wife," "negro mistress," "concubine," "mulattress," "black mistress," and "negro paramour," were often young, attractive, and assertive.[20]

As owners of other human beings, white men were in a position that allowed them to exploit and coerce female slaves; yet it appears that when sexual relationships with female property were involved, the exercise of power was not always one-sided. Indeed, in some cases, a reversal of power appears to have taken place, if the testimony of aggrieved wives, visitors, neighbors, and friends is to be believed. They charged black women with enticing, tempting, and luring husbands away from their wives. There was little doubt, a spurned Virginia wife informed the court, that the slave Maria made overtures toward the master, who possessed "a large estate of land & negroes." She toyed with him, invited his embraces, and permitted him to kiss her in the presence of others; she also slept with him, sometimes on a pallet in the wife's chamber, at other times in a room adjoining the house. A family friend who lived on the plantation for five months said that the husband was "strongly attached to a servant girl of the family with whom he habitually had illicit & criminal intercourse." He often embraced and kissed her in front of the friend, invited her to a seat at the dining table with the family, and "appeared to be passionately attached to her."[21]

This type of relationship was, in fact, not highly unusual in families in the midst of splitting apart. In some cases, adult family members testified about the behavior of their aging fathers. They made similar observations about men becoming attached to certain black women, playing with them in front of family members, and as one son said, "catching hold of her & she of him & laughing together." The fathers were not only playful but intimate with the women while permitting them to do as they pleased and not compelling them to work in the same manner as the other slaves. They also refused to punish them for insulting members of the white family. In North Carolina, the slave Silvia, as indicated in several accounts, flirted with her elderly owner, a man in his seventies. She whispered in his ear and ran off into the woods knowing he would follow. She moved into the owner's house and forced the wife out of her own bed; she secured the keys to the corncrib, smokehouse, bedroom, and family chest; and she put chains around two storage containers, one belonging to the owner's wife, the other to the owner's 105-year-old mother. Occasionally she physically chastised the mistress. Silvia gave birth to two children. One, described as black, was born dead; the other, live-born, was described as "brighter than negroes are commonly" and almost certainly the child of the owner.[22]

As a result of the attachment white men felt for them, some slave women exerted authority over white women, the white women's children, and sometimes their fellow slaves. Indeed, there were probably very few communities with sizable populations of slaves where some black women did not assume the role of mistress of the household, where some so-called black concubines did not become mistresses of farms or plantations, assuming "control & management" of the master's affairs as well as the affairs of his children. In return, they could expect special privileges, kinder treatment, additional allowances, better clothing, protection of their own children, and the ability to travel to see relatives. Whatever the circumstances, it is safe to assume that many viewed their connection with the owner as an opportunity to improve their situation within the constraints of the slave system, perhaps even to begin a journey with their children toward freedom.[23]

The complaints of wives suing for divorce and the testimonies offered on their behalf are replete with anecdotes of plantation life suggesting that some female slaves who ascended to such positions in their owners' households viewed white women with contempt and used their privileged status to usurp their power. Such was at least the perception of some mistresses who said they were made to feel like outcasts in their own homes and subservient to their slaves. Black mistresses stripped white women of their authority over their own slaves, prohibited fellow slaves from obeying their orders, and encouraged slaves to poke fun at the wives. They forced wives, as did a "negro paramour" in Alabama, to submit to "caprices and tyranny," insults and humiliations, while acting as "a kind of guardian and mistress" over the plantation. They also sought revenge for past mistreatment of themselves as well as members of their families or struck out because of their anger and frustration at being enslaved. A "negro wench" in South Carolina welcomed the advances of her master, a farmer and mill owner who possessed seven slaves. As the relationship evolved, the black woman disciplined the couple's seven children, beat one of them severely for being disrespectful to her, and set up housekeeping in the nearby mill with the husband. When the wife protested the "illicit & criminal intercourse" as well as the mistreatment of her children, the husband went to the farmhouse and gave his wife "a cruel & severe beating."[24]

Although most slave women who, in the words of one wife, "gained precedent" over a family's domestic affairs did so by virtue of their sexual relationships with their male owners, some also attained positions of authority due to their superior organizational and administrative abilities. They sought to undermine the mistresses' authority by demonstrating their own unique talents managing household affairs. Slave women who tried to gain a measure of power through such tactics were most often older, boasting years of experience managing people, white and black, adults and children, and possessing personality traits and skills that made them valuable to their owners. They were able to maneuver within the politics of the plantation by finding ways to strengthen their relationships with their male owners and at the same time scheming to lessen the authority of the white mistresses. As time passed, they exerted more and more authority in the households and thus often felt at liberty to be impertinent, hostile, and abusive toward their mistresses. The mulatto woman Caroline, a Kentucky slave owned by Edward Coleman, gradually gained control over her owner's household. In a position of authority, with "unbounded influence" over the master, as the wife said, Carolina became rude, insolent, and aggressive. In another case, shortly after his marriage, a Virginia slave owner told his bride that his slave cook would exercise the authority of mistress. It did not take long for the young wife to recognize that the unnamed cook possessed "all control and authority" over domestic matters.[25]

In these and other instances, it was clear that, from the perspective of the wives at least, some slave women sought, even relished, the power and authority they exercised over the white women. As de facto heads of domestic affairs, they organized meals, disciplined white children, and scolded, directed, and mistreated wives. Some, including a female servant in Charles County, Maryland, who managed her owner's affairs, were in their twenties, but most, like a slave woman in Alabama, were older and had risen to their positions over a number of years.[26]

Another tactic adopted by some female slaves to reverse the dynamics of power and subservience was to spread rumors about their owners' wives. A slave owned by Thomas Garner in Alabama circulated gossip, the nature of which the complaining wife did not disclose, about her white mistress. The wife defended herself by asserting she had always "remained faithful to the honor and interests" of her husband, but the husband believed the slave. In other instances, slaves spied on white women and reported back to their owners, turned over letters from clandestine lovers, and worked in various ways to undermine the reputations of their mistresses.[27]

In households where female slaves gained authority over their white mistresses, through sexual relationships or otherwise, husbands invariably sided with them when a dispute arose. As a result, the black women who managed households, acting as de facto wives, were at liberty to chastise white women with insulting language, "opprobrious epithets," and verbal abuse, lowering the wives, as one white mistress in Mississippi said, "to the level with the said negro servant." They were often described by white women as haughty, impudent, belligerent, arrogant, and abusive. Despite the black women's condition in bondage, the white women said, they perceived themselves as having achieved "status" and "position" over the mistresses. A few were permitted by their male owners to inflict physical chastisements on white women. One Georgia slave who engaged in "illicit & carnal commerce" with a husband beat and whipped the man's wife during an argument.[28]

Such reversal of roles encouraged other slaves to treat the white women with contempt and hostility, especially when slaveholding husbands either condoned or encouraged such behavior. The wife of one South Carolina slave owner said "she was not only treated by her husband with severity and disrespect, but her servants, observing the conduct of their master, were habitually rude, insolent and disobedient." Sarah Smith of Alabama said that her husband cursed and threatened her and, even worse, stood idly by as one of his slaves hit her with "hands, sticks & whips." Once they realized that she could not "exercise any control of the servants about their common dwelling," one Louisiana wife explained that most of the slaves on the plantation became disobedient and unruly.[29]

It should be noted that the reversal of roles occurred in families in the midst of marital crises, and the evidence comes from aggrieved wives and/or white witnesses testifying in their behalf. In some ways, therefore, the evidence is biased. But because subordination of a wife to a slave mistress is one of the most consistent and pervasive symptoms of family turmoil described by slave-owning wives suing for divorce or alimony, there can be little doubt that many black women in troubled households probably took the lead in fostering the development of such relationships, or at least encouraged them in order to gain advantages for themselves and their families. Although there were undoubtedly many instances of white men forcing themselves upon female slaves, and some scholars have, in fact, argued that all relationships between masters and slaves are by nature coerced, it appears in the study cases cited above that the exploitation between owners and slaves could go both ways. The detailed depictions of domestic life in households where the reversal of roles took place support the view that, no matter how harsh the system was, it did not entirely take away the ability of slaves to take initiatives in order to improve their lives by finding cracks in the system and using them to their advantage.

However strong and dominant a position some black women appeared to have reached, their situation was always precarious, subject to the whim of an owner or a turn of circumstance. Even giving birth to their owners' children did not provide female slaves with continued protection or stability, as the culture of the slaveholding community weighed against status thus acquired. Wives often spent months, even years, attempting to regain the affection and respect of their husbands, calling on relatives, friends, neighbors, clergy, and others to intervene. A number of other factors

African American nanny and her white charge. This rare unidentified ambrotype of a black woman and a white child is typical of the few extant daguerreotypes, tintypes, and ambrotypes of slave women. Though the woman portrays the myth of the dutiful slave who loved her master's white children, her countenance and facial expression reveal a measure of hostility. In families in crisis, a number of slave women not only rejected this stereotype but acted to replace white women, albeit for brief periods, as female household heads. (Courtesy Cowan's Auction, Inc., Cincinnati, Ohio.)

worked against such authority conferred upon female slaves. The great majority of slave women involved in sexual relationships with white men were young and could bring a good price if put on the auction block, and thus the lure of profit could be used by those who sought to dislodge them from their position. Moreover, many of their white protectors were older and subject to the vagaries of age, disease, and economic change.[30]

The results of such unpredictable events were at play when the Mississippi slave Emily, in her late teens and described by her owner James Whitehead as "the finest girl he ever saw," took over the management of his household affairs. By all accounts, Emily was a young woman of extraordinary intelligence, ability, vitality, and beauty. After seventeen years of marriage and the birth of five children, the owner's wife said, her husband had become "so infatuated by his passion for the said Emily that he has neither the power nor the desire to conceal the nature of his intercourse with her." His "undisguised fondness and caresses" alienated his children and drew the attention of many people in the community. For her part, Emily quickly asserted her dominance in the domestic sphere, ordering the wife about, chastising her in front of her children, demeaning her in front of fellow slaves, and prohibiting her from giving commands. Emily's authority on the farm and dominance over her white mistress, however, proved to be temporary. Less than a year after he had purchased her at the Forks of the Road near Natchez, under pressure from family and friends, James Whitehead sold "the finest girl he ever saw."[31]

As suggested by the examples cited in the preceding section, marital conflicts revealed the extraordinary personal and racial dynamics at work in slave-owning households, especially laying bare the great variety of interracial and gender relationships that would likely otherwise have remained buried under the surface, perhaps known by the surrounding society but certainly not openly discussed, much less accepted. Indeed, the regularity with which certain themes emerge from these cases, even as each case is woven into a unique tapestry, points to the reality that the domestic situations thus described occurred with far greater frequency than the limited sample of divorce and separation petitions that constitute this study would otherwise suggest.[32]

■ Eliza Ransom believed she had done everything she could to meet her obligations as a wife as required "by Religious morality and the Customs of Society." But no act of forbearance or goodwill, she believed, "would ever awaken in his bosom a sense of duty, or even the ordinary feelings of humanity." Fearing for her life after her own beating and the whipping of her favorite slave, Sally, she fled from her husband's plantation to the home of her friend and the trustee of her separate estate, Cornelius K. Ayer, whose wife almost certainly was the recipient of the pickles prepared by Sally, an incident that sparked Dr. Ransom to become so outraged. It was the series of violent outbursts against her slaves and herself that made Eliza realize she had made a tragic mistake. During the legal proceedings of property separation, Dr. Ransom refused to turn over information about the estate's debts; continued to manage the slaves, including Sally; and asserted he had every right to sell any portion or all of his wife's property as he saw fit. It appears that he was largely successful. Although Eliza claimed in her suit that her husband's "doings and pretenses" were "contrary to equity and good conscience" and asked to be allowed to live separate and apart on her own "settled estate," her husband continued to maintain control of most of the land and slaves and soon began disposing of the property. It is not known what became of Eliza's favorite slave, Sally, but in subsequent years, Eliza was not listed in the census returns anywhere in the state; neither was her husband nor their slaves. After the Civil War, sixty-four-year-old Eliza Ransom lived with her son Charles Taylor (from her first marriage) and his family on their farm in Bedford County, Tennessee.[33]

CONCLUSION

The Civil War swept away the old regime in the South and, in doing so, changed southern society forever. After the war, divorce became largely a male purview, and most of the suits, brief and nondescript, were filed by men. Nor would slavery ever again enter the equation, as former slaves not only could legally marry but could legally obtain a divorce. White women did not have to contend with the interracial sexual dynamics between their husbands and female slaves, nor did they have to fight to retain control of their slave property. Thus, the pre–Civil War decades were unique in many ways, not the least of which was the fact that during that era, primarily white women filed petitions for divorce, separation, and alimony, and they detailed the reasons for doing so with lengthy narratives of their marriages, their lives, and their anguish.

The story of antebellum families in crisis shows a part of the slave regime that was hidden, including the pervasive nature of domestic violence and white women who asserted themselves and left oppressive husbands. In taking action, the women probably helped push the political process of revising and amending divorce and alimony statutes as well as the laws governing married women's property, as the legal codes and protections for women evolved during the decades before the Civil War. There is little doubt that some of the white women who made their marital woes public found it difficult to sustain themselves and their children. The high proportion of divorce cases that ended in compromise and reconciliation reflected this. At the same time, despite the mores and customs of the society in which they lived, these women exhibited a great deal of courage and resiliency by standing up for what they considered to be their marital rights. The contention that married women possessed few, if any, legal rights during the period and were less independent and less successful than the women in the eighteenth century is not borne out by an examination of divorce and alimony cases. White women filed increasing numbers of petitions to general assemblies and, later, to equity, or chancery, courts, often without male "next friends," and they succeeded in a number of instances in obtaining favorable rulings. They did so despite economic hardship and the opprobrium of society. Nor were women from the most prosperous families more likely to obtain favorable decrees than those from middling or non-slave-owning families.

The divorce cases also showed how slaveholding men chose a variety of sexual partners and were more apt to have affairs with white women than with their own slaves; non-slave-owning men who filed for divorce overwhelmingly charged their wives with having sexual affairs with black men, despite the dangers such encounters posed for the men involved, whether slave or free. At the same time, in the midst of marital conflicts, black women saw opportunities to protect themselves and their children by accepting the advances of the slave-owning household heads. This occurred in a number of instances, sometimes even when the slave women were not mentioned by name. Female slaves usurped the authority of the white mistress and asserted themselves as the female heads of households. Of course, they still remained the property of the owner, and if the husband and wife reconciled or if the husband changed his mind, black women and their children could, and on occasion were, sold, sometimes because of the threatening demands of white wives.

Most of the marital clashes occurred on farms and plantations, often in remote and isolated areas some distance from the nearest town or city. While some white women who filed for divorce and alimony, even in out-of-the-way locations, could call on friends, relatives, neighbors, and others for assistance, others could not. They remained isolated and alone, with few friends or relatives, and neighbors were often unwilling to offer aid or disagreed with the concept of divorce. The emphasis by many historians on the networks of friends and family who came to the rescue of women seeking divorce and separation has probably been exaggerated, especially as southerners migrated from the eastern seaboard to states in the West and Southwest. Many women were forced to find and hire lawyers on their own and, after fleeing from their homes, had difficulty sustaining themselves and their children.

As time passed, state statutes and chancery courts became increasingly important in determining the outcome of divorce suits. In fact, transformations in localized law and keeping the peace occurred after 1830, as state legislatures turned away from passing private acts and focused on enacting laws for the public welfare. Reputations, or the "credit," of plaintiffs and defendants were still important, but certainly less so than a generation before. This was especially true in the circuit, district, and superior chancery courts, where divorce litigation was tried, as the civil codes of each state governed the process and decisions of judges and juries. The proceedings followed the legal rules and regulations established by each state. Those who brought strong cases, citing specific laws, producing credible witnesses, and submitting pertinent documents, could often expect to win even if their reputations in the community were less than exemplary or their characters were attacked during trials.

Despite the ability of some black women to maneuver within the system, when divorce pleas reached the courts, it was clear that slaves were considered property. White women struggled to maintain slave ownership, despite rules of coverture and property laws favoring men. To protect their human property, a few women obtained prenuptial agreements or arranged for their premarital property to be put into trusts. In those agreements, they required their husbands to allow them "sole and separate" use of slaves and other property. Some wives received inheritances from their parents or other family members during their marriages and secured deeds allowing them to keep the property separate from their husband's holdings. The deeds often said that the future children of female slaves would be similarly protected for the separate use of the women. As time passed, white women seeking separation not only demanded that they be allowed to keep their premarital and trust property, but they sought to secure communal property as well, including slaves. They also argued that their husbands' creditors should not be permitted to confiscate their separate estates.

White women fared better than white men in their pleas for divorce and separation, even when submitting their causes to the three general assemblies where adequate data is available—Maryland, Virginia, and Tennessee. Women filed one-third more legislative petitions and were twice as likely to receive favorable results. In the chancery, or equity, suits, women filed substantially more petitions than did men, and four out of five among them obtained a divorce or separation or alimony. The comparatively small number of men who filed court suits for divorce obtained favorable decrees in about three-fourths of the cases. In short, women proved to be relatively successful before the general assemblies and highly successful in their filing of divorce petitions in chancery.

In addition, the picture painted by some historians of the affectionate relationship between plantation mistresses and a few privileged female slaves did not occur in these households. In fact, in a number of cases, their roles were reversed, as slave women became de facto mistresses of the households and white women were put under their control. Nor is the picture of the well-meaning master who felt some attachment to his black charges accurate. Just the opposite was true, as white men and women fought over ownership of human property. Indeed, in some measure, a divorce was not unlike what occurred after an owner died and his estate was probated. At the same time, while the evidence confirms what some scholars have argued about how slaveholding men abused rather than respected their wives, there is little evidence that by bringing the ill treatment to public scrutiny white women were threatening to disrupt the social system.

Some historians have described divorce and alimony laws in various southern states (as well as certain states in the North) as "conservative" or "progressive" or "liberal," but such terms tend to obfuscate rather than illuminate what was occurring in the legislatures and equity courts. In South Carolina, where divorce was not permitted by law, and Alabama, where the final decision was made by the state legislature throughout the period, the chancery court decisions revealed that to simply say these states were "conservative" fails to describe the marital struggles that occurred and the results of those struggles. Nor does a description of Louisiana as "progressive" or Tennessee as "liberal" with regard to divorce, separation, and alimony tell us about the workings of the chancery courts in those states. In all, it is clear that the southern states were in many ways similar to states in the North and Northwest in the legal changes that occurred over time concerning marital disunion. The difference in the South occurred in the applications of the laws with regard to the South's peculiar institution. Indeed, race and slavery were inextricably intertwined with the marital lives of most southerners, both slave owners and non–slave owners.

AN ESSAY ON SOURCES AND METHODOLOGY

Several factors recommend antebellum equity, or chancery, court records as a remarkable source for understanding divorce, slavery, and the law in the Old South. First, most contemporary sources—diaries, correspondence, notebooks, tracts, autobiographies, reminiscences, newspaper accounts, and magazine articles—rarely discuss failed marriages and almost completely ignore the bitterness, anger, frustration, infidelity, and violence of some domestic relationships. Perhaps the best example of this is the famous 1,380-page diary written by Ella Gertrude Clanton Thomas, the wife of a Georgia planter. Spanning more than four decades, beginning in 1848, Gertrude Thomas admitted that she never wrote about her "inmost thoughts," even though the temptation to write about the feelings that agitated her heart were "almost irresistible." Consequently, she and many other members of slaveholding families kept their deepest and darkest secrets hidden. In Thomas's case, she never divulged, except circuitously, that both her father and her husband had "outside wives and children" or that her husband became an alcoholic. Nor did she or others discuss domestic violence or the sexual abuse of slaves and children committed by neighbors and friends. Thus, what grieved Gertrude the most went unsaid and unrecorded.

Many other southerners who kept journals and diaries were equally silent on such subjects, especially white women who omitted the most wrenching and revealing as well as emotionally significant events in their lives. They did so in accordance with the mores and the cultural values of the time. As historian Nell Irvin Painter observed, southern elites were adept at keeping secrets and preserving appearances. Not until private pain or public shame had reached the breaking point and the legal steps required to dissolve a marriage and break up a family had been taken were reticence overcome and decorum set aside, laying bare what had been carefully concealed or silenced in many families.[1]

Second, the equity, or chancery, court divorce and alimony records from the antebellum years are far more complete than those that came before or after, in terms of length, complexity, detail, family history, court record, and testimony. The records offer a rich assortment of related documents, including amended petitions, oaths, affidavits, court orders, depositions, court testimony, interrogatories, defendants' answers, decrees, and judges' opinions. Prior to the American Revolution, only a few states even permitted divorce, and witness testimony offered in cases of separation of property was sketchy at best and in most cases nonexistent. After the Civil War, divorce petitions became extremely brief; they were filed primarily by men, whereas those filed before the war were filed primarily by women, and the men's cases often lacked witness testimony. The postwar cases, as one authority writes, "took on a purely legalistic mode of argument," and the narrative form of the antebellum era was replaced with a "formulaic outline."[2]

The divorce records of the antebellum era provide a wealth of material about failing domestic relationships and offer unique insights into the lives of all the household members, including slaves. Offering a sharp contrast to the usual reserve found in private diaries and correspondence, those who filed petitions to dissolve their marriages were frank and candid about their deepest feelings and their domestic lives. They often provided the names, dates, places, and descriptions of acts of adultery; described drunken rampages, interracial sex, and brutal whippings and beatings; and revealed acts of desertion, incest, and insanity. Not only did plaintiffs and defendants tell their stories, but witnesses gave depositions that were read at trial or testified in person before judges and juries. The evidence they offered also tells how slaves responded to their owners' marital problems. The records show what it meant to own other human beings and how the ownership of slaves permeated virtually every aspect of southern life. Despite the legal phraseology and the tendency of some plaintiffs and defendants to exaggerate the truth, the testimony found in these cases exposes with wrenching clarity the brutality and sexual exploitation inherent in the slave system, the suffering it engendered in both white and black families alike, and the inextricable intertwining of the lives of blacks and whites, adults and children, women and men, and slave owners and non-slave owners.

Although neither divorce nor separation was commonplace in the antebellum south, the cases tell us a great deal about families in crisis and, in doing so, reveal in their most extreme form some of the social and cultural mores of the period. For we can safely say that for the few who dared or were forced to violate society's taboo against the dissolution of marriage, there were many others with similar grievances who did not come forward. Indeed, the language used by the women and men who were called to testify in these cases, although often expressing a sense of reprobation or sometimes outrage toward the conduct of a wife beater, an adulterer, or a drunk, does not convey the sense that such cases were exceptional or unheard of in the community. Similarly, the graphic depictions of slave women who chose or had no choice but to side with the head of the household in domestic conflicts provides direct insight into the broad and complex web of personal interactions among slaveholders and slaves, men and women, across the various levels of authority and submission in the tightly hierarchical slave-owning households. For it can be argued that the difficult choices of allegiance slave men and women were forced to make for their protection when drawn to the center of domestic conflicts could not have been confined to situations of marital strife, but had to have been made in myriad other daily domestic interactions with their owners, male and female.

Finally, as suggested above, the wide geographical, topographical, demographic, and temporal distribution of the cases in this study provides an opportunity for uncovering trends that a study more restrictive in its scope could not have afforded. The petitions were filed in legislatures and county courts across every geographical area of the South, in towns and cities as well as in rural areas. The cases were filed in a total of 211 counties and parishes and the District of Columbia. In short, although no single body of evidence is perfect, the scope of this study, drawn as it is from cases spanning such a wide geographic area over many decades and across different swaths of society, is broad enough to offer a good understanding of families in crisis and the circumstances surrounding the dissolution of marriages in a slaveholding society.[3]

Some of the petitions included in this study were presented to state legislatures. Legislative records present many challenges for the researcher attempting to achieve a perspective on divorce in the antebellum era. As historian Richard Chused observed concerning Maryland, the acts issued as rulings in such cases were often opaque, hiding the reasons for the conflicts. The legislative acts often included only a simple, unedifying one-line statute such as the one issued in the case of Eliza Gibson of the city of Baltimore, who was, the statute said, divorced from her husband, Edmund D. Gibson, *a vinculo matrimonii*. In addition, only the plaintiff's side of the argument is often available, except in later decades when some states required that a trial be held and court records be kept before a state assembly was allowed to pass a divorce act. Concerning the records of Maryland, Chused noted that the original petitions, committee reports, and case files were routinely destroyed, making legislative records quite sparse. The same could be said for most other southern states, with the exception of Virginia, North Carolina, and Tennessee.[4]

This study relies in part on statistical evidence. Only a few scholars of race and slavery today trust or make use of statistical evidence. In fact, some historians argue that statistical breakdowns in analyzing the antebellum era are without merit. Part of the reason, they argue, is that cliometricians, as they were called, of the 1970s and 1980s made bold claims based on limited amounts of evidence, the most famous example being *Time on the Cross: The Economics of American Negro Slavery*, by Nobel laureate Robert William Fogel and distinguished historian Stanley Engerman. Yet, the gathering, examining, and analyzing of statistical evidence *can* provide answers to questions that otherwise could not be answered. This is especially true in examining the class structure in a region. In addition, there are studies that have successfully employed this methodology to expand our knowledge about divorce and slavery.[5]

Although I do not purport the evidence that emerges from the statistics to be definitive, it comes from every southern state and from virtually every year. As a result, it suggests patterns that could be found in other divorce and alimony cases, at least in rough dimensions. The statistical tables are straightforward. They list the jurisdictions governing the granting of divorces; show the proportion of petitioners who cited adultery, violence, abandonment, alcoholism, or a combination as causes for divorce; provide the gender breakdowns for those submitting petitions; and assess slave ownership and wealth among the families of those seeking divorce or separation.

Estimates regarding the economic position of those filing for divorce, separation, or alimony are derived from the number of slaves they owned. Indeed, slave ownership provides the best barometer of wealth for our purposes, especially because in the great majority of cases, the court records list the number of slaves or cite them by name; much less frequently, the records include inventories of other types of property. The information on slave ownership taken from the petitions and the related documents is supplemented with information found in the U.S. census returns, including the number of slaves in each household. For the years 1790 through 1810, the census data provides the aggregate number of enslaved black people in each household; for the years 1820 through 1840, it provides the number of slaves in each household, including males and females in age groupings; and for the years 1850 and 1860, it provides a list of slaves owned, each slave being identified by age, gender, and color but not by name. One caveat is in order regarding the census records for the years 1790 through 1840. The data for those years does not specify whether the slaves listed in the household were the property of the head of the household or merely hired or living in the household as part of an estate. It can be assumed, however, that the overwhelming majority of slaves listed in such a manner were owned by the household head.

It should also be noted that although the information in the documentation of divorce cases is very good for assessing the scale of slaveholding by a household or individual slave owner in terms of the number of slaves owned, it does not provide, for the most part, the monetary value of these holdings. Therefore, the value of slaveholdings used as part of this study's statistical evidence was derived by applying several assumptions based on findings generally agreed upon by historians regarding the market value of slaves. Among the 550 cases of divorce filed by white women from slaveholding families, for example, the exact number of slaves was ascertained in 503 cases, but the slaves' market value was provided in only 84 of these 503 cases, or about 17 percent; among the 54 cases of divorce filed by white men who owned slaves, the exact number of slaves was ascertained in 44 cases, but the slaves' market value was found in only 7 of these 44 cases, or about 16 percent. Historians have estimated that roughly 60 percent of a slaveholder's estate was held in the value of his or her slaves. They have also shown that the price of a "Prime Field Hand," an able-bodied but unskilled young man, was about twice the price of the "average" slave. "Prime" or "likely" women sold for less than "prime" or "likely" men. Youngsters as well as slaves in their forties, fifties, and sixties sold for substantially less than those in their teens and twenties. Some adults sold for less than $100, and others, as was the case for an elderly black man in Virginia, found themselves valued at "Fifty dollars less than nothing." Using one-half of the value of a "prime field hand," adjusted for market and year as shown in Table 6, as representing the mean or average around which the value of slaveholdings in a typical household were distributed, the value of an individual's slaveholdings can be estimated with a relative measure of accuracy by taking into account how many slaves he or she owned and where (in relation to the table's 6 location markets) and when (in relation to the table's eleven key years) he or she lived. Using this estimate in conjunction with the ratio of slaveholding to total estate mentioned above, the estimated value of an individual's total estate can then be derived, again with some measure of certainty.[6]

In reality, of course, the proportion of slave property to total estate varied by individual slave owner or, more specifically, by type of slave owner. Among those who acquired only a few slaves, the proportion was often less than 60 percent of the value of their total estate; for those who owned many slaves working on large plantations, the proportion was often greater. But the average is probably close to being accurate over time in

Sources and Methodology | 123

various sections of the South. In a few instances, inventories of slaves and estimates of real and personal property are included with the court proceedings of divorce cases or found in the U.S. census returns in 1850 and 1860. These tend to corroborate the percentage.

Table 6 was used to determine the appropriate market value to be applied to the family's slave property based on where and when that family lived, within the ranges shown in the table. The average value thus selected was then multiplied by the number of slaves owned by that individual as provided in the documentation of a specific divorce case, if available, or the U.S. census records. The estimate of the family's total estate was then calculated using the assumption that the slave property accounted for about 60 percent of that total. Given that slave prices and estate values fluctuated constantly, estimates thus calculated are only approximations, but they do reveal not only the economic position but the social and class standing of those involved in divorce and separation cases in this study.

Among the most difficult problems I encountered in dealing with the cases used in this study was ascertaining the final result of each divorce, separation, or alimony application. The legislative records often do not connect the cause for divorce with the result; the chancery court records sometimes do not include a final decree. In some instances, the minutes of the courts have been consulted, but they are not always extant. The "no decree" category was thus unavoidable. In other instances, cases were dismissed after an agreement was reached by the parties, and the compromise was not indicated in the record (as with Sarah H. Black, in Chapter 2, for example). In a few cases, the plea was "partially granted" and then dismissed. "Partially granted" did not necessarily mean that the case was decided in the plaintiff's favor, only that the court had agreed to some of the requests and the final adjudication was not included in the record. In short, the records do not permit definitive answers to the questions about final outcomes, but only a rough gauge of the results and the attitudes of judges and juries.

Most of the statistical evidence presented is derived from data found in the approximately 8,000 pages of documentary evidence in legislative and equity court case files and analyzed using Microsoft Excel spreadsheet software, one of the simplest and most basic tools for creating a database. The variables include the state and county where the case was filed; date of filing; the name, gender, and color of the plaintiff; whether the plaintiff was a slave owner and how many slaves he or she owned; the petition result; the number of years the petitioner had been married when the case was filed; the number of children; whether a reconciliation with the estranged

TABLE 6 Average Prices of Prime Field Hands (in dollars)

	1800	1808	1813	1818	1828	1837	1843	1848	1853	1856	1860
Washington/ Richmond/ Norfolk	350	500	400	700	450	900	500	700	1,250	1,300	1,200
Charleston	500	550	450	850	500	1,200	600	900	900		1,400
Louisville	400		550	800	700	1,200	650	800	1,200	1,000	1,800
Mid-Georgia	450	650	450	1,000	600	1,300	600	900	1,250	1,500	1,600
Montgomery				800	700	1,200					1,800
New Orleans	500	600		1,000		1,300					

Source: Ulrich Bonnell Phillips, *The South in the Building of the Nation*, 12 vols. (Richmond, Va.: Southern Historical Publication Society, 1909), 5:127.

spouse had taken place; the estimated value of slaves, real estate, and total estate owned by the plaintiff and/or defendant; the specific "prayer" of the plaintiff (divorce, separation, protection of property, alimony, maintenance, custody of children, or subpoena); the specific grounds for filing a suit (adultery, intemperance, abandonment, abuse, insanity, impotence, or felony, among others); the number of years the plaintiff had been separated from his or her spouse before filing for divorce; and any indication of involvement of slaves in the dispute (property dispute; sexual partner; favoritism of slave; mistreatment of slaves; intervention of slaves in the dispute, sale, division, hiring, jailing, and trading of slaves; and slaves who had run away).

A word should be added about petitions for divorce submitted for consideration to general assemblies. The primary objective of this study is to understand the reasons for divorce and separation involving race and slavery. In this regard, most General Assembly records offer meager information. In many cases, even where there are extant petitions, there is very little supporting evidence showing why private bills were either enacted or rejected. In Alabama, for example, the chancery court clerks sent copies of divorce and alimony proceedings, minutes, and decrees to the General Assembly, but as in Maryland and most other states, none of this supporting evidence has survived to show how and why the legislatures took the action they did. As a result, this study has relied primarily on chancery, or equity, court records, which provide a rich resource for understanding divorce, alimony, slavery, and the law in the Old South.

APPENDIX 1

TABLE 7 Complaints and Decrees in Chancery, or Equity, Court, 1779-1867

	TOTALS		ADULTERY		Extreme abuse	DESERTION		Excessive drinking
	Women	Men	Women	Men	Women*	Women	Men	Women*
Agreement	8	1	6	1	4		1	3
Dismissed by plaintiff	25	1	9		9	4		7
Settled	12		1		8			5
TOTAL	45	2	16	1	21	4	1	15
Granted	247	40	97	27	95	83	18	73
Granted *pro confesso*	11		1		5	3	1	2
Partly granted	85		28	1	36	16		30
Partly granted, dismissed	10		1		4	4		5
Reasonable		3						
TOTAL	353	43	127	28	140	106	19	110
Denied	6	2	1	2	2			1
Dismissed	29	9	9	4	14	9	6	8
Rejected	4		2		3	1		
TOTAL	39	11	12	6	19	10	6	9
TOTAL	437	56	155	35	180	120	26	134
Percent granted	81	77	82	80	78	88	73	82
Unusual outcomes								
Abated	4		4		1	1		1
Both sides	1							
Default		1		1			1	
Mistrial		1		1			1	
Transferred	1		1		1			1
Withdrawn	3		1		2			2
TOTAL	9	2	6	2	4	1	2	4

TABLE 7 (continued)

	TOTALS		ADULTERY		Extreme abuse	DESERTION		Excessive drinking
	Women	Men	Women	Men	Women*	Women	Men	Women*
Data not available, no decree	127	25	50	20	44	36	10	36
GRAND TOTAL	573	83	211	57	228	157	38	174

Source: Compiled from Divorce and Alimony Excel File Database; includes data from chancery, or equity, court records.

Note: The results are taken from the wording in the case files and court minutes. Thus, "agreement," "dismissed by plaintiff," and "settled" all represented various forms of a compromise agreement between the parties; "granted" in its various forms usually represented a victory for the plaintiff; "denied," "dismissed," and "rejected" usually signified a victory for the defendant. The accusations sometimes overlapped, and thus the plaintiffs' charges do not add up to the total number of cases.

*With two or three exceptions, all of the complaints regarding extreme abuse and excessive drinking were filed by wives against their husbands.

TABLE 8 Decrees and Slave Ownership among Plaintiffs' Families, 1779–1867

No. of slaves	1–4		5–9		10–19		20+		OTHER OWNERS*		NONOWNERS		TOTALS	
	Women	Men	Women	Men	Women	Men	Women	Men	Women	Men	Women	Men	Women	Men
Agreement	3		2		2		1						8	1
Dismissed by plaintiff	6	10	9	1	3		3		3		1	1	25	12
Settled	5		2		4		1						12	
TOTAL	14	11	13	1	9		5		3		1	1	45	2
Granted	101	10	43	3	31	5	25	1	21	2	26	19	247	40
Granted pro confesso	5		4				1		1		2		13	
Partly granted	27	1	21		19		12		4	1		1	83	3
Partly granted, dismissed	5		3		2								10	
TOTAL	138	11	71	3	52	5	38	1	26	3	28	20	353	43
Denied	2	1	1		1		1		1	1			6	2
Dismissed	9	3	5	2	7		5	1	1	2	2	1	29	9
Rejected	2		1								1		4	
TOTAL	13	4	7	2	8		6	1	2	3	3	1	39	11
TOTAL	165	15	91	6	69	5	49	2	31	6	32	22	437	56

TABLE 8 Continued

No. of slaves	1–4		5–9		10–19		20+		OTHER OWNERS*		NONOWNERS		TOTALS	
	Women	Men	Women	Men	Women	Men	Women	Men	Women	Men	Women	Men	Women	Men
Unusual outcomes														
Abated	1		1		1		1						4	
Both sides			1										1	
Default												1	1	1
Mistrial				1										1
Transferred							1						1	
Withdrawn	1				1				1				3	
TOTAL	2		2	1	2		2		1			1	9	2
Data not available, no decree	42	4	22	2	24	2	12	1	7	2	20	14	127	25
GRAND TOTAL	209	19	115	9	95	7	63	3	39	8	52	37	573	83

Source: Compiled from Divorce and Alimony Excel File Database.

Note: Cases during and following the Civil War involved slave ownership prior to the war or former slaves filing for divorce in its aftermath; slave ownership is derived from chancery court records as well as U.S. census returns.

The results are taken from the wording in the case files and court minutes. Thus, "agreement," "dismissed by plaintiff," and "settled" all represented various forms of a compromise agreement between the parties; "granted" in its various forms usually represented a victory for the plaintiff; "denied," "dismissed," and "rejected" usually signified a victory for the defendant. The accusations sometimes overlapped, and thus the plaintiffs' charges do not add up to the total number of cases.

*The "other owners" category includes families who were slaveholders for whom data on the number of slaves was not available.

APPENDIX 2

Petitioners to General Assemblies and to Chancery, or Equity, Courts, 1779–1867

State	County	Year	Plaintiff	Slave owner[1]			Number of slaves[2]	Result[3]
Va.	Amelia	1779	Rebecca Bass	F	W	Y	9	granted
Va.	Pittsylvania	1786	Ann Phillips	F	W	Y		dismissed
Va.	Sussex	1796	Elizabeth Wilkinson	F	W	Y		granted
Va.*	Fluvanna	1802	Dabney Pettus	M	W			reasonable
N.C.	Rowan	1803	Betsey Caldwell	F	W	Y	1	no decree
N.C.*	Beaufort	1803	Euphan Rhodes	F	W	Y		granted
Va.*	Norfolk	1803	Benjamin Butt	M	W			**granted**
N.C.*	Mecklenburg	1804	Cassandra Houston	F	W	Y	3	rejected
N.C.*		1805	Sarah Johnson	F	W	Y	9	rejected
Va.*	Accomack	1805	Ayres Tatham	M	W			reasonable
N.C.*	Edgecombe	1805	Eli Manning	M	W			granted
N.C.*	Rowan	1805	Christian Limbaugh	M	W			rejected
Ga.	Greene	1806	Mary Jackson	F	W	Y	1	no decree
Va.*	Culpeper	1806	Charlotte Ball	F	W	Y	19	rejected
Va.	Southampton	1806	Penelope Parker	F	W			granted
Va.*	Prince William	1806	Daniel Rose	M	W			**granted**
Va.*	Fauquier	1807	Ambrose Walden	M	W	Y	7	rejected
N.C.*	Chatham	1808	Milly Farrar	F	W	Y	4	granted
S.C.	Washington	1808	Jannett Prather	F	W	Y	6	granted
N.C.*	Person	1808	Lucy Crockett	F	W	Y		granted
Va.*	Loudon	1808	Isaac Fouch	M	W			reasonable
Ky.	Jefferson	1809	Eliza Bainbridge	F	W	Y	1	granted
N.C.*	Franklin	1809	Frances Murdin	F	W	Y	8	granted
D.C.	Washington	1809	Mary Belt	F	W	Y	11	granted
S.C.	Charleston	1809	Mary Rain	F	W	Y		pg
Va.*	Amherst	1809	William Howard	M	W			reasonable
N.C.*	Ashe	1809	Alexander Smith	M	W			granted
Ky.	Harrison	1810	Elizabeth Branning	F	W	Y	1	granted
Ga.	Oglethorpe	1810	Margarett Compton	F	W	Y	5	dismissed
Ky.	Fayette	1810	Rebecca Looney	F	W	Y	4	no decree
S.C.	Washington	1810	Judith Williams	F	W	Y	11	granted
N.C.*	Duplin	1810	Barbara Wilkinson	F	W	Y		granted
N.C.*	Wake	1810	Young Utley	M	W			granted
N.C.*	Edgecombe	1810	Isaac Bracewell	M	W			rejected
Tenn.	Rhea	1810	Hannah Morris	F	W			dismissed

State	County	Year	Plaintiff	Slave owner[1]			Number of slaves[2]	Result[3]
N.C.	Lincoln	1811	Elinor Hart	F	W	Y	1	no decree
S.C.	Charleston	1811	Ann Prentiss	F	W	Y	3	pg
Ky.	Jefferson	1811	Elizabeth Perry	F	W	Y	10	granted
Va.*	Richmond City	1811	John Pryor	M	W	Y		rejected
Ky.	Barren	1812	Nancy Summers	F	W	Y	2	granted
S.C.	Charleston	1812	Charlotte Price	F	W	Y	153	no decree
N.C.*	Camden	1813	Sarah Bell	F	W	Y		rejected
N.C.*	Gates	1813	James Hoffler	M	W			granted
N.C.*	Wake	1813	Joseph Hancock	M	W			rejected
Ky.	Harrison	1814	Harriet Night	F	W	Y	1	no decree
N.C.*	Gates	1814	Love Brady	F	W	Y	4	granted
D.C.	Washington	1814	Sarah Burford	F	W	Y	5	pg
Va.*	Augusta	1814	Ellen Dunlap	F	W	Y	5	rejected
S.C.	Washington	1814	Sarah Pester	F	W	Y	9	no decree
S.C.	Columbia	1814	Mary McAdams	F	W	Y		granted
Va.*	Northampton	1814	Richard Jones	M	W			granted
D.C.	Washington	1815	Ann Roberts	F	W	Y	2	pg
N.C.	Stokes	1815	Hannah Hussey	F	W	Y	2	no decree
S.C.	Washington	1815	Jane Griffin	F	W	Y	13	settled
Va.*	Powhatan	1815	Hezekiah Mosby	M	W			bill drawn
Va.*	Campbell	1816	Robert Wright	M	B	Y	1	rejected
S.C.	Columbia	1816	Jane McKinney	F	W	Y	1	granted
Ky.	Harrison	1816	Elizabeth McMillen	F	W	Y	2	granted
S.C.	Washington	1816	Rosannah Moore	F	W	Y	1	pg
S.C.	Columbia	1816	Anna Allen	F	W	Y	7	granted
N.C.*	New Hanover	1816	Harriet Laspeyre	F	W	Y	10	granted
La.	Pointe Coupee	1816	Marie Pourciau	F	W	Y	11	withdrawn
La.	E. Baton Rouge	1816	Mary Gayle	F	W	Y	19	granted
Va.*	Fauquier	1816	Abraham Newton	M	W			**granted**
S.C.	Washington	1817	Mary Strain	F	W	Y	1	pg
S.C.	Washington	1817	Margarett Summers	F	W	Y	1	pg
Ky.	Barren	1817	Susannah Hendrick	F	W	Y	2	granted
S.C.	Charleston	1817	Elizabeth Cole	F	W	Y	2	pg
S.C.	Columbia	1817	Martha Upthegrove	F	W	Y	7	no decree
La.	St. Landry	1817	Celeste Collins	F	W	Y	6	granted
S.C.	Charleston	1817	Rebecca E. Scott	F	W	Y	8	pg
Va.	Southampton	1817	Polly Gray	F	W	Y	17	no decree
N.C.*	Sampson	1817	Bernard Laspeyre	M	W	Y		rejected
Va.*	Bedford	1817	Sopha Dobyns	F	W	Y		bill drawn
Va.	Henrico	1817	Mary Bain	F	W	Y		granted
N.C.	Richmond	1818	Jane Robinson	F	W	Y	5	no decree
La.	Orleans	1818	Clara Doggett	F	W	Y	4	granted

State	County	Year	Plaintiff	Slave owner[1]			Number of slaves[2]	Result[3]
S.C.	Darlington	1818	Mercy Standley	F	W	Y	5	no decree
S.C.	Chester	1818	Elizabeth Ratteree	F	W	Y	8	pg
S.C.	Columbia	1818	Sarah Carter	F	W	Y	33	granted
S.C.	Newberry	1819	Catharine Lowry	F	W	Y	4	granted
La.	Feliciana	1819	Rebecca Harvey	F	W	Y	11	pg
N.C.	Wake	1819	Sarah Davis	F	W	Y		no decree
Va.*	Louisa	1819	Barbara Pettus	F	W	Y		**granted**
La.	Orleans	1819	Victorine Destrehan	F	W	Y		granted
Tenn.*	Franklin	1819	Hardy Doyle	M	W			no act
Tenn.*	Davidson	1819	Norfleet Perry	M	W			no act
La.	Orleans	1819	Genevieve Menard	F	B			granted
D.C.	Washington	1820	Anne Logan	F	W	Y	1	granted
N.C.	Stokes	1820	James Larimore	M	W	Y	1	granted
S.C.	Fairfield	1820	Sarah Beam	F	W	Y	1	granted
S.C.	Chester	1820	Rosanna Maxwell	F	W	Y	2	dismissed
La.	W. Baton Rouge	1820	Victoria Stark	F	W	Y	9	no decree
Tenn.*	Stewart	1820	Harriet Gibson	F	W	Y	10	granted
La.	W. Baton Rouge	1820	Alexis Trudeau	M	W	Y		denied
La.	W. Baton Rouge	1820	Julie Trudeau	F	W	Y		granted
Tenn.*	Sumner	1821	Elizabeth Street	F	W	Y	1	no act
Ga.	Wilkes	1821	Elizabeth McMickins	F	W	Y	3	granted
Tenn.*	Williamson	1821	Catherine Smith	F	W	Y	4	reasonable
Tenn.*	Robertson	1821	Henry Gardner	M	W	Y	22	no act
Tenn.	Williamson	1821	Keziah Berryman	F	W	Y	23	pg
N.C.	Stokes	1821	Molly Hutcheson	F	W	Y		no decree
Tenn.*		1821	Mary Logue	F	W			no act
Tenn.*	Grainger	1821	Kimble Midkiff	M	W			reasonable
S.C.	Newberry	1822	Margarett Parham	F	W	Y	1	granted
La.	E. Baton Rouge	1822	Ann Miller	F	W	Y	1	pg
La.	Pointe Coupee	1822	Susan Black	F	W	Y	3	withdrawn
S.C.	Charleston	1822	Martha Simpson	F	W	Y	5	granted
Ky.	Todd	1822	Elizabeth Wright	F	W	Y	13	no decree
Tenn.*	Montgomery	1822	William McClure	M	W	Y	15	no act
N.C.	Orange	1822	Ellenor Gappins	F	W	Y		pg
N.C.	Haywood	1823	Elizabeth Cline	F	W	Y	1	no decree
S.C.	Newberry	1823	Maria Cromer	F	W	Y	1	granted
S.C.	Spartanburg	1823	Patsy Silmon	F	W	Y	1	no decree
N.C.*	Randolph	1823	Jane Welborn	F	W	Y	5	granted
S.C.	Pendleton	1823	Margaret Castleberry	F	W	Y	10	dismissed
N.C.	Nash	1823	Jonathan Wells	M	W			no decree
Va.*	Louisa	1823	Lewis Bourne	M	W			bill drawn
Mo.	Boone	1824	Mary Strode	F	W	Y	2	granted

State	County	Year	Plaintiff	Slave owner[1]			Number of slaves[2]	Result[3]
Ky.	Barren	1824	Betsy Watts	F	W	Y	2	no decree
La.	Orleans	1824	Emilie Heno	F	W	Y	1	granted
S.C.	Columbia	1824	Martha Taylor	F	W	Y	2	granted
Md.	Baltimore	1824	Sarah Warfield	F	W	Y	3	dismissed
N.C.	Perquimans	1824	Sarah Oneel	F	W	Y	8	no decree
Va.*	King William	1824	Evelina Roane	F	W	Y	11	granted
La.	St. Landry	1824	John Lyons	M	W	Y	19	granted
S.C.	Newberry	1824	Jane Griffin	F	W	Y		no decree
N.C.*	Wake	1824	Lewis Tombereau	M	W			granted
N.C.*	Washington	1824	John Barber	M	W			rejected
N.C.	Granville	1825	Sarah Chandler	F	W	Y	5	granted
La.	St. Landry	1825	Caroline Prudhome	F	W	Y	4	granted
Va.	Henrico	1825	Elizabeth Oliver	F	W	Y	7	granted
Ky.	Barren	1825	Mary Smith	F	W	Y	15	no decree
La.	West Feliciana	1825	Susan Black	F	W	Y	8	pg
Tenn.	Williamson	1825	Peggy Mallory	F	W	Y	17	pg
La.	Iberville	1825	Izabelle Questi	F	W	Y	11	dbp
S.C.	Laurens	1825	Frances Pyles	F	W	Y	14	no decree
La.	Iberville	1825	Mary Ellis	F	W	Y	12	dismissed
La.	Natchitoches	1825	Celeste Langlois	F	W	Y	13	dismissed
La.	West Feliciana	1825	Sarah Rawlings	F	W	Y	18	granted
La.	Natchitoches	1825	Marie Castro	F	W	Y		granted
S.C.	Newberry	1825	Mary Cannon	F	W	Y		withdrawn
Ky.	Fayette	1825	Deidamia Rutherforth	F	W			dbp
N.C.*	Haywood	1825	John Chambers	M	W			granted
S.C.	Fairfield	1825	Christina Stanton	F	W			no decree
Va.*	Sussex	1826	Macy Gay	F	W	Y	1	**granted**
Tenn.*	Sumner	1826	Elizabeth Wilson	F	W	Y	2	rejected
D.C.	Washington	1826	Ann Gibson	F	W	Y	13	pg
N.C.	Lincoln	1826	Catharine Rhyne	F	W	Y	4	granted
Va.*	Nansemond	1826	David Parker	M	W	Y	4	bill drawn
S.C.	Sumter	1826	Charlotte Wiggins	F	W	Y	4	pg
Va.	Lynchburg	1826	Patsey Hawkins	F	W	Y	5	granted
S.C.	Newberry	1826	Lucinda Payne	F	W	Y	13	settled
La.	W. Baton Rouge	1826	Margaret McDougald	F	W	Y	49	no decree
S.C.	Charleston	1826	Mary Kinloch	F	W	Y	60	no decree
Ky.	Christian	1826	Mary Lacey	F	W	Y		dbp
Ky.	Pike	1827	Polly Thompson	F	W	Y	1	granted
N.C.*	New Hanover	1827	Jonathan Bryan	M	W	Y	4	rejected
N.C.*	Wayne	1827	Jesse Barden	M	W			granted
Ky.	Jefferson	1828	Mary Johnson	F	W	Y	1	granted
La.	Orleans	1828	Leocadie Beauregard	F	W	Y	2	granted

State	County	Year	Plaintiff	Slave owner[1]			Number of slaves[2]	Result[3]
Ky.	Harrison	1828	Polley Reno	F	W	Y	4	no decree
Tenn.	Montgomery	1828	Lucy Brantley	F	W	Y	13	pg
La.	Iberville	1828	Pauline Bergeron	F	W	Y	17	dismissed
Ky.	Woodford	1828	Nancy Fleming	F	W	Y	40	dismissed
La.	St. Landry	1828	Victorin Ledeé	M	B			dbp
N.C.	Craven	1828	Graham Bishop	M	W			no decree
Ky.	Fayette	1829	Melinda Poston	F	W	Y	1	pg
N.C.	Lincoln	1829	Catharine Goble	F	W	Y	1	granted
Ky.	Bourbon	1829	Charles Oneal	M	W	Y	2	granted
La.	West Feliciana	1829	Polly Allyn	F	W	Y	4	granted
Tenn.	Montgomery	1829	Abraham Brantley	M	W	Y	13	granted
N.C.	Caswell	1829	Frances Womack	F	W	Y	10	granted
Tenn.	Maury	1829	Jane McKee	F	W	Y	14	pg
N.C.	Wayne	1829	Lydia Edwards	F	W	Y	16	granted
La.	St. Landry	1829	Jean Guillory	M	B	Y	18	granted
N.C.	Granville	1829	Elizabeth Wheeler	F	W	Y		granted
N.C.	Chatham	1829	Rachel Hamlet	F	W			no decree
Tenn.*		1829	Caroline Hill	F	W			no act
Tenn.*	Maury	1829	John Rich	M	W			no act
Ky.	Bourbon	1830	Louisa King	F	W	Y	2	granted
La.	Pointe Coupee	1830	Hetty Mitchell	F	W	Y	3	rejected
N.C.	Nash	1830	Charity Westray	F	W	Y	3	granted
S.C.	Union	1830	Augusta A. Jeter	F	W	Y	5	granted
Md.	Charles	1830	Martha Turner	F	W	Y	4	granted
Ala.	Bibb	1830	Sarah Goodgame	F	W	Y	4	dbp
S.C.	Charleston	1830	Margaret Vause	F	W	Y	7	granted
Ky.	Fayette	1830	Matilda Payne	F	W	Y	7	pg
Va.	Lynchburg	1830	Elizabeth Shomaker	F	W	Y	8	no decree
S.C.	Richland	1830	Rebecca Maguire	F	W	Y	14	granted
La.	St. Landry	1830	Frances Harris	F	W	Y	9	granted
Ky.	Christian	1830	Sally Patton	F	W	Y	17	pg
Ga.	Jones	1830	Mary McMath	F	W	Y	21	granted
N.C.	Guilford	1830	Andrew Whittington	M	W			no decree
Ky.	Jefferson	1831	Mary Mills	F	W	Y	1	granted
Ky.	Jefferson	1831	Elizabeth Jones	F	W	Y	1	settled
N.C.	Buncombe	1831	Phebe Osborne	F	W	Y	6	granted
S.C.	Charleston	1831	Jane Schmidt	F	W	Y	12	no decree
Fla.	Escambia	1831	Victoria Le Sassier	F	W	Y	20	granted
Ala.	Mobile	1831	James Puckett	M	W			granted
N.C.	Perquimans	1831	Gabriel Goodwin	M	W			granted
N.C.	Granville	1831	Charles Mitchell	M	W			no decree
N.C.	Granville	1831	William Hickman	M	W			no decree

Appendix 2 | 135

State	County	Year	Plaintiff	Slave owner[1]			Number of slaves[2]	Result[3]
La.	St. Landry	1832	Elizabeth Collins	F	W	Y	3	pg
N.C.*	Halifax	1832	Mary Reid	F	W	Y	31	granted
Del.*	Sussex	1832	Francis Ludenum	M	B			denied
N.C.	Nash	1832	Piety Tisdale	F	W			granted
La.	Natchitoches	1833	Marie Quierry	F	W	Y	2	granted
La.	Orleans	1833	Maria Webb	F	W	Y	6	granted
Va.	Petersburg	1833	Aminta Williams	F	W	Y	7	grantedpc
Va.	Princess Anne	1833	Susan Sorey	F	W	Y	8	pgd
N.C.	Caswell	1833	Nancy Swift	F	W	Y	8	granted
N.C.	Wake	1833	Elizabeth Smith	F	W	Y	9	granted
Tenn.*	Franklin	1833	Susan Doolin	F	W	Y	10	no act
S.C.	Union	1833	Barsheba Burns	F	W	Y	14	granted
S.C.	Chester	1833	Melinda McCalla	F	W	Y	18	no decree
La.	W. Baton Rouge	1833	Céleste Molaison	F	W	Y	41	granted
N.C.	Guilford	1833	Olivia Fields	F	W			granted
N.C.	Caswell	1833	Andrew Whittington	M	W			granted
N.C.	Wake	1833	Elisha Lee	M	W			no decree
Va.*	James City	1833	Joseph Gresham	M	W			**granted**
N.C.	Craven	1833	Henry Richardson	M	B			no decree
S.C.	Newberry	1834	Mary Gruber	F	W	Y	2	no decree
Ky.	Jefferson	1834	Mary Allen	F	W	Y	2	pgd
La.	Orleans	1834	Adeline Porter	F	W	Y	3	granted
N.C.	Person	1834	Martha Evans	F	W	Y	5	granted
N.C.	Wayne	1834	Richard Jernigan	M	W	Y	9	no decree
N.C.	Northampton	1834	Margaret Moore	F	W	Y	25	no decree
La.	Iberville	1834	Hélène Rimbaud	F	W	Y	11	granted
La.	West Feliciana	1834	Elizabeth Overbay	F	W	Y	21	granted
La.	W. Baton Rouge	1834	Marie Daigle	F	W	Y	34	pg
N.C.*	Burke	1834	Ellena Cobb	F	W			granted
N.C.	Pasquotank	1835	Ann Sawyer	F	W	Y	2	granted
N.C.	Rowan	1835	Ann West	F	W	Y	4	granted
N.C.	Macon	1835	Polly Pearson	F	W	Y	3	no decree
Va.	Scott	1835	Nancy Grigsby	F	W	Y	4	pgd
N.C.	Rockingham	1835	Polly Orrin	F	W	Y	5	granted
N.C.	Pasquotank	1835	Nancy Wilson	F	W	Y	7	no decree
La.	E. Baton Rouge	1835	Mary Carr	F	W	Y	5	granted
S.C.	Charleston	1835	Eliza Byrnes	F	W	Y	11	pg
S.C.	Newberry	1835	Mary Graham	F	W	Y	13	no decree
Tenn.	Davidson	1835	Winnefrid Richmond	F	W	Y	20	granted
Va.*	Norfolk	1835	Thomas Culpepper	M	W			rejected
Fla.*	Monroe	1836	Eliza Patterson	F	W	Y	1	no act
N.C.	Granville	1836	Susan Phillips	F	W	Y	1	granted

State	County	Year	Plaintiff	Slave owner[1]			Number of slaves[2]	Result[3]
N.C.	Granville	1836	Margaret Strother	F	W	Y	1	granted
Ky.	Christian	1836	Martha Dabney	F	W	Y	3	no decree
N.C.	Guilford	1836	Nancy Jenkins	F	W	Y	2	no decree
Tenn.	Williamson	1836	Judith Word	F	W	Y	2	granted
N.C.	Pasquotank	1836	Elizabeth Brozier	F	W	Y	5	granted
N.C.	Wayne	1836	Margaret Kornegay	F	W	Y	7	no decree
La.	West Feliciana	1836	Abraham Jones	M	W	Y	5	dbp
Tenn.	Williamson	1836	Nancy Hughes	F	W	Y	6	settled
Md.	Charles	1836	Martha Turner	F	W	Y	9	granted
Ky.	Barren	1836	Catherine Bishop	F	W	Y	26	pg
S.C.	Fairfield	1836	Drucilla Rook	F	W	Y		pg
Va.*	King William	1836	Ann Eubank	F	W			**granted**
La.	E. Baton Rouge	1836	Ann Bienville	F	B			granted
Va.	Petersburg	1837	Sarah Evans	F	W	Y	1	denied
N.C.	Wilkes	1837	Elizabeth Bently	F	W	Y	1	granted
Va.	Lynchburg	1837	Adelia Turner	F	W	Y	2	pg
La.	Iberville	1837	Marcellite Sellier	F	W	Y	2	granted
Va.	Southampton	1837	Mary Pope	F	W	Y	4	granted
S.C.	Charleston	1837	Eliza Prince	F	W	Y	3	granted
Va.	Petersburg	1837	Martha Weeks	F	W	Y	14	granted
La.	St. Landry	1837	Mary Beauchamp	F	W	Y	3	granted
Ky.	Floyd	1837	Eleanor Morgan	F	W	Y	15	granted
Tenn.	Williamson	1837	Jane Owen	F	W	Y	16	pg
S.C.	Fairfield	1837	Elizabeth Hassan	F	W	Y	20	pg
Tenn.	Williamson	1837	Louisiana Reid	F	W	Y	45	granted
Va.*	King William	1837	Elizabeth Pannill	F	W			**granted**
Va.	Southampton	1837	Polly Gardner	F	W			granted
N.C.	Lincoln	1838	Unicy Martin	F	W	Y	1	granted
Va.*	Bedford	1838	Sally Ballinger	F	W	Y	1	**granted**
S.C.	Charleston	1838	Maria Carpenter	F	W	Y	1	no decree
Tenn.	Carter	1838	Nancy Rowe	F	W	Y	2	pg
Miss.	Lauderdale	1838	Elizabeth McQueen	F	W	Y	2	granted
Tenn.	Williamson	1838	Parilee Adcock	F	W	Y	4	granted
Ala.	Madison	1838	Mary Hall	F	W	Y	3	dismissed
Ala.	Mobile	1838	Mary Acre	F	W	Y	5	no decree
Mo.	Cape Girardeau	1838	Malinda Morris	F	W	Y	7	pg
Fla.	Escambia	1838	Margaret Garner	F	W	Y	11	no decree
La.	E. Baton Rouge	1838	Mournin Headen	F	W	Y	37	granted
N.C.	Orange	1838	Mary Clark	F	W	Y		dbp
Va.*	Orange	1838	Richard Hall	M	W			**granted**
Ky.	Jefferson	1838	Milly Boston	F	B			no decree
La.	E. Baton Rouge	1838	Elizabeth Blake	F	W			no decree

Appendix 2 | 137

State	County	Year	Plaintiff	Slave owner[1]			Number of slaves[2]	Result[3]
N.C.	Nash	1838	Thomas Flowers	M	W			granted
La.	St. Landry	1839	Marguerite Godin	F	W	Y	1	no decree
Va.	Petersburg	1839	Eliza Gallee	F	B	Y	4	grantedpc
N.C.	Caswell	1839	Elizabeth Broughton	F	W	Y	9	no decree
Ala.	Shelby	1839	Eveline Whetstone	F	W	Y		granted
N.C.	Davidson	1839	Juliana Bringle	F	W			granted
N.C.	Guilford	1839	Martha Brannock	F	W			no decree
N.C.	Burke	1839	Samuel Jimeson	M	W			no decree
Tex.	Nacogdoches	1839	Susan Colwell	F	W			pg
N.C.	Guilford	1840	William King	M	W	Y	1	no decree
Ala.	Talladega	1840	Josiah Houston	M	W	Y	1	dismissed
N.C.	Ashe	1840	Christina Walters	F	W	Y	2	pg
N.C.	Lincoln	1840	Sarah Ramsay	F	W	Y	3	granted
La.	E. Baton Rouge	1840	Patience Havis	F	W	Y	3	pg
N.C.	Burke	1840	Anne Wilson	F	W	Y	4	agreement
Ky.	Harrison	1840	Casander Paul	F	W	Y	2	granted
Va.*	Richmond City	1840	Mary Lawson	F	W	Y	10	no act
N.C.	Rutherford	1840	Elizabeth Hamrick	F	W	Y	13	granted
Ala.	Benton	1840	Martha Nabors	F	W	Y	9	dbp
La.	E. Baton Rouge	1840	Jane Johnston	F	W	Y	18	granted
S.C.	Newberry	1840	Harriet Young	F	W	Y	17	granted
La.	Orleans	1840	Elizabeth Charbonnet	F	W	Y		granted
Va.	Campbell	1840	Amanda Crow	F	W	Y		**granted**
Va.	Campbell	1840	Sarah Robinson	F	W	Y		granted
Va.*	Nansemond	1840	Bryant Rawls	M	W			bill drawn
N.C.	Davidson	1841	Fanny Sowers	F	W	Y	1	granted
La.	Orleans	1841	Hubert Dénisse	M	B	Y	1	granted
Ala.	Shelby	1841	Elizabeth Langford	F	W	Y	1	granted
Ala.	Talladega	1841	John Farley	M	W	Y	1	granted
N.C.	Randolph	1841	Mary Moffitt	F	W	Y	3	no decree
N.C.	Orange	1841	Mary Whitsell	F	W	Y	4	no decree
N.C.	Wake	1841	Sarah Hunter	F	W	Y	9	no decree
Va.	Halifax	1841	Sarah Womack	F	W	Y	16	no decree
Ala.	Mobile	1841	Margaret Garner	F	W	Y	17	no decree
Ky.	Woodford	1841	Caroline Turner	F	W	Y	16	dismissed
Miss.	Lowndes	1841	Mary Shotwell	F	W	Y	38	granted
Tex.	Brazoria	1841	Isabella Andrews	F	W	Y	60	granted
S.C.	Barnwell	1841	Eliza Ransom	F	W	Y	46	no decree
Ala.	Pickens	1841	Jacob Smith	M	W	Y		dismissed
Fla.	Leon	1841	Francis Whiting	M	W	Y		no decree
Va.*	Campbell	1841	Sarah Robinson	F	W	Y		rejected
Va.*	Frederick	1841	Thomas Cain	M	W			bill drawn

State	County	Year	Plaintiff	Slave owner[1]		Number of slaves[2]	Result[3]
Va.*	Preston	1841	Jacob Plum	M	W		**granted**
N.C.	Surry	1841	Ruth Steelman	F	W		rejected
Va.	Franklin	1841	Henry Payne	M	W		dismissed
Ala.	Sumter	1842	William Hill	M	W Y	1	dismissed
Tenn.	Smith	1842	Mary A. Harper	F	W Y	2	granted
Md.	St. Mary's	1842	Jane Rock	F	W Y	2	no decree
Ky.	Jefferson	1842	Elizabeth Gray	F	W Y	3	granted
Tenn.	Maury	1842	Martha Farrar	F	W Y	5	granted
N.C.	Lincoln	1842	Mary Falls	F	W Y	6	no decree
Ala.	Shelby	1842	Lucretia Chambers	F	W Y	5	dismissed
Va.	Campbell	1842	Frances Callaham	F	W Y	10	dismissed
Ala.	Shelby	1842	John Chambers	M	W Y	9	dbp
Md.	Charles	1842	Louisa Holmes	F	W Y	17	granted
Ala.	Talladega	1842	Sarah Smith	F	W Y	23	dbp
Ala.	Lowndes	1842	Margaret Oliver	F	W Y	54	granted
Fla.	Leon	1842	Sarah Whiting	F	W Y		no decree
N.C.	Chatham	1842	Milly Buckner	F	W Y		no decree
N.C.	Rowan	1842	Emeline Adderton	F	W		granted
N.C.	Caswell	1842	Harriet Bouldin	F	W		no decree
Ala.	Mobile	1842	Margaret Garner	F	W		no decree
Mo.	Boone	1842	Robert Chiles	M	W		default
Tenn.	Shelby	1842	William M. Patterson	M	W		granted
Ala.	Sumter	1843	Catharine Underwood	F	W Y	1	abated
S.C.	Newberry	1843	Louisa Suber	F	W Y	2	grantedpc
La.	Pointe Coupee	1843	Azeline Sicard	F	W Y	2	granted
N.C.	Davidson	1843	Rebecca Wood	F	W Y	3	dismissed
N.C.	Guilford	1843	Laura Vanstore	F	W Y	3	granted
Va.	Campbell	1843	Mary Perkins	F	W Y	3	pgd
Md.	Charles	1843	Mary Spedden	F	W Y	3	granted
N.C.	Lincoln	1843	Elizabeth Clubb	F	W Y	5	both sides
N.C.	Stokes	1843	Henry Shouse	M	W Y	7	granted
S.C.	Barnwell	1843	Harriet Sanders	F	W Y	8	pg
Tenn.	Sumner	1843	Martha Stone	F	W Y	8	granted
Ga.	Coweta	1843	Mary Davis	F	W Y	10	granted
Fla.*		1843	John Mangham	M	W Y	24	no act
N.C.	Randolph	1843	Margaret Johnston	F	W Y		no decree
Md.	Baltimore	1843	Margaret Jorden	F	W		no decree
Ala.	Autauga	1843	Martha Gray	F	W		dismissed
Md.	Baltimore	1843	Elizabeth Tinges	F	W		no decree
Va.*	Culpeper	1843	Mary Lawry	F	W		rejected
Va.	Franklin	1844	Siney Barnes	F	W Y	1	pgd
N.C.	Hyde	1844	Rebecca Mason	F	W Y	2	no decree

State	County	Year	Plaintiff	Slave owner[1]			Number of slaves[2]	Result[3]
N.C.	Nash	1844	Mary Daniel	F	W	Y	2	rejected
S.C.	Charleston	1844	Margaret Burbage	F	W	Y	2	grantedpc
N.C.	Wake	1844	Thomas Oliver	M	W	Y	3	no decree
Ky.	Scott	1844	Mary Owens	F	W	Y	3	granted
Tenn.	Marshall	1844	Mary Fitzpatrick	F	W	Y	4	pg
S.C.	Sumter	1844	Hannah Evans	F	W	Y	8	grantedpc
Ky.	Nicholas	1844	Elizabeth Hyatt	F	W	Y	15	granted
N.C.	Montgomery	1844	Rebecca Mask	F	W	Y	41	granted
Ala.	Chambers	1844	Winney Jeter	F	W	Y	43	pg
La.	Iberville	1844	Rachel Hudnall	F	W	Y	174	granted
Ala.	Mobile	1844	Maria St. Guirons	F	W			granted
Md.	Baltimore	1844	Henry Houck	M	W			granted
Md.	Baltimore	1844	Jane Lyons	F	W			no decree
N.C.	Robeson	1844	Edward Karsey	M	B			dismissed
N.C.	Lincoln	1844	Elizabeth Cody	F	W			no decree
Ala.	Sumter	1845	William Hill	M	W	Y	1	dismissed
S.C.	Chester	1845	Hannah Neil	F	W	Y	2	granted
N.C.	Pitt	1845	Margaret Moore	F	W	Y	5	no decree
N.C.	Granville	1845	Eliza Cooke	F	W	Y	6	no decree
S.C.	Fairfield	1845	Sarah Ann Simpson	F	W	Y	6	pg
N.C.	Northampton	1845	Nancy Vasser	F	W	Y	4	no decree
Ala.	Chambers	1845	Sarah Trimble	F	W	Y	5	dbp
Ala.	Montgomery	1845	Elizabeth Stacy	F	W	Y	6	abated
Ala.	Talladega	1845	Catherine Jordan	F	W	Y	5	granted
Mo.	Ste. Genevieve	1845	Elizabeth Hunt	F	W	Y	10	no decree
Tenn.	Shelby	1845	Thomas Burkley	M	W	Y	14	granted
Ala.	Lowndes	1845	Ruth Balderee	F	W	Y	24	pg
N.C.	Wayne	1845	Eveline Fort	F	W	Y	33	granted
Ky.	Jefferson	1845	Esther Schleisinger	F	W	Y	36	dismissed
Tenn.	Maury	1845	Cornelia Long	F	W	Y	31	dismissed
Ala.	Madison	1845	Sarah Hall	F	W	Y	45	dbp
Tex.	San Augustine	1845	Harriet Dell	F	W	Y		granted
N.C.	Craven	1845	Wesley Gray	M	W			no decree
Tenn.*	Anderson	1845	Mary Hookins	F	W			rejected
Md.	Baltimore	1845	Elizabeth Collins	F	W			granted
N.C.	Randolph	1845	Isaac Routh	M	W			granted
Va.	Halifax	1846	Lethe Hicks	F	W	Y	1	granted
Ala.	Lowndes	1846	Martha Gray	F	W	Y	1	granted
Tenn.	Marshall	1846	Priscilla Russell	F	W	Y	1	granted
Ky.	Christian	1846	Elizabeth Chick	F	W	Y	1	granted
Ala.	Sumter	1846	Eliza Glover	F	W	Y	2	dismissed
Tenn.	Davidson	1846	Matilda Kingston	F	W	Y	2	no decree

State	County	Year	Plaintiff	Slave owner[1]			Number of slaves[2]	Result[3]
Ala.	Mobile	1846	Elizabeth Humphreyville	F	W	Y	2	pg
Tenn.	Smith	1846	Ruth Moore	F	W	Y	4	settled
Ala.	Mobile	1846	Catherine Snow	F	W	Y	6	pg
Mo.	Clay	1846	Sarah Duncan	F	W	Y	8	dismissed
Ky.	Scott	1846	Ann Gunnell	F	W	Y	10	dismissed
Va.	Petersburg	1846	Susan Bryan	F	W	Y	23	pg
Ala.	Barbour	1846	Maria Betts	F	W	Y	22	granted
Ky.	Harrison	1846	Agnes Coleman	F	W	Y	24	agreement
Va.	Halifax	1846	Mary Murphy	F	W	Y	25	granted
S.C.	Fairfield	1846	Eley A. Hall	F	W	Y	26	settled
Va.*	Richmond City	1846	Helen Hamilton	F	W	Y		no act
Ky.	Pike	1846	John King	M	W			granted
N.C.	Wake	1846	Sarah Strickland	F	W			no decree
Ala.	Mobile	1847	Sarah Debose	F	W	Y	2	pg
Md.	Montgomery	1847	Ann Magruder	F	W	Y	3	granted
Tenn.	Bedford	1847	Sophia Swales	F	W	Y	3	no decree
Va.	Franklin	1847	Rebecca Ayers	F	W	Y	4	no decree
Ala.	Mobile	1847	Harriet Johnson	F	W	Y	4	dismissed
Ky.	Butler	1847	Susan Brown	F	W	Y	3	granted
Va.	Albemarle	1847	Ann Chick	F	W	Y	6	pgd
Tenn.	Maury	1847	Margaret Hackney	F	W	Y	32	granted
Ala.	Sumter	1847	Eliza Glover	F	W	Y		granted
N.C.	Granville	1847	William Wilson	M	W			pg
S.C.*	Barnwell	1847	Marmaduke Jones	M	W			no decree
Ky.	Boyle	1847	Permelia Russell	F	B			dismissed
La.	St. Landry	1847	Jane Edmunds	F	B			granted
N.C.	Granville	1847	Amanda Walker	F	W			granted
Mo.	Cape Girardeau	1848	Lydia Crump	F	W	Y	1	granted
Fla.	Leon	1848	James Oates	M	W	Y	1	granted
Ala.	Tallapoosa	1848	Sarah Claffey	F	W	Y	2	granted
Tenn.	Knox	1848	Sarah Arnold	F	W	Y	3	pg
Miss.	Adams	1848	Renette O'Blenis	F	W	Y	4	granted
La.	Pointe Coupee	1848	Mary Grace	F	W	Y	3	pg
Ala.	Mobile	1848	Henry Hunt	M	W	Y	5	dismissed
Ala.	Mobile	1848	Harriet Johnston	F	W	Y	4	granted
Ala.	Pickens	1848	Epsey McMath	F	W	Y	6	granted
N.C.	Cleveland	1848	Lelia Weathers	F	W	Y	9	agreement
Tenn.	Maury	1848	Elizabeth Hamilton	F	W	Y	9	granted
Tenn.	Marshall	1848	Drucilla Secrest	F	W	Y	14	pg
S.C.	Newberry	1848	Mary Nix	F	W	Y	14	settled
Ala.	Tallapoosa	1848	Elizabeth Holley	F	W	Y	15	pg
Va.*	Henry	1848	Lucy Norman	F	W	Y	19	**granted**

State	County	Year	Plaintiff	Slave owner[1]			Number of slaves[2]	Result[3]
N.C.	Richmond	1848	Stephen Cole	M	W	Y	27	granted
Ala.	Montgomery	1848	Albert Wray	M	W	Y	87	dismissed
Ala.	Tallapoosa	1848	Henry Norrell	M	W	Y		no decree
Tex.	Brazoria	1849	Mary Prewitt	F	W	Y	1	granted
Mo.	Jefferson	1849	Martha Huskey	F	W	Y	2	dbp
Va.	Petersburg	1849	Armstrong Blick	M	W	Y	2	granted
Miss.	Adams	1849	Margaret O'Conner	F	W	Y	2	dbp
Miss.	Adams	1849	Margaret O'Conner	F	W	Y	2	granted
Tenn.	Bradley	1849	Mary Hall	F	W	Y	3	no decree
N.C.	Pasquotank	1849	Elisabeth Bright	F	W	Y	4	no decree
Va.	Fluvanna	1849	Nancy Holland	F	W	Y	5	granted
Ky.	Barren	1849	Mary Ferrell	F	W	Y	5	granted
Ky.	Christian	1849	Robert Lewis	M	W	Y	5	granted
Tenn.	Bradley	1849	Margaret Twomey	F	W	Y	7	pg
Tenn.	Williamson	1849	Sarah Haley	F	W	Y	10	no decree
Tenn.	Blount	1849	Mary Williams	F	W	Y	10	no decree
Ala.	Montgomery	1849	Armstrong Mitchell	M	W	Y	15	granted
Ala.	Sumter	1849	Mary Heison	F	W	Y	10	agreement
S.C.	Fairfield	1849	Mary Ann Stokes	F	W	Y	22	pg
Tenn.	Marshall	1849	Milly Morris	F	W	Y	17	no decree
N.C.	Perquimans	1850	Parthena Foster	F	W	Y	1	no decree
Md.	Baltimore	1850	Jane Collins	F	W	Y	1	no decree
Tenn.	Knox	1850	Martha Weaver	F	W	Y	2	granted
Tex.	Jefferson	1850	Queen Nogess	F	W	Y	1	pg
La.	Catahoula	1850	Alley Ross	F	W	Y	2	granted
Md.	Charles	1850	Ann Beall	F	W	Y	8	pg
N.C.	Ashe	1850	Sarah Schoat	F	W	Y	6	granted
Tenn.	Knox	1850	Sarah Price	F	W	Y	6	granted
La.	E. Baton Rouge	1850	Alcy Ingram	F	W	Y	6	granted
N.C.	Randolph	1850	Andrew Amick	M	W	Y	8	mistrial
N.C.	Craven	1850	Harriet Foy	F	W	Y	12	no decree
Ky.	Bourbon	1850	Mary Adams	F	W	Y	14	granted
Va.	Albemarle	1850	Mary Rhodes	F	W	Y	12	granted
Miss.	Claiborne	1850	Misella Henry	F	W	Y	26	granted
Ala.	Coosa	1850	Milley David	F	W	Y	31	dismissed
Ala.	Perry	1850	Rachael Sanders	F	W	Y	48	abated
Ala.	Mobile	1850	Gasper Nelins	M	W	Y		granted
N.C.	Wayne	1850	Daniel Griffin	M	W			granted
N.C.	Wayne	1850	John Sykes	M	W			granted
Va.*	Goochland	1850	Mary Terry	F	W			**granted**
Fla.	Marion	1850	Georgia Rivers	F	W			granted
La.	Natchitoches	1850	Marie Metoyer	F	B			granted

State	County	Year	Plaintiff	Slave owner[1]		Number of slaves[2]	Result[3]
Miss.	Lauderdale	1850	Mary Williamson	F	W		no decree
Va.	Albemarle	1850	Hillary Wood	M	W		granted
Ala.	Mobile	1851	Tabitha Pope	F	W Y	1	dismissed
N.C.	Guilford	1851	Beulah Huzza	F	W Y	2	no decree
N.C.	Granville	1851	Nancy Hunt	F	W Y	2	no decree
La.	Catahoula	1851	Sarah Garrett	F	W Y	3	granted
S.C.	Newberry	1851	Mary Ann Warner	F	W Y	4	settled
Tex.	Jefferson	1851	Rachael Cotton	F	W Y	3	granted
Tenn.	Williamson	1851	Naomi Johnson	F	W Y	6	dismissed
Ky.	Scott	1851	James Griffith	M	W Y	15	granted
Va.	Lynchburg	1851	Stella Rucker	F	W Y	10	granted
Ala.	Tallapoosa	1851	Narcissa Henderson	F	W Y	87	no decree
Ala.	Lowndes	1851	Joseph Crow	M	W Y		dismissed
Ala.	Lowndes	1851	Emily Manning	F	W Y		denied
Tenn.	Williamson	1851	Mary Owen	F	W Y		granted
Ky.	Jefferson	1851	Sophia Victoria	F	W		granted
Ark.	Bradley	1852	James Marks	M	W Y	1	no decree
Mo.	Jefferson	1852	Benjamin Boucher	M	W Y	1	granted
Va.	Petersburg	1852	Virginia Hughes	F	W Y	1	granted
Mo.	Platte	1852	John Freeland	M	W Y	2	granted
N.C.	Northampton	1852	Susan Outland	F	W Y	2	no decree
S.C.	Charleston	1852	Harriet Rembert	F	W Y	2	granted
Ala.	Sumter	1852	Dorcus Eakin	F	W Y	2	granted
Miss.	Lowndes	1852	Elizabeth Campbell	F	W Y	2	granted
Tex.	Bexar	1852	Mary Trimble	F	W Y	2	no decree
Va.	Lancaster	1852	Sarah Hinton	F	W Y	2	no decree
Tenn.	Davidson	1852	Margaret Demoss	F	W Y	5	granted
Tenn.	Lincoln	1852	Sarah Raines	F	W Y	6	no decree
Ala.	Dallas	1852	Jane Bizzell	F	W Y	10	abated
Tenn.	Smith	1852	Elizabeth Cornwell	F	W Y	10	granted
Ala.	Madison	1852	Emily Cornelius	F	W Y	25	pg
N.C.	Person	1852	Matilda Brooks	F	W		granted
Tenn.	Washington	1852	George Conley	M	B		no decree
Va.	Petersburg	1852	Watkins Jones	M	B		granted
N.C.	Chatham	1853	Mary Williams	F	W Y	1	no decree
Ala.	Mobile	1853	Margaret Wickes	F	W Y	1	dbp
Tenn.	Davidson	1853	Mary Clinard	F	W Y	1	granted
Tenn.	Williamson	1853	John Smith	M	W Y	1	denied
S.C.	Charleston	1853	Maria Boyce	F	W Y	2	grantedpc
N.C.	Craven	1853	Mary Richardson	F	W Y	2	no decree
N.C.	Buncombe	1853	Mary Fulton	F	W Y	3	no decree
Ala.	Dallas	1853	Jane Chapman	F	W Y	3	dbp

State	County	Year	Plaintiff	Slave owner[1]			Number of slaves[2]	Result[3]
S.C.	Anderson	1853	Eliza Felton	F	W	Y	8	granted
Tenn.	Davidson	1853	Nancy Greer	F	W	Y	9	dbp
Ky.	Todd	1853	Mary Miller	F	W	Y	11	pg
N.C.	Nash	1853	Sarah Williamson	F	W	Y	12	pg
Tenn.	Franklin	1853	Edney Harrison	F	W	Y	11	granted
Miss.	Adams	1853	Alzonuth Whitehead	F	W	Y	12	pg
Va.	Franklin	1853	Mary Perdue	F	W	Y	10	granted
Fla.	Leon	1853	Christena Strong	F	W	Y	19	no decree
Ala.	Perry	1853	Dionytia Bondurant	F	W	Y		granted
Ga.	Richmond	1853	Eliza Abbot	F	W			granted
N.C.	Yadkin	1853	Rebecca Chamberlain	F	W			granted
La.	Orleans	1853	Paul Motzenbecker	M	W			granted
N.C.	Granville	1853	Eliza Ellis	F	W			no decree
N.C.	Nash	1854	Harriet Bailey	F	W	Y	1	granted
S.C.	Darlington	1854	Leorna Kelly	F	W	Y	3	pg
N.C.	Guilford	1854	Sidney Peters	F	W	Y	2	granted
La.	E. Baton Rouge	1854	Susan O'Neal	F	W	Y	2	dbp
Va.	Petersburg	1854	Archibald Drew	M	W	Y	2	granted
N.C.	Montgomery	1854	Nancy Davis	F	W	Y	4	no decree
Ala.	Talladega	1854	William Brewer	M	W	Y	4	granted
Tenn.	Williamson	1854	Narcissa Davis	F	W	Y	5	grantedpc
N.C.	Wayne	1854	Penelope Smith	F	W	Y	4	granted
Ala.	St. Clair	1854	Mary Edwards	F	W	Y	7	granted
Tenn.	Bradley	1854	Eliza Graves	F	W	Y	7	pg
Va.	Campbell	1854	Martha S. Mattox	F	W	Y	6	rejected
Tenn.	Washington	1854	Jane Fitzgerald	F	W	Y	10	granted
N.C.	Guilford	1854	Nancy Donnell	F	W	Y	13	pg
Ga.	Houston	1854	Curtis Leary	M	W	Y	6	no decree
S.C.	Barnwell	1854	Maria Holly	F	W	Y	16	pg
Ala.	Talladega	1854	Lydia Rawdon	F	W	Y	20	granted
Ga.	Jones	1854	Frances Paul	F	W	Y	18	granted
Fla.	St. Johns	1854	Susan VanHantsckee	F	W	Y	96	no decree
S.C.	Sumter	1854	Marion Converse	F	W	Y	222	grantedpc
Ky.	Barren	1854	Susan Butler	F	W	Y		granted
Va.	Petersburg	1854	Joseph Magee	M	W	Y		granted
N.C.	Stanly	1854	Andrew Troutman	M	W			granted
Tenn.	Williamson	1855	Susan Littleton	F	W	Y	1	granted
N.C.	Guilford	1855	Martha Rainey	F	W	Y	1	granted
Tenn.	Wilson	1855	Lucy A. Pruitt	F	W	Y	1	granted
Tenn.	Davidson	1855	Elizabeth Lyon	F	W	Y	1	granted
S.C.	Barnwell	1855	Ann Watson	F	W	Y	2	grantedpc
Ky.	Barren	1855	Mary Galloway	F	W	Y	2	granted

State	County	Year	Plaintiff		Slave owner[1]		Number of slaves[2]	Result[3]
La.	Orleans	1855	Francis Terence	M	B	Y	2	granted
Tenn.	Smith	1855	Frances Barrett	F	W	Y	3	granted
Tenn.	Maury	1855	Elizabeth Covington	F	W	Y	3	granted
N.C.	Yadkin	1855	Nancy Speer	F	W	Y	4	granted
Tenn.	Davidson	1855	Samuella Fussell	F	W	Y	5	dbp
D.C.	Washington	1855	Mary Maryman	F	W	Y	5	pg
N.C.	Duplin	1855	Blany Williams	M	W	Y	7	granted
S.C.	Newberry	1855	Mary M. Boland	F	W	Y	7	dbp
Tenn.	Davidson	1855	Nancy Greer	F	W	Y	8	denied
Va.	Petersburg	1855	Mary E. Chappell	F	W	Y	7	dismissed
Tenn.	Bedford	1855	Elizabeth Tune	F	W	Y	10	denied
Va.	Franklin	1855	Catharine Ross	F	W	Y	11	dbp
Va.	Scott	1855	Rebeccah Dykes	F	W	Y	9	dbp
Va.	Franklin	1855	Elizabeth Wade	F	W	Y	17	dbp
Tenn.	Davidson	1855	Sarah Baker	F	W	Y	22	granted
Ark.	Phillips	1855	Levisa Dobbin	F	W	Y	42	pg
Tex.	Brazoria	1855	Sarah Black	F	W	Y	53	dbp
Miss.	Lowndes	1855	Martha Harvey	F	W	Y	41	granted
Ala.	Baldwin	1855	Martha Crow	F	W	Y		pg
Ky.	Jefferson	1855	Elizabeth Wilhoyte	F	W	Y		granted
Ala.	Talladega	1855	Angeline Simmons	F	W	Y		dbp
Tenn.	Davidson	1855	Laura Wynne	F	W	Y		granted
N.C.	Wake	1855	Abigail Carpenter	F	W			granted
La.	St. Landry	1855	Evelina Collins	F	B			pg
N.C.	Lincoln	1855	Frances Courtney	F	W			granted
Tenn.	Washington	1855	Clarissa Jones	F	W			granted
Va.	Albemarle	1855	Susan A. Gully	F	W			granted
Va.	Petersburg	1855	John Brooks	M	W			granted
N.C.	Davidson	1856	Sarah Thomas	F	W	Y	1	granted
N.C.	Franklin	1856	Mary Williams	F	W	Y	2	no decree
Ky.	Scott	1856	Judith Wilson	F	W	Y	2	granted
Tenn.	Williamson	1856	Jesse Johnson	M	W	Y	2	granted
Ga.	Meriwether	1856	Frances Jenkins	F	W	Y	2	granted
Tenn.	Davidson	1856	Mary Davis	F	W	Y	3	granted
Tenn.	Davidson	1856	Laticia Henley	F	W	Y	4	pgd
Md.	Anne Arundel	1856	Harriet Watkins	F	W	Y	3	no decree
N.C.	Guilford	1856	Mary Garrett	F	W	Y	7	pg
Va.	Franklin	1856	Sally Odineal	F	W	Y	5	pg
N.C.	Wake	1856	Elizabeth Page	F	W	Y	5	no decree
S.C.	Charleston	1856	Eliza Egan	F	W	Y	10	granted
N.C.	Guilford	1856	Anne Gilchrist	F	W	Y	8	pg
N.C.	Mecklenburg	1856	Caroline Wallace	F	W	Y	20	no decree

State	County	Year	Plaintiff	Slave owner[1]			Number of slaves[2]	Result[3]
N.C.	Richmond	1856	Mary Cole	F	W	Y	37	pg
Va.	Mecklenburg	1856	Lucy Burwell	F	W	Y	30	pg
Miss.	Adams	1856	Lydia Ireson	F	W	Y	34	granted
Ala.	Mobile	1856	Caroline Stevens	F	W	Y		granted
N.C.	Richmond	1856	Mary Stuart	F	W			granted
N.C.	Montgomery	1856	Nancy Graves	F	W			granted
N.C.	Guilford	1856	Lydia Dean	F	W			granted
N.C.	Guilford	1856	Jane Milton	F	B			granted
N.C.	Yadkin	1856	Kennedy Williams	M	W			no decree
Tenn.	Davidson	1857	Hester Dodd	F	W	Y	1	granted
Tenn.	Davidson	1857	Madison Taylor	M	W	Y	1	pg
Ky.	Harrison	1857	Emily Conner	F	W	Y	1	pg
Md.	Anne Arundel	1857	Margery A. Wells	F	W	Y	4	pg
S.C.	Barnwell	1857	Rebecca Hair	F	W	Y	3	grantedpc
N.C.	Chatham	1857	Ruth Watson	F	W	Y	2	granted
N.C.	Ashe	1857	Sarah Edwards	F	W	Y	4	granted
N.C.	Stokes	1857	Martha Joyce	F	W	Y	5	granted
Miss.	Lowndes	1857	Charlotte Smith	F	W	Y	3	granted
S.C.	Fairfield	1857	Frances Boulware	F	W	Y	9	no decree
Tenn.	Washington	1857	Evelina E. Gillespie	F	W	Y	9	grantedpc
N.C.	Perquimans	1857	Matilda Everton	F	W	Y	10	pgd
N.C.	Yadkin	1857	Antoinette Matthews	F	W	Y	16	pg
Miss.	Jefferson	1857	Louisa Hamberlin	F	W	Y	10	no decree
Miss.	Jefferson	1857	Mary Cogan	F	W	Y	24	granted
N.C.	Guilford	1857	Elisha Dodson	M	W			no decree
Ala.	Tallapoosa	1857	Mary Turner	F	W			granted
N.C.	Guilford	1857	William Hanner	M	W			no decree
N.C.	Guilford	1857	Robert Mitchell	M	B			granted
Fla.	Escambia	1857	Catherine Llopis	F	B			granted
Tenn.	Davidson	1857	Mary Gilbert	F	W			no decree
Va.	Petersburg	1857	Eliza Parham	F	B			granted
Tenn.	Knox	1858	Isabella King	F	W	Y	1	granted
Fla.	Leon	1858	Sarah Miller	F	W	Y	1	granted
Va.	Campbell	1858	Jane Hughes	F	W	Y	1	settled
Va.	Lynchburg	1858	Jane Williamson	F	W	Y	3	granted
Ky.	Butler	1858	Frances Puckett	F	W	Y	2	dismissed
Ala.	Sumter	1858	Mary Merriman	F	W	Y	4	pg
Miss.	Claiborne	1858	Caroline Dungan	F	W	Y	3	granted
N.C.	Guilford	1858	Mary Caffey	F	W	Y	4	pg
Ky.	Barren	1858	Elizabeth Hord	F	W	Y	6	pg
S.C.	Laurens	1858	Rebecca Dean	F	W	Y	9	granted
Ky.	Harrison	1858	Louisa Williams	F	W	Y	7	no decree

State	County	Year	Plaintiff	Slave owner[1]			Number of slaves[2]	Result[3]
Ga.	Houston	1858	Elsie Hamilton	F	W	Y	12	settled
Ky.	Jefferson	1858	Ann Harrell	F	W	Y	10	no decree
Ky.	Bourbon	1858	Francis Troutman	M	W	Y	14	no decree
Ky.	Fayette	1858	Melissa Chevis	F	W	Y	16	granted
Va.	Scott	1858	Rebecca Dykes	F	W	Y	12	granted
Ala.	Shelby	1858	Margarett Campbell	F	W	Y	17	no decree
Miss.	Washington	1858	Mary Morris	F	W	Y	15	pgd
Miss.	Noxubee	1858	Lerona Foster	F	W	Y	31	transferred
Miss.	Yalobusha	1858	Ruth Rayburn	F	W	Y		granted
N.C.	Randolph	1858	Benjamin Millican	M	W			granted
N.C.	Guilford	1858	Henry Brady	M	W			no decree
Md.	Anne Arundel	1858	William Hall	M	B			granted
Miss.	Claiborne	1858	Susanah Bailey	F	W			granted
N.C.	Randolph	1858	Rhodes Riley	M	W			agreement
Ky.	Warren	1859	Sarah Manor	F	W	Y	1	granted
Tex.	Travis	1859	Sarah Fowler	F	W	Y	1	pg
N.C.	Davidson	1859	Nancy Hanes	F	W	Y	2	granted
Ala.	Mobile	1859	Catherine Moore	F	W	Y	5	no decree
Miss.	Lowndes	1859	Elizabeth Askew	F	W	Y	6	granted
Va.	Chesterfield	1859	Polly A. Cox	F	W	Y	5	no decree
N.C.	Rowan	1859	Jane Hyde	F	W	Y	8	pg
Ala.	Mobile	1859	Isabella Kelly	F	W	Y	10	no decree
Va.	Mecklenburg	1859	Ellen Field	F	W	Y	8	granted
S.C.	York	1859	Mariah Sutton	F	W	Y	11	no decree
Va.	Franklin	1859	Victoria C. Clement	F	W	Y	10	pg
La.	West Feliciana	1859	Ann Richardson	F	W	Y	9	dbp
N.C.	Cleveland	1859	Sarah McCombs	F	W	Y	15	agreement
Va.	Halifax	1859	Rebecca Spragins	F	W	Y	18	granted
Tenn.	Williamson	1859	Mary Owen	F	W	Y	33	no decree
Tenn.	Maury	1859	Fanny Caldwell	F	W	Y		grantedpc
N.C.	Guilford	1859	Mary Shackleford	F	W			granted
N.C.	Wilson	1859	Nancy Haybarger	F	W			no decree
N.C.	Wake	1859	Emeline Smith	F	W			no decree
N.C.	Hanover	1859	Hannah Hansley	F	W			pg
Va.	Petersburg	1859	John Taylor	M	B			no decree
Fla.	Leon	1860	Elizabeth Freeman	F	W	Y	3	granted
Ala.	Mobile	1860	Mary Holcombe	F	W	Y	1	no decree
Ala.	Dallas	1860	Mary Davis	F	W	Y	1	dismissed
Fla.	Leon	1860	Elizabeth Hill	F	W	Y	4	no decree
La.	Iberville	1860	Cecilia Hart	F	W	Y	1	granted
N.C.	Henderson	1860	Sarah Rucker	F	W	Y	1	agreement
Ala.	Perry	1860	Margaret Winn	F	W	Y	12	no decree

State	County	Year	Plaintiff	Slave owner[1]			Number of slaves[2]	Result[3]
S.C.	Anderson	1860	Elizabeth Mattison	F	W	Y	8	granted
La.	Natchitoches	1860	Sarah Ann Robinson	F	W	Y	7	dbp
Ga.	Houston	1860	Elizabeth Jones	F	W	Y	6	settled
Miss.	Noxubee	1860	Carolina Walker	F	W	Y	16	no decree
N.C.	Rockingham	1860	Charlotte Allen	F	W	Y	21	no decree
Ky.	Barren	1860	Laura Bell Garvan	F	W	Y	38	dismissed
S.C.	Sumter	1860	Susan Colclough	F	W	Y	70	no decree
N.C.	Craven	1860	Graham Jones	M	W			no decree
Va.	Petersburg	1860	Bryant Day	M	B			dbp
N.C.	Hyde	1860	Pearley Farrow	F	W			no decree
Va.	Petersburg	1860	Elizabeth Armistead	F	B			granted
Va.	Lynchburg	1860	William Cochran	M	W			granted
La.	Iberville	1861	Rosina Davis	F	W	Y	1	pg
N.C.	Caldwell	1861	Elizabeth Hood	F	W	Y	1	no decree
N.C.	Randolph	1861	Margaret Gray	F	W	Y	1	agreement
Fla.	Leon	1861	Levina Johnson	F	W	Y	22	denied
Ala.	Talladega	1861	Margaret Merritt	F	W	Y	7	granted
D.C.	Washington	1861	Jane Mackall	F	W	Y	7	pg
Tex.	Nacogdoches	1861	Hannah Crawford	F	W	Y	8	agreement
N.C.	Nash	1861	Mary Moore	F	W	Y	8	pg
Tenn.	Franklin	1861	Mary Clarke	F	W	Y	11	granted
Md.	Charles	1861	Alice Canter	F	W	Y	13	no decree
S.C.	Richland	1861	Laura Ann Myers	F	W	Y	17	pg
Md.	Anne Arundel	1861	Stephen Lee	M	W	Y	24	no decree
D.C.	Washington	1861	Rhoda Strother	F	W			granted
Ky.	Barren	1861	Mathew Gilmore	M	W			granted
N.C.	Randolph	1861	Nancy Brooks	F	W			no decree
Va.	Petersburg	1861	Rebecca Dowdy	F	B			granted
Ky.	Fayette	1862	Ann Boyd	F	W	Y	4	settled
Md.	Anne Arundel	1862	Harriet Schwrar	F	W	Y	5	no decree
Md.	Charles	1862	Catherine Brayfield	F	W	Y	7	granted
Va.	Franklin	1862	Elizabeth Wade	F	W	Y	24	granted
N.C.	Guilford	1862	Jane Brown	F	W	Y	18	pg
Fla.	Leon	1862	Mary Chaires	F	W	Y	66	granted
Miss.	Lowndes	1862	Lerona Foster	F	W	Y		granted
Ala.	Mobile	1862	Elizabeth Ribet	F	W			no decree
D.C.	Washington	1862	Kate McConnell	F	W			granted
Va.	Franklin	1863	Sarah M. Mason	F	W	Y	6	pgd
Ala.	Mobile	1863	James Slater	M	W	Y	11	no decree
Ga.	Houston	1863	Sarah York	F	W	Y	7	granted
Md.	Anne Arundel	1863	Emma Weedon	F	W	Y	23	no decree
Ala.	Mobile	1863	Catharine Chastang	F	B			granted

State	County	Year	Plaintiff	Slave owner[1]			Number of slaves[2]	Result[3]
Va.	Petersburg	1863	Mary Eliza Butler	F	B			granted
Va.	Petersburg	1863	William Green	M	B			no decree
Va.	Petersburg	1863	Cornelius Jackson	M	B			no decree
Tex.	Jefferson	1864	Euphrasia Tivis	F	W	Y	1	denied
N.C.	Mecklenburg	1864	Elizabeth Rea	F	W	Y	6	granted
Tex.	Grayson	1865	B. Carr	M	W	Y	2	no decree
Md.	Montgomery	1865	Julia Patterson	F	W	Y		no decree
Md.	Anne Arundel	1865	Philip Schwrar	M	W	Y		pg
Ala.	Henry	1866	Eugenia Atwell	F	W	Y	7	granted
Va.	Albemarle	1866	Elizabeth Bailey	F	W	Y	6	dismissed
N.C.	Davidson	1866	Rachel Miller	F	W	Y	8	pg
N.C.	Wake	1866	John Green	M	W			granted
N.C.	Buncombe	1866	Nathan Miller	M	W			granted
N.C.	Rowan	1866	Jacob Bostian	M	W			no decree
N.C.	Guilford	1866	Mary Hubbard	F	B			no decree
N.C.	Guilford	1866	Ziphire Goings	F	B			no decree
N.C.	Buncombe	1866	Mary Lytle	F	W			no decree
Va.	Albemarle	1866	Jack Robinson	M	B			granted
Va.	Albemarle	1867	Daniel Lee	M	B			dismissed

*petition to General Assembly

[1] B = black; F = female; M = male; W = white; Y = slave owner

[2] **Bold** number indicates number of slaves as listed in the U.S. census

[3] dbp = dismissed by plaintiff; grantedpc = granted *pro confesso*; pg = partially granted; pgd = partially granted, dismissed

Bold result from Wesley Pippenger, *Connections and Separations, Divorce, Name Change and other Genealogical Tidbits from the Acts of the General Assembly [of Virginia]* (Westminster, Md.: Willow Bend Books, 2000).

NOTES

A Note on Petition Analysis Records (PARs)

Included with the citation for each case and related documents in this study is a Petition Analysis Record (PAR) number. The first digit in the number identifies legislative (1) versus county court (2 or 3) petitions. The next two digits indicate the state where the petition was filed. The numbering is in state alphabetical sequence. Since only the fifteen slaveholding states and the District of Columbia are represented in the collection, the numbering is from 01 (Alabama) to 16 (Virginia). The next three numbers represent the last three numbers of the filing year. The last two digits are used to identify a petition among petitions filed in the same year and the same state. This number points researchers to the original petition and related documents in the Race and Slavery Petitions Project microfilm edition. All of the cases with PARs can be found in microfilm edition, which includes 151 reels of film and seven guide/indexes, totaling about 4,000 pages, published by LexisNexis. All or part of the microfilm edition can be found in a number of research libraries and archives, which are listed, along with a description of the project and collection process, in the online Digital Library on American Slavery, http://library.uncg.edu/slavery/. Consult the Digital Library for further information on the names of slaves in each case. The Petitions Project also published a two-volume, selected book edition: Loren Schweninger, ed., *The Southern Debate over Slavery*, vol. 1, *Petitions to Southern Legislatures, 1778–1864* (Urbana: University of Illinois Press, 2001), and Loren Schweninger, ed., and Marguerite Howell and Nicole Mazgaj, asst. eds., *The Southern Debate over Slavery*, vol. 2, *Petitions to Southern County Courts, 1775–1867* (Urbana: University of Illinois Press, 2008). It should also be noted that the outcome of each case used in the text is cited in the endnote citation, and the outcomes of all the cases under study can be found in Appendix 2.

Abbreviations

AAETSU	Archives of Appalachia, East Tennessee State University, Johnson City
ADAH	Alabama Department of Archives and History, Montgomery
CCA	Clerk of Court Archives
CCCO	Circuit Court Clerk's Office
CCH	County Courthouse
KDLA	Kentucky Division of Libraries and Archives, Frankfort
LC	Louisiana Collection, New Orleans Public Library
LP	Legislative Petitions
LV	Library of Virginia, Richmond
MoSA	Missouri State Archives, Jefferson City
MSA	Maryland State Archives, Annapolis
NA	National Archives, Washington, D.C.

NCSA	North Carolina State Archives, Raleigh
PAR	Petition Analysis Record (see A Note on Petition Analysis Records [PARs])
PCH	Parish Courthouse
SAF	State Archives of Florida, Tallahassee
SC	Schweninger Collection
SCDAH	South Carolina Department of Archives and History, Columbia
TSLA	Tennessee State Library and Archives, Nashville
UALS	University of Arkansas at Little Rock, School of Law
USAA	University of South Alabama Archives, Mobile
USMSAC	United States Manuscript Agricultural Census
USMSPC	United States Manuscript Population Census
USMSSC	United States Manuscript Slave Census

Preface

1. Grossberg, "Guarding the Altar," 197. The first government summaries of divorce were published after the Civil War. See U.S. Bureau of Labor, *Marriage and Divorce in the United States*; U.S. Department of Commerce and Labor, *Special Reports*.

2. Johnson, *Ante-Bellum North Carolina*, 191 (quote of lawmaker); Decree, May Term 1848, Joseph W. Lesesne, Chancellor of the Southern District of Alabama, with Petition of Martha M. Gray and James Porter to the Chancery Court of Lowndes County, Alabama, 21 May 1846, *Martha M. Gray and James Porter v. Joshua Gray*, in Alabama Supreme Court Records, Record Book, 1848, pp. 1–12, 64–69, ADAH, PAR #20184502; Joel Prentiss Bishop, *Commentaries on the Law of Marriage and Divorce, and Evidence in Matrimonial Suits* (Boston: Little, Brown, 1852), v, quoted in Grossberg, *Governing the Hearth*, 31; Wates, "Precursor to the Victorian Age," 3–14; Fox-Genovese, "Family and Female Identity in the Antebellum South," 15–31.

3. Drake, "Notes and Documents," 434–35; Ferrell, "Early Statutory and Common Law," 604 n. 1; Buckley, *Great Catastrophe of My Life*, 50–51, 55–58; Bourne, *Marriage Indissoluble and Divorce Unscriptural*, 12, 86.

4. McCurry, *Masters of Small Worlds*, 88.

5. Jacobson, *American Marriage and Divorce*, 21, 89–91; Kleinberg, *Women in the United States*, 141; Blake, *Road to Reno*, 52–56; Ferrell, "Early Statutory and Common Law," 607 n. 17. For "self-divorce," see Basch, "Marriage and Domestic Relations," 255–56; Edwards, "Law, Domestic Violence, and the Limits of Patriarchal Authority," 768; Hartog, "Marital Exits and Marital Expectations," 122–23. For related topics, see Basch, *In the Eyes of the Law* and *Framing American Divorce*; Riley, *Divorce*; Waldrep and Nieman, *Local Matters*.

6. Clark, "Matrimonial Bonds"; Aptheker, *Woman's Legacy*, 46; Fernandez, *From Chaos to Continuity*, 53–87; Bynum, *Unruly Women*, 63–69; Censer, "'Smiling through Her Tears,'" 37, 47.

7. Grossberg, *Judgment for Solomon*, xi, xiii; Grossberg and Tomlins, *Cambridge History of Law in America*, 2:vii–xiii; Hall, Finkelman, and Ely, *American Legal History*, 145–48; Penningroth, "African American Divorce," 24–25; Mann, *Republic*

of Debtors, 72–77; Brewer, *By Birth or Consent*, 369–75; Hartog, *Man and Wife in America*, 1–5. Also see Pascoe, *What Comes Naturally*; Welke, *Law and the Borders of Belonging in the Long Nineteenth Century*; Silkenat, *Moments of Despair*.

8. Gross, *Double Character*, 6–8, 45; Edwards, *People and Their Peace*, 3.

9. Brewer, "Transformation of Domestic Law," 298; Sturtz, *Within Her Power*, 90, 181; Gundersen and Gampel, "Married Women's Legal Status in Eighteenth-Century New York and Virginia"; Berkin, "Clio's Daughters"; Shammas, "Early American Women and Control over Capital." Also see Brown, *Good Wives, Nasty Wenches, and Anxious Patriarchs*; Isaac, *Transformation of Virginia*; Salmon, *Women and the Law of Property*.

Chapter 1

1. Petition of Harriet Laspeyre to the General Assembly of North Carolina, New Hanover County, 18 December 1816, in General Assembly, Session Records, Divorce and Alimony Petitions, November–December 1816, *Harriet Laspeyre v. Bernard Laspeyre*, NCSA, granted, PAR #11281601. Harriet's father, Revolutionary War major general John Ashe, and grandfather, John Baptista Ashe, had both served as speakers of the colonial assembly; her uncle, Samuel Ashe, became the ninth governor of the state. See http://www.enotes.com/topic/John_Ashe_(general), (10 August 2010). For information about the Laspeyres' slaves, farm, and vineyard, see USMSPC, New Hanover County, North Carolina, 1800, p. 8; Alden Spooner, *The Cultivation of American Grape Vines and the Making of Wine*, 2nd ed. (Brooklyn, N.Y.: Alden Spooner, 1858), 14–15; Liberty Hyde Bailey, *Sketch of the Evolution of Our Native Fruits* (Bedford, Mass.: Applewood Books, 1906), 66–67.

2. Salmon, *Women and the Law of Property*, 60–64. The literature on the subject for the New England and middle colonies during the colonial period includes Cott, "Eighteenth-Century Family and Social Life" (quotes p. 23) and "Divorce and the Changing Status of Women"; Riddell, "Legislative Divorce in Colonial Pennsylvania"; Weisberg, "Under Great Temptations Here"; Spalletta, "Divorce in Colonial New York"; Brewer, "Transformation of Domestic Law."

3. Bardaglio, *Reconstructing the Household*, 32–33; Salmon, *Women and the Law of Property*, 62–63; Van Ness, "On Untieing the Knot."

4. Stone, *Broken Lives*, 9–10; Stone, *Road to Divorce*, 24–27, 183–84; Zaher, "When a Woman's Marital Status Determined Her Legal Status," 459–61; Ferrell, "Early Statutory and Common Law," 604; Oldham, *English Common Law in the Age of Mansfield*, 335; William Blackstone, *Commentaries on the Laws of England (1765–1769)*, bk. 1, chap. 15, pp. 421–29, and chap. 16, p. 444, http://www.lonang.com/exlibris/blackstone/bla115.htm (20 November 2007). Both Massachusetts and the mother country viewed marriage as a civil contract, but they differed on what type of court should rule on marital questions and when and how the contract could be broken.

5. Konig, "Regionalism in Early American Law," 152–53. Colonial Massachusetts, Connecticut, and Pennsylvania did not have separate courts of equity in the English fashion. See Katz, "Politics of Law in Colonial America"; Salmon, "Women and Property in South Carolina," 659 n. 10.

6. Konig, "Regionalism in Early American Law," 167, 173–75, 177; Brewer, "Transformation of Domestic Law," 288–89, 298; Sturtz, *Within Her Power*, 7, 16, 20; Hadden, "Fragmented Laws of Slavery."

7. U.S. Congress, *Federal and State Constitutions*, 2:777–90 (Georgia 1777, 1789); 3:1687–1705 (Maryland 1776); 5:2787–99 (North Carolina 1776); 6:3241–3306 (South Carolina 1776, 1778, 1790, 1868, 1895); Kerber, *Women of the Republic*, 139 (common law). For attitudes toward divorce in the Palmetto State, see McCurry, *Masters of Small Worlds*, 86–87; Frierson, "Divorce in South Carolina."

8. Petition of James Hathaway to the Delaware General Assembly, 16 June 1786, http://archives.delaware.gov/exhibits/document/petitions (December 2007); Hodes, *White Women, Black Men*, 245–46 n. 12; Petition of Benjamin Butt Jr. to the Virginia General Assembly, Norfolk County, 7 December 1803, in LP, LV; Related Documents: Depositions, Ivy Holstead, Nancy Butt, Anna Murdan, Benjamin Butt, 31 October 1803; Affidavit, Elizabeth Holstead, ca. 1803; Bill of Divorce, 2 June 1803, with ibid., reasonable, reported, PAR #11680301; Riley, "Legislative Divorce in Virginia"; Higginbotham and Kopytoff, "Racial Purity and Interracial Sex," 110 n. 144; Kierner, *Beyond the Household*, 126–27. For separation and property acts, see *Laws of North Carolina at a General Assembly, begun and held at the city of Raleigh*, 43, 68; Kierner, *Southern Women in Revolution*, 195–98.

9. Chused, *Private Acts in Public Places*, 47; Johnson, *Ante-Bellum North Carolina*, 218–19; Ferrell, "Early Statutory and Common Law," 604 n. 1; McBride, "Divorces, Separations, and Security of Property," 43; Censer, "'Smiling through Her Tears,'" 26 n. 8.

10. *Acts of the General Assembly of the State of Georgia*, 47–48.

11. *Statute Laws of the State of Tennessee, of a Public and General Nature*, 1:74–76 (copy of 1799 law plus revisions in 1809 and 1819 concerning jurisdiction, procedures, and causes for divorce); Bamman and Spero, *Tennessee Divorces*, ii, iii; *Compilation of the Statutes of Tennessee*, 256–62 (revision of divorce laws and transfer to circuit chancery courts); *Statute Laws of the State of Tennessee, of a General Character*, 149–51 (revisions to divorce laws during the period 1840 to 1846); *Code of Tennessee*, 482–86 (summary and expansion of divorce laws). A "next friend" was a person who appeared in a lawsuit to act for the benefit of an incompetent or minor plaintiff who did not have full legal capacity. The term *prochein ami* was used. After 1836, Tennessee women were not required to have a "next friend"; see Goodheart, Hanks, and Johnson, "'Act for the Relief of Females,'" pt. 1, p. 324.

12. *Statute Law of Kentucky*, 4:19–20 (circuit court jurisdiction law passed 31 January 1809), 5:365 (divorce appeal, writ of error, had to be filed within three years of the divorce decree); *Revised Statutes of Kentucky*, 389–93 (grounds for divorce in chancery courts); Howard, *History of Matrimonial Institutions*, 3:42 (Kentucky residents continue to petition General Assembly); Johnson, *Ante-Bellum North Carolina*, 218–19; Ferrell, "Early Statutory and Common Law," 604 n. 1; Censer, "'Smiling through Her Tears,'" 26 n. 8 (North Carolina); *Digest of the Laws of Virginia, Which Are of a Permanent Character and General Operation*, 287–89 (includes 1827 divorce law).

13. Howard, *History of Matrimonial Institutions*, 3:42–72.

14. *The Digest of 1808*, reproduced by Louisiana State University Law Center, http://www.law.lsu.edu/index.cfm (14 December 2009); Schafer, *Slavery, the Civil Law, and the Supreme Court of Louisiana*, 17. During the early years, petitioners seeking separation of bed and board referred to the "Civil Code," meaning the *Digest of 1808*, by title headings, chapter, article, and page number. See, for example, Petition of Mary Gayle to the District Court of East Baton Rouge Parish, Louisiana, 25 September 1816, in Records of the Third Judicial District Court, *Mary Gayle v. Christopher Gayle*, Case #414, CCA, Baton Rouge, La.; Related Documents: Order, 25 September 1816; Order, 27 September 1816; Sheriff's Return, 30 September 1816; Inventory, 30 September 1816; Judgment, ca. September 1816, with ibid., granted, PAR #20881608.

15. Basch, *Framing American Divorce*, 48; Schafer, *Slavery, the Civil Law, and the Supreme Court of Louisiana*, 16; McMillen, *Southern Women*, 43; Pascal, "Sources of Order," 920, 929; *Civil Code of the State of Louisiana*, 77–87; Kent, *Commentaries on American Law*, 2:81; Fernandez, *From Chaos to Continuity*, 80–88; *Consolidation and Revision of the Statutes of the State*, 226–28 (includes 1827 statute and revisions); *Revised Statutes of Louisiana*, 184–86; Censer, "'Smiling through Her Tears,'" 26 n. 8.

16. Censer, "'Smiling through Her Tears,'" 208 (North Carolina divorce law); U.S. Congress, *Federal and State Constitutions*, 1:590 (Delaware 1831); *Laws of the State of Delaware*, 148–50; Munroe, *History of Delaware*, 170; Blake, *Road to Reno*, 17, 55, 56, 247 (Delaware Assembly continued to pass private acts); *Maryland Code*, 75–77 (1842 law); Howard, *History of Matrimonial Institutions*, 3:31–32, 33, 35, 56 (Maryland 1830). The nine laws passed by the Maryland Assembly between 1830 and 1850 can be found in Chused, *Private Acts in Public Places*, 183–89.

17. U.S. Congress, *Federal and State Constitutions*, 6:3439 (Tennessee 1834); 2:805 (Georgia 1833); 5:2797 (North Carolina 1835); 1:281; 3:1424 (Louisiana 1845); 7:3842 (Virginia 1850); 4:2173 (Missouri); 1:281 (Arkansas 1836); 2:680 (Florida 1838); 6:3561 (Texas 1845).

18. In 1849, the Arkansas Supreme Court listed these "personal indignities"; see Phillips, *Untying the Knot*, 145–46. See also Phillips, *Putting Asunder*, 446; Riley, *Divorce*, 42; Censer, "'Smiling through Her Tears,'" 29. From its founding in 1801, the District of Columbia turned divorce cases over to the circuit court; see *Revised Code of the District of Columbia*, 294–97.

19. The term "mulatto" is used here and in other sections of this study as contemporaries employed it to describe persons of mixed racial origin. I have also used such terms as "mixed race," "interracial," "mixed blood," "colored," and "negro" when spoken or written by contemporaries.

20. Bardaglio, *Reconstructing the Household*, 51 (colonial Maryland and Virginia laws); Hening, *Statutes at Large*, 3:86–88 (1691 Virginia law); Higginbotham and Kopytoff, "Racial Purity and Interracial Sex," 110 n. 144; Rothman, "'Notorious in the Neighborhood,'" 74; John Codman Hurd, *The Law of Freedom and Bondage in the United States*, 2 vols. (Boston: Little, Brown, 1862; reprint, New York: Negro University Press, 1968), 2:92 (Tennessee statute); *Laws of the State of North Carolina, Passed by the General Assembly*, 33; *Code of Virginia*, 740. For a summary of these laws, see Bardaglio, *Reconstructing the Household*, 256–59 nn. 94–100; Farnam,

Chapters in the History of Social Legislation, 194. For South Carolina, see Wikramanayake, *World in Shadow*, 76; Johnson and Roark, *Black Masters*, 169; Schweninger, Howell, and Mazgaj, *Southern Debate over Slavery*, 2:105–6.

21. Grossberg, "Guarding the Altar," 202–3; Bardaglio, "'Shameful Matches,'" 119. For an anthology of important articles, see Hall, *Law, Society, and Domestic Relations*.

22. *Replication of the Project of the Civil Code of Louisiana*, 298; *Civil Code of the State of Louisiana*, 511–12.

23. Dougan, "Arkansas Married Woman's Property Law," 13–16; Chused, "Married Women's Property Law," 1398–99; *Acts and Resolutions*, 24–25; *Laws of the State of Mississippi: Passed at an Adjourned Session of the Legislature*, 72–73; Moncrief, "Mississippi Married Women's Property Act"; *Laws of the State of Mississippi, Passed at A Regular Biennial Session of the Legislature*, 152–55; Basch, "Marriage and Domestic Relations," 246, 260; McMillen, *Southern Women*, 43; Bardaglio, *Reconstructing the Household*, 32; Warbasse, *Changing Legal Rights of Married Women*, 48, 138, 167. For dower rights, see Morris, *Southern Slavery and the Law*, 93–96.

24. Petition of Bernard Laspeyre to the General Assembly, Sampson County, North Carolina, 11 December 1817, in General Assembly, Session Records, Divorce and Alimony Petitions, November–December 1817, *Bernard Laspeyre v. Harriet Laspeyre*, NCSA, rejected, PAR #11281703. In 1830, in his sixties, Bernard Laspeyre headed a household in Bladen County consisting of a boy under five and a woman in her twenties, along with seven slaves and two free blacks. He died in 1837. See USMSPC, Bladen County, North Carolina, 1830, p. 88; USMSPC, Brunswick County, North Carolina, 1830, p. 329; USMSPC, New Hanover County, North Carolina, Wilmington, 1840, p. 12, and 1850, p. 434; USMSSC, New Hanover County, North Carolina, 1850, p. 28 (William H. Laspeyre). For the Ashe family, see http://genforum.genealogy.com/ashe/messages/273.html (9 August 2010).

Chapter 2

1. Petition of Sarah H. Black to the District Court of Brazoria County, Texas, 26 March 1855, in Records of the District Court, *Sarah H. Black v. James E. Black*, Case #1835, CCH, Angleton, Tex.; Related Documents: Interrogatories, 21 April 1855; Order, 25 May 1855; Partial Copy of Order, 25 May 1855; Order, ca. 1855, with ibid., dismissed, PAR #21585501; USMSPC, Abbeville District, South Carolina, 1820, p. 3; 1830, p. 20; and Henry County, Tennessee, 1840, p. 439 (the printed page number, for both the page and facing page, is used in this and other citations of the manuscript population census returns; they were viewed on ancestry.com).

2. USMSPC, Brazoria County, Texas, 1850, p. 381; USMSSC, Brazoria County, Texas, 1850, pp. 177, 225; USMSAC, Brazoria County, Texas, 1850, pp. 84–85; DeBow, *Statistical View of the United States*, 95.

3. The literature on the subject has expanded significantly in recent years. See Pascoe, *What Comes Naturally*; Gross, *What Blood Won't Tell*; Wallenstein, *Tell the Court I Love My Wife*; Kennedy, *Interracial Intimacies*; Hollinger, "Amalgamation and Hypodescent"; Robinson, *Dangerous Liaisons*; Sommerville, *Rape and Race in the Nineteenth-Century South*; Rothman, *Notorious in the Neighborhood*; Block, *Rape*

and Sexual Power in Early America; Buckley, "Unfixing Race"; Bardaglio, "'Shamefull Matches'"; Block, "Lines of Color, Sex, and Service"; Hodes, *White Women, Black Men*.

4. For contemporary accounts, which focus on planters and slave women, see James S. Buckingham, *The Slave States of America*, 2 vols. (London: Fisher, Son, 1842), 2:213–14; Blane, *Excursion through the United States and Canada*, 204; Kemble, *Journal of a Residence in America*, 15. See also Clinton, *Fanny Kemble's Civil Wars*, 124, and "Caught in the Web of the Big House."

5. Petition of Priscilla Hunter Russell to the Chancery Court of Marshall County, Tennessee, 9 September 1846, in Chancery Court, Loose Records, *Priscilla Hunter Russell v. John Russell*, Case #136, TSLA; Related Documents: Compromise, Priscilla Russell and John Russell, 8 October 1847; Decree, ca. 9 September 1846; Clerk and Master's Report, ca. 9 September 1846, with ibid., granted, PAR #21484611; Petition of Lelia Weathers to the Superior Court of Cleveland County, North Carolina, 29 November 1848, in County Court Divorce Records, *Lelia Weathers v. William Weathers*, NCSA; Related Documents: Oath, Lelia Weathers, 29 November 1848; Order, 30 November 1848, with ibid. (cold and distant), agreement, PAR #21284814; Petition of Nancy Summers to the Circuit Court of Barren County, Kentucky, 17 March 1812, in Records of the Circuit Court, Equity Judgments, *Nancy Summers v. John Summers*, Case #15, KDLA; Related Documents: Amended Bill, 15 February 1813; Order, 15 February 1813; Depositions, Adron Lane, Sarah Lane, and William Johnson, 4 March 1813; Decree, ca. 1812, with ibid., granted, PAR #20781204.

6. Petition of Rhoda Strother to the Circuit Court of Washington, Washington, D.C., 19 January 1861, in Records of the United States District Court, Chancery Records, Old Divorces, *Rhoda Strother v. Robert Slaughter Strother*, Case #4, NA; Related Documents: Decree, 27 May 1861; Newspaper Article, Robert Strother, 20 February 1860, with ibid., granted, PAR #20486103. Her husband left the city a short time later and moved to the Kansas Territory.

7. *Civil Code of the State of Louisiana*, article 1468; Schafer, *Slavery, the Civil Law, and the Supreme Court of Louisiana*, 185; Frederick Law Olmsted, *The Cotton Kingdom: A Traveller's Observations on Cotton and Slavery in the American Slave States*, ed. Arthur Schlesinger (New York: Knopf, 1953), 235–37; Petition of Rachel Hudnall to the District Court of Iberville Parish, Louisiana, 22 March 1844, in Records of the Fourth Judicial District Court, *Rachel Douglass Hudnall v. Thomas Hudnall*, Cases #2147 and #2181, PCH, Plaquemine, La.; Related Documents: Order, 22 March 1844; Supplemental Petition, 11 April 1844; Petition Service Acknowledgment, 10 April 1844; Testimonies, John Terrell, Edward Moore, 13 April 1844; Judgment, 22 April 1844, with ibid., granted, PAR #20884407. The couple had recently migrated from Mississippi. In 1840, Thomas Hundall (Hundell) headed a household consisting of 9 other whites and 174 slaves. See also USMSPC, Madison County, Mississippi, 1830, pp. 602–3, and Southern District, 1840, p. 96; Petition of Celeste Langlois to the District Court of Natchitoches Parish, Louisiana, 18 October 1825, in Records of the District Court, *Celeste Vergen Langlois v. Auguste Langlois*, Case #854, PCH, Natchitoches, La.; Related Documents: Court Record, 11 November 1825; Judgment, November Term 1826, with ibid., dismissed, PAR #20882525.

8. Petition of Elizabeth Stacy and David Chambliss to the Chancery Court of Montgomery County, Alabama, 1845, in Records of the Circuit Court, Records, 1845–46, pp. 538–40, *Elizabeth Stacy and David Chambliss v. William Stacy*, CCH, Montgomery, Ala.; Related Documents: Answer, William Stacy, 14 February 1846; Agreement, 29 October 1845, with ibid., abated, PAR #20184522; Petition of Caroline Dungan and David Hurlong to the District Court of Claiborne County, Mississippi, 9 September 1858, in Records of the Chancery Court, *Caroline Dungan and David Hurlong v. Jacob Dungan*, Case #57, CCH, Port Gibson, Miss.; Related Documents: Depositions, Michael McGee and Joshua D. Goza, 22 March 1859; Final Decree, 22 April 1859, with ibid. ("as white as any white children, with straight hair"), granted, PAR #21085813; Petition of Eley Parker Hall to the Equity Court of Fairfield District, South Carolina, 15 June 1846, in Records of the Equity Court, Bills, *Eley Parker Hall v. Laban Hall*, Case #1847, SCDAH; Related Documents: Decree, 17 July 1847; Answer, Laban Hall, 26 November 1846, with ibid., partially granted, PAR #21384639; Petition of Mary Jackson and Samuel Buckhan to the Superior Court of Greene County, Georgia, 1806, in Records of the Superior Court, *Mary Jackson and Samuel Buckhan v. Joseph Jackson*, Proceedings, 1808–9, 125–27, CCH, Greensboro, Ga.; Related Documents: Summons, Joseph Jackson, 22 January 1806, no decree with petition, PAR #20680602.

9. For community sentiment, see Jabour, *Scarlett's Sisters*, 91; Bancroft, *Slave-Trading in the Old South*, 38, 50–51, 57, 102, 328; Johnson, *Soul by Soul*, 113; Tadman, *Speculators and Slaves*, 125–27; Deyle, *Carry Me Back*, 126–27; Johnston, *Race Relations in Virginia and Miscegenation in the South*, 240; Loren Schweninger, ed., *From Tennessee Slave to St. Louis Entrepreneur: The Autobiography of James Thomas*, foreword by John Hope Franklin (Columbia: University of Missouri Press, 1984), 108, 117; Franklin and Schweninger, *In Search of the Promised Land*, 171; Petition of Sarah Smith and James H. Hill to the Chancery Court of Talladega County, Alabama, 19 May 1842, in Records of the Circuit Court, Final Records, 1841–42, pp. 249–53, *Sarah Smith and James H. Hill v. John Smith*, Talladega County Judicial Building, Talladega, Ala.; Related Documents: Order, 19 May 1842; Subpoena, 19 May 1842; Dismissal, 7 June 1842, with ibid., dismissed, PAR #20184205.

10. Bardaglio, *Reconstructing the Household*, 49; Robinson, *Dangerous Liaisons*, 5; Petition of Martha Upthegrove and Alexander Fuller to the Equity Court of Richland District, South Carolina, 7 July 1817, in Records of the Equity Court, Bills, Richland District, *Martha Upthegrove and Alexander Fuller v. Henry Upthegrove*, SCDAH; Related Documents: List of Witnesses for Complainant, ca. 7 July 1817, with ibid., no decree with petition, PAR #21381725; Petition of Ellen Dunlap to the Virginia General Assembly, Augusta County, 12 October 1814, in LP, LV; Related Documents: Affidavit, James and Thomas Shields, 1 October 1814; Affidavit, Rachel and Peggy Shields, 1 October 1814; Affidavit, Samuel Torbet, 4 October 1814, with ibid., rejected, PAR #11681419; Petition of Winnefrid Richmond to the Chancery Court of Davidson County, Tennessee, 9 December 1835, in Supreme Court Cases, Middle Tennessee, *Winnefrid Richmond and Lewis Garrett v. Braddock Richmond*, box 72, TSLA; Related Documents: Amended Bill, 8 June 1836; Bond, Braddock Richmond, ca. June 1836; Subpoena, 12 December 1835; Answer, Braddock

Richmond, 12 May 1836; Replication (incomplete), ca. 1836; Decree and Notice of Appeal, ca. February 1837; Appeal Bond, 18 February 1837; Depositions, William Gillam, Samuel Sparkman, Robert Butler, John Adams, James Cooper, William Robinson, Mrs. Bivens, Anna Ridley, Mrs. Buchanan, Joseph Alley, O. Tucker, ca. 1836; Supreme Court Decree, 5 February 1839; Order, Decree, Opinion, ca. 1837 1843, with ibid., granted, appealed, affirmed, PAR #21483520.

11. Petition of Anna Allen to the Equity Court of Richland District, South Carolina, 14 December 1816, in Records of the Equity Court, Bills, *Anna Allen v. John Allen and Turner Stark*, SCDAH; Related Documents: Order, 14 December 1816; Commissioner's Report, February Term 1817; Report on Sale, June Term 1817, with ibid., granted, PAR #21381606; USMSPC, Sumter District, South Carolina, Claremont, 1810, p. 219.

12. Petition of Ann Eliza Eubank to the Virginia General Assembly, King William County, Virginia, 9 December 1836, in LP, LV; Related Documents: Copy of Record of Circuit Superior Court, King William County, November 1835, with ibid., granted, PAR #11683601.

13. Petition of Jane Robinson to the Superior Court of Richmond County, North Carolina, 30 June 1818, in County Court Divorce Records, *Jane Robinson v. William Robinson*, NCSA; Related Documents: Summons, September 1817; Depositions of William Powell and Alamander[?] Hunt, [22] June 1818, James Kelly, 23 June 1818, Betsy Stansill (also spelled Stancill), 25 June 1818, Hannah Cole, June 1818, James Cole, 27 June 1818, with ibid., no decree with petition, PAR #21281803. The superior court minutes for Richmond County, which would contain the results of the trial, are not extant. As indicated by this and other cases, white men forcing themselves upon slave women was a civil matter. The reverse, black men forcing themselves on white women, was a criminal offense sometimes punishable by death. See Sommerville, "'I Was Very Much Wounded'"; Getman, "Sexual Control in the Slaveholding South," 136–40.

14. Kemble, *Journal of a Residence on a Georgian Plantation*, 238–39, 270.

15. Farnam, *Chapters in the History of Social Legislation*, 185, 205; Bardaglio, *Reconstructing the Household*, 65–66 (Cobb on laws concerning trespass on a female slave); Bynum, *Unruly Women*, 109; Sommerville, *Rape and Race in the Nineteenth-Century South*, 75; Hodes, *White Women, Black Men*, 3, 5, 30, 65, 87.

16. Botham, *Almighty God Created the Races*, 56–59; Hodes, *White Women, Black Men*, 3–5, 19–38, 54–59; Sommerville, *Rape and Race in the Nineteenth-Century South*, 16, 86–101; Bynum, *Unruly Women*, 69–70, 98–99; Kennedy, *Interracial Intimacies*, 59–69; Rothman, "'To be Freed from Thate Curs and Let at Liberty'"; Wyatt-Brown, *Southern Honor*, 315–16; Wyatt-Brown, *Honor and Violence in the Old South*, 98–105; Morris, *Southern Slavery and the Law*, 302–5.

17. Forret, *Race Relations at the Margins*, 215.

18. Petition of Dabney Pettus to the Virginia General Assembly, Fluvanna County, 13 December 1802, in LP, LV; Related Documents: Affidavit, Elizabeth G. Meryman, 2 December 1802; Affidavit, Susanna Herndon, 2 December 1802; Affidavit, Rach[ae]l Puckett, 2 December 1802; Statement, Elizabeth Pettus, 25 October 1801; Statement, John Brishwood, 27 November 1802; Dabney Pettis to Elizabeth

Pettis [sic], 29 November 1802, with ibid., reasonable, reported, PAR #11680206; Petition of John Rich to the Tennessee General Assembly, Maury County, 1829, in LP, TSLA; Related Documents: List of Subscribers, ca. 1829, with ibid., no act with petition, PAR #11482912; Petition of Josiah Houston to the Chancery Court of Talladega County, Alabama, 29 February 1840, in Records of the Circuit Court, Final Records, 1843-46, pp. 55-56, *Josiah Houston v. Matilda Houston*, Talladega County Judicial Building, Talladega, Ala.; Related Documents: Subpoena, Matilda Houston, 29 February 1840; Order, February 1841; Continuance, November 1842; Dismissal, December 1843, with ibid., dismissed, PAR #20184004.

19. Petition of Marmaduke Jones to the South Carolina General Assembly, Barnwell District, November 1847, in General Assembly, Petitions, *Marmaduke Jones v. Ann Jones*, Case #1847-44-01, SCDAH; Related Documents: Oath, Jonathan Jones, 29 October 1847; Oath, Owen M. Daniel et al., 9 November 1847; Affidavit, Elizabeth Hair, 8 November 1849, no act with petition, PAR #11384706. See also Petition of Young Utley to the North Carolina General Assembly, Wake County, 11 December 1810, in General Assembly, Session Records, NCSA, read and referred, PAR #11281010.

20. Petition of Ayres Tatham to the Virginia General Assembly, Accomack County, 13 December 1805, in LP, LV; Related Documents: List of Subscribers, ca. 1805; Bill of Divorce, 28 March 1804, with ibid., reasonable, reported, PAR #11680503; Petition of Robert Chiles to the Chancery Court of Boone County, Missouri, 25 April 1842, in Records of the Circuit Court, Microfilm Reel C16671, *Robert Chiles v. Celia Lambert Chiles*, Case #1646, MoSA; Related Documents: Newspaper Notice, 15 January 1842; Deposition, Elizabeth Caton, 13 August 1842; Copy of Petition, Robert Chiles, 26 November 1841; Subpoena, James Payne Jr., 16 August 1842; Sheriff's Return, 17 August 1842; Notice, Robert Chiles, 8 August 1842; Summons, Celia Chiles, 26 November 1841; Sheriff's Return, ca. 26 November 1841; Docket Page, ca. August 1842, with ibid., no decree with petition, PAR #21184216.

21. Higginbotham, *In the Matter of Color*, 46; Petition of David Parker to the General Assembly, Nansemond County, Virginia, 8 December 1826, in LP, LV; Related Documents: Notice, unidentified newspaper, 12 October [1826]; Affidavit, Washington Smith, 23 November 1826, with ibid., bill drawn, PAR #11682601. In 1830, Parker owned four slaves; see USMSPC, Nansemond County, Virginia, Eastern District, 1830, p. 232. In Virginia, if a white husband could prove that his wife gave birth to a mixed-race child, it was not necessary to identify the African American father to obtain a divorce. See *Acts Passed at a General Assembly of the Commonwealth of Virginia*, 145; Petition of Daniel Griffin to the Superior Court of Wayne County, North Carolina, 1850, in Records of the County Court, Slaves and Free Persons of Color, *Daniel Griffin v. Leah Griffin*, NCSA; Related Documents: Decree, ca. 1850; Deposition of Richard Grant, 2 May 1857, with ibid., granted, PAR #21285022.

22. Petition of Henry Shouse to the Superior Court of Stokes County, North Carolina, 20 March 1843, in County Court Divorce Records, *Henry Shouse v. Ann Shouse*, NCSA; Related Documents: Oath, Henry Shouse, 20 March 1843; Order, 20 March 1843, with ibid., granted, PAR #21284313; USMSPC, Stokes County, North Carolina, Bethania District, 1840, p. 142. For a similar case, see Petition of William

Hickman to the Superior Court of Granville County, North Carolina, September 1831, in County Court Divorce Records, *William Hickman v. Nancy Hickman*, NCSA, no decree with petition, PAR #21283110.

23. Petition of Thomas Flowers to the Equity Court of Nash County, North Carolina, n.d., in County Court Divorce Records, *Thomas Flowers v. Temperance Flowers*, NCSA; Related Documents: Decree, n.d., with ibid., granted, PAR #21200001.

24. Petition of James Larimore to the Superior Court of Stokes County, North Carolina, 1820, in County Court Divorce Records, *James Larimore v. Catharine Larimore*, NCSA; Related Documents: Deposition of Winney Westbrook, ca. 1820, with ibid., granted, PAR #21282001; USMSPC, Stokes County, North Carolina, 1820, p. 355, and 1840, p. 200.

25. Petition of William H. Cochran to the Circuit Court of Lynchburg, Virginia, May 1860, in Circuit Court of Chancery Papers, *William H. Cochran v. Lucinda Dowdy Cochran*, LV; Related Documents: Depositions, Henry W. Wright and Thomas Brooks, 15 May 1860; Decree, June Term 1860, with ibid., granted, PAR #21686012.

26. Sommerville, *Rape and Race in the Nineteenth-Century South*, 34; Hodes, *White Women, Black Men*, 139; Catterall, *Judicial Cases Concerning American Slavery*, 2:63, 64, 76; Petition of Andrew Whittington to the Superior Court of Guilford County, North Carolina, 27 October 1830, in County Court Divorce Records, *Andrew Whittington v. Lucy Whittington*, NCSA; Related Documents: Summons, Lucy Whittington, September 1830; Answer, Lucy Whittington, 26 April 1831, with ibid., granted, PAR #21283003; Petition of Andrew Whittington to the Superior Court of Caswell County, North Carolina, 18 February 1833, in County Court Divorce Records, *Andrew Whittington v. Lucy Whittington*, NCSA; Related Documents: Depositions, Lucresay Sprout, ca. 1834; Joseph Whittington, Guilford County, 13 February 1834; Thomas Underwood, ca. 1834; David Clark, M. Arthur, Guilford County, 7 November 1835; Aaron Clymer, Guilford County, 3 November 1834, with ibid., granted, PAR #21283309. The birth of a "colored child" occurred after the couple's separation. See also Petition of Norfleet Perry to the Tennessee General Assembly, Davidson County, 29 September 1819, in LP, TSLA; Related Documents: Certificate, William Donelson, Justice of the Peace, 28 September 1819; Affidavit, Thomas Walton, 27 September 1819; Affidavit, Josiah Perry, 23 September 1819; Affidavit, Edward Phillips, 15 September 1819, with ibid., referred to select committee, PAR #11481926. See Rothman, "'To be Freed from Thate Curs,'" 443–81; Buckley, *Great Catastrophe of My Life*, 123; John Rankin, *Letters on American Slavery, Addressed to Mr. Thomas Rankin, Merchant at Middlebrook, Augusta Co., Va.*, 5th ed. (Boston: Garrison and Knapp, 1839), 63, in Hodes, *White Women, Black Men*, 214 n. 5.

27. Petition of James Carmichael, V. D. Jamison, David Rumph, Samuel P. Jones, Sanders Glover Jr., et al., to the South Carolina General Assembly, Orangeburgh District, South Carolina, 12 December 1812, in Records of the General Assembly, Case #1812-111, SCDAH, referred to Judiciary Committee, PAR #11381203.

28. See Petition of William Brewer to the Chancery Court of Talladega County, Alabama, 25 November 1854, in Records of the Chancery Court, Minutes and Dockets, 1857–61, pp. 21–32, 36–41, 44–51, *William Brewer v. Jane C. Brewer*,

Shelby County Archives, Columbiana, Ala.; Related Documents: Copies of Answer, Jane C. Brewer, ca. August 1855; Cross Bill, Jane C. Brewer, ca. August 1855 (filed 31 December 1855); Amendments to Original Bill, 21 June 1855; Answer to Cross Bill, William C. Brewer, 2 August 1855; Suppression of Depositions, 22 March 1856; Summons Order of Register, 3 November 1856; Agreement, William Brewer and Jane Brewer, ca. 1856; Report of Register, 27 November 1856; Exceptions to Report of Register, William Brewer, 27 November 1856; Record, 21 April 1857; Report of Register, 21 April 1857; Opinion and Decrees, July 1856, 4 September 1856; Orders, November 1856, July 1857, with ibid., granted, PAR #20185421; Petition of Kennedy M. Williams and William W. Patterson to the Superior Court of Yadkin County, North Carolina, 8 April 1856, in County Court Divorce Records, *Kennedy M. Williams and William W. Patterson v. Mary Eliza Williams*, NCSA, no decree with petition, PAR #21285609; Petition of Nancy Speer to the Equity Court of Yadkin County, North Carolina, 4 September 1855, in County Court Divorce Records, *Nancy Speer v. Samuel Speer*, NCSA; Related Documents: Order, ca. 1855, with ibid., granted, PAR #21285504.

29. Petition of Joseph W. Magee to the Circuit Court of Petersburg, Virginia, March 1854, in Records of the Circuit Superior Court of Chancery, Drawer 64–66, *Joseph W. Magee v. Margaret Marks Magee*, CCCO, Petersburg, Va.; Related Documents: Depositions, Sarah E. Gresham, William Miller, and Benjamin Payne, 27 March 1854; Decree, May Term 1854, with ibid., granted, PAR #21685420; USMSPC, Dinwiddie County, Virginia, Petersburg, South Ward, 1860, p. 340; USMSSC, Dinwiddie County, Virginia, Petersburg, South Ward, 1860, p. 25. In 1839, Eliza Gallee filed her own petition for divorce; see Petition of Eliza Gallee and Catharine A. Cooke to the Circuit Superior Court of Petersburg, Virginia, August 1839, in Records of the Circuit Superior Court of Chancery, Drawer 38–40, *Eliza Gallee and Catharine A. Cooke v. Joseph Gallee*, CCCO, Petersburg, Va.; Related Documents: Notice to Take Depositions, 15 October 1840; Certification of Delivery of Notice, 31 October 1840; Depositions, Samuel Epes, John Paterson, Freeman G. Walker, William H. Williams, William Fenn, John H. Bailey, 28 October 1840; Note for Decree, ca. October 1840, with ibid., granted pro confesso, PAR #21683920; Petition of Thomas M. Oliver to the Superior Court of Wake County, North Carolina, 1844, in County Court Divorce Records, *Thomas M. Oliver v. Frances M. Oliver*, NCSA; Related Documents: Answer, Frances Oliver, 30 March 1844; Deposition, Margaret Savage, New York City, ca. 1844, with ibid., no decree with petition, PAR #21284406; USMSPC, Wake County, North Carolina, Raleigh, 1850, p. 277; USMSSC, Wake County, North Carolina, Raleigh, 1850, p. 659; Petition of James Puckett to the Circuit Court of Mobile County, Alabama, 16 November 1831, in Records of the Chancery Court, Divorce Cases, *James Puckett v. Elizabeth Puckett*, Case #162, USAA; Related Documents: Substitute for Original Bill, James Puckett, 17 May 1832; Answer, Elizabeth Puckett, ca. 1832; Affidavit, John Reynolds, 21 March 1832; Affidavit, W. M. Walker, 22 March 1832; Affidavit, Rebecca Pettis, 30 March 1832; Decree, 21 May 1832, with ibid., granted, PAR #20183103; Petition of John H. Brooks to the Chancery Court of Petersburg, Virginia, 3 March 1855, in Records of the Circuit Superior Court of Chancery, Drawer 132–33, *John H. Brooks v. Eliza Jane*

Brooks, CCCO, Petersburg, Va.; Related Documents: Depositions, James R. Pride and Edward B. White, 1 May 1855; Correspondence, Fanny B. to Dr. John Crowder, ca. 1855; Order, May Term 1855, with ibid., granted, PAR #21685512.

30. DeBow, *Statistical View of the United States*, 95. Of course, by virtue of this study's focus on race and the institution of slavery, wives from nonslaveholding families who cited white women as their husbands' sexual partners in cases of divorce were included only if slaves or free persons of color were associated in some way with their cases. For example, mentioned in the case of Martha Brannock, who charged her husband with committing adultery with white women, is the fact that she had received a slave woman as a personal servant from her father, a large slave owner. See Petition of Martha Brannock to the Superior Court of Guilford County, North Carolina, 22 February 1839, in County Court Divorce Records, *Martha Brannock v. Wright Brannock*, NCSA; Related Documents: Answer, Wright Brannock, 25 April 1839, with ibid., no decree with petition, PAR #21283911. The proportional distribution of this study's slaveholding families in terms of the size of their slaveholdings, defined by the number of slaves owned within predefined ranges as well as the average number of slaves owned across the study population, must be viewed as a rough assessment. In 1860 in the South, there were 385,000 slave owners and 4 million slaves, or an average of about 10 slaves per owner, as compared with an average of 11 in this study's divorcing families. See Stampp, *Peculiar Institution*, 30.

31. Among the 87 families in the first category (men accused of adultery with their own slaves or other slaves), 75 possessed slaves, and in 66 cases the number of slaves could be determined. Among the 111 families in the second category (men accused of adultery with white women or white and/or black women), 103 were slave owners, and in 95 cases the number of slaves could be determined. Of course, it is probable that, in the contemporary southern culture, some wives accepted without complaint their husbands' "colored families" or ignored their spouses' sexual advances toward black women, viewing their husbands' adultery with other white women as more of a threat to their marriage, thus somewhat skewing the study's statistics; yet the evidence here still suggests that adultery by white men with white women was commonplace, at least as revealed in divorce and alimony cases.

32. Isenberg, *Sex and Citizenship in Antebellum America*, 127; Jabour, *Scarlett's Sisters*, 91.

33. See n. 1 above.

34. USMSPC, Brazoria County, Texas, 1860, p. 78; USMSSC, Brazoria County, Texas, 1860, p. 61; Brazoria County Probate Index thru 1900, http://www.texasgen.org/ (19 August 2010). The $107,875 in 1860 would be the equivalent of about $2,585,952 today. See: http://www.westegg.com/inflation/infl.cgi/ (21 December 2011).

Chapter 3

1. Petition of Lydia Rawdon (also spelled Rardon, Rhoden, and Rowden) and William M. McPherson to the Chancery Court of Talladega County, Alabama,

5 June 1854, in Records of the Circuit Court, Records, 1856–57, 9:230–36, *Lydia Rawdon and William M. McPherson v. Isaac Rawdon*, Talladega County Judicial Building, Talladega, Ala.; Related Documents: Affidavit, John Morgan, 5 June 1854; Order for Publication and Posting, 5 June 1854; Certification of Publication and Posting, 24 July 1854, with ibid., granted pro confesso, PAR #20185403. In the 1840 census, the son was listed as being between ten and fifteen. In her 1854 petition, Lydia said he had "grown almost to manhood" although he was in his twenties. The father, Isaac, was not listed in either the 1850 or 1860 returns; see USMSPC, Talladega County, Alabama, Northern District, 1840, p. 276. See also *Reports of Cases Argued and Determined in the Supreme Court of Alabama*, 565–67; Catterall, *Judicial Cases Concerning American Slavery*, 3:209.

2. In 1852, the Alabama Insane Hospital, a large, four-story facility, opened in nearby Tuscaloosa. Lydia could have had Isaac committed there but chose an asylum in another state. See Cooledge, "[Samuel] Sloan Check List"; Yanni, "Linear Plan for Insane Asylums," 33; Petition of Lydia Rawdon and William M. McPherson to the Chancery Court of Talladega County, Alabama, 5 June 1854, in n. 1 above; Related Documents: Consent to be Guardian ad litem, Robert Chapman, 20 December 1854; Copies of Decretal Order, 23 December 1854; Answer, R. H. Chapman, Guardian ad litem, 23 December 1854, with ibid., granted, PAR #20185404; Petition of Thomas Rawdon to the Chancery Court of Talladega County, Alabama, 28 February 1855 (Isaac's brother asked that Lydia provide an account of her financial activities and that the court appoint a "Committee or Guardian for the estate"); Related Documents: Deposition, John P. Rawdon, 17 January 1855; Agreement of Counsel, 1855; Order, 2 March 1855; Memorandum, Testimony in Trial, 3 March 1855; Decree, 9 April 1855; Affirmed by Supreme Court, 10 March 1856; Notice of Reference, 12 June 1856; Notice of Execution of Reference, 12 September 1856; Report of Register, 10 January 1857, with ibid., dismissed, appealed, affirmed, PAR #20185530. In 1840, Isaac Rawdon, in his forties, headed a household consisting of a boy between the ages of ten and fifteen, a woman in her thirties, and seven slaves; see USMSPC, Talladega County, Alabama, Northern District, 1840, p. 276.

3. Hartog, *Man and Wife in America*, 1–5; Edwards, *People and Their Peace*, 169–72; Pascoe, *What Comes Naturally*; Welke, *Law and the Borders of Belonging in the Long Nineteenth Century*. As mentioned in the Preface, some husbands and wives simply went their separate ways, what some authors have termed "self-divorce," moving to a different state, even remarrying without a legal divorce. These cases rarely found their way into the courts. See Basch, "Marriage and Domestic Relations," 255–56; Hartog, "Marital Exits and Marital Expectations," 122–23; Edwards, "Law, Domestic Violence, and the Limits of Patriarchal Authority," 768. For desertion, see O'Hear, "'Some of the Most Embarrassing Questions,'" 1512; Feigenson, "Extraterritorial Recognition of Divorce," 119, 123.

4. For the difficulties of diagnosing various diseases, see Stowe, *Doctoring the South*, 148.

5. Savitt, *Medicine and Slavery*, 245–51; Petition of Nancy Rowe to the Chancery Court of Washington County, Tennessee, 22 March 1838, in Washington County Court Records, Chancery Court, *Nancy Rowe v. Thomas Rowe, Lorenzo D. Rowe*,

Samuel L. Rowe, John L. Rowe, and Gilliad Rowe, AAETSU; Related Documents: Order, 22 March 1838, with ibid., partially granted, PAR #21483803.

6. Petition of Madison Taylor to the Chancery Court of Davidson County, Tennessee, 16 January 1857, in Records of the Chancery Court, Case Files, *Madison Taylor v. Nancy P. Taylor, Espy Taylor, and L. K. Spain*, Case #1757, Metropolitan Nashville–Davidson County Archives; Related Documents: Order, 15 January 1857; Answer, Nancy P. Taylor, 5 May 1857 (information taken from the answer); Decree, 5 December 1857, with ibid., partially granted, settled, PAR #21485703; USMSPC, Davidson County, Tennessee, Nashville, 1850, p. 142, and Nashville, Fifth Ward, 1860, p. 417; USMSSC, Davidson County, Tennessee, Nashville, Fifth Ward, 1860, p. 254.

7. Petition of Elizabeth Mary Cole, John M. Fraser, Samuel Fraser Cole, and Mary Louisa Fraser Cole to the Equity Court of Charleston District, South Carolina, 16 September 1817, in Records of the Equity Court, Bills, *Elizabeth Mary Cole, John M. Fraser, Samuel Fraser Cole, and Mary Louisa Fraser Cole v. Richard Cole*, SCDAH; Related Documents: Court Record, 29 September 1817; Summons, Richard Cole, 16 September 1817; Depositions, C. C. Chitty, J. M. Fraser, ca. 29 September 1817, with ibid., partially granted, PAR #21381717; Petition of Rebecca Looney to the Circuit Court of Fayette County, Kentucky, 20 September 1810, in Records of the Circuit Court, Case Files, *Rebecca Looney v. Robert Looney*, KDLA, no decree with petition, PAR #20781007; Petition of Rebecca Looney to the Chancery Court of Fayette County, Kentucky, 17 March 1812, in Records of the Circuit Court, Case Files, *Rebecca Looney v. Robert Looney and John Edwards*, KDLA; Related Documents: Amended Bill, 21 March 1812; Bill of Exceptions, 22 March 1812; Affidavit, Absolom Bainbridge, ca. 1812, with ibid. ("strongly diseased"), no decree with petition, PAR #20781208.

8. Petition of Elizabeth D. Lyon and Asbury Kent to the Chancery Court of Davidson County, Tennessee, 15 June 1855, in Records of the Chancery Court, Case Files, *Elizabeth D. Lyon and Asbury Kent v. James M. Lyon*, Case #1421, Metropolitan Nashville–Davidson County Archives; Related Documents: Order, 15 June 1855; Pledge for Security, R. McLain, 15 June 1855; Decree, 22 June 1855, with ibid., granted, PAR #21485529. The family had migrated to Tennessee from Ohio. In 1840, James M. Lyon, in his thirties, headed a family in Cincinnati consisting of a woman in her twenties and four girls under ten; see USMSPC, Hamilton County, Ohio, Cincinnati, First Ward, 1840, p. 44.

9. Petition of Sarah H. Claffey and James Calloway to the Chancery Court of Tallapoosa County, Alabama, 30 September 1848, *Sarah H. Claffey and James Calloway v. Matthew Claffey*, in Records of the Circuit Court, Minutes and Decrees, Chancery Court, 1848–52, pp. 262–71, CCH, Dadeville, Ala.; Related Documents: Copies of Order, 2 October 1848; Subpoenas, 30 October 1848; Bond, 9 October 1848; Amendment to Bill, April 1849; Rules of Register and Master, 2 April, 7, 19 May 1849; Interrogatories, 8 May 1849; Deposition, Mary Ann R. Calloway, 22 May 1849; Decree, 29 May 1849, with ibid., granted, PAR #20184821; Petition of Victoria C. Smith Clement and John Anthony Smith to the Circuit Court of Franklin County, Virginia, 1 September 1859, in Chancery Court Papers, *Victoria Smith Clement and John Anthony Smith v. James R. Clement*, LV; Related Documents: Order, 31 Au-

gust 1859; Statement, James R. Clement, 20 September 1859, with ibid., partially granted, PAR #21685914. See also Petition of Fanny Caldwell and George F. Everett to the Chancery Court of Maury County, Tennessee, 4 April 1859, in Records of the Chancery Court, Case Files, *Fanny Caldwell and George F. Everett v. David A. Caldwell*, Maury County Archives, Columbia, Tenn.; Related Documents: Deposition, Hugh C. Harrison, 28 March 1860; Amended Petition, ca. March 1860; Order, 19 September 1867, with ibid., granted pro confesso, PAR #21485948.

10. Petition of Martha Weeks and Sarah Pennington to the Circuit Superior Court of Petersburg, Virginia, May 1837, in Records of the Circuit Superior Court of Chancery, *Martha Weeks and Sarah Pennington v. William Weeks*, Drawer 31–34, CCCO, Petersburg, Va.; Related Documents: Court Record, June 1837; Commissioners' Reports, 1 August 1837, 26 November 1838, with ibid., granted, PAR #21683716; Howard, *History of Matrimonial Institutions*, 3:31–33 (information on Maryland).

11. McCandless, *Moonlight, Magnolias, and Madness*, 166–67, 195–96; Grob, *Mad among Us*, 84–85; Cahow, *People, Patients, and Politics*, 23 ("unbending Providence").

12. Petition of Eveline B. Fort and Eveline Fort to the Superior Court of Wayne County, North Carolina, 27 February 1856, in Wayne County Divorce Records, *Eveline B. Fort and Eveline Fort v. William B. Fort*, NCSA; Related Documents: Oath, 27 February 1856; Copy of Order, Fall Term 1856, with ibid., no decree with petition, PAR #21285635; Petition of Mary Owen and J. W. Cowan to the Chancery Court of Williamson County, Tennessee, 10 March 1859, in Records of the Chancery Court, *Mary Owen and J. W. Cowan v. Everett Owen, Joshua W. Owen, and John Owen*, Williamson County Archives, Franklin, Tenn.; Related Documents: Acknowledgment of Security, L. H. Moseley, 10 March 1859, with ibid., no decree with petition, PAR #21485910; Petition of Mary J'On Kinloch, Thomas L. Kinloch, Martha Kinloch, Cleland Kinloch, and Thomas Lowndes to the Equity Court of Charleston District, South Carolina, 28 August 1826, in Records of the Equity Court, Bills, *Mary J'On Kinloch, Thomas L. Kinloch, Martha Kinloch, Cleland Kinloch, and Thomas Lowndes v. Jacob Bond J'On, Frederick Kinloch, Francis Kinloch, Henry A. Middleton, Harriet Middleton, and Charles Mayrant*, SCDAH, no decree with petition, PAR #21382616. In 1820, Frederick Kinloch, between sixteen and twenty-six, headed a household with his wife in the same age grouping as the only other household member. He possessed sixty slaves. See USMSPC, Georgetown District, South Carolina, Santee, 1820, p. 72.

13. Petition of John M. Smith to the Chancery Court of Williamson County, Tennessee, 26 May 1853, in Records of the Chancery Court, Record Book, 18:487–501, *John M. Smith v. Martha E. Smith, Nathan O. McAdams, and Hiram H. Holt*, CCH, Franklin, Tenn.; Related Documents: Answer, Martha E. Smith, 1 June 1853; Cross Bill, Martha E. Smith, 20 December 1853; Answer, John Smith, 17 June 1854; Order, 3 October 1854; Decree, 5 October 1854, with ibid. (cut out the heart), dismissed, cross bill granted, PAR #21485335; Petition of Jane E. Owen and Samuel F. Bittick to the Chancery Court of Williamson County, Tennessee, 28 June 1837, in Records

of the Chancery Court, *Jane E. Owen and Samuel F. Bittick v. Sterling Owen*, Williamson County Archives, CCH, Franklin, Tenn.; Related Documents: Order, 28 June 1837; Supplemental Bill, 16 July 1837; Order, 14 July 1837; Answer, Sterling Owen, 25 October 1837; Account of Trust, ca. 1839; Copy of Petition, 28 June 1837; Petition of Sterling Owen, 21 February 1838; Writ of Habeas Corpus, 22 February 1838; Sheriff's Report, 23 February 1838; Indictment for Assault, *State of Tennessee vs. Sterling Owen*, 12 July 1837; Affidavit, Dr. F. T. Reid, 15 March 1838, with ibid., partially granted, PAR #21483703. For a similar case, see Petition of Ellen A. Field and George S. Hayes to the Circuit Court of Mecklenburg County, Virginia, August 1859, in Chancery Court Causes, *Ellen A. Field and George S. Hayes v. James Wistar Field*, LV; Related Documents: Copy of Decree, September Term 1868; Affidavit, T. F. Goode, 28 June 1866, with ibid., granted, PAR #21685903.

14. Petition of Catharine Lowry and Simon Cary to the Equity Court of Newberry District, South Carolina, 1 February 1819, in Records of the Equity Court, Bills, *Catharine Lowry and Simon Cary v. Johnston Lowry*, Case #1822-12, SCDAH; Related Documents: Order, 15 February 1819; Joint Answer, James Kincaid and William Huston, 25 February 1822, with ibid., granted pro confesso, PAR #21381918.

15. Rorabaugh, *Alcoholic Republic*, ix; Bernard, "American Drinking Tradition"; Lender and Martin, *Drinking in America*, 46–47; Dabney, *Mountain Spirits*; Tyrrell, "Drink and Temperance in the Antebellum South."

16. Johnson, *Ante-Bellum North Carolina*, 169; Dougan, "Arkansas Married Woman's Property Law," 15 (Mississippi and Arkansas laws); Petition of John Jones, Gaines F. Fletcher, Charles Ready, John Leiper, and R. G. Ellis to the Tennessee General Assembly, Rutherford County, 19 December 1849, in LP, TSLA, no act with petition, PAR #11484904; Petition of David B. Taylor, William B. Chowning, B. F. Brown, et al., to the County Court of Westmoreland County, Virginia, May 1855, in County Court Papers, LV, no decree with petition, PAR #21685521; Petition of the Citizens of Charleston Neck to the South Carolina General Assembly, 1840, in Records of the General Assembly, Document #ND-#2125, SCDAH; Related Document: "A Bill For the better Regulation of the Commissioners of Cross Roads for Charleston Neck," n.d., sponsored by James Smith Rhett, Christ Church Parish, with ibid., referred to Judicial Committee, PAR #11384012.

17. Petition of Mary Jane Horn Clinard to the Chancery Court of Davidson County, Tennessee, 13 January 1853, in Records of the Chancery Court, Case Files, *Mary Jane Horn Clinard v. Henderson Clinard*, Case #956, Metropolitan Nashville–Davidson County Archives; Related Documents: Order, 12 January 1853; Pledge for Security, 13 January 1853; Order, 24 May 1853; Sheriff's Statement, 19 June 1854; Sheriff's Return, 26 June 1854; Decree, 5 May 1854, with ibid., granted, PAR #21485329; Petition of Penelope Smith to the Equity Court of Wayne County, North Carolina, 19 August 1854, in Records of the County Court, *Penelope Smith v. William B. Smith*, NCSA; Related Documents: Order, 23 August 1854, with ibid., granted, PAR #21285434; Petition of Ann Rebecca Watson and Samuel Williams to the Equity Court of Barnwell District, South Carolina, 24 December 1855, in Records of the Equity Court, Bills, *Ann Rebecca Watson and Samuel Williams v.*

Arthur Watson, SCDAH; Related Documents: Order, 13 February 1856; Court Record Concerning the Death of Watson's Next Friend, Samuel Williams, 3 February 1858, with ibid., granted pro confesso, PAR #21385519.

18. Petition of Elizabeth Anderson Covington to the Chancery Court of Maury County, Tennessee, 24 June 1855, in Records of the Chancery Court, Case Files, *Elizabeth Anderson Covington v. Eldrige A. Covington*, Maury County Archives, Columbia, Tenn.; Related Documents: Order, 25 June 1855; Supplemental Petition, 16 July 1855; Order, 16 July 1855; Decree, 22 September 1855, with ibid., granted, PAR #21485532.

19. Petition of Emily Cornelius and Robert True to the Chancery Court of Madison County, Alabama, 31 August 1852, in Records of the Chancery Court, Chancery Records, 1857, Book C-24-26, pp. 605–18, *Emily Cornelius and Robert True v. William Cornelius*, Madison County Public Library Archives, Huntsville, Ala.; Related Documents: Copies of Schedule A—Inventory of Land and Slaves, William Cornelius, 1852; Summons, William Cornelius, 1 September 1852; Answer, William Cornelius, 1852; Orders, 3 December 1852, 30 May 1853, 1 February, 7 December 1854, 8 June 1855; Final Decree, 9 June 1855; Complainant's Exceptions, June 1855; Defendant's Exceptions, June 1855; Appeal Bond, 29 June 1855; Decree, Alabama Supreme Court, 8 January 1858. See also Copy of Bill of Complaint, Emily Cornelius, 1 August 1852, and related documents, in Alabama Supreme Court, Cases, *Cornelius v. Cornelius*, vol. 221, January 1858, pp. 1–8, 88–89, ADAH, partially granted, appealed, PAR #20185204; Censer, "'Smiling through Her Tears,'" 44–45.

20. Petition of Louisa Word and Jacob Everly to the Pleas and Quarter Sessions Court of Williamson County, Tennessee, April 1832, in Records of the County Court, *Louisa Word and Jacob Everly v. America Word*, Williamson County Archives, Franklin, Tenn.; Related Documents: Guardian's Account for January 1830, 5 July 1831; Decree, 13 April 1832, with ibid., granted, PAR #21483210; Petition of Mary A. Murphy and John Mills to the Circuit Superior Court of Halifax County, Virginia, 25 February 1846, in Records of the Circuit Superior Court of Chancery, Finals, *Mary A. Murphy and John Mills v. James Murphy*, Halifax Circuit Court Building, Halifax, Va.; Related Documents: Decree, ca. 1846, with ibid., partially granted, PAR #21684614; Petition of Judith Word and Andrew B. Ewing to the Circuit Court of Williamson County, Tennessee, 12 January 1836, in Records of the County Court, *Judith Word and Andrew B. Ewing v. Thomas H. Word*, Williamson County Archives, Franklin, Tenn.; Related Documents: Order, 11 January 1836; Acknowledgment of Security, John Marshall, 12 January 1836; Decree, 7 April 1836, with ibid., granted, PAR #21483606; Petition of Ann West to the Superior Court of Rowan County, North Carolina, 1835, in County Court Divorce Records, *Ann West v. Thomas West*, NCSA; Related Documents: Decree, Fall Term 1835, with ibid., granted, PAR #21283502; Petition of Eleanor Morgan to the Circuit Court of Floyd County, Kentucky, 9 November 1837, in Records of the Circuit Court, Case Files, *Eleanor Morgan v. David Morgan, Susan Morgan, Ann Morgan, Thomas Morgan, Rebecca Morgan, Eleanor Morgan, and David Morgan*, Case #61, KDLA; Related Documents: Answer, Susan, Ann, Thomas, Rebecca, Eleanor, and David Morgan, ca. 1837; Answer, David Morgan, ca. 1837; Decree, 17 August 1838, with ibid., granted, PAR #20783721.

21. Petition of Elizabeth Anderson Covington to the Chancery Court of Maury County, Tennessee, 24 June 1855, in Records of the Chancery Court, Case Files, *Elizabeth Anderson Covington v. Eldrige A. Covington*, Maury County Archives, Columbia, Tenn.; Related Documents: Order, 25 June 1855; Supplemental Petition, 16 July 1855; Order, 16 July 1855; Decree, 22 September 1855, with ibid. (grog shop), granted, PAR #21485532; Petition of Margaret A. Winn and Romulus W. Moore to the Chancery Court of Perry County, Alabama, 27 December 1860, in Records of the Chancery Court, Case Papers, *Margaret A. Winn and Romulus W. Moore v. Pyramus Winn*, ADAH; Related Documents: Copies of Deposition, Thomas C. Hill, 14 February 1862; Decretal Order, August 1861; Decretal Order, n.d., with ibid., no decree with petition, PAR #20186029. At the divorce hearing it was revealed that Winn, despite being "considerably intoxicated," performed an operation on a black woman who was delivering a child.

22. In addition to the five states cited in Censer ("'Smiling through Her Tears,'" 28 n. 12), Missouri passed similar legislation in 1845; see *Revised Statutes of the State of Missouri*, 426–29.

23. Quoted in Oakes, *Ruling Race*, 77 ("Alabama fever"), 79 ("the entire population").

24. Johnson, *Ante-Bellum North Carolina*, 221 ("eloped to the Louisiana country"); Petition of Betsy Caldwell to the County Court of Rowan County, North Carolina, 27 September 1803, in County Court Divorce Records, *Betsy Caldwell v. Thomas Caldwell*, NCSA; Related Documents: Depositions, Archibald Cathey, Andrew Hannah, Henry Conner, Adam Brevard, 29 July 1805, with ibid., no decree with petition, PAR #21280301; Petition of Mary Strode and George Harrison to the Circuit Court of Boone County, Missouri, 11 February 1824, in Records of the Circuit Court, *Mary Strode and George Harrison v. Stephen Strode*, Case #75, MoSA; Related Documents: Affidavit, Nathaniel Potter, 9 October 1824; Newspaper Notice, Mary Strode v. Stephen Strode, June Term 1824; Order, ca. June Term 1824; Summons, Stephen Strode, 21 July 1824; Sheriff's Return, 9 October 1824; Decree, 13 October 1824; Summons, Stephen Strode, 25 March 1824; Sheriff's Return, 4 May 1824, with ibid., granted, PAR #21182405.

25. *Statute Law of Kentucky*, 4:19–20; *Acts Passed at the Second Session of the General Assembly of the State of Alabama*, 79; *Maryland Code*, 75–77 (1842 law); *Digest of the Laws of Virginia of a Civil Nature and of a Permanent Character*, 588–94 (abandonment for five years, passed in 1852–53). See also *Laws of the State of Delaware*, 148–50; Censer, "'Smiling through Her Tears,'" 28 n. 12.

26. Petition of Sophia Swales to the Chancery Court of Bedford County, Tennessee, 16 October 1847, Records of the Chancery Court, vol. D, pp. 699, 701, *Sophia Swales v. John Swales*, CCH, Shelbyville, Tenn., no decree with petition, PAR #21484701; Petition of Betsy Watts to the Circuit Court of Barren County, Kentucky, 1824, in Records of the Circuit Court, Equity Judgments, Microfilm Reel #209796, *Betsy Watts v. David Watts*, Case #245, KDLA; Related Documents: Deposition, George Richardson, 10 September 1824; Newspaper Publication, ca. March 1824; Signed Statement, Terence Cooney, 20 June 1824, with ibid., no decree with petition, PAR #20782408; Petition of Hannah Neil and William Walker to the

Equity Court of Chester District, South Carolina, 30 October 1845, in Records of the Equity Court, Bills, *Hannah Neil and William Walker v. Benjamin Neil*, Case #1845-199, SCDAH; Related Documents: Order, 30 October 1845, with ibid., granted, PAR #21384519.

27. Petition of Melinda McCalla and Philander Moore to the Chancery Court of Chester District, South Carolina, 24 December 1833, in Records of the Equity Court, Bills, *Melinda McCalla and Philander Moore v. James McCalla*, Case #1833-99, SCDAH; Related Documents: Order, 24 December 1833; Affidavit, Philander Moore, 24 December 1833, with ibid., partially granted, PAR #21383315. For the husband's slaveholdings, see USMSPC, Chester District, South Carolina, 1810, p. 275; 1820, p. 57; and 1830, p. 339; Petition of Misella Ann Henry and Martin O. Hopkins to the Chancery Court of Claiborne County, Mississippi, 25 December 1850, in Records of the Vice Chancery Court, *Misella Ann Henry and Martin O. Hopkins v. Oliver C. Henry*, Case #606, CCH, Natchez, Miss.; Related Documents: Final Decree, 2 January 1852, with ibid., granted, PAR #21085031; Petition of Rebecca E. Askew Hair and William Butler Matheny to the Equity Court of Barnwell District, South Carolina, 7 October 1857, in Records of the Equity Court, Bills, Microfilm Reel BW85, frames 651–55, *Rebecca Askew Hair and William Butler Matheny v. Irvine R. Hair*, SCDAH; Related Documents: Answer, Irvine R. Hair, ca. 7 October 1857; Orders, ca. 7 October 1857, 8 October 1857, with ibid. (crops in the field), granted, PAR #21385776; Petition of Elizabeth McQueen to the Circuit Court of Lauderdale County, Mississippi, 22 May 1838, in Records of the Circuit Court, Case Files, *Elizabeth McQueen v. Peter McQueen*, Case #70, Lauderdale County Archives, Meridian, Miss.; Related Documents: Decree, May Term 1839; Order, July 1838; Commissioner's Report, 19 November 1838; Order and Copy of Orders, 27 August, 3 December 1838; Interrogatories, 18 August 1838; Deposition, Thomas P. C. Lott, 4 April 1839, with ibid., granted, PAR #21083805.

28. Petition of Mary E. Moore to the Superior Court of Nash County, North Carolina, 18 July 1861, in County Court Divorce Records, *Mary E. Moore v. Richard Moore*, NCSA; Related Documents: Order, 24 July 1861; Oath, Mary E. Moore, July 18, 1861; Writ of Sequestration, 2 August 1861, with ibid., partially granted, PAR #21286117; Petition of Elinor Hart and John Beaty to the County Court of Lincoln County, North Carolina, 10 August 1811, in County Court Divorce Records, *Elinor Hart and John Beaty v. William Hart and Andrew Hart*, NCSA, no decree with petition, PAR #21281101. Most deserted women received favorable rulings from the courts. See Petition of Mary Ann Shackleford to the Superior Court of Guilford County, North Carolina, 15 September 1859, in County Court Divorce Records, *Mary Ann Shackleford v. Armsted Shackleford*, NCSA; Related Documents: Order, Fall Term 1860, with ibid., granted, PAR #21285918; Petition of Laticia Henry Henley and Beverly W. Henry to the Chancery Court of Davidson County, Tennessee, 28 February 1856, in Records of the Chancery Court, Case Files, *Laticia Henry Henley and Beverly W. Henry v. Richard L. Henley*, Case #1574, Metropolitan Nashville–Davidson County Archives; Related Documents: Order, 28 February 1856, with ibid., partially granted, PAR #21485604; Petition of Nancy Summers to the Circuit Court of Barren County, Kentucky, 17 March 1812, in Records of the Circuit Court, Equity Judgments, *Nancy*

Summers v. John Summers, Case #15, KDLA; Related Documents: Amended Bill, 15 February 1813; Order, 15 February 1813; Depositions, Henry Bishong, Adron Lane, Sarah Lane, William Johnson, and Mathew Campbell, 4 March 1813; Decree, ca. 1812, with ibid., granted, PAR #20781204.

29. O'Hear, "'Some of the Most Embarrassing Questions,'" 1512, 1514, 1519; Feigenson, "Extraterritorial Recognition of Divorce," 119. For filing in a different state, see Petition of Susan Bryan and Michael Dunn to the Circuit Superior Court of Petersburg, Virginia, 12 November 1846, in Records of the Circuit Superior Court of Chancery, Drawer 83–85, *Susan Bryan and Michael Dunn v. Thomas Bryan*, CCCO, Petersburg, Va.; Related Documents: Supplemental Petition, 28 November 1846; Decree, ca. November 1846, with ibid., partially granted, PAR #21684617; Petition of Sarah Johnson to the North Carolina General Assembly, 29 November 1805, in General Assembly, Session Records, Divorce Petitions, November–December 1805, *Sarah Johnson v. John L. D. Johnson*, NCSA, rejected, PAR #11280504. For a search with children in tow, see Petition of Frances S. Harris to the District Court of St. Landry Parish, Louisiana, 1 April 1830, in Records of the Fifth Judicial District Court, *Frances S. Harris v. Gowin Harris*, Case #1662, PCH, Opelousas, La.; Related Documents: Copy of Supplemental Petition, 2 April 1830; Order, 2 April 1830; Sheriff's Report, 3 April 1830; Judgment, 8 June 1831, with ibid., granted, PAR #20883008.

30. Petition of Betsy Watts to the Circuit Court of Barren County, Kentucky, 1824, in Records of the Circuit Court, Equity Judgments, Microfilm Reel #209796, *Betsy Watts v. David Watts*, Case #245, KDLA; Related Documents: Deposition, George Richardson, 10 September 1824; Newspaper Publication, ca. March 1824; Signed Statement, Terence Cooney, 20 June 1824, with ibid., no decree with petition, PAR #20782408; Petition of Hannah Neil and William Walker to the Equity Court of Chester District, South Carolina, 30 October 1845, in Records of the Equity Court, Bills, *Hannah Neil and William Walker v. Benjamin Neil*, Microfilm Reel CS75, frames 333–37, 340, Case #1845-199, SCDAH; Related Documents: Order, 30 October 1845, with ibid., granted, PAR #21384519; Petition of Penelope Gardner Parker to the Chancery Court of Southampton County, Virginia, 21 January 1806, in Chancery Court Papers, Oversized, *Penelope Parker v. Ivy Parker, John Lee, Josiah Murdough, James Harrison, Hardy Cobb, Theophilus Daughtrey, and Henry Gardner*, Case #10-1806, LV; Related Documents: Order, ca. 21 January 1806; Answer, Henry Gardner, ca. 21 January 1806; Summons, Ivy Parker, 21 January 1806, with ibid., granted, PAR #21680606.

31. Brearley, "Pattern of Violence," 685–88; Owsley, *Plain Folk of the Old South*, 117–18; Wilbur Cash, *The Mind of the South* (New York: Knopf, 1941; reprint, Garden City, N.Y.: Doubleday Anchor, 1956), 34–35; Franklin, *Militant South*, 36–37; Wyatt-Brown, *Southern Honor*, 252–61; Wyatt-Brown, *Honor and Violence in the Old South*, 144–53; Ayers, *Vengeance and Justice*, 9–33. For domestic violence, see Baptist, "'My Mind Is to Drown You and Leave You Behind'"; Whitman, "'I have Got the Gun and Will Do As I Please with Her'"; Edwards, "Law, Domestic Violence, and the Limits of Patriarchal Authority," 738 n. 8; Edwards *People and Their Peace*, 74; Gross, *Double Character*, 51, 52, 116–17.

32. For the wording in various statutes, see *Statute Laws of the State of Tennessee, of a Public and General Nature*, 1:74–76; *Revised Statutes of Kentucky*, 389–93; *Digest of the Laws of Virginia, Which Are of a Permanent Character and General Operation*, 287–89; Johnson, *Ante-Bellum North Carolina*, 218. See also Petition of Beulah Huzza to the Superior Court of Guilford County, North Carolina, 24 March 1851, in County Court Divorce Records, *Beulah Huzza v. William Huzza*, Case #42, NCSA, no decree with petition, PAR #21285115.

33. Griswold, "Evolution of the Doctrine of Mental Cruelty," 128–29. North Carolina and three other states, including Tennessee, Arkansas, and Texas, granted divorces on the grounds of cruelty without physical violence. See Censer, "'Smiling through Her Tears,'" 28.

34. Petition of Mary L. Heison and Stephen Horton to the Circuit Court of Sumter County, Alabama, 19 February 1849, in Records of the Circuit Court, Estates, *Mary L. Heison and Stephen Horton v. Ferdinand Heison*, Case #316, CCH, Livingston, Ala.; Related Documents: Order, 20 February 1849; Decree, 2 March 1849, with ibid. ("half dozen severe and heavy blows"), agreement, PAR #20184906; Petition of Matilda Roach Kingston to the Chancery Court of Davidson County, Tennessee, 14 July 1846, in Records of the Chancery Court, Case Files, *Matilda Roach Kingston v. William Kingston, Martin Forehand, and William Cummings*, Case #54, Metropolitan Nashville–Davidson County Archives; Related Documents: Pledge of Security, L. W. Roach, ca. 20 July 1846, with ibid., no decree with petition, PAR #21484612; USMSPC, Davidson County, Tennessee, Middle District, 1840, p. 348; Petition of Mary Davis to the Superior Court of Coweta County, Georgia, 1843, in Records of the Superior Court, Writs, 1839–49, pp. 124–27, *Mary Davis v. William J. Davis*, CCH, Newnan, Ga.; Related Documents: Summons, William J. Davis, 13 December 1843; Schedule of Property, William J. Davis, 25 November 1843; Affidavit, Mary Davis, 13 December 1843; Sheriff's Return, 13 December 1843; Jury Verdict, ca. 1844; Court Record, ca. 1844, with ibid., granted, PAR #20684310.

35. Petition of Jane McKee and Alvis J. Riggs to the Circuit Court of Maury County, Tennessee, 28 April 1829, in Records of the Chancery Court, Case Files, *Jane McKee and Alvis J. Riggs v. William McKee*, CCH, Columbia, Tenn.; Related Documents: Order, 28 April 1829; Bond, William D. Ray, 28 April 1829, with ibid., partially granted, PAR #21482905; Petition of Misella Ann Henry and Martin O. Hopkins to the Chancery Court of Claiborne County, Mississippi, in n. 27 above; Petition of Mary Logue to the Tennessee General Assembly, 8 September 1821, in LP, TSLA; Related Documents: List of Subscribers, ca. 1821, with ibid., no act with petition, PAR #11482109.

36. Petition of Rebecca Boyd Dean and J. H. Baker to the Chancery Court of Laurens District, South Carolina, 4 February 1858, in Records of the Equity Court, Bills, *Rebecca Boyd Dean and J. H. Baker v. Walter D. A. Dean*, Case #1858-20, SCDAH; Related Documents: Depositions, A. Dribble, Sheriff W. Arnold, W. B. Veerdesin, Robert Vance, ca. 4 February 1858, J. W. B. Deen [Dean], 4 February 1858, with ibid., no decree with petition, PAR #21385839; USMSPC, Laurens District, South Carolina, 1830, p. 235; 1840, p. 13; and 1850, p. 240; USMSSC, Laurens District, South Carolina, 1850, p. 857; Petition of Elizabeth Rogers Collins to the District Court

of St. Landry Parish, Louisiana, 29 June 1832, in Records of the Fifth Judicial District Court, *Elizabeth Collins v. William Collins*, Case #1967, PCH, Opelousas, La.; Related Documents: Answer and Countersuit, ca. 1832; Interrogatories, ca. 1832; Judgment, 3 June 1835, with ibid., partially granted, PAR #20883209; Petition of Elizabeth Wilkinson and James Wilkinson to the Chancery Court of Sussex County, Virginia, November 1796, in County Court Papers, Microfilm Reel 120, frames 542, 547–49, *Elizabeth Wilkinson and James Wilkinson v. William Wilkinson*, LV; Related Documents: Court Record, November 1796–August 1797; Deposition, Betty Wilkerson [Wilkinson], 2 November 1796, with ibid., granted, PAR #21679606.

37. Petition of Augusta A. Jeter and David Johnson to the Equity Court of Union District, South Carolina, 13 August 1830, in Records of the Equity Court, Bills, *Augusta A. Jeter and David Johnson v. Richard Jeter*, Case #1831-198, SCDAH; Related Documents: Statement, David Johnson, 14 August 1830; Order, 13 August 1830, with ibid., partially granted, granted pro confesso, PAR #21383020.

38. Schweninger, "Vass Slaves," 481; Petition of Sarah L. Vass Womack and Daniel F. Morris to the Circuit Superior Court of Halifax County, Virginia, 7 March 1841, in LP, Halifax County, 1 March 1848, *Sarah L. Vass Womack and Daniel F. Morris v. Edward Womack*, LV; Related Documents: Copy of Answer, Edward Womack, 12 April 1841; Copy of Deposition, Mary C. Carlton, 17 July 1841; Depositions, Isaac Medley, John S. Lewellen, 4 September 1841; Court Record, 1 March 1848, with ibid., no decree with petition, PAR #21684125. For a similar complaint, see Petition of Louisa Holmes to the Equity Court of Charles County, Maryland, 12 August 1842, in SC, *Louisa Holmes v. William Holmes Sr.*, Case #339, MSA; Related Documents: Supplemental Petition, Louisa Holmes, 19 August 1842; Deposition, Washington A. Posey, 24 August 1842; Order, 25 August 1842; Voucher, William Holmes to George Brent, 26 August 1842; Affidavit, Edward Adams, 28 November 1842; Order, 28 November 1842; Deposition, Washington A. Posey, 6 March 1843; Deposition, Eleanor Holmes, 15 March 1843; Decree, 1 November 1844; Auditor's Report, Accounts of Louisa and William Holmes, ca. November 1844, with ibid., granted, PAR #20984202.

39. Petition of Elizabeth McMickins and John Cooper to the Superior Court of Wilkes County, Georgia, 1821, in Records of the Superior Court, Record Book, 1822–23, pp. 142–44, *Elizabeth McMickins and John Cooper v. Nathaniel McMickins*, CCH, Washington, Ga.; Related Documents: Subpoena, Nathaniel McMickins, 15 August 1821; Sheriff's Return, 17 August 1821; Jury Verdict, 23 July 1822; Order, ca. 1822, with ibid., granted, PAR #20682119; Petition of Rebecca Wood to the Superior Court of Davidson County, North Carolina, 18 February 1843, in Records of the County Court, *Rebecca Wood v. Lorenzo D. Wood*, NCSA; Related Documents: Order, 18 February 1843; Opinion, Supreme Court of North Carolina, June Term 1845, with ibid., granted, appealed, reversed and dismissed, PAR #21284306.

40. For typical arrest cases, see Petition of Rosannah McClelland Moore and John McClelland to the Equity Court of Washington District, South Carolina, 5 January 1816, in Records of the Equity Court, Bills, *Rosannah McClelland Moore and John McClelland v. James Moore*, Case #1816-1, SCDAH; Related Documents: Order, 5 January 1816, with ibid., partially granted, PAR #21381616; Petition of

Abigail Carpenter to the Superior Court of Wake County, North Carolina, 13 April 1855, in County Court Divorce Records, *Abigail Carpenter v. James Carpenter*, NCSA; Related Documents: Oath, Abigail Carpenter, 13 April 1855; Deposition, Mary Ford, ca. 1855, with ibid., granted, PAR #21285506; Petition of Keziah Berryman and Keziah Scruggs to the Circuit Court of Williamson County, Tennessee, 23 October 1821, in Records of the County Court, *Keziah Berryman and Keziah Scruggs v. Anderson Berryman*, Williamson County Archives, Franklin, Tenn.; Related Documents: Order, 22 October 1821; Transcript of Record, *John W. Pope v. Anderson Berryman*, 18 January 1822; Order, August 1821; Authorization to Release Anderson Berryman from Jail, Keziah Berryman, ca. October 1821, with ibid., partially granted, PAR #21482102. In 1820, Anderson Barriman [Berryman], over age 45, headed a household consisting of two boys under 10, a boy between 10 and 16, a male 16 to 18, a male 16 to 26, and a woman between 26 and 44. He possessed twenty-three slaves. See USMSPC, Williamson County, Tennessee, 1820, p. 357.

41. Petition of Elizabeth Mattison and Hamilton L. Eaton to the Equity Court of Anderson District, South Carolina, 22 May 1860, in Records of the Equity Court, Bills, *Elizabeth Stone Trussell Mattison and Hamilton L. Eaton v. Leroy W. Mattison and Jeptha F. Wilson*, Microfilm Order #27, Reel D1267, Box/Drawer 7, Document/Case #1860—303, SDAH; Related Documents: Order, 22 May 1860; Statement, Hamilton L. Eaton, 22 May 1860; Order, 25 June 1860; Decree (incomplete), 4 February 1861, with ibid., granted, referred to commissioners, PAR #21386043; Petition of Susan Sorey and Lemuel Butt to the Circuit Superior Court of Princess Anne County, Virginia, 25 May 1833, in Chancery Court Causes, *Susan Sorey and Lemuel Butt v. Nathaniel Sorey*, Case #7-1837, LV; Related Documents: Answer, Nathaniel Sorey, 4 September 1833; Copy of Decree, 28 May 1834; Court Record, April 1833–May 1837; Receipts, 1 September 1835, 9 November 1835, with ibid., granted, PAR #21683309. See also Petition of Sarah Trimble and James Cooke to the Chancery Court of Chambers County, Alabama, 1 March 1845, in Records of the Circuit Court, Record Book Middle Chancery District, 1841–53, pp. 260–70, *Sarah Trimble and James Cooke v. John Trimble*, CCH, Lafayette, Ala.; Related Documents: Order, 25 March 1845; Subpoena, 31 March 1845; Bond, 31 March 1845; Answer, John B. Trimble, 12 May 1845, with ibid., dismissed, PAR #20184505.

42. Alexis de Tocqueville, *Democracy in America*, ed. J. P. Mayer and Max Lerner (New York: Harper and Row, 1966), 319.

43. Petition of Cassandra Houston to the North Carolina General Assembly, Mecklenburg County, 22 November 1804, in General Assembly, Session Records, Divorce Petitions, November–December 1804, *Cassandra Houston v. James Houston*, NCSA; Related Documents: Testimony, Augustus Alexander, 10 November 1804; Depositions of Cassandra Houston, George Alexander, Augustus Alexander, Marshall Alexander, A. Alexander, Francis B. Smart, John McCullock, Jane Alexander, Paris Alexander, Thomas Greer, and George W. Smart, 19 October 1804, George W. Smart, 10 November 1804, with ibid., rejected, PAR #11280405. See also Petition of Cornelia J. Long and Claborne Gee to the Chancery Court of Maury County, Tennessee, 1845, in Records of the Chancery Court, Case Files, *Cornelia J. Long and Claborne Gee v. Nicholas J. Long*, Maury County Archives, Columbia, Tenn.; Related

Documents: Answer, Nicholas J. Long, 20 March 1845; Decree, March 1846, with ibid., dismissed, PAR #21484523; USMSPC, Maury County, Tennessee, Western District, 1830, p. 357, and Middle District, 1840, p. 327; Petition of Joseph Gresham to the Virginia General Assembly, James City, 10 December 1833, in LP, LV; Related Documents: Copy of Record of Superior Court, 14 November 1832, 25 October 1833, with ibid., rejected, PAR #11683312; Petition of Eli Manning and Winny Manning to the North Carolina General Assembly, Edgecombe County, 9 December 1805, in General Assembly, Session Records, Divorce Petitions, November–December 1805, NCSA, granted, PAR #11280516; Petition of Eliza Byrnes and James C. Perry to the Equity Court of Charleston District, South Carolina, 11 July 1835, in Records of the Equity Court, Bills, *Eliza Byrnes and James C. Perry v. John P. Byrnes*, Case #1835-11, SCDAH; Related Documents: Deposition (incomplete), James C. Perry, ca. 1835; Order, 11 July 1835, with ibid., partially granted, PAR #21383514.

44. Petition of Eveline M. Whetstone and William Ratcliff to the Chancery Court of Shelby County, Alabama, 27 August 1839, in Records of the Chancery Court, Record Book, 1839–41, pp. 363–67, *Eveline M. Whetstone and William Ratcliff v. Evans L. Whetstone*, Shelby County Archives, Columbiana, Ala.; Related Documents: Subpoena, Evans L. Whetstone, 29 August 1839; Order, August 1839; Second Order, February 1840; Order and Decree, February 1841, with ibid., granted, PAR #20183913; Petition of Harriet Bouldin to the Superior Court of Caswell County, North Carolina, 1842, in County Court Divorce Records, *Harriet Bouldin v. Edward C. Bouldin*, NCSA, no decree with petition, PAR #21284207; Petition of Martha Taylor and Meschech Battee to the Equity Court of Columbia District, South Carolina, 19 April 1824, in Records of the Equity Court, Bills, Richland District, *Martha Taylor and Meschech Battee v. Mary Taylor, Henry Taylor, and Needham Dudley*, SCDAH; Related Documents: Order, ca. 1824, with ibid., granted pro confesso, PAR #21382446; Petition of Ruth Fick to the Equity Court of Charleston District, South Carolina, 7 March 1825, in Records of the Equity Court, Bills, *Ruth Fick v. John Concklin*, Case #1825-14, SCDAH, no decree with petition, PAR #21382520.

45. Petition of Elizabeth Tinges to the Equity Court of Baltimore County, Maryland, 25 October 1843, in SC, *Elizabeth Tinges v. William Tinges*, Case #C333, MSA; Related Documents: Answer, William Tinges, 5 December 1843; Copy of Answer, William Tinges, 5 December 1843, with ibid., no decree with petition, PAR #20984302. Apparently he could easily pass as a white person. A census taker in 1840 listed him as white, in his forties, and the head of a family consisting of a white woman in her forties and a white boy and white girl in their teens; see USMSPC, Baltimore County, Maryland, 1840, p. 143.

46. Censer, "'Smiling through Her Tears,'" 27–28.

47. Ibid., 29; Petition of Susan Littleton and William Haynes to the Chancery Court of Williamson County, Tennessee, 26 February 1855, in Records of the Chancery Court, Record Book, 19:609–16, *Susan Littleton and William Haynes v. Joseph Littleton and Isaac G. Neely*, CCH, Franklin, Tenn.; Related Documents: Order, 24 February 1855; Answer, Joseph Lewis Littleton, 3 April 1855; Answer, Isaac G. Neely, 3 April 1855; Decrees, 9 April 1855, December Term 1855; Order, April Term 1856; Court Record, April Term 1857; Order, April Term 1858, with ibid., partially

granted, PAR #21485513; Petition of Flora L. Cheatham Ewing and Milton P. Wheat to the Chancery Court of Bedford County, Tennessee, 27 July 1850, in Supreme Court Cases, Middle Tennessee, *Flora Cheatham Ewing and Milton P. Wheat v. Joseph Thompson, Nicholas P. Cheatham, Edmond B. Cheatham, and William Little*, TSLA; Related Documents: Court Transcript (incomplete), 27 July 1850 and ca. 1852; Deposition, Nicholas P. Cheatham, County Court, Adair County, Kentucky, 18 and 19 February 1851; Decree, State Supreme Court, ca. March 1852, with ibid., granted, appealed, affirmed, ("such As a Gentleman would not employ to his Slave"), PAR #21485017.

48. Petition of Dorcas Eakin and Thomas Lacy to the Chancery Court of Sumter County, Alabama, 27 October 1852, in Records of the Circuit Court, Estates, *Dorcas Eakin and Thomas Lacy v. Samuel S. Eakin*, Case #413, CCH, Livingston, Ala.; Related Documents: Deposition, Clara Browning, 26 January 1853; Decree, 4 March 1853, with ibid., granted, PAR #20185207.

49. Petition of Celeste Leonard Collins to the District Court of St. Landry Parish, Louisiana, 6 October 1817, in Records of the Fifth Judicial District Court, *Celeste Leonard Collins v. William L. Collins*, Case #338, PCH, Opelousas, La.; Related Documents: Judgment, 22 November 1817; Deed of Gift, 23 June 1812, certified 15 November 1812, with ibid., granted, PAR #20881710; Petition of Elizabeth Overbay to the District Court of West Feliciana Parish, Louisiana, 20 October 1834, in Records of the Third Judicial District Court, *Elizabeth Overbay v. Henry Overbay*, Case #1420, PCH, St. Francisville, La.; Related Documents: Order, 17 October 1834; Order, 18 October 1834; Judgment, 20 December 1834, with ibid., granted, PAR #20883417; Petition of Rebecca A. Harvey to the District Court of Feliciana Parish, Louisiana, 21 July 1819, in Records of the Third Judicial District Court, *Rebecca A. Harvey v. James Harvey*, Case #1147, Clerk of Court Archives, Baton Rouge, La.; Related Documents: Transcript of Court Records, 3 August 1819–22 March 1826, including Inventory, 17 August 1819; Judgment, 21 August 1819; Countersuit, James Harvey, 1 October 1819; Judgment, 24 April 1820; and Order of Sequestration, 20 May 1823; Petition, James Harvey, ca. 14 November 1822; Promissory Note, Rebecca Harvey to James Harvey, 7 April 1821; Summons, 14 November 1822; Sheriff's Return, 27 November 1822; Answer, Rebecca Harvey, ca. November 1822 (incomplete) with ibid., partially granted, protested, reversed, motion for new trial, amended, PAR #20881991; Petition of Victorine Fortier Destrehan to the District Court of Orleans Parish, Louisiana, 24 December 1819, in Records of the First Judicial District Court, Case Records, *Victorine Fortier Destrehan v. Nicolas Noel Destrehan*, Case #2796, LC; Related Documents: Order, 24 December 1819; Verdict, 5 April 1820; Judgment, 21 April 1820, with ibid., granted ("damned whore and drunken bitch"), PAR #20881931.

50. *Statute Law of Kentucky*, 4:19–20; *Laws of the State of Mississippi, Passed at a Regular Session of the Mississippi Legislature*, 118; *Revised Statutes of the State of Missouri*, 426–29; Censer, "'Smiling through Her Tears,'" 28 n. 12; Petition of Azeline Conner to the District Court of Pointe Coupee Parish, Louisiana, 7 August 1843, in Records of the Fourth Judicial District Court, *Azeline Conner v. Adolphe Conner*, Case #1460, PCH, New Roads, La.; Related Documents: Order, 10 July 1843; Judg-

ment, 25 November 1843; Copy of Judgment, 9 December 1843, with ibid., granted, PAR #20884326; Petition of Hannah A. Hansley to the Superior Court of New Hanover County, North Carolina, 14 October 1859, in County Court Divorce Records, *Hannah A. Hansley v. William M. Hansley*, NCSA, partially granted, PAR #21285946.

51. Haskel and Smith, *Complete Descriptive and Statistical Gazetteer*; DeBow, *Statistical View of the United States*, 95; Alyce Billings Walker, ed., *Alabama: A Guide to the Deep South* (New York: Federal Writers Project, 1941; reprint, New York: Hastings House, [1975]), 311.

52. USMSPC, Talladega County, Alabama, Talladega District, 1850, p. 358, and Southern Division, 1860, p. 871; USMSSC, Talladega County, Alabama, Talladega District, 1850, p. 469; USMSAC, Talladega County, Alabama, Talladega District, 1850, pp. 737–38; USMSPC, Talladega County, Alabama, Southern Division, 1860, p. 871; USMSSC, Southern Division, 1860, p. 360; USMSAC, Talladega County, Alabama, Southern Division, 1860, pp. 11–12.

Chapter 4

1. Petition of Sarah Duncan to the Circuit Court, Clay County, Missouri, 28 July 1846, in Records of the Supreme Court, Case Files, *Sarah Duncan v. William Duncan*, Case #19, MoSA; Related Documents: Transcript of Court Record, 27 July 1846–August 1847; Copy of Decree, February 1848; Supreme Court Opinion, 21 December 1848, with ibid., granted, appealed, reversed, dismissed, PAR #21184601. For William Duncan, see USMSPC, Clay County, Missouri, 1830, p. 274; 1840, p. 18; and Clay County, Missouri, Fishing River Township, 1850, p. 377; USMSSC, Clay County, Missouri, Fishing River Township, 1850, p. 458. William Duncan married Sarah Ratliff on 5 August 1838 in Clinton County, Missouri; see Jordan Dodd, Missouri Marriages to 1850, ancestry.com (14 April 2009). In 1840, William Duncan headed a household with Sarah and four children ages 5 to 20. He possessed eleven slaves, including three boys and three girls under 10, one male 10 to 24, one man and two women ages 24 to 36, and one woman 36 to 55. See USMSPC, Clay County, Missouri, 1840, p. 18, and Clay County, Missouri, Fishing River Township, 1850, p. 377; USMSSC, Clay County, Missouri, Fishing River Township, 1850, p. 458.

2. *Revised Statutes of the State of Missouri*, 428–29. Sarah Duncan "signed" an oath before a justice of the peace affirming the truthfulness of her statements with "her X mark." See Oath, Sarah Duncan, 27 July 1846, in Transcript of Court Record, 27 July 1846–August 1847, cited in n. 1 above. See also *Laws of A Public and General Nature, of the District of Louisiana*, 1:517 (1817 law); *Laws of a Public and General Nature of the State of Missouri*, 2:360–61 (1833 law).

3. Petition of Sarah Duncan cited in n. 1 above.

4. Order for Injunction, 28 July 1846; Writ of Injunction, 28 July 1846; Injunction Bond, Sarah Duncan and John Reed, 4 August 1846; Summons, Samuel Gillery, Clerk of Clay County Court, 4 August 1846; Order for Alimony, 4 October 1846; Answer, William Duncan, 26 February 1847; Cross Bill, William Duncan, ca. 26 February 1847; Replication, Sarah Duncan, 26 February 1847; Decree, February 1848, in Transcript of Court Record, 27 July 1846–August 1847, in n. 1 above.

5. Bertram Wyatt-Brown, for example, suggested that women were powerless

"before the bench and assembly overseeing divorces," and pleas initiated in their behalf were uniformly unsuccessful; see Wyatt-Brown, *Southern Honor*, 283, 286.

6. Popkin, *Statutes in Court*, 61–62, 67, http://books.google.com/books (14 September 2009); Glymph, *Out of the House of Bondage*, 60. In 1820, Joseph Story, called the father of American equity, wrote that the ablest lawyers "found the courts of common law the most lucrative, as well as the most attractive for the display of their talents." This may have been true during the early years of the nineteenth century, but by the 1820s and later, equity court lawyers found good opportunities for making money and displaying their talents as attorneys. See Story, *Miscellaneous Writings*, 270; Warbasse, *Changing Legal Rights of Married Women*, 39–40. Perhaps the leading southern proponent of the continued partnering of "equity" and statutory law in judicial rulings was South Carolina College professor of law and political economist Francis Lieber, a German-born author who published in 1839 *Legal and Political Hermeneutics*. Although Lieber warned judges against an equitable interpretation and judicial construction of statutes, he nevertheless emphasized that lawyers and judges should consider not only the wording but also the spirit of the law. See Binder and Weisberg, *Literary Criticisms of Law*, 47–52.

7. Johnson, *Ante-Bellum North Carolina*, 614; Bishir, *North Carolina Architecture*, 206–12; Kaye, *Joining Places*, 168–72; Durrill, "Tale Of Two Courthouses," 661–63; Edwards, *People and Their Peace*, 70.

8. Petition of Winnefrid Richmond and Lewis Garrett to the Chancery Court of Davidson County, Tennessee, 9 December 1835, in Supreme Court Cases, Middle Tennessee, *Winnefrid Richmond and Lewis Garrett v. Braddock Richmond*, box 72, TSLA; for Related Documents see Chap. 2, n. 10; granted, appealed, affirmed, PAR #21483520. In the great majority of cases, lawyers were either identified by surnames or not identified. For the lawyers in this case, see USMSPC, Davidson County, Tennessee, Nashville, 1830, p. 277, and Fourth Ward, 1840, p. 284 (G. W. Campbell); USMSPC, Davidson County, Tennessee, Nashville, 1830, p. 281, and Fifth Ward, 1840, p. 291 (Thomas H. Fletcher); USMSPC, Davidson County, Tennessee, Civil District 22, 1840, p. 282 (David Scott).

9. USMSPC, Jefferson County, Kentucky, Louisville, 1830, p. 92, and 1840, p. 138; Petition of Eliza Bainbridge to the Circuit Court of Jefferson County, Kentucky, 16 October 1809, in Records of the Circuit Court, Case Files, *Eliza Bainbridge v. Absolom Bainbridge*, Case #49, KDLA; Related Documents: Amended Bill, ca. 1809; Correspondence, Absolom Bainbridge to E. Bainbridge, 1 December 1809; Depositions, John C. Sullivan, 21 March 1810, William T. Limrall, ca. 1810; Decree, 21 November 1810, with ibid., granted, PAR #20780903; Petition of Louisa Holmes to the Equity Court of Charles County, Maryland, 12 August 1842, in SC, *Louisa Holmes v. William Holmes Sr.*, Case #339, MSA; Related Documents: Supplemental Petition, Louisa Holmes, 19 August 1842; Depositions, Washington A. Posey, 24 August 1842, 6 March 1843, Eleanor Holmes, 15 March 1843; Order, 25 August 1842; Voucher, William Holmes to George Brent, 26 August 1842; Affidavit, Edward Adams, 28 November 1842; Order, 28 November 1842; Decree, 1 November 1844; Auditor's Report, Accounts of Louisa and William Holmes, ca. November 1844, with ibid., granted, PAR #20984202; Petition of Margery A. Ryon Wells

to the Equity Court of Anne Arundel County, Maryland, 16 December 1857, in SC, *Margery A. Ryon Wells v. James H. Wells*, Case #OS195, MSA; Related Documents: Order, 19 December 1857; Injunction Bond and Certification, Margery A. Wells, Calvert Brown, Catharine A. Ryon, et al., 12 December 1857; Answer, James H. Wells, 4 February 1858; Amended Petition, Margery Wells, 16 February 1858; Orders, 19 February 1858, 29 May 1858; List of Property and Debts, James Wells, 10 March 1858; Depositions, Catherine M. Ryon (daughter), William Ryon, Samuel Anderson, William Wickham, Judson Clark, Edward C. Mills, 19 July 1858; Depositions, Thomas R. Beard, Francis L. Newman, 27 July 1858; Depositions, Catherine M. Ryon, Zealous A. Gray, Robert T. Ryon, 13 August 1858; Court Record, 3 October 1858; Subpoena, 13 August 1858, with ibid., granted, PAR #20985703.

10. DeSaussure, *Reports of Cases*; Edwards, *People and their Peace*, 30, 38, 115, 176; Petition of Sarah Beam and Richardson Mayo to the Equity Court of Fairfield District, South Carolina, 9 May 1820, in Records of the Equity Court, Bills, *Sarah Beam and Richardson Mayo v. Albert Beam*, Case #1821-7, SCDAH; Related Documents: Court Costs, ca. 1820; Answer, Albert Beam, 19 June 1820; Subpoena, Albert Beam, 8 May 1820; Sheriff's Return, 11 May 1820; Subpoenas, Betsey Beams [Beam], Nancy Mayo, Richardson Mayo, et al., 8 May 1820; Sheriff's Return, 12 May 1820; Subpoenas, Betsey Beam, Nancy Mayo, John Floyd, et al., January 1821; Sheriff's Report, 27 January 1821; Sheriff's Returns, 13 February 1821; Subpoenas, Betsey Beam, Nancy Mayo, John Floyd, et al., 25 May 1821; Decree, 19 June 1821, with ibid., partially granted, PAR #21382020.

11. Petition of Mary E. Cogan to the Chancery Court of Jefferson County, Mississippi, 10 October 1857, in Records of the Chancery Court, *Mary E. Cogan v. Charles S. L. Cogan*, Case #3, CCH, Fayette, Miss.; Related Documents: Depositions, Michael W. Trimble, Meyer Eiseman, William A. Trimble, 20 April 1861, Robert Duncan, 23 April 1861; Attorneys' Statement, 23 April 1861; Decree, 26 April 1861, with ibid., granted, PAR #21085703.

12. See, for example, Petition of Mary Strode and George Harrison to the Circuit Court of Boone County, Missouri, 11 February 1824, in Records of the Circuit Court, Microfilm Reel C-16662, *Mary Strode and George Harrison v. Stephen Strode*, Case #75, MoSA; Related Documents: Affidavit, Nathaniel Potter, 9 October 1824; Newspaper Notice, June Term 1824; Order, ca. June Term 1824; Summons, Stephen Strode, 25 March 1824; Sheriff's Return, 4 May 1824; Summons, Stephen Strode, 21 July 1824; Sheriff's Return, 9 October 1824; Decree, 13 October 1824, with ibid., granted, PAR #21182405.

13. Petition of Melinda W. Poston to the Circuit Court of Fayette County, Kentucky, 9 November 1829, in Records of the Circuit Court, Case Files, *Melinda W. Poston v. Richard Poston*, KDLA; Related Documents: Order, 9 October 1829; Depositions, Joseph Cabell Harrison, Sophia R. Harrison, and James Devore, 6 April 1830, with ibid., no decree with petition, PAR #20782921.

14. USMSPC, Shelby County, Alabama, 1850, p. 207, and 1860, p. 311; USMSSC, Shelby County, Alabama, 1850, p. 14 (name spelled Alfonso), and 1860, p. 124 (Alphonso A. Sterrett); USMSPC, Talladega County, Alabama, Talladega, 1850, p. 395, and Dallas County, Alabama, Selma, 1860, p. 839; USMSSC, Talladega

County, Alabama, Talladega, 1850, p. 523, and Dallas County, Alabama, Selma, 1860, p. 144 (Alexander White); Petition of William Brewer to the Chancery Court of Talladega County, Alabama, 25 November 1854, in Records of the Chancery Court, Minutes and Dockets, 1857–61, pp. 21–32, 36–41, 44–51; *William Brewer v. Jane C. Brewer*, Shelby County Archives, Columbiana, Ala.; for Related Documents, see Chap. 2, n. 28, granted, PAR #20185421. Judge Clark did, however, allow Jane to keep, as alimony, nearly $1,000 that she had received from the estate of her first husband's mother.

15. Petition of Charles Oneal to the Circuit Court of Bourbon County, Kentucky, 19 August 1829, in Records of the Circuit Court, Case Files, *Charles Oneal v. Eliza Isham Oneal*, CCH, Paris, Ky.; Related Documents: Copy of Indenture, Charles Oneal and Eliza Oneal, 15 March 1823; Final Decree, 21 May 1830, with ibid., granted, PAR #20782911.

16. Petition of Robert D. Lewis to the Circuit Court of Christian County, Kentucky, 12 November 1849, in Records of the Circuit Court, Petitions in Equity, *Robert D. Lewis v. Virginia A. Lewis*, KDLA; Related Documents: Answer, Virginia A. Lewis, 4 March 1850; Depositions, 30 October 1850; Decree, ca. 1850, with ibid., granted, PAR #20784914; USMSPC, Christian County, Kentucky, Second District, 1850, p. 367. A missing page in the decree prevents us from knowing exactly what happened to the five slaves. It is clear that the court gave custody of the children to the wife, but she argued that the husband did not, in fact, turn over the slaves as he claimed.

17. Petition of Margaret Garner to the Superior Court of Escambia County, Florida, 24 September 1838, in Chancery Court, Divorce Cases, Mobile County, Alabama, *Margaret Garner v. Thomas Garner*, Case #745, USAA; Related Documents: Summons, Thomas Garner, 28 September 1838; Execution of Summons, 2 October 1838, with ibid., no decree with petition, PAR #20583803; Petition of Margaret Garner to the Superior Court of Escambia County, Florida, 1 October 1838, in Chancery Court, Divorce Cases, Mobile County, Alabama, *Margaret Garner v. Thomas Garner*, Case #745, USAA; Related Documents: Order for Writ of Sequestration, 1 October 1838; Execution of Orders, 2 October 1838; Order to Seize Thomas Garner, 1 October 1838; Execution of Order, 2 October 1838; Authorization to Release Thomas Garner, 2 October 1838; Dismissal, 24 November 1838; Certification of Court Transcript, 21 April 1841, with ibid., dismissed, PAR #20583804. In 1840, Margaret's counsel, B. D. Wright, in his forties, headed a family consisting of a woman in her thirties and five children, including three boys under age five. He owned nine slaves. In the household, census takers listed one person in the category "learned professional engineers." See USMSPC, Escambia County, Florida Territory, 1840, p. 14.

18. Fisher, "Ideology and Imagery in the Law of Slavery," 73; Applebaum, "Miscegenation Statutes," 49–50; Getman, "Sexual Control in the Slaveholding South"; Petition of Mary Hall and William F. Hall to the Circuit Court of Madison County, Alabama, 25 June 1838, in Records of the Chancery Court, Madison County, Alabama, Chancery Record 1839, vol. K, pp. 242–48, *Mary Hall and William Hall v. Nathaniel Hall, Logan Brandon, Michael Houghton, and William Houghton*, 25 June

1838, Madison County Public Library Archives, Huntsville, Ala.; Fiat, Mary Hall, 2 July 1838; Bond, Nathaniel Hall, 10 October 1838; Writ of Attachment, Nathaniel Hall, 16 July 1838; Order and Continuance, 26 October 1838; Answer and Affidavit, Nathaniel Hall, 9 October 1839; Answer, Logan Brandon (two pages missing), ca. 1839; Depositions, Robert Bailey (also spelled Baily), John Lusk, Joseph Sharp, John Heathcock, Robert Bailey (second deposition), John Sharp, 12 June 1839; Certification of Depositions, 12 June 1839; Dismissal, 21 December 1839, with ibid., dismissed, PAR #20183802; Petition of Tabitha Pope to the Chancery Court of Mobile County, Alabama, 25 February 1851, in Records of the Chancery Court, Divorce Cases, *Tabitha Pope v. William O. Pope*, Case #1646, USAA; Related Documents: Interrogatories, Dewit Fuller, David Walker, 1 April 1851; Decree, ca. 1851, with ibid., dismissed, PAR #20185109.

19. Kent, *Commentaries on American Law*, 2:81.

20. Petition of Nancy Fleming to the Circuit Court of Woodford County, Kentucky, 12 June 1828, in Records of the Circuit Court, Case Files, *Nancy Fleming v. Leonard Fleming*, KDLA; Related Documents: Order, 12 June 1828; Answer, Leonard Fleming, 18 September 1828, with ibid., dismissed, PAR #20782814.

21. Petition of Harriet S. Johnson and Jose Green to the Chancery Court of Mobile County, Alabama, 6 March 1847, in Records of the Chancery Court, Divorce Cases, *Harriet S. Johnson and Jose Green v. Daniel L. Johnson*, Case #1342, USAA; Related Documents: Newspaper Notice, *Mobile Herald and Tribune*, March 1847; Decree, ca. 1847, with ibid., dismissed, PAR #20184701. The judge was Joseph Lesesne. Also, Petition of Margarett Smith Compton and James Smith to the Superior Court of Oglethorpe County, Georgia, 31 July 1810, in Records of the Superior Court, Minutes, 1810-13, pp. 123-33, *Margarett Smith Compton and James Smith v. John Compton*, CCH, Lexington, Ga.; Related Documents: Order, 31 July 1810; Summons, John Compton, 3 August 1810; Sheriff's Return, 6 August 1810; Answer, John Compton, 8 November 1810; Order, March Term 1811, with ibid., dismissed, PAR #20681023; Petition of Cornelia J. Long and Claborne Gee to the Chancery Court of Maury County, Tennessee, 1845, in Records of the Chancery Court, Case Files, *Cornelia J. Long and Claborne Gee v. Nicholas J. Long*, Maury County Archives, Columbia, Tenn.; Related Documents: Answer, Nicholas J. Long, 20 March 1845; Decree, March 1846, with ibid., dismissed, PAR #21484523.

22. Petition of Sarah Goodgame and William McCullers to the Circuit Court of Bibb County, Alabama, April 1830, in Records of the Circuit Court, Record Book, 1826-36, pp. 54-56, *Sarah Goodgame and William McCullers v. John Goodgame*, CCH, Centreville, Ala.; Related Documents: Subpoena, John Goodgame, 13 May 1830; Decree, September 1830, with ibid., dismissed, PAR #20183001; Petition of Permelia Russell, free woman of color, to the Circuit Court of Boyle County, Kentucky, 4 October 1847, in Records of the Circuit Court, Equity/Chancery Cases, *Permelia Russell v. Willis Russell*, free man of color, KDLA; Related Documents: Answer, Willis Russell, 2 March 1848; Depositions, Manerva Doneghy, Jane Green, Polly Gray, et al., 1 March 1848; Court Record, September 1848, with ibid. (violence, adultery, and excessive drinking), dismissed, PAR #20784713; Petition of Martha S. Huskey to the Circuit Court of Jefferson County, Missouri, 23 April 1849, in Records

of the Circuit Court, *Martha S. Huskey v. Silas Huskey*, Case #1408, CCH, Hillsboro, Mo.; Related Documents: Order, 23 April 1849; Motion to Dismiss, 8 November 1849, with ibid. (desertion), partially granted, dismissed, PAR #21184903; Petition of Ann D. Harbour Richardson to the District Court of West Feliciana Parish, Louisiana, 20 June 1859, in Records of the Seventh Judicial District Court, *Ann D. Harbour Richardson v. Jared N. Richardson*, Case #1325, PCH, St. Francisville, La.; Related Documents: Order, 11 June 1859; Supplemental Petition, 14 March 1860; Decree, 6 June 1867 [*sic*], with ibid. ("excesses, cruel treatment, and outrages"), dismissed, PAR #20885917.

23. Goodheart, Hanks, and Johnson, "'Act for the Relief of Females,'" pt. 1, p. 331, and pt. 2, p. 405.

24. *Acts Passed at the Seventh Annual Session of the General Assembly of the State of Alabama*, 102–3; *Acts Passed at the Third Annual Session of the General Assembly of the State of Alabama*, 107; *Laws of North Carolina at a General Assembly, begun and held in Raleigh, on the Twentieth Day of November*, 14; *Laws of North Carolina at a General Assembly, begun and held in Raleigh, on the Third Monday*, 48; *Laws of the State of North-Carolina, Enacted in the Year 1816*, 50, 52. Occasionally, an act did contain pertinent information. The act granting Daniel Rose a divorce in 1806, for example, noted that seven months after his marriage, his wife "was delivered of a mulatto child" (Pippenger, *Connections and Separations*, 11 [Daniel Rose]). See also the summaries provided in Bamman and Spero, *Tennessee Divorces*, drawn from 750 legislative petitions and acts; Chused, *Private Acts in Public Places*, tables 5, 8; Buckley, *Great Catastrophe of My Life*, tables A1, A2, A4; Goodheart, Hanks, and Johnson, "'Act for the Relief of Females,'" pt. 2, table 4.

25. The ratio of 8 to 1, women to men, who filed suits with the judiciary, as revealed in the overall statistics of this study, is probably too high. In North Carolina, where the best records were found, 125 women and 34 men filed in the superior courts, a ratio of about 4 to 1; this ratio is probably more representative. Still, it is clear that women were far more likely to petition the courts than petition legislatures and were far more successful in doing so. See Schweninger, "'To the Honorable.'"

26. See n. 1 above. Louis Houck, ed., *Reports of Cases Determined in the Supreme Court of the State of Missouri from July 1848 to October 1849* (Sacramento: California State Law Library, 2004), 12:53–57 (*Nagel v. Nagel*), http://homepages.rootsweb.ancestry.com/~dobson/mo/moclay.htm (26 July 2009).

27. USMSPC, Clay County, Missouri, Fishing River Township, 1850, p. 377; USMSSC, Clay County, Missouri, Fishing River Township, 1850, p. 458. In 1850, Virginia-born Sarah Duncan lived in a household headed by Kentucky-born farmer John Reed, age fifty-four, his thirty-seven-year-old wife Mary, and their four children. Reed owned land worth $11,000 and sixteen slaves. In the next census, Sarah Duncan was not listed. See USMSPC, Clinton County, Missouri, District Sixteen, 1850, p. 424; USMSSC, Clinton County, Missouri, District Sixteen, 1850, p. 472; USMSPC, Clinton County, Missouri, Hardin Township, 1860, p. 50; USMSSC, Clinton County, Missouri, Hardin Township, 1860, p. 207.

Chapter 5

1. Petition of Louisiana Reid and William W. Dabney to the Chancery Court of Williamson County, Tennessee, 7 June 1837, in Records of the County Court, *Louisiana Reid and William W. Dabney v. Thomas McDaniel Reid and David Campbell*, Williamson County Archives, Franklin, Tenn.; Related Documents: Pledge of Surety, R. Alexander, 7 June 1837; Supplemental Bill, 6 July 1837; Indenture, Thomas McDaniel Reid to William Dabney, 13 June 1837; Decree, 16 November 1838; Commissioners' Report, 13, 14 December 1838, with ibid. (incomplete), granted, PAR #21483702. Louisiana's children, listed in the commissioners' report in 1838, included John G. Banks, James M. Banks, Thomas C. Banks, Leonard D. Banks, and Mary M. Banks. See Petition of Louisiana Reid and Thomas W. Cash to the Chancery Court of Williamson County, Tennessee, 26 April 1838, in Records of the Chancery Court, 11:479–81, 506–7, *Louisiana Reid and Thomas W. Cash v. David Campbell, James M. Banks, John G. Banks, Thomas C. Banks, Mary Banks, Leonard Banks, and Thomas M. Reid*, CCH, Franklin, Tenn., granted, appealed, PAR #21483808; Haskel and Smith, *Complete Descriptive and Statistical Gazetteer*, 730. For the probating of the will in 1835, see Johnson, *Probate Genealogy*, 10.

2. The will is quoted in Petition of Louisiana Reid and William W. Dabney to the Chancery Court of Williamson County, Tennessee, 7 June 1837, cited in n. 1 above. In her 1838 petition, Louisiana noted that by the time her husband died in late May or early June 1835, she had given birth to six children: John G. Banks; James M. Banks; Thomas C. Banks; William Banks, "who since died intestate without issue"; Mary Banks; and Steward Banks. The 1838 commissioner's report cited five children: John G. Banks, James M. Banks, Thomas Banks, Leonard D. Banks, and Mary M. Banks. The will, written before 1835, therefore, divided the property into sevenths, for Louisiana and their six children. By the time the will was probated, one son had died; another son, Steward, died shortly afterward; and Leonard had not been born. "Child yet unborn [later to be Leonard D. Banks]" is cited in Johnson, *Probate Genealogy*, 147.

3. Petition of Louisiana Reid and William W. Dabney to the Chancery Court of Williamson County, Tennessee, 7 June 1837 (see n. 1 above); Petition of Louisiana Reid and Thomas W. Cash to the Chancery Court of Williamson County, Tennessee, 26 April 1838, in Records of the Chancery Court, 11:479–81, 506–7, *Louisiana Reid and Thomas W. Cash v. David Campbell, James M. Banks, John G. Banks, Thomas C. Banks, Mary Banks, Leonard Banks, and Thomas M. Reid*, CCH, Franklin, Tenn.; Related Documents: Copy of Order Granting Letters Testamentary to David Campbell, January 1836; Answer, John G. Banks, James M. Banks, et al., 23 October 1838; Decree and Appeal, 16 November 1838, with ibid., granted, appealed, PAR #21483808.

4. Edwards, *People and Their Peace*, 159, 173 (quote), 174–76, 345 n. 41, 348–49 n. 10; see Lebsock, *Free Women of Petersburg*; Faust, *Mothers of Invention*; Friedman, *Enclosed Garden*; Kierner, *Southern Women in Revolution* and *Beyond the Household*; Kerber, *Women of the Republic*; McMillen, *Motherhood in the Old South*; Varon, *We Mean to Be Counted*; Weiner, *Mistresses and Slaves*; Hodes, *White Women, Black Men*; Jabour, *Scarlett's Sisters*; Cashin, *Our Common Affairs*. At the time of her

marriage, a woman legally became a *feme covert*, and although she still could file suits, any property she owned became part of her husband's estate. When she died, if she was survived by a husband and children, any property she might have inherited or possessed during marriage became a life estate in her husband's name, through the principle of curtsey.

5. Warbasse, *Changing Legal Rights of Married Women*, 5-6, 48; McMillen, *Southern Women*, 43; Morris, *Southern Slavery and the Law*, 93-96. For the state of Louisiana, see *Replication of the Project of the Civil Code of Louisiana*, 298; *Civil Code of the State of Louisiana*, 511-12; *Laws of the State of Mississippi: Passed at an Adjourned Session of the Legislature*, 72.

6. *Civil Code of the State of Louisiana*, 511. See Section III, Article 2361; Warbasse, *Changing Legal Rights of Married Women*, 48-49; Petition of Marie Pourciau Olinde to the District Court of Pointe Coupee Parish, Louisiana, 14 November 1816, in Records of the Fourth Judicial District Court, *Marie Robillard Pourciau v. Barthelemy Olinde*, Case #350, PCH, New Roads, La.; Related Documents: Amended Petition (incomplete), 20 May 1817; Judgment, 22 November 1817, with ibid., withdrawn, PAR #20881610; Petition of Marguerite Lejeune LeBleu Godin to the District Court of St. Landry Parish, Louisiana, 21 August 1839, in Records of the Fifth Judicial District Court, *Marguerite Lejeune LeBleu Godin v. Ernest Godin*, Case #2734, PCH, Opelousas, La.; Related Documents: Order, 30 August 1839, with ibid., partially granted, PAR #20883917; Petition of Alcy Ingram to the District Court of East Baton Rouge Parish, Louisiana, 9 August 1850, in Records of the Sixth Judicial District Court, *Alcy Ingram v. Robert C. Ingram*, Case #658, CCA, Baton Rouge, La.; Related Documents: Order, 9 August 1850; Judgment, 4 November 1850, with ibid., granted, PAR #20885007.

7. Petition of Mary Belt and Walter Hellen to the Circuit Court of Washington, Washington, D.C., 15 November 1809, in Records of the United States Circuit Court, Chancery Dockets and Rule Case Files, Record Group 21, box 10, Case #132, *Mary Belt and Walter Hellen v. Hiram Belt*, NA; Related Documents: Decree, 1 July 1812; Copy of Schedule of Property of Mary Belt, ca. 1809, with ibid., granted, PAR #20480901. For the early period, see also Petition of Elinor Hart and John Beaty to the County Court of Lincoln County, North Carolina, 10 August 1811, in County Court Divorce Records, *Elinor Hart and John Beaty v. William Hart and Andrew Hart*, NCSA, no decree with petition, PAR #21281101; Petition of Harriet Night to the Circuit Court of Harrison County, Kentucky, 23 March 1814, in Records of the Circuit Court, Case Files, Drawer 166-68, Case #4894, *Harriet Night v. William Night and Aaron Ashbrook*, CCH, Cynthiana, Ky.; Related Documents: Amended Petitions, ca. 1814, 20 September 1814; Depositions, Mycajah Cleveland, Jacob Night, and Shadrack Night, 23 May 1815, Hugh Bell, Jane Brown, Rebeckah McFarland, William McFarland Sr., William McFarland Jr., Archilaus Vanhook, Jane Bell, Margaret Bell, and George Nesbit, 18 and 19 May 1815, with ibid., no decree with petition, PAR #20781403.

8. Petition of Elizabeth Hamilton and William Hassell to the Chancery Court of Maury County, Tennessee, 21 September 1848, in Supreme Court Cases, Middle Tennessee, *Elizabeth Hamilton and William Hassell v. Alexander C. Hamilton*, TSLA;

Related Documents: Transcript of Chancery Court Record (incomplete), 21 September 1848–22 April 1850; Answer, Alexander C. Hamilton, 22 February 1849; Bill of Sale, Joseph Hassell to Alexander C. Hamilton, 9 December 1843; Bill of Sale, Alexander and Elizabeth Hamilton to Joseph Hassell, 9 December 1843; Copy of Petition, 21 September 1848; Copy of Order, 21 September 1848; Copy of Decree, ca. 21 September 1848, with ibid., granted, appealed, affirmed, PAR #21484825; *Statute Laws of the State of Tennessee, of a General Character*, 149.

9. Petition of Mary Miller to the Circuit Court of Harrison County, Kentucky, 27 August 1833, in Records of the Circuit Court, Case Files, *Mary Miller v. Adam Miller, John B. Raine, and Henry F. Wilson*, Drawer 221-24, Case #6068, CCH, Cynthiana, Ky.; Related Documents: Order, H. O. Brown, 27 August 1833; Last Will and Testament, William Allentharp, 26 April 1833; Certified Copy of Newspaper Notice, 8 January 1834; Decree, ca. 1834, with ibid., granted, PAR #20783311. See also Petition of Evalina Gillespie and Alfred Taylor to the Chancery Court of Washington County, Tennessee, 5 December 1853, in Washington County Court Records, Chancery Court, *Evalina E. C. Gillespie and Alfred M. C. Taylor v. Charles K. Gillespie and Alfred E. Jackson*, Record Group 18, box 167, folder 6, AAETSU; Related Documents: Order, 30 November 1853, with ibid., granted, PAR #21485303.

10. Petition of Jane McKinney and Jonathan Harris to the Equity Court of Columbia District, South Carolina, 10 July 1816, in Records of the Equity Court, Bills, Fairfield District, *Jane McKinney and Jonathan Harris v. Benjamin McKinney*, Case #1816-3, SCDAH; Related Documents: Subpoena, Richard Harrison, Miss Strawburgh, John Pagan, General Starke, June 1817; Sheriff's Returns, 20, 28 February 1818; Writ of Habeas Corpus, Benjamin McKinney, 1 January 1818, with ibid., partially granted, PAR #21381615.

11. Petition of Margaret Garner to the Chancery Court of Mobile County, Alabama, 1 March 1841, in Records of the Chancery Court, Divorce Cases, Case #745, *Margaret Garner v. Thomas Garner*, USAA; Related Documents: Decree, 20 November 1841; Certification of Court Transcripts of Divorce Case in Florida and Oath of Judge Dillon Jordan, 21 April 1841. These transcripts were entered as Exhibit B in this proceeding and appear in their entirety in PARs #20583803 and #20253804. No decree with petition, PAR #20184113. Petition of Charlotte Smith and Shannon R. Bell to the Chancery Court of Lowndes County, Mississippi, 7 September 1857, in Records of the Chancery Court, box 11, Case #32, *Charlotte Smith and Shannon R. Bell v. George Smith and Samuel Butler*, Billups-Garth Archives, Lowndes County Public Library, Columbus, Miss.; Related Documents: Order, 7 September 1857; Affidavit, Shannon R. Bell, 6 November 1857; Amended Bill, Charlotte Smith, 5 November 1857; Deposition, Shannon R. Bell, 14 May 1858; Demurrer, Samuel Butler, 31 October 1857; Decree, 26 October 1858, with ibid., partially granted, PAR #21085724; Petitions of Mary T. McMath to the Superior Court of Jones County, Georgia, 24 June 1830, 12 September 1831, in Records of the Superior Court, Writs 1831-35, pp. 105-13, *Mary T. McMath v. William McMath*, CCH, Gray, Ga.; Related Documents: Schedule of Property, William McMath, ca. 1831; Subpoena, William McMath, 28 June 1830; Sheriff's Return, 30 June 1830; Answer, William McMath, October Term 1830; Jury Verdict, 19 April 1831; Court Ruling, 22 April 1831; Ap-

peal, William McMath, 20 April 1831; Certification, 12 September 1831, with ibid., granted, PAR #20683009. The related documents for the 12 September 1831 petition above included Schedule of Property, William McMath, ca. 1831; Order, 14 September 1831; Injunction and Subpoena, William McMath, 16 September 1831; Oath, Mary McMath, 13 September 1831; Sheriff's Return, 17 September 1831; Jury Verdict, April Term 1832; Court Ruling, ca. April Term 1832, with ibid., granted, PAR #20683118.

12. Petition of Harriet B. Young and John B. O'Neall to the Equity Court of Newberry District, South Carolina, 2 January 1840, in Records of the Equity Court, Bills, *Harriet B. Young and John B. O'Neall v. John T. Young*, Case #1840-5, SCDAH; Related Documents: Orders, 2 January 1839, 24 June 1840, with ibid., granted, PAR #21384028; Petition of Mary Mills to the Circuit Court of Jefferson County, Kentucky, 28 July 1831, in Records of the Circuit Court, Case Files, *Mary Mills v. William Mills*, Case #1561, KDLA; Related Documents: Decree, 12 October 1831, with ibid., granted, PAR #20783119; Petition of Lucinda Chappell Payne and John Chappell to the Equity Court of Newberry District, South Carolina, 29 June 1826, in Records of the Equity Court, Bills, *Lucinda Chappell Payne and John Chappell v. John W. Payne*, Case #1826-7, SCDAH; Related Documents: Order, 30 June 1826; Settlement, Lucinda Payne and John Payne, 29 August 1826, with ibid., partially granted, settled, PAR #21382623. The couple remained together in later years. In 1850, John W. Payne, a farmer age fifty-eight, still lived with Lucinda, age forty-five. He owned $15,000 worth of real estate and forty-five slaves. See USMSPC, Laurens District, South Carolina, 1850, p. 204; USMSSC, Laurens District, South Carolina, 1850, p. 735; Petition of Lucy Smith Brantley, James Herring, and Samuel Smith to the Chancery Court of Montgomery County, Tennessee, 12 July 1828, in Supreme Court Cases, Middle Tennessee, *Lucy Smith Brantley, James Herring, and Samuel Smith v. Abraham Brantley*, TSLA. For similar cases, see Catterall, *Judicial Cases Concerning American Slavery*, 1:145; Burdett A. Rich and M. Blair Wailes, eds., *American Law Reports Annotated* (Rochester, N.Y.: E. R. Andrews, 1920), 6:56; Petition of Mary Ann Andrews and Clay Stennett to the Chancery Court of Limestone County, Alabama, 21 March 1856, in Alabama Supreme Court Cases, Supreme Court Record 1859, 234:1–5, 153–54, *Mary Ann Andrews and Clay Stennett v. Richard J. Andrews*, ADAH; Related Documents: Copy of Final Decree, 20 May 1858; Copy of Appeal Bond, Richard J. Andrews et al., 25 May 1858, with ibid., granted, appealed, dismissed, PAR #20185625.

13. Petition of Harriet S. Johnson and Jose Green to the Chancery Court of Mobile County, Alabama, 6 March 1847, in Records of the Chancery Court, Divorce Cases, *Harriet S. Johnson and Jose Green v. Daniel L. Johnson*, Case #1342, USAA; Related Documents: Newspaper Notice, *Mobile Herald and Tribune*, March 1847; Decree, ca. 1847, with ibid., dismissed, PAR #20184701; Petition of Harriet L. Johnston and John Roulufs to the Chancery Court of Mobile County, Alabama, 18 September 1848, in Records of the Chancery Court, *Harriet L. Johnston and John Roulufs v. David L. Johnston*, Case #1436, USAA, no decree with petition, PAR #20184806; Petition of Lethe Hicks to the Circuit Superior Court of Halifax County, Virginia, January 1846, in Records of the Circuit Superior Court of Chancery, Finals, *Lethe*

Hicks v. Joseph Hicks, Halifax Circuit Court Building, Halifax, Va.; Related Documents: Decree, ca. January 1846; Court Record, February 1846, with ibid., granted, PAR #21684612. In the censuses, Lethe Hicks was listed as the head of household for many years. In 1860, at age sixty-eight, she owned one adult female slave. See USMSPC, Halifax County, Virginia, Eastern District, 1830, p. 404; 1840, p. 57; Southern District, 1850, p. 110; and 1860, p. 125; USMSSC, Halifax County, Virginia, Southern District, 1860, p. 80.

14. Shammas, "Re-assessing the Married Women's Property Acts"; Lebsock, *Free Women of Petersburg*, 67, 72–76; Censer, *North Carolina Planters and Their Children*, 74–75; Chused, "Married Women's Property Law," 1371, 1379; Lazarou, *Concealed under Petticoats*, 75–79; Warbasse, *Changing Legal Rights of Married Women*, 42, 47–48, 55.

15. Petition of Margaret A. Winn and Romulus W. Moore to the Chancery Court of Perry County, Alabama, 27 December 1860, in Records of the Chancery Court, Case Papers, *Margaret A. Winn and Romulus W. Moore v. Pyramus Winn*, ADAH; Related Documents: Copies of Deposition, Thomas C. Hill, 14 February 1862; Decretal Order, August 1861; Decretal Order, n.d., with ibid., no decree with petition, PAR #20186029.

16. Salmon, *Women and the Law of Property*, 88–89; Petition of Eley A. Parker Hall to the Equity Court of Fairfield District, South Carolina, 15 June 1846, in Records of the Equity Court, Bills, *Eley A. Hall v. Laban Hall*, Case #1847-2, SCDAH; Related Documents: Decree, 17 July 1847; Answer, Laban Hall, 26 November 1846, with ibid., partially granted, PAR #21384639; Petition of Harriet J. Foy to the Superior Court of Craven County, North Carolina, 1850, in County Court Divorce Records, *Harriet J. Foy v. Thomas D. Foy*, NCSA; Related Documents: Subpoena, 3 October 1850; Answer, Thomas D. Foy, 3 April 1851; Indenture, Thomas Foy to Harriet and Elizabeth Smith, 6 January 1844, with ibid., no decree with petition, PAR #21285023.

17. Lebsock, *Free Women of Petersburg*, 72; Petition of Adelia Cohen Turner and Samuel J. Wiatt to the Circuit Superior Court of Lynchburg, Virginia, 28 August 1837, in Ended Chancery Court Causes, *Adelia Turner and Samuel J. Wiatt v. John S. Turner and John Bothingham*, LV; Related Documents: Court Record, 28 August 1837–May 1838; Injunction, 26 August 1837; Marriage Contract, 22 December 1832; Decree, 27 October 1837, with ibid., injunction granted, dismissed, PAR #21683717; USMSPC, Campbell County, Virginia, Eastern District, 1840, p. 66.

18. Petition of Mary Hall to the Chancery Court of Bradley County, Tennessee, 2 February 1847, in Records of the Chancery Court, Case Files, *Mary Hall v. Alexander Hall*, Case #344B, TSLA; Related Documents: Supplemental Petition, 8 January 1849; Order, 8 January 1849; Writ of Injunction, August 1849, with ibid., no decree with petition, PAR #21484721; USMSPC, Bradley County, Tennessee, Twenty-sixth Subdivision, 1850, pp. 228, 246, and Seventh District, 1860, p. 215; USMSSC, Bradley County, Tennessee, Seventh District, 1860, p. 77; Petition of Narcissa Davis to the Chancery Court of Williamson County, Tennessee, 23 September 1854, in Records of the Chancery Court, *Narcissa Davis v. Nicholas Knight and James T. Davis*, Williamson County Archives, Franklin, Tenn.; Related Documents:

Deed of Trust, James T. Davis to Nicholas Knight, 11 July 1854; Order, ca. 5 April 1855; Decree, 5 April 1855, with ibid. (suit against trustee), partially granted, PAR #21485413; Petition of Mary Rhodes and John Bishop to the Circuit Court of Albemarle County, Virginia, 22 August 1850, in Ended Chancery Court Causes, *Mary Rhodes and John Bishop v. John Rhodes*, Case #383, LV; Related Documents: Decree, 21 October 1851, with ibid., granted, PAR #21685027. While she was successful in protecting her separate estate in this instance, Mary Rhodes noted that her husband had already sold the land and slaves she had inherited from her father. See also Petition of Christena Strong to the Circuit Court of Leon County, Florida, 22 December 1853, in Chancery Case Files, *Christena Strong v. Christopher B. Strong*, SAF, no decree with petition, PAR #20585309.

19. Warbasse, *Changing Legal Rights of Married Women*, 47; Petition of Margaret Vause to the Equity Court of Charleston District, South Carolina, 13 February 1830, in Records of the Equity Court, Bills, *Margaret Vause v. John Vause*, Case #1833-83, SCDAH; Related Documents: Orders, 12 February, 5 May, 29 December 1830; Answer, John Vause, 22 February 1830, with ibid., partially granted, PAR #21383018.

20. Petition of Maria Betts and John Wellborn to the Circuit Court of Barbour County, Alabama, 17 March 1846, in Records of the Circuit Court, Records, *Maria Betts and John Wellborn v. Elisha Betts, Samuel N. Brown, Thomas A. Brannon, Francis S. Jackson, and George W. Gunn*, vol. C, pp. 1528–36, 1556–68, 1624–25, Barbour County Clerk's Office, Clayton, Ala.; Related Documents: Copies of Deed, Elisha Betts to George W. Gunn, 20 March 1843; Deed of Trust, Burke County, Georgia, Moses Walker to Maria Nelson, 29 November 1827; Subpoena, 7 April 1846; Decree, Fall 1846; Fiat, 6 April 1846; Deposition, C. C. Mills, 7 November 1846; Interrogatories, 4 September 1846; Deposition, Abram Greeson, Walton County, Georgia, 10 October 1846; Register's Orders, 17 September 1846; Interrogatories, 4 September 1846; Deposition, Green B. Haynes, Walton County, Georgia, 10 October 1846; Decree, November 1846, with ibid., granted, PAR #20184621. She won her case a few months after the state passed an act that prohibited creditors from confiscating a married woman's property for her husband's prenuptial debts. See Warbasse, *Changing Legal Rights of Married Women*, 170. See also Petition of Sarah Jett and John Dezam to the Chancery Court of Washington County, Tennessee, 5 January 1846, in Washington County Court Records, Chancery Court, *Sarah Jett and John Dezam v. Starke Jett, Jacob Merchant, Ransom Moree, and E. D. Rader*, AAETSU, no decree with petition, PAR #21484618.

21. Petition of Elizabeth Oliver and John Bath to the Chancery Court of Henrico County, Virginia, 5 September 1825, in Ended Chancery Court Causes, *Elizabeth Oliver and John Bath v. James Oliver*, LV; Related Documents: Court Record, 5 September 1825; Decree, ca. 1825, with ibid., granted, PAR #21682508. During a protracted legal battle, Elizabeth died; her slaves and other property, however, were turned over to the administrator of her estate. See also Petition of Sarah Welsh and David White to the Chancery Court of Mobile County, Alabama, 18 July 1839, in Records of the Chancery Court, Divorce Cases, *Sarah Welsh and David White v. Dennis R. Welsh and Richard Redwood*, Case #507, USAA; Related Documents: Writ of Arrest, Dennis Welsh, 18 July 1839; Agreement to Lower Bond, 23 July 1839; In-

denture, Sarah Barnes and Dennis Welsh, 22 November 1836; Affidavit, 24 January 1837; Certification of Transcript, 23 August 1837; Bill for Injunction, Dennis Welsh, ca. July 1839, with ibid., granted, PAR #20183911.

22. Petition of Margarett A. Campbell and John C. Tomlinson to the Chancery Court of Shelby County, Alabama, 13 July 1858, in Alabama Supreme Court Cases, Supreme Court Record [1861], *Margarett A. Campbell and John C. Tomlinson v. John C. Campbell*, frame/pages 1–21, 77–86, vol. 248, ADAH; Related Documents: PAR #20185941; Copies of Deed of Gift, Margarett Ann Campbell to John C. Tomlinson, 19 December 1853; Subpoena, John C. Campbell, 15 July 1858; Answer, John C. Campbell, 13 December 1858; Amended Bill of Complaint, 9 December 1859; Original Deed, Exhibit B—Margarett Ann Campbell to John C. Tomlinson, 17 December 1853; Answer to Amended Bill, John C. Campbell, 9 December 1859; Petition, Margarett A. Campbell, ca. 1859; Answer to Petition for Receiver, John C. Campbell, ca. 1859; Order Before Register, 31 January 1859; Orders, 1858–60, with ibid., partially granted, appealed, reversed, remanded, PAR #20185836.

23. Salmon, "Women and Property in South Carolina," 674–75; Petition of Elizabeth Ann Jones to the Superior Court of Houston County, Georgia, 1 May 1860, in Records of the Superior Court, Writs, 1856–66, pp. 467–68, *Elizabeth Ann Jones v. Efferd H. Jones*, Georgia Department of Archives and History, Atlanta; Related Documents: Schedule of Property, Efferd H. Jones, 1 May 1860; Schedule of Property, Trust Estate of Elizabeth Ann Jones, 1 May 1860; Summons, Efferd H. Jones, 2 May 1860; Court Record, ca. 1860, with ibid., settled, PAR #20686005; Petition of Sarah Hall and Joseph Holloway to the Chancery Court of Madison County, Alabama, 18 August 1845, in Records of the Chancery Court, Record 1846–47, pp. 252–65, *Sarah Hall and Joseph Holloway v. Adam Hall*, Madison County Public Library Archives, Huntsville, Ala.; Related Documents: Sale of Property, ca. 1845; Order, 18 August 1845; Bond, 19 August 1845; Subpoena, 19 August 1845; Bond, 20 September 1845; Answer, Adam Hall, 29 September 1845; Schedules of Property of Adam Hall, With Marriage, Prior to Marriage, After Marriage, ca. 1845; Final Decree, June 1846, with ibid., agreement between the parties, bill dismissed, PAR #20184511; Petition of James Griffith to the Circuit Court of Scott County, Kentucky, 10 August 1851, in Records of the Circuit Court, Case Files, *James Griffith v. Margaret Griffith, John McMurtry, and David McMurtry*, Case #4593, KDLA; Related Documents: Indenture, James Griffith and Margaret McMurtry, 20 June 1850; Decree, 25 August 1852, with ibid., granted, PAR #20785108; USMSSC, Scott County, Kentucky, First District, Eastpart, 1850, n.p.; USMSPC, Scott County, Kentucky, First District, Eastpart, 1850, p. 401 (James Griffith); USMSSC, Fayette County, Kentucky, First District, 1850, p. 177; USMSPC, Fayette County, Kentucky, First District, 1850, p. 189 (McMurtry family). In this case, the husband sought a divorce and enforcement of their marriage contract as it pertained to the separation of their property.

24. Petition of Mary M. Clarke to the Chancery Court of Franklin County, Tennessee, 1 July 1861, in Miscellaneous Court Records, *Mary M. Clarke v. William Clarke*, Case #23, TSLA; Related Documents: Order, 1 July 1861; Amended Petition, 23 August 1861; Order, 24 August 1861; Decree, 20 February 1867, with ibid., granted, PAR #21486103.

25. Schafer, *Slavery, the Civil Law, and the Supreme Court of Louisiana*, 127; Petition of Mary Ann Warner and Aaron M. Dominick to the Equity Court of Newberry District, South Carolina, 21 May 1851, in Records of the Equity Court, Bills, *Mary Ann Warner and Aaron M. Dominick v. Jacob Warner*, Case #1851-17, SCDAH; Related Documents: Consent of Next Friend, 21 May 1851; Order, ca. 28 May 1851; Attorney's Note, 28 May 1851; Receipt for Court Costs, 28 May 1851, with ibid., settled, PAR #21385138; Petition of Elizabeth Hamilton and Christopher C. Hudson to the Chancery Court of Dallas County, Alabama, 1850, in Records of the Circuit Court, Chancery Records, 1852–54, vol. J, pp. 542–44, *Elizabeth Hamilton and Christopher C. Hudson v. Alexander C. Hamilton*, CCH Annex, Selma, Ala., no decree with petition, PAR #20185007. This Tennessee case was filed in Alabama. See also Petition of Mary H. Miller and William France to the Circuit Court of Todd County, Kentucky, 26 January 1853, in Records of the Circuit Court, Equity Case Files, *Mary H. Miller and William France v. James M. Miller*, KDLA; Related Documents: Order, 19 January 1853, with ibid., no decree with petition, PAR #20785304; Petition of Sarah Trimble and James Cooke to the Chancery Court of Chambers County, Alabama, 1 March 1845, in Records of the Circuit Court, Record Book Middle Chancery District, 1841–53, pp. 260–70, *Sarah Trimble and James Cooke v. John Trimble*, CCH, Lafayette, Ala.; Related Documents: Order, 25 March 1845; Subpoena, 31 March 1845; Bond, 31 March 1845; Answer, John B. Trimble, 12 May 1845, with ibid., dismissed, PAR #20184505.

26. DeBow, *Statistical View of the United States*, 95. The general profile changed slightly in 1860. See Stampp, *Peculiar Institution*, 31; Berlin, *Slaves without Masters*, 397. For estimating property ownership from available contemporary data during the early period, see Soltow, *Distribution of Wealth and Income*, 176, 179, and *Men and Wealth*, 82–83. Soltow projects the percentages of slaveholding families in the South (though he and others define the South in different ways) to be 36 percent in 1790, 36 percent in 1830, 31 percent in 1850, and 25 percent in 1860. In 1860, the average total estate for adult white males in the region was $3,978, nearly twice the amount for adult white males in the North, with most of the difference found in the value of slaves. See Soltow, *Men and Wealth*, 65–66.

27. Wood, *Masterful Women*, 150–57.

28. Sumter Diary, 1 July, 24 October, 10 December 1840, quoted in Weiner, *Mistresses and Slaves*, 37; Scarborough, *Overseer*, 16; Wiethoff, *Crafting the Overseer's Image*; Wood, *Masterful Women*, 3–4; Kierner, *Beyond the Household*, 144; Varon, *We Mean to Be Counted*, 104.

29. Wood, *Masterful Women*, 3, 150; Martha Cocke to Caroline Cocke, 9 April [1811?], Cocke Family Papers, quoted in Wood, "'Strongest Ties,'" 135.

30. Petition of Stella Jones Rucker and William H. Wooten to the Circuit Court of Lynchburg, Virginia, 20 September 1851, in Records of the Circuit Court of Chancery, *Stella Jones Rucker and William H. Wooten v. Tinsley Rucker and Pleasant Labby*, LV; Related Documents: Order, October Term 1851; Decree, December Term 1851, with ibid., granted, PAR #21685120; USMSPC, Lynchburg, Campbell County, Virginia, 1850, p. 115 (Stella Rucker signed a prenuptial agreement); Petition of Rachel Miller to the Equity Court of Davidson County, North Carolina, 4 March 1866,

in County Court Divorce Records, *Rachel Miller v. Isaac B. Miller,* NCSA; Related Documents: Agreement, Rachel Miller and Isaac B. Miller, 28 May 1866, with ibid., granted, PAR #21286608.

31. Petition of Adelia Cohen Turner and Samuel J. Wiatt to the Circuit Superior Court of Lynchburg, Virginia, 28 August 1837, in Ended Chancery Court Causes, *Adelia Turner and Samuel J. Wiatt v. John S. Turner and John Bothingham,* LV; Related Documents: Court Record, 28 August 1837–May 1838; Injunction, 26 August 1837; Marriage Contract, 22 December 1832; Decree, 27 October 1837, with ibid., injunction granted, dismissed, PAR #21683717; Petition of Margaret Fischer and George Keyser to the Chancery Court of Mobile County, Alabama, 10 March 1856, in Records of the Chancery Court, Divorce Cases, *Margaret Fischer and George Keyser v. John Fischer,* Case #2020, USAA; Related Documents: Proof of Publication, 15 April 1856; Interrogatories, 15 December 1856, with ibid., no decree with petition, PAR #20185612; Petition of Sarah E. York to the Superior Court of Houston County, Georgia, August 1863, in Records of the Superior Court, Minutes, 1858–67, pp. 482–83, *Sarah E. York v. William York,* Georgia Department of Archives and History, Atlanta; Related Documents: Order, 13 November 1863; Acknowledgment, August 1863; Order, 31 August 1863, with ibid., granted, PAR #20686309; Petition of Matilda Everton to the Superior Court of Perquimans County, North Carolina, 16 September 1857, in County Court Divorce Records, *Matilda Everton v. Major Everton,* NCSA; Related Documents: Amendment to Petition, Matilda Everton, 2 October 1857; Answer, Major Everton, 21 October 1857; Answer to Amended Bill, Fall Term 1857; Interlocutory Order, Fall Term 1857; Copy of Petition of Matilda Everton, 16 September 1857; Copy of Answer, Major Everton, 21 October 1857; Reports of Cases at Law, Supreme Court of North Carolina, December 1857–August 1858, pp. 202–13, with ibid., partially granted, PAR #21285713; Petition of Elizabeth Gray, George F. Gray, John P. Gray, Henry Gray, Mary Ann Gray, and Joseph Gray to the Chancery Court of Jefferson County, Kentucky, 2 December 1842, in Records of the Circuit Court, Case Files, *Elizabeth Gray, George F. Gray, John P. Gray, Henry Gray, Mary Ann Gray, and Joseph Gray v. Edward Crutchfield, Reason Butler, Josephus Turnham, and William Crutchfield,* Case #3846, KDLA; Related Documents: Amended Bills, 16 August 1843 and 29 October 1844; Bill of Revivor, 21 June 1844; Last Will and Testament, John S. Gray, 1 January 1836; Decree, 2 May 1845; Order of Sale, 4 March 1845; Public Notice, 27 March 1845, with ibid., granted, PAR #20784216; Petition of Sarah Ann Manor to the Equity Court of Warren County, Kentucky, 30 September 1859, in Records of the Circuit Court, Equity/Chancery Cases, *Sarah Ann Manor v. A. J. Manor,* KDLA; Related Documents: Notice, 11 July 1861; Decree, 8 August 1862; Amended Petition, 1 November 1859; Order, 1 November 1859, with ibid., partially granted, PAR #20785914.

32. Harriett Anne Beard's announcements were discussed when William Watkins filed a petition appealing his wife's divorce suit. Petition of William Watkins to the Equity Court of Anne Arundel County, Maryland, ca. 1854, in SC, *William Watkins v. Harriett Anne Watkins,* MSA; Related Documents: Appointment of Commissioner, 30 May 1854; Testimony, Benjamin Beard, Mary A. Black, William Black, 28 June 1854; Testimony, Francis Brashears, William Bird, John W. Williams, Fay-

ette Ball, 10 August 1854; Testimony, Thomas Davidson, Samuel Dorsett, Benjamin Watkins, Benjamin H. Harwood, Daniel Davis, 7 September 1854; Testimony, Francis Brashears, 28 September 1854; Commissioner's Statement, 27 November 1854; List of Interrogatories, Harriett Watkins, ca. 1854; List of Cross Interrogatories, William Watkins, ca. 1854; Commissioner's Oath and Clerk's Oath, 8 December 1854, with ibid., granted, PAR #20985646; USMSPC, Anne Arundel County, Maryland, First District, 1850, p. 314; USMSSC, Anne Arundel County, Maryland, First District, 1850, p. 299; Petition of Mary H. Davis and Robert Graham to the Chancery Court of Davidson County, Tennessee, 21 April 1856, in Records of the Chancery Court, Case Files, *Mary H. Davis and Robert Graham v. Henry L. Davis*, Case #1610, Metropolitan Nashville–Davidson County Archives; Related Documents: Decree, 27 May 1856, with ibid., granted. PAR #21485616; Petition of Mary Ann Merriman and Benjamin Lancaster to the Chancery Court of Sumter County, Alabama, 19 February 1858, in Records of the Circuit Court, Estates, *Mary Ann Merriman and Benjamin Lancaster v. William B. Merriman*, Case #470, CCH, Livingston, Ala.; Related Documents: Affidavit, Mary Ann Merriman, 19 February 1858; Writ of Seizure, 19 February 1858, with ibid., granted, PAR #20185826. Merriman failed to obtain her divorce, but the judge issued a writ of seizure for a slave named Polly before she could be sold. See Petition of Mary Ann Merriman and Benjamin Lancaster to the Chancery Court of Sumter County, Alabama, 12 June 1858, in ibid.; Related Documents: Decree, 1858, with ibid., dismissed, PAR #20185853. See *Acts of the Seventh Biennial Session, of the General Assembly of Alabama*, 119–29; Petition of Levisa Dobbin to the Circuit Court of Phillips County, Arkansas, 29 May 1855, in Arkansas Supreme Court, Records and Briefs, *Levisa Dobbin v. Wilson D. Dobbin*, Case #586, UALS; Related Documents: Copies of Marriage Contract, Wilson D. Dobbin and Levisa Pillow, 24 January 1853; Indenture, 26 March 1855; Deeds, 17 June 1855, 19 September 1854; Appeal to Arkansas Supreme Court, 5 June 1856, with ibid., denied, PAR #20285516.

33. See n. 1 above.

34. USMSPC, Williamson County, Tennessee, Middle District, 1840, p. 179, and Eleventh Civil District, 1850, p. 264 (both L. D. and Thomas Banks); USMSSC, Williamson County, Tennessee, Eleventh Civil District, 1850, p. 885 (Thomas Banks), and First District, 1860, pp. 514 (L. D. Banks), 484, 494 (Thomas Banks); USMSAC, Williamson County, Tennessee, Eleventh Civil District, 1850, pp. 583–84, and First District, 1860, pp. 7 (Thomas Banks), 15 (second Thomas Banks), 29 (L. D. Banks); USMSPC, Williamson County, Tennessee, Eleventh Civil District, 1870, pp. 191 (L. D. Banks), 174 (Thomas Banks), and 1880, p. 169 (Louisiana Banks). In 1870, L. [Louisiana] D. Banks, age sixty-five, owned $8,000 worth of real estate and $1,000 worth of personal property. She lived with her son Leonard, listed as a farmer age thirty-five. Her other son, Thomas, was a merchant in Williamson County, living with his family. In 1880, seventy-five-year-old Louisiana Banks lived with her son Leonard, a farmer age forty-four, her daughter-in-law Ella, and her grandchildren, Fannie, age five; John, age four; and Mary, age two. In the same household were Andy McKissac, a twenty-year-old black laborer, and Jane Scruggs, an eighteen-year-old mulatto servant.

Chapter 6

1. Petition of Eliza Taylor Ransom to the Equity Court of Barnwell District, South Carolina, 8 October 1841, in Records of the Equity Court, Bills, Microfilm Reel BW83, frames 116–24, *Eliza Taylor Ransom v. Dr. Thomas S. Ransom*, SCDAH, no decree with petition, PAR #21384101. For slave and free white populations in Barnwell District, each about 10,500, see Haskel and Smith, *Complete Descriptive and Statistical Gazetteer*, 50. In 1830, Eliza's late husband, John Taylor, owned a plantation and 28 slaves, including 17 ages ten and older. Taylor was in his thirties, while Eliza was in her twenties. Among the Ransoms' 46 slaves cited in the census in 1840, there were 5 boys and 10 girls under age ten, but 12 males and 12 females between ten and under thirty-six, with the others over age thirty-six. Twenty-four were listed as "employed in agriculture." The only whites cited at the residence were Eliza and her husband, both in their thirties. See USMSPC, Barnwell District, South Carolina, 1830, p. 164, and 1840, p. 182.

2. Petition of Mary Ann Rain and John Herring to the Equity Court of Charleston District, South Carolina, 13 June 1809, in Records of the Equity Court, Bills, *Mary Ann Rain and John Herring v. Samuel Rain*, Case #1810-52, SCDAH; Related Documents: Order, 13 June 1809, with ibid., partially granted, PAR #21380906; Petition of Ellen Dunlap to the Virginia General Assembly, Augusta County, 12 October 1814, in LP, LV; Related Documents: Affidavit, James and Thomas Shields, 1 October 1814; Affidavits, Rachel Shields, Peggy Shields, 1 October 1814, and Samuel Torbet, 4 October 1814, with ibid., rejected, PAR #11681419; Petition of Ann West to the Superior Court of Rowan County, North Carolina, 1835, in County Court Divorce Records, *Ann West v. Thomas West*, NCSA; Related Documents: Decree, Fall Term 1835, with ibid., granted, PAR #21283502; Petition of Edward F. Kemp and Sarah C. Kemp to the Chancery Court of Monroe County, Mississippi, 13 April 1855, in Records of the Chancery Court, *Edward F. Kemp and Sarah C. Kemp v. Felix G. Hawkins*, Case #240, CCH, Aberdeen, Miss.; Related Documents: Order, 12 April 1855; Decree, 1 July 1858, with ibid., dismissed, PAR #21085518.

3. There were also the following: "Negro fellow," "negro paramour," "negro mistress," "Negro woman slave" "grown negroes," "young negroes," and as found in a Louisiana court case, "seventeen head of slaves." See Petition of Pauline Bergeron to the District Court of Iberville Parish, Louisiana, 23 September 1828, in Records of the Fourth Judicial District Court, *Pauline Bergeron v. Baptiste Bergeron*, Case #709, PCH, Plaquemine, La.; Related Documents: Order, 22 September 1828; Answer, Baptiste Bergeron, 22 October 1828; Court Record of Case Dismissal, 28 April 1829, with ibid., dismissed, PAR #20882837.

4. Petition of William McClure to the County Court, Montgomery County, Tennessee, 16 July 1822, in LP, TSLA; Related Documents: Affidavit, James McClure, 16 July 1822, with ibid., no act with petition; PAR #11482202. In 1830, William McClure, a single white person, lived with his 16 slaves, including 5 boys and 4 girls under age ten, 3 males and 2 females between ages ten and twenty-four, and 1 woman age twenty-four to thirty-six. McClure was in his forties. See USMSPC, Montgomery County, Tennessee, 1830, p. 38; Petition of Frances G. Pyles and Alexander Winn to the Chancery Court of Laurens District, South Carolina, 20 April

1825, in Records of the Equity Court, *Frances G. Pyles and Alexander Winn v. Abner Pyles*, Case #1826 15, SCDAH; Related Documents: Answer, Abner Pyles, 20 April 1825; Agreement to Provide Support for Child, Abner Pyles, 15 November 1824, with ibid., no decree with petition, PAR #21382508. The "conspiracy" between the female house servant and his wife is detailed in the husband's answer.

5. Petition of Emilie Brout Heno to the District Court of Orleans Parish, Louisiana, 22 January 1824, in Records of the First Judicial District Court, Case Records, *Emilie Brout Heno v. Ursin Heno*, Case #5862, LC; Related Documents: Order, 5 February 1824, with ibid., granted, PAR #20882407; Petition of Jonathan Bryan to the North Carolina General Assembly, New Hanover County, 29 November 1827, in General Assembly, Session Records, NCSA; Related Documents: Depositions of John Larkins, Moses Larkins, Levin Mesick, and I. Messick [*sic*], Betsy Allen, Mary Mitchell, John Sikes, ca. 1825, Margret Sikes, 17 November 1825; Correspondence, Jonathan Bryan to Ann Jane Bryan, 9 November 1825, with ibid., House: read, referred, report unfavorable, PAR #11282712.

6. Petition of John H. Brooks to the Chancery Court of Petersburg, Virginia, 3 March 1855, in Records of the Circuit Superior Court of Chancery, *John H. Brooks v. Eliza Jane Brooks*, CCCO, Petersburg, Va.; Related Documents: Depositions, James R. Pride and Edward B. White, 1 May 1855; Correspondence, Fanny B. to Dr. John Crowder, ca. 1855; Order, May Term 1855, with ibid. (a young slave girl delivered love notes), granted, PAR #21685512; Petition of Mary Ann Williams to the Superior Court of Franklin County, North Carolina, 1856, in County Court Divorce Records, *Mary Ann Williams v. Lansford Williams*, NCSA (a "little negro boy" accompanied a wife to meet with her lawyer), no decree with petition, PAR #21285636; Petition of Louisa Williams to the Circuit Court of Harrison County, Kentucky, 23 August 1858, in Records of the Circuit Court, Case Files, *Louisa Williams v. Asa Williams*, Case #12743, KDLA; Related Documents: Depositions, John Doyle (quote), John Nevel (Nevil), and Lucy Anderson, 1 October 1858; Copy of Rule, May 1861, with ibid., granted, PAR #20785818.

7. Petition of Emily Conner to the Circuit Court of Harrison County, Kentucky, 23 March 1857, in Records of the Circuit Court, Case Files, *Emily Conner v. John Conner*, Case #12339, CCH, Cynthiana, Ky.; Related Documents: Order, 23 March 1857; Answer, John Conner, 11 April 1857; Depositions, Jacob Russell, 7 May 1857, Philemon Conner, Richard Tuttle, Thomas C. White, 28 April 1857; Order, 3 April 1857; Amended Petition, 31 March 1857, with ibid., no decree with petition, PAR #20785704.

8. Petition of Susan Ann Brown to the Circuit Court of Butler County, Kentucky, 25 September 1847, in Records of the Circuit Court, Equity Cases, *Susan Ann Brown v. John G. Brown, Harvey Taylor, and Hiram Brown*, Case #1303, KDLA; Related Documents: Depositions, William E. Dixon, 24 September 1847, Moses T. Reed, Richard Haws, C. C. Porter, 25 September 1847; Answer, John G. Brown, 30 September 1847; Decree, ca. 1847, with ibid., granted, PAR #20784712.

9. Petition of Ann Wingfield Chick and John J. Wingfield to the Circuit Superior Court of Albemarle County, Virginia, 8 May 1847, in Ended Chancery Court Causes, *Ann Wingfield Chick and John J. Wingfield v. Littleton W. Chick, Francis Meri-*

wether L. Chick, Elizabeth Ann Chick, Littleton Eugene Chick, Charles W. Chick, and Otho B. Chick, LV; Related Documents: Court Record, 26 May–25 October 1847; Order, 30 June 1847; Summons, 4 June 1847, with ibid., injunction granted, PAR #21684726; Petition of Margaret Garner to the Chancery Court of Mobile County, Alabama, 30 March 1841, in Records of the Chancery Court, Divorce Cases, *Margaret Garner v. Thomas Garner*, Case #745, USAA; Related Documents: Affidavits, Thomas Bobe, 20, 29 March 1841, Andreas Corral, John Mulligan, 26 March 1841, Ezekiel Salomon, D. Quinn, 29 March 1841; Order, 30 March 1841, with ibid., no decree with petition, PAR #20184114; Petition of Anna Allen to the Equity Court of Columbia District, South Carolina, 14 December 1816, in Records of the Equity Court, Bills, Richland District, *Anna Allen v. John Allen and Turner Stark*, SCDAH; Related Documents: Order, 14 December 1816; Commissioner's Report, February Term 1817; Report on Sale, June Term 1817, with ibid., granted, PAR #21381606.

10. Petition of Jane E. M. Mackall to the Circuit Court of Washington, Washington, D.C., 7 January 1861, in Records of the United States District Court, Chancery Records, Old Divorces, Case #4, *Jane E. M. Mackall v. Brooke Mackall*, NA; Related Documents: Answer, Brooke Mackall, 28 May 1861, with ibid., no decree with petition, PAR #20486105; Petition of Matilda Payne to the Circuit Court of Fayette County, Kentucky, 16 August 1830, in Records of the Circuit Court, Case Files, *Matilda Payne v. Hugh Payne*, Case #723, KDLA; Related Documents: Order, 14 August 1830, with ibid., dismissed, PAR #20783016. Matilda feared that the husband planned to carry out his threat "to take the rest of the negroes and run them off and sell them."

11. Petition of Harriet Night to the Circuit Court of Harrison County, Kentucky, 23 March 1814, in Records of the Circuit Court, Case Files, *Harriet Night v. William Night and Aaron Ashbrook*, Case #4894, CCH, Cynthiana, Ky.; Related Documents: Amended Petitions, ca. 1814, 20 September 1814; Depositions, Mycajah Cleveland, Jacob Night, Shadrack Night, 23 May 1815, Hugh Bell, Jane Brown, Rebeckah McFarland, William McFarland Sr., William McFarland Jr., Archilaus Vanhook, Jane Bell, Margaret Bell, and George Nesbit, 18, 19 May 1815, with ibid. (hire of a nine-year-old boy some distance from his home and the sale of another young boy), no decree with petition, PAR #20781403. In 1820, Aaron Ashbrook possessed five slaves. See USMSPC, Harrison County, Kentucky, 1820, p. 206; Petition of Mary Hall and William F. Hall to the Circuit Court of Madison County, Alabama, 25 June 1838, in Records of the Chancery Court, Chancery Record 1839, vol. K, pp. 211–13, 217–19, 242–48, *Mary Hall and William F. Hall v. Nathaniel Hall, Logan Brandon, Michael Houghton, and William Houghton*, Madison County Public Library Archives, Huntsville, Ala. (sale of two young girls and an elderly black man, despite wife's desperate pleas); for Related Documents see Chap. 4, n. 18; dismissed, PAR #20183802; Petition of Maria Glover Holly and James G. Wilkinson to the Equity Court of Barnwell District, South Carolina, October 1854, in Records of the Equity Court, Bills, Microfilm Reel BW69, frames 35–40, *Maria Glover Holly and James G. Wilkinson v. Joshua Holly*, SCDAH; Related Documents: Order, ca. 1854; Court Record, ca. 1854, with ibid., partially granted, PAR #21385416; USMSPC, Barnwell District, South Carolina, 1850, p. 412; USMSSC, Barnwell District, South Carolina, 1850, p. 667.

12. Petition of Martha Stone to the Circuit Court of Sumner County, Tennessee, 18 September 1843, in Records of the Circuit Court, Loose Records, *Martha Stone v. Lewis Stone*, Case #534, TSLA; Related Documents: Bond, Martha Stone, William Garret to Lewis Stone, 10 September 1843; Order, 1 November 1845, with ibid., granted, PAR #21484353. Charity Hunter was the woman referred to in the petition. In 1840, she owned four female slaves, two under age ten and two between ten and twenty-four. See USMSPC, Cumberland County, Kentucky, 1840, p. 371.

13. For slave women who attempted to abscond, either alone or with their children, see Petition of Benjamin Browne to the Virginia General Assembly, 16 December 1809, Surry County, LP, LV; *Charleston Mercury*, 14 August 1826; *New Orleans Bee*, 15 March, 9, 12 May 1834; *New Orleans Picayune*, 3 July 1839, 4 July 1840; *Charleston Mercury*, 4 May 1830; *Richmond Enquirer*, 17 May 1850; *Republican Banner* (Tenn.), 1 October 1841, 18 April 1842; Franklin and Schweninger, *Runaway Slaves*, 25, 65; Petition of Josiah Houston to the Chancery Court of Talladega County, Alabama, 29 February 1840, in Records of the Circuit Court, Final Records, 1843-46, pp. 55-56, *Josiah Houston v. Matilda Houston*, Talladega County Judicial Building, Talladega, Ala.; Related Documents: Subpoena, Matilda Houston, 29 February 1840; Order, February 1841; Continuance, November 1842; Dismissal, December 1843, with ibid., dismissed, PAR #20184004. The husband Josiah wrote that "to his great astonishment," his wife was "delivered of a black child, the fruits of an illicit intercourse carried on between the said Matilda [his wife] and a negro slave" belonging to her father. The case was dismissed because Josiah left the state. See also Petition of Patience Cassity Havis to the District Court of East Baton Rouge Parish, Louisiana, 28 November 1840, in Records of the Third Judicial District Court, *Patience Cassity Havis v. John Havis*, Case #2942, CCA, Baton Rouge, La.; Related Documents: Orders, 25 November 1840, 23 January 1843; Supplemental Petition, 10 December 1840; Order, 16 December 1840; Supplemental Petition, 31 January 1842; Order, 21 January 1842; Copy of Supplemental Petition and Order, 16 December 1840; Supplemental Petition, ca. 13 February 1841; Order, 13 February 1841; Writ of Injunction, 30 November 1840, with ibid., partially granted, final judgment postponed, PAR #20884032; USMSPC, East Baton Rouge Parish, Louisiana, Eastern District, 1840, p. 85. Patience, who had left her husband, asked that the court release the three slaves into her possession if she executed a bond with good security. The court granted the request.

14. Petition of Stephen L. Lee to the Equity Court of Anne Arundel County, Maryland, 1 April 1861, in SC, *Stephen L. Lee v. Caroline Lee*, Case #OS298, MSA, no decree with petition, PAR #20986103; USMSPC, Anne Arundel County, Maryland, 1840, p. 128, and First District, 1850, p. 317; USMSSC, Anne Arundel County, Maryland, First District, 1850, p. 323; USMSPC, Anne Arundel County, Maryland, First District, 1860, p. 963; USMSSC, Anne Arundel County, Maryland, First District, 1860, p. 10. See also Petition of Caroline Duncan Lee to the Circuit Court of Anne Arundel County, Maryland, 31 July 1861, in SC, *Caroline Lee v. Stephen L. Lee*, Case #OS298, MSA; Related Documents: Order, 13 January 1862; Answer, Stephen Lee, 13 January 1862; Order, 7 February 1862, with ibid., partially granted, PAR #20986104.

15. Petition of Martha S. Huskey to the Circuit Court of Jefferson County, Missouri, 23 April 1849, in Records of the Circuit Court, *Martha S. Huskey v. Silas Huskey*, Case #1408, CCH, Hillsboro, Mo.; Related Documents: Order, 23 April 1849; Motion to Dismiss, 8 November 1849, with ibid., partially granted, dismissed, PAR #21184903; Petition of Rebecca Askew Hair and William Butler Matheny to the Equity Court of Barnwell District, South Carolina, 7 October 1857, in Records of the Equity Court, Bills, Microfilm Reel BW85, frames 651–55, *Rebecca Askew Hair and William Butler Matheny v. Irvine R. Hair*, SCDAH; Related Documents: Answer, Irvine R. Hair, ca. 7 October 1857; Orders, ca. 7 October 1857, 8 October 1857, with ibid., granted, PAR #21385776.

16. Douglass, *Narrative*, 60.

17. Petition of Elizabeth Cornwell to the Chancery Court of Smith County, Tennessee, 27 July 1852, in Records of the Chancery Court, Microfilm Reel 256, frames 1045–50, 1069–85, *Elizabeth A. Toney Cornwell v. Pleasant F. Cornwell*, Case #485, TSLA; Related Documents: Answer, Pleasant F. Cornwell, 7 August 1852; Decree, 11 August 1852, with ibid., granted, PAR #21485234; USMSPC, Smith County, Tennessee, North of Cumberland and East of Caney Fork rivers, 1850, p. 216; Petition of Nancy Haybarger to the Superior Court of Wilson County, North Carolina, 1859, in County Court Divorce Records, *Nancy Haybarger v. Robert H. Haybarger*, NCSA; Related Documents: Oath, 8 May 1860, with ibid., no decree with petition, PAR #21285912; Petition of Jane McCalop Johnston to the District Court of East Baton Rouge Parish, Louisiana, 18 May 1840, in Records of the Third Judicial District Court, *Jane McCalop Johnston v. William Johnston*, Case #2875, CCA, Baton Rouge, La.; Related Documents: Judgment, 23 July 1840, with ibid., granted, PAR #20884020.

18. Petition of Melinda W. Poston to the Circuit Court of Fayette County, Kentucky, 9 November 1829, in Records of the Circuit Court, Case Files, *Melinda W. Poston v. Richard Poston*, KDLA; Related Documents: Order, 9 October 1829; Depositions, Joseph Cabell Harrison, Sophia R. Harrison, and James Devore, 6 April 1830, with ibid., no decree with petition, PAR #20782921; Petition of Catherine Bishop to the Circuit Court of Barren County, Kentucky, 12 July 1836, in Records of the Circuit Court, Equity Judgments, *Catherine Bishop v. Lowry Bishop*, Case #849, KDLA; Related Documents: Order, 12 July 1836; Answer, Lowry Bishop, 17 October 1836; Amended Bill, ca. 1836; Notice of Bond Posted, Lowry Bishop, 18 July 1836; Depositions, Granville Hall and Edmund Duff, 16 May 1837, with ibid., no decree with petition, PAR #20783616; Petition of Mary Gayle to the District Court of East Baton Rouge Parish, Louisiana, 25 September 1816, in Records of the Third Judicial District Court, *Mary Gayle v. Christopher Gayle*, Case #414, CCA, Baton Rouge, La; for Related Documents, see Chap. 1, n. 14; granted, PAR #20881608.

19. See Fox-Genovese, "Family and Female Identity in the Antebellum South," 15–31, and *Within the Plantation Household*, chap. 3; Weiner, *Mistresses and Slaves*, chap. 4; Petition of Martha Brannock to the Superior Court of Guilford County, North Carolina, 22 February 1839, in County Court Divorce Records, *Martha Brannock v. Wright Brannock*, NCSA; Related Documents: Answer, Wright Brannock, 25 April 1839, with ibid., no decree with petition, PAR #21283911; Petition of Lydia

Jane Ireson and Alexander Boyd to the Chancery Court of Adams County, Mississippi, 13 December 1853, in Records of the Chancery Court, *Lydia Jane Ireson and Alexander Boyd v. Lansford O. Ireson*, Case #5, CCH, Natchez, Miss., no decree with petition, PAR #21085335; Petition of Lydia Jane Ireson and Robert T. Lessly to the Circuit Court of Adams County, Mississippi, 9 April 1856, in Records of the Chancery Court, *Lydia Jane Ireson and Robert T. Lessly v. Lansford O. Ireson*, with Case #5, CCH, Natchez, Miss.; Related Documents: Answer, Lansford O. Ireson, 9 May 1856; Amended Bill, Lydia Jane Ireson, 14 November 1856; Interrogatories, Charles N. Vaughan (visitor), Dr. Caleb Farrar, ca. 1856; Final Decree, 18 May 1857, with ibid., granted, PAR #21085631; Petition of Isabella Duncan King to the Chancery Court of Knox County, Tennessee, 27 August 1858, in Records of the Chancery Court, *Isabella Duncan King v. David King*, Case #1020, TSLA; Related Documents: Order, 27 August 1858; Decree, 9 April 1859, with ibid., granted, PAR #21485830; Petition of Martha Ann Crow and A. W. Bryant to the Chancery Court of Baldwin County, Alabama, 18 September 1855, in Records of the Chancery Court, Divorce Cases, *Martha Ann Crow and A. W. Bryant v. John F. Crow*, Case #1978, USAA; Related Documents: Affidavit, Martha A. Crow, 15 September 1855; Order for Injunction, 18 September 1855, with ibid., partially granted, PAR #20185523.

20. Petition of Elizabeth Cline to the Superior Court of Haywood County, North Carolina, October 1823, in Records of the County Court, *Elizabeth Cline v. Daniel Cline*, NCSA, no decree with petition, PAR #21282301; Petition of Sarah Carter and Charles Fralick to the Equity Court of Columbia District, South Carolina, 1 October 1818, in Records of the Equity Court, Bills, Richland District, *Sarah Carter and Charles Fralick v. Benjamin Carter*, SCDAH; Related Documents: Order, ca. 1 October 1818, with ibid., granted pro confesso, PAR #21381807. In 1820, Benjamin Carter, over forty-five years old and the only white person in the household, possessed thirty-three slaves. Among the slaves, twelve were engaged in agriculture and three in "manufacturing." See USMSPC, Richland District, South Carolina, 1810, p. 326, and Kershaw District, South Carolina, 1820, p. 148 (Benjamin Carter); Petition of Margaret G. Castleberry and James McGriffin to the Equity Court of Pendleton District, South Carolina, 10 December 1823, in Records of the Equity Court, Bills, *Margaret G. Castleberry and James McGriffin v. Asa Castleberry*, SCDAH; Related Documents: Deposition, Margaret Castleberry, 18 November 1823, with ibid., partially granted, dismissed, PAR #21382317.

21. Petition of Lucy W. Norman to the Virginia General Assembly, Henry County, 20 December 1848, in LP, LV; Related Documents: Extracts from Depositions, Wilmouth Edwards (family friend), Catharine Carter, Elizabeth Murphy, ca. 1848; Copy of Court Record, 3 October 1848, with ibid., referred to Committee for Courts of Justice, PAR #11684814.

22. Petition of Maria W. Webb to the District Court of Orleans Parish, Louisiana, 7 August 1833, in Records of the First Judicial District Court, Case Records, *Maria W. Webb v. William Webb*, Case #10742, LC; Related Documents: Order, 7 August 1833; Judgment, 14 March 1835; Testimonies, Clements Daniel (son) et al., 17 February 1834, with ibid., granted, PAR #20883314; Petition of Anne Wilson to the Equity Court of Burke County, North Carolina, 19 November 1840, in County Court Di-

vorce Records, *Anne Wilson v. William Wilson*, NCSA; Related Documents: Order, 19 November 1840; Answer, William Wilson, 25 November 1840; Depositions, Isabella Wilson, Martha Cuthbertson, Nathaniel Cuthbertson, David Cuthbertson, Elizabeth Browning, Elijah Browning, 22 December 1840, with ibid., agreement, PAR #21284004. The couple owned four slaves: "Sylvey," Lucinda, Cynthia, and Jacob. See USMSPC, Burke County, North Carolina, 1830, following p. 204, and 1840, p. 284. In describing the "dead born" baby, Martha Cuthbertson said that "its Head was mashed and the bones of the head broken." In all likelihood this was the result of a difficult delivery with the use of forceps, despite the fact that physicians, rather than midwives or slaves, usually employed forceps. See Jensen, *Loosening the Bonds*, 33–34.

23. Buckley, "'Placed in the Power of Violence,'" 36; Petition of Mary Strain and Abijah Penson to the Equity Court of Washington District, South Carolina, 7 October 1817, in Records of the Equity Court, Bills, *Mary Strain and Abijah Penson v. William Strain*, Case #1818 8, SCDAH; Related Documents: Oath, Abijah Penson, 6 October 1817; Order, ca. 7 October 1817, with ibid., partially granted, PAR #21381723; Petition of Elizabeth Clubb to the Superior Court of Lincoln County, North Carolina, 1843, in County Court Divorce Records, *Elizabeth Clubb v. David Clubb*, NCSA; Related Documents: Oath, Elizabeth C. Clubb, 9 December 1841; Answer, David Clubb, 9 September 1843, with ibid., settled, PAR #21284303; Petition of Elizabeth Hill to the Circuit Court of Leon County, Florida, 13 July 1860, in Chancery Case Files, *Elizabeth Hill v. John M. Hill*, SAF, no decree with petition, PAR #20586003; USMSPC, Leon County, Florida, Tallahassee, 1860, p. 8; USMSSC, Leon County, Florida, Tallahassee, 1860, p. 247.

24. Petition of Lucretia Chambers and Thomas McGinnis to the Chancery Court of Shelby County, Alabama, 6 July 1842, in Records of the Chancery Court, Court Record, 1839–46, 2:220–25, *Lucretia Chambers and Thomas McGinnis v. John Chambers*, CCH, Columbiana, Ala.; Related Documents: Subpoena, John Chambers, 7 July 1842; Sheriff's Return, 13 July 1842; Answer, John Chambers, n.d.; Order, n.d.; Dismissal, 7 August 1844, with ibid., dismissed, PAR #20184219; Petition of Anna Allen to the Equity Court of Columbia District, South Carolina, 14 December 1816, in Records of the Equity Court, Bills, Richland District, *Anna Allen v. John Allen and Turner Stark*, SCDAH; Related Documents: Order, 14 December 1816; Commissioner's Report, February Term 1817; Report on Sale, June Term 1817, with ibid., granted, PAR #21381606. In Richmond, Va., slave owner Robert Hamilton gave the keys to his "coal room" to a young black woman who was responsible for doling out coal to the owner's wife. See Petition of Helen Hamilton to the Virginia General Assembly, Richmond City, Virginia, 14 December 1846, in LP, LV, referred to Committee for Courts of Justice, PAR #11684604.

25. Catterall, *Judicial Cases Concerning American Slavery*, 5:235; Petition of Agnes Coleman to the Circuit Court of Harrison County, Kentucky, 2 July 1846, in Records of the Circuit Court, Case Files, *Agnes Coleman v. Edward Coleman*, Case #9024, CCH, Cynthiana, Ky.; Related Documents: Answer, Edward Coleman, 30 July 1846; Decree, 24 September 1846, with ibid., dismissed, PAR #20784612. Coleman owned twenty-four slaves. Petition of Mary W. Lawson to the Virginia

General Assembly, Richmond City, Virginia, 8 January 1840, in LP, LV; Related Documents: Statement of Mary W. Lawson, 23 February 1839; Copy of Indenture, 26 September 1837, with ibid., referred to Committee for Courts of Justice, PAR #11684005.

26. Petition of Martha Turner to the Equity Court of Charles County, Maryland, 27 March 1830, in SC, *Martha Turner v. Thomas Turner*, Case #11576, MSA; Related Documents: Separation Agreement, *Thomas Turner and Martha Turner*, 21 October 1829; Depositions, Dr. Edward Miles, Benjamin Stonestreet, 13 March 1831, Susan Courtney, Mary Ann Courtney, Philip Turner, Jane King, Dr. Celestus Lancaster, Lewis E. Turner, Thomas O'Brian, Henry H. Freeman, Samuel Stiggs, Jane Turner, Elizabeth Turner and Henrietta Turner, 14 March 1831, with ibid., no decree with petition, PAR #20983011. In 1830, Thomas Turner, in his fifties, headed a household with three boys under age fifteen and a girl in her late teens. His wife had left the previous year (separation agreement above). He possessed four slaves. See USMSPC, Charles County, Maryland, Bryantown, 1830, p. 164; Petition of Mary Jane Davis and Sarah Blalock to the Equity Court of Dallas County, Alabama, 23 January 1860, in Records of the Circuit Court, Record 1858–60, vol. O, pp. 151–72, *Mary Jane Davis and Sarah Blalock v. Daniel Davis*, CCH, Selma, Ala.; Related Documents: Copies of Notice of Petition, 13 August 1860; Decretal Order, 1860; Report of Register, 16 August 1860; Order, August 1860; Schedule to Report, 15 August 1860; Exceptions to Register's Report, 17 August 1860; Report of Register on Exceptions, 17 August 1860; Order, August 1860; Decretal Order for Temporary Alimony, August 1860; Orders, August 1860, January 1861; Notice of Motion for Attachment, 7 January 1861; Order Denying Motion for Attachment, January 1861; Exceptions of Complainant to Testimony, 1861; Exceptions of Defendant to Testimony, 1861; Consent of Parties as to Testimony, 1861; Order, January 1861; Copies of Summons, 23 January 1860; Answer, Daniel Davis, 14 February 1860; Opinion and Decree, January 1861, with ibid., dismissed, PAR #20186033.

27. Petition of Margaret Garner to the Chancery Court of Mobile County, Alabama, 1 March 1841, in Records of the Chancery Court, Divorce Cases, *Margaret Garner v. Thomas Garner*, Case #745, USAA; Related Documents: Decree, 20 November 1841; Certification of Court Transcripts of Divorce Case in Florida and Oath of Judge Dillon Jordan for Said Case, 21 April 1841. These transcripts were entered as Exhibit B in this proceeding and appear in their entirety in PARs #20583803 and #20253804, with ibid.; no decree with petition, PAR #20184113. See also Petition of Caroline Augusta Turner to the Circuit Court of Woodford County, Kentucky, 6 July 1841, in Records of the Circuit Court, Case Files, *Caroline Augusta Turner v. Fielding Turner*, KDLA; Related Documents: Deposition, James E. Davis, 4 January 1842; Copy of Letter, N. Turner to Caroline Turner, 13 March 1831, with ibid., dismissed, PAR #20784112.

28. Petition of Margaret Ann O'Conner and James E. R. Chisholm to the Chancery Court of Adams County, Mississippi, 21 April 1849, in Records of the Vice Chancery Court, *Margaret Ann O'Conner and James E. R. Chisholm v. Luke O'Conner*, CCH, Natchez, Miss.; Related Documents: Dismissal, 5 May 1849; Consents, Margaret Ann O'Conner and James E. R. Chisholm, 21 April 1849; Affidavit, James E. R. Chis-

holm, 21 April 1849; Order, 23 April 1849, with ibid., partially granted, dismissed, PAR #21084908; Petition of Margaret O'Conner and J. E. R. Chisholm to the Chancery Court of Adams County, Mississippi, 24 November 1849, in Records of the Vice Chancery Court, *Margaret O'Conner and J. E. R. Chisholm v. Luke O'Conner*, Case #496, CCH, Natchez, Miss.; Related Documents: Order, 22 November 1849; Notice, 6 December 1849; Depositions, Henry Brown and John Sullivan, 8 December 1849; Final Decree, 7 January 1850; Receipt, Margaret O'Conner, 14 January 1850; Commissioner's Report, 14 January 1850, with ibid., granted, PAR #21084914; Petition of Harriet Rembert and Edward Hamlin to the Equity Court of Charleston District, South Carolina, 21 January 1852, in Records of the Equity Court, Bills, *Harriet Rembert and Edward Hamlin v. Isaac Rembert*, Case #1852-77, SCDAH; Related Documents: Consent of Next Friend, Edward Hamlin, 21 January 1852; Order, 21 January 1852; Master's Report, 4 February 1854, with ibid., granted, PAR #21385247; Petition of Mary Jackson and Samuel Buckhan to the Superior Court of Greene County, Georgia, 1806, in Records of the Superior Court, Proceedings 1808-9, pp. 125-27, *Mary Jackson and Samuel Buckhan v. Joseph Jackson*, CCH, Greensboro, Ga.; Related Documents: Summons, Joseph Jackson, 22 January 1806, with ibid., no decree with petition, PAR #20680602.

29. Petition of Jane E. Holmes Schmidt and John L. Holmes to the Equity Court of Charleston District, South Carolina, 29 June 1831, in Records of the Equity Court, Bills, *Jane E. Holmes Schmidt and John L. Holmes v. John W. Schmidt*, Case #1833-78, SCDAH; Related Documents: Order, 11 January 1833; Answer, John W. Schmidt, 25 November 1831; Affidavit to Postpone Case, John W. Schmidt, 20 January 1832, with ibid., partially granted, postponed, PAR #21383110; Petition of Jacob Smith to the Chancery Court of Pickens County, Alabama, 25 October 1841, in Records of the Circuit Court, Estates, *Jacob Smith v. Sarah Smith*, Case #3, CCH, Carrollton, Ala.; Related Documents: Answer, 20 December 1841; Decree, ca. 1844; Interrogatories, 20 May 1844; Depositions, James W. Smith, John Smith, Fielding S. Smith, 1 July 1843, with ibid., dismissed, PAR #20184105. In 1840, Jacob Smith, in his forties, was listed with eight children—4 boys and 4 girls under twenty—and 4 female slaves, 2 under ten and 2 between ten and twenty-four. See USMSPC, Pickens County, Alabama, 1840, p. 318; Petition of Ann Harbour Richardson to the District Court of West Feliciana Parish, Louisiana, 20 June 1859, in Records of the Seventh Judicial District Court, *Ann Harbour Richardson v. Jared N. Richardson*, Case #1325, PCH, St. Francisville, La.; Related Documents: Order, 11 June 1859; Decree, 6 June 1867; Supplemental Petition, 14 March 1860, with ibid., dismissed, PAR #20885917.

30. Petition of Izabelle Questi to the District Court of Iberville Parish, Louisiana, 15 April 1825, in Records of the Fourth Judicial District Court, *Izabelle Questi v. Giovanni Questi*, Case #546, PCH, Plaquemine, La.; Related Documents: Order, 15 April 1825; Judgment, 22 October 1825, with ibid., dismissed with the consent of the parties, PAR #20882508.

31. Petition of Alzonuth M. Whitehead and Alexander K. Farrar to the Chancery Court of Adams County, Mississippi, 18 March 1853, in Records of the Vice Chancery Court, *Alzonuth M. Whitehead and Alexander K. Farrar v. James H. White-*

head, Case #748, CCH, Natchez, Miss.; Related Documents: PARs #21085314, #21085315; Order, 23 March 1853, with ibid., granted, PAR #21085313; Petition of Alzonuth M. Whitehead and Alexander K. Farrar to the Chancery Court of Adams County, Mississippi, 31 December 1853, with ibid.; Related Documents: Order to Sheriff, 28 March 1853; Sheriff's Report, 5 April 1853; Interrogatories and Testimony, Timothy Thomas, David Thomas, Turner Ewell (quote), Henry C. Whitehead, 22 December 1853, Ann Eliza Davis, Mary Holmes, and Thomas G. James, 23 December 1853; Commissioner's Report, 31 December 1853, with ibid., no decree with petition, PAR #21085315.

32. See, for example, Petition of Mary A. Harper to the Chancery Court of Smith County, Tennessee, 5 September 1842, in Records of the Chancery Court, Microfilm Reel 319, frames 1503–7, 1513–14, 1520–26, 1528–29, *Mary A. Harper v. Alfred Harper*, Case #3627, TSLA; Related Documents: Order, 2 September 1842; Answer, Alfred Harper, 16 January 1843; Depositions, William Richardson, James Richardson, John Carter, 8 July 1843; Related Petition, ca. August 1843, with ibid., granted, PAR #21484215; Petition of Margery Ryon Wells to the Equity Court of Anne Arundel County, Maryland, 16 December 1857, in SC, *Margery Ryon Wells v. James H. Wells*, MSA; for Related Documents, see Chap. 4, n. 9; granted, PAR #20985703; Petition of Marie Louise Castro to the District Court of Natchitoches Parish, Louisiana, 18 October 1825, in Records of the District Court, *Marie Louise Castro v. Jose Maria Castro*, Case #852, PCH, Natchitoches, La.; Related Documents: Verdict, ca. November 1825; Judgment, November Term 1825; List of Court Costs, 15 November 1825; Plaintiff's Evidence, November Term 1825, with ibid., granted, PAR #20882526.

33. See n. 1 above. In 1840, Cornelius K. Ayer, still in his thirties, owned 95 slaves, including 50 field hands, on a nearby plantation. He and his wife had three children. See USMSPC, Barnwell District, South Carolina, 1840, p. 32; USMSPC, Bedford County, Tennessee, Tenth District, 1870, p. 293.

Essay on Sources and Methodology

1. Painter, "Soul Murder and Slavery," 37; Burr, *Secret Eye*, 100.

2. Silkenat, *Moments of Despair*, 116; Penningroth, "African American Divorce." For the nature of petitioning in other places during different time periods, see Mann, *Republic of Debtors*, 72–77; Davis, *Fiction in the Archives*, 3–8, 45, 85.

3. The counties are distributed by state as follows: Alabama 20, Arkansas 2, Delaware 1, Florida 5, Georgia 8, Kentucky 15, Louisiana 10, Maryland 5, Missouri 6, Mississippi 8, North Carolina 49, South Carolina 16, Tennessee 21, Texas 7, and Virginia 38, plus the District of Columbia.

4. Chused, *Private Acts in Public Places*, 12.

5. Robert William Fogel and Stanley L. Engerman, *Time on the Cross: The Economics of American Negro Slavery*, 2 vols. (Boston: Little, Brown, 1974); Chused, *Private Acts in Public Places*, 163–83; Buckley, *Great Catastrophe of My Life*, 269–71; Tadman, *Speculators and Slaves*, tables 2–8; Pargas, *Quarters and the Fields*, tables 1.1–1.6, 5.1–5.3.

6. For comparative purposes, see Evans, "Economics of American Negro Slavery," 199–202; Tadman, *Speculators and Slaves*, 189–91. For the price of the "average" slave being about one-half of the price of a prime male field hand as well as the relative proportion of slaves in a total estate, see Deyle, *Carry Me Back*, 56–59; Ransom, *Conflict and Compromise*, 63, 75; Ransom and Sutch, "Capitalists without Capital," 137.

BIBLIOGRAPHY

Primary Sources

MANUSCRIPTS
Alabama
Abbeville (Henry County)
   Records of the Circuit Court, Final Records, vol. B–C, 1866
Carrollton (Pickens County)
   Records of the Circuit Court, Estates, 1841–48
Centerville (Bibb County)
   Records of the Bibb County Circuit Court
      Record Books, 1826–36, 1836–46
Clayton (Barbour County)
   Records of the Circuit Court
      Records, vol. C, 1846
Columbiana (Shelby County)
   Shelby County Archives, Records of the Chancery Court
      Record Book 1, 1839–41; Record Book 2, 1839–46
      Records of the Talladega County Chancery Court, Minutes and Dockets:
          Divorces, Slaves, Estates, 1857–61
Dadeville (Tallapoosa County)
   Records of the Circuit Court
      Chancery Cases Involving Slaves, 1848–51
      Chancery Court, Minutes and Decrees, 1848–52, 1855–67
Hayneville (Lowndes County)
   Records of the Circuit Court
      Final Record, vol. 1, 1842; vol. 4, 1845; vol. 7, 1851; vol. 8, 1851
Huntsville (Jefferson County)
   Madison County Public Library Archives
      Chancery Record, C-23-9, vol. K, 1839; C-23-13, vol. O, 1846–47; C-24-26,
         vol. V, 1852
Lafayette (Chambers County)
   Records of the Circuit Court, Record Book Middle Chancery District, 1841–53
Livingston (Sumter County)
   Records of the Circuit Court, Estates, 1842–58
Mobile (Mobile County)
   University of South Alabama Archives
      Chancery Cases, 1838
      Records of the Chancery Court, Case Files, 1848–63
      Records of the Chancery Court, Divorce Files, 1841–63
Montgomery (Montgomery County)
   Alabama Department of Archives and History

Alabama Supreme Court Records, Case Record Books, 1848–61
Records of the Montgomery County Circuit Court, Records, 1845–46
Records of the Perry County Chancery Court, Case Papers, 1850–53
Montgomery County Courthouse
Records of the Circuit Court, Chancery Records, 1849–50
Selma (Dallas County)
Records of the Circuit Court
Chancery Records, 1852–54, 1858–60
Talladega (Talladega County)
Records of the Circuit Court
Final Records, 1839–41, 1841–42, 1843–46, 1846–69; Record, 1836–47; Records, 1856–57

Arkansas
Little Rock (Pulaski County)
University of Arkansas at Little Rock, School of Law
Arkansas Supreme Court Records and Briefs, 1855
Warren (Bradley County)
Records of the Circuit Court
Old Circuit Court Papers, 1830–60

Delaware
Dover
Delaware State Archives
Legislative Papers, 1832

District of Columbia
District of Columbia (Washington County)
National Archives
Records of the United States Circuit Court
Chancery Dockets and Rules Case Files, 1809–61
Chancery Records, Old Divorces, 1861–62

Florida
Ocala (Marion County)
Records of the Circuit Court
Chancery Case Files, 1850
Pensacola (Escambia County)
Copy of Records of the Chancery Court, Mobile County, Alabama, Divorce Case, 1838
Records of the Probate Court, 1831–57
Records of the Superior Court, 1831–45
St. Augustine (St. Johns County)
Records of the Circuit Court, 1854
Tallahassee (Leon County)

State Archives of Florida
    Records of the Circuit Court of Leon County, Chancery Case Files, 1848–62
    Records of the Superior Court of Leon County, Chancery Case Files, 1841–42
    Records of the Territorial Legislative Council, 1839–43

Georgia
Atlanta (Fulton County)
    Georgia Department of Archives and History
        Records of the Superior Court of Houston County
            Minutes, 1858–67; Writs, 1856–66
Augusta (Richmond County)
    Records of the Superior Court, Writs, 1853–55
Greensboro (Greene County)
    Records of the Superior Court, Proceedings, 1808–9
Greenville (Meriwether County)
    Records of the Superior Court, Writs, 1857–60
Grey (Jones County)
    Records of the Superior Court, Minutes, 1847–71; Writs, 1831–35
Lexington (Oglethorpe County)
    Records of the Superior Court, Minutes, 1810–13
Newnan (Coweta County)
    Records of the Superior Court, Writs, 1839–49
Washington (Wilkes County)
    Records of the Superior Court, Record Book, 1822–23

Kentucky
Cynthiana (Harrison County)
    Records of the Circuit Court, Case Files, 1810–58
Frankfort (Franklin County)
    Kentucky Division of Libraries and Archives
        Records of the Chancery Court of Todd County
            Equity Case Files, 1822–53
        Records of the Circuit Court of Barren County
            Equity Judgments, 1812–61
        Records of the Circuit Court of Boyle County
            Equity/Chancery Cases, 1847
        Records of the Circuit Court of Butler County
            Equity Cases, 1847–58
        Records of the Circuit Court of Christian County
            Petitions in Equity, 1825–49
        Records of the Circuit Court of Fayette County
            Case Files, 1810–62
        Records of the Circuit Court of Floyd County
            Case Files, 1837
        Records of the Circuit Court of Jefferson County

        Case Files, 1809–58
        Records of the Circuit Court of Nicholas County
            Case Files, 1844
        Records of the Circuit Court of Pike County
            Case Files, 1827–46
        Records of the Circuit Court of Scott County
            Case Files, 1844–56
        Records of the Circuit Court of Warren County
            Equity/Chancery Cases, 1859
        Records of the Circuit Court of Woodford County
            Case Files, 1828–41
Paris (Bourbon County)
    Records of the Circuit Court, Case Files, 1829–58

Louisiana
Baton Rouge (East Baton Rouge Parish)
    East Baton Rouge Parish Clerk of Court Archives
        Records of the Third Judicial District Court
            Case Files, 1816–40
        Records of the Sixth Judicial District Court
            Case Files, 1850–54
Harrisonburg (Catahoula Parish)
    Records of the District Court, Case Files, 1850–51
Natchitoches (Natchitoches Parish)
    Records of the District Court, Case Files, 1825–60
New Orleans (Orleans Parish)
    Louisiana Collection, New Orleans Public Library
        Records of the First Judicial District Court
            Case Records, 1818–41
        Records of the Fifth Judicial District Court
            Suit Records, 1853–55
New Roads (Pointe Coupee Parish)
    Records of the Fourth Judicial District Court
        Case Files, 1816–43
    Records of the Ninth Judicial District Court
        Case Files, 1848
Opelousas (St. Landry Parish)
    Records of the Fifth Judicial District Court
        Case Files, 1817–39
    Records of the Fifteenth Judicial District Court
        Case Files, 1847–55
Plaquemine (Iberville Parish)
    Records of the Fourth Judicial District Court
        Case Files, 1825–44
    Records of the Sixth Judicial District Court

    Case Files, 1860–61
Port Allen (West Baton Rouge Parish)
  Records of the Fourth Judicial District Court
    Case Files, 1820–34
St. Francisville (West Feliciana Parish)
  Records of the Third Judicial District Court
    Case Files, 1825–36
  Records of the Seventh Judicial District Court
    Case Files, 1859

Maryland
Annapolis
  Maryland State Archives' Schweninger Collection
    Records of the Anne Arundel County Equity/Chancery Court, 1856–65
    Records of the Baltimore County Equity/Chancery Court
      Case Files, 1824–50
    Records of the Charles County Equity/Chancery Court
      Case Files, 1830–62
    Records of the Montgomery County Equity/Chancery Court
      Case Files, 1847–65
    Records of the St. Mary's County Equity/Chancery Court
      Case Files, 1842

Mississippi
Coffeeville (Yalobusha County)
  Records of the Chancery/Probate Courts, Case Files, 1858
Columbus (Lowndes County)
  Billups-Garth Archives, Lowndes County Public Library
    Records of the Chancery Court
      Case Files, 1857–62; Minutes, 1845–53
        Record, Noxubee County Chancery Court, 1858
Fayette (Jefferson County)
  Records of the Chancery Court, 1857
Greenville (Washington County)
  Records of the Chancery Court
    Final Record in Chancery, 1858
Macon (Noxubee County)
  Records of the Chancery Court, Case Files, 1842–60
Meridian (Lauderdale County)
  Lauderdale County Archives
    Records of the Circuit Court
      Divorce Case Files, 1838–55
Natchez (Adams County)
  Record of the Claiborne County Chancery Court, 1850
  Records of the Vice Chancery Court, 1848–53

Port Gibson (Claiborne County)
    Records of the Chancery Court, Case Files, 1858
Woodville (Wilkinson County)
    Records of the Probate Court, 1856

Missouri
Hillsboro (Jefferson County)
    Records of the Circuit Court, Case Files, 1849–52
Jackson (Cape Girardeau County)
    Records of the Circuit Court, Case Files, 1838–48
Jefferson City (Cole County)
    Missouri State Archives
        Records of the Circuit Court of Boone County
            Case Files, 1824–42
        Records of the Supreme Court
            Record of the Chancery Court of Clay County
                Case File, 1846
            Record of the Circuit Court of Platte County
                Case File, 1852
Ste. Genevieve (Ste. Genevieve County)
    Records of the Circuit Court, Case File, 1845

North Carolina
Raleigh (Wake County)
    North Carolina State Archives
        General Assembly, Session Records
            Divorce Petitions, 1803–34
            House Committee Reports, Divorce, Alimony, and Internal
                Improvements, 1825
            Joint Committee Reports, Divorce, Alimony, Finance, 1809
            Joint Committee Reports, Divorce and Alimony, 1808
            Senate Committee Reports, Claims and Military, 1827
        Records of Superior Court of Davidson County
            Slaves and Free Persons of Color, 1826–96
        Records of the Equity Court of Wayne County
            Case File, 1854
        Records of the State Supreme Court
            Record of the Equity Court of Orange County, 1822
        Records of the Superior Court
            Divorce Records, Case Files
                Ashe County, 1840–57
                Buncombe County, 1831–66
                Burke County, 1839–40
                Caldwell County, 1861
                Caswell County, 1829–42

    Chatham County, 1829–57
    Cleveland County, 1848
    Craven County, 1828–60
    Davidson County, 1839–66
    Duplin County, 1856
    Franklin County, 1856
    Granville County, 1826–53
    Guilford County, 1830–66
    Henderson County, 1860
    Hyde County, 1860
    Lincoln County, 1811–55
    Macon County, 1835
    Mecklenburg County, 1856–64
    Montgomery County, 1844–56
    Nash County, 1823–61
    Northampton County, 1834–52
    Orange County, 1838–41
    Pasquotank County, 1835–49
    Perquimans County, 1824–57
    Person County, 1834–52
    Randolph County, 1841–61
    Richmond County, 1818–56
    Robeson County, 1844
    Rockingham County, 1835–60
    Rowan County, 1835–66
    Rutherford County, 1840
    Stanly County, 1854
    Stokes County, 1815–57
    Surry County, 1841
    Wake County, 1819–66
    Wayne County, 1829–56
    Wilson County, 1859
    Yadkin County, 1853–57
Records of the Superior Court of Haywood County
    Case File, 1823
Records of the Superior Court of Wayne County
    Slaves and Free Persons of Color, 1789–1869
Records of the Superior Court of Wilkes County
    Miscellaneous Records, 1837
William Blount Rodman Legal Papers
    Record of the Superior Court of Hyde County, 1844

South Carolina
Columbia (Richland County)
    South Carolina Department of Archives and History

General Assembly, Petitions, 1847
Records of the Equity Court, Bills
    Anderson District, 1853-60
    Barnwell District, 1841-57
    Charleston District, 1809-56
    Chester District, 1818-45
    Columbia District, 1814-24
    Darlington District, 1818-54
    Fairfield District, 1820-57
    Laurens District, 1825-58
    Newberry District, 1819-55
    Pendleton District, 1823
    Richland District, 1830-61
    Spartanburg District, 1823
    Sumter District, 1826-60
    Union District, 1830-33
    Washington District, 1810-17
    York District, 1859

Tennessee
Columbia (Maury County)
    Maury County Archives
        Records of the Chancery Court, Case Files, 1842-59
        Records of the Circuit Court, Case File, 1829
Fayetteville (Lincoln County)
    Records of the Chancery Court, Minutes, 1847-54
Franklin (Williamson County)
    Record of the Chancery Court of Williamson County, 1855 (courthouse)
    Williamson County Archives
        Records of the Chancery Court, Case Files, 1836-59
        Records of the Circuit Court, Case Files, 1821-56
Johnson City (Washington County)
    Archives of Appalachia, East Tennessee State University
        Records of the Chancery Court, Washington County, Civil Case Files, 1838-57
Memphis (Shelby County)
    Memphis and Shelby County Archives
        Records of the Circuit Court, Case Files, 1842-45
Nashville (Davidson County)
    Metropolitan Nashville-Davidson County Archives
        Records of the Chancery Court, Case Files, 1846-57
    Tennessee State Library and Archives
        Legislative Petitions, 1819-45
        Records of the Chancery Court, Case Files/Loose Records
            Blount County, 1849 (found in Knox County records)

       Bradley County, 1847–54
       Franklin County, 1861, Miscellaneous Court Records
       Knox County, 1848–58
       Marshall County, 1844–49
       Rhea County, 1810
       Smith County, 1842–55
       Sumner County, 1843
   Supreme Court of Middle Tennessee Case Files
       Record of Chancery Court Proceedings
          Bedford County, 1855
          Davidson County, 1835–55
          Franklin County, 1853
          Maury County, 1848
          Montgomery County, 1828
          Wilson County, 1855
Shelbyville (Bedford County)
   Records of the Chancery Court, Case Files, 1847

Texas
Angleton (Brazoria County)
   Records of the District Court, Case Files, 1841–55
Austin (Travis County)
   Records of the District Court, Case File, 1859
   Texas State Library and Archives
      Records of the Texas Supreme Court
          District Court of Bexar County, Case File, 1852
Beaumont (Jefferson County)
   Records of the District Court, Case Files, 1850–64
Nacogdoches (Nacogdoches County)
   East Texas Research Center, Stephen F. Austin University
      Records of the District Court of San Augustine County, 1845
   Records of the District Court, Case Files, 1839–61
Sherman (Grayson County)
   Records of the District Court, Case File, 1865

Virginia
Halifax (Halifax County)
   Records of the Circuit Superior Court, Chancery Finals, 1846
Petersburg (corporation of)
   Records of the Circuit Superior Court, Case Files, 1835–63
Richmond (corporation of)
   Library of Virginia
      Legislative Petitions, 1802–50
         Halifax County Circuit Superior Court Record, 1841
      Records of the Chancery Court

Albemarle County Ended Chancery Causes, 1847–67
Amelia County Court Papers, Judgments, 1779–90
Campbell County Superior Court Records, 1840–54
Chesterfield County Chancery Court Causes, 1859
Fluvanna County Ended Chancery Causes, 1849
Franklin County Chancery Court Papers, 1841–63
Henrico County Ended Chancery Causes, 1817–25
Lancaster County Circuit Court Chancery Papers, 1852
Lynchburg Ended Chancery Causes, 1826–60
Mecklenburg County Chancery Court Causes, 1856–59
Pittsylvania County Court Papers, Judgments, 1787
Princess Anne County Chancery Court Causes, 1833
Scott County Determined Chancery Causes, 1835–58
Southampton County Chancery Papers, 1806–37
Sussex County Court Papers, 1796
Rustburg (Campbell County)
Records of the Circuit Superior Court, Case Files, 1842–59

PUBLISHED SOURCES

Acts and Resolutions, passed by the Legislative Council, of the Territory of Florida, at its Third Session, Begun and Held in the City of Tallahassee, on Monday, January 6, 1845. Tallahassee: W. and C. J. Bartlett, 1845.

Acts of the General Assembly of the State of Georgia, Passed in Milledgeville, at an Annual Session in November and December 1833. [Milledgeville]: Polhill and Fort, 1834.

Acts of the Seventh Biennial Session, of the General Assembly of Alabama, Held in the City of Montgomery, Commencing on the Second Monday in November, 1859. Montgomery: Sorter and Reid, 1860.

Acts Passed at a General Assembly of the Commonwealth of Virginia, Begun and Held at the Capitol in the City of Richmond, on Monday the Tenth Day of October, in the Year of Our Lord, One Thousand Eight Hundred and Fourteen. Richmond: Thomas Richie, 1815.

Acts Passed at the Second Session of the General Assembly of the State of Alabama. Begun and held in the Town of Cahawba, on the first Monday in November, one thousand eight hundred and twenty. Cahawba: Allen and Brickell, 1820.

Acts Passed at the Seventh Annual Session of the General Assembly of the State of Alabama, Begun and Held in the Town of Cahawba, on the Third Monday in November, One Thousand Eight Hundred and Twenty-five. Cahawba: William A. Allen and Co., 1826.

Acts Passed at the Third Annual Session of the General Assembly of the State of Alabama, Begun and Held in the Town of Cahawba, on the First Monday in November, One Thousand Eight Hundred and Twenty-one. Cahawba: William A. Allen and Co., 1822.

Blane, William N. *An Excursion through the United States and Canada during the Years 1822–23.* London: Baldwin, Cradock, and Joy, 1824.

Bourne, George. *Marriage Indissoluble and Divorce Unscriptural*. Harrisonburg, Va.: Davidson and Bourne, 1813.

Civil Code of the State of Louisiana, Preceded by the Treaty of Cession with France, The Constitution of the United States of America, and of the State. N.p.: Citizen of Louisiana, 1825.

The Code of Tennessee Enacted by the General Assembly of 1857–'8. Nashville: Eastman and Company, 1858.

The Code of Virginia: with the Declaration of Independence and the Constitution of the United States. Richmond: William F. Ritchie, 1849.

A Compilation of the Statutes of Tennessee, of a General and Permanent Nature, From the Commencement of the Government to the Present time . . . . Nashville: James Smith, 1836.

The Consolidation and Revision of the Statutes of the State, of a General Nature. New Orleans: Bee Office 1852.

DeBow, J. D. B., comp. *Statistical View of the United States, Embracing its Territory, Population—White, free colored, and Slave—Moral and Social Condition, Industry, property, and Revenue . . . Being a Compendium of the Seventh Census*. Washington, D.C.: Beverly Tucker, 1854.

DeSaussure, Henry William. *Reports of Cases Argued and Determined in the Court of Chancery of the State of South-Carolina, and in the Court of Appeals in Equity*. 4 vols. Columbia, S.C.: Daniel and J. J. Faust, 1817–19.

Digest of the Laws of Virginia, Which Are of a Permanent Character and General Operation; Illustrated by Judicial Decisions: to which is added, An Index of the Names of the Cases in the Virginia Reporters. Richmond: Smith and Palmer, 1841.

Digest of the Laws of Virginia of a Civil Nature and of a Permanent Character and General Operation: Illustrated by Judicial Decisions. 2 vols. Richmond: J. W. Randolph, 1856.

Douglass, Frederick. *Narrative of the Life of Frederick Douglass, an American Slave, Written by Himself*. Boston: Anti-slavery Office, 1846.

Haskel, Daniel, and J. Calvin Smith. *A Complete Descriptive and Statistical Gazetteer of the United States of America*. New York: Sherman and Smith, 1847.

Hening, W. W., ed. *The Statutes at Large; Being a Collection of All the Laws of Virginia from the First Session of the Legislature in 1619*. 13 vols. Richmond, 1809–23.

Kemble, Frances Anne. *Journal of a Residence in America*. Paris: A. and W. Galignani, 1835.

Kent, James. *Commentaries on American Law*. 11th ed. 4 vols. Boston: Little, Brown and Company, 1866.

Laws of a Public and General Nature, of the District of Louisiana, of the Territory of Louisiana, of the Territory of Missouri, and of the State of Missouri, up to the Year 1824. 2 vols. Jefferson City: W. Lusk and Son, 1842.

Laws of a Public and General Nature of the State of Missouri, Passed Between the Years 1824 and 1836, Not Published in the Digest of 1825, Nor in the Digest of 1835. 2 vols. Jefferson City: W. Lusk and Son, 1842.

Laws of North Carolina at a General Assembly, begun and held at the city of Raleigh, on the twenty-first Day of November, in the Year of our Lord One thousand seven hundred and ninety-six . . . . [1797].

Laws of North Carolina at a General Assembly, begun and held in Raleigh, on the Third Monday the Nineteenth Day of November, in the year of our Lord One Thousand Eight Hundred and Ten. Raleigh: n.p. [1811].

Laws of North Carolina at a General Assembly, begun and held in Raleigh, on the Twentieth Day of November, in the year of our Lord One Thousand Seven Hundred and Ninety-seven. Halifax, N.C.: Abraham Hodge, 1797.

Laws of the State of Delaware, Passed at a Session of the General Assembly, Commenced and Held at Dover, on Tuesday the Third Day of January, in the year of our Lord, One Thousand Eight Hundred and Thirty-Two. George Town: James M'Calla, 1832.

Laws of the State of Mississippi: Passed at an Adjourned Session of the Legislature, Held in the City of Jackson, From January 7, to February 16, A. D. 1839. Jackson: B. D. Howard, 1839.

Laws of the State of Mississippi, Passed at a Regular Biennial Session of the Legislature, Held in the City of Jackson in January, February and March, A. D. 1846. Jackson: C. M. Price and G. R. Fall, 1846.

Laws of the State of Mississippi, Passed at a Regular Session of the Mississippi Legislature, Held in the City of Jackson, January, February, and March, 1850. Jackson: Fall and Marshall, 1850.

Laws of the State of North-Carolina, Enacted in the Year 1816. Raleigh: Thomas Henderson, 1817.

Laws of the State of North Carolina, Passed by the General Assembly, at the Session of 1838–'39. Raleigh: J. Gales and Son, 1839.

The Maryland Code. Public General Laws, Compiled by Otho Scott, and Hiram M'Cullough, Commissioners; Adopted by the Legislature of Maryland, January Session, 1860. Baltimore: John Murphy and Co., 1860.

The Replication of the Project of the Civil Code of Louisiana, 1825. New Orleans: Thomas J. Moran's Sons, 1937.

Reports of Cases Argued and Determined in the Supreme Court of Alabama, During January Term 1856. Montgomery: Barrett and Wimbish Printers, 1856.

The Revised Code of the District of Columbia, Prepared Under the Authority of the Act of Congress, Entitled "An act to improve the Laws of the District of Columbia, and to Codify the Same," Approved March 3, 1855. Washington, D.C.: A. O. P. Nicholson, 1857.

The Revised Statutes of Kentucky by C. A. Wickliffe, S. Turner, and S. S. Nicholas, Commissioners Appointed by the Legislature, Approved and Adopted by the General Assembly, 1851 and 1852. Frankfort: A. G. Hodges, 1852.

The Revised Statutes of Louisiana, Compiled by U. B. Phillips, Under the Direction of a Joint Committee of the Legislature. New Orleans: John Claiborne, 1856.

The Revised Statutes of the State of Missouri, Revised and Digested by the Thirteenth General Assembly, during the Session of Eighteen Hundred and Forty-four and Eighteen Hundred and Forty-five. St. Louis: J. W. Dougherty, 1845.

The Statute Law of Kentucky; with Notes, Praelections, and Observations on the Public Acts. 5 vols. Frankfort: Butler and Wood, 1819.

Statute Laws of the State of Tennessee, of a General Character; Passed since the Compilation of the Statutes by Caruthers and Nicholson, in 1836, and Being a Supplement to That Work, with Several Titles Arranged in Alphabetical Order. Nashville: J. G. Shepard, 1846.

The Statute Laws of the State of Tennessee, of a Public and General Nature; Revised and Digested by John Haywood and Robert L. Cobbs, by Order of the General Assembly. 2 vols. Knoxville: F. S. Heiskell, 1831.

Story, Joseph. *The Miscellaneous Writings, Literary, Critical, Juridical, and Political of Joseph Story, Now First Collected.* Boston: James Munroe and Company, 1835.

U.S. Bureau of Labor. First Special Report of the Commissioner of Labor. *Marriage and Divorce in the United States, 1867 to 1886; Including an Appendix Relating to Marriage and Divorce in Certain Countries in Europe.* Washington, D.C.: Government Printing Office, 1897.

U.S. Congress. House. *The Federal and State Constitutions, Colonial Charters, and other Organic Laws of the States Territories, and Colonies.* 59th Cong., 2nd sess., 1909. 7 vols. Washington, D.C.: Government Printing Office, 1909.

U.S. Department of Commerce and Labor. Bureau of the Census. *Special Reports: Marriage and Divorce, 1867–1906.* Part 1, *Summary, Laws, Foreign Statistics.* Washington, D.C.: Government Printing Office, 1909.

Secondary Sources

Applebaum, Harvey M. "Miscegenation Statutes: A Constitutional and Social Problem." *Georgetown Law Journal* 53 (1964): 49–91.

Aptheker, Bettina. *Woman's Legacy: Essays on Race, Sex, and Class in American History.* Amherst: University of Massachusetts Press, 1982.

Ayers, Edward. *Vengeance and Justice: Crime and Punishment in the 19th-Century American South.* New York: Oxford University Press, 1984.

Bamman, Gale W., and Debbie W. Spero. *Tennessee Divorces, 1797–1858, Taken from 750 Legislative Petitions and Acts.* Nashville: Gale W. Bamman, 1985.

Bancroft, Frederic. *Slave-Trading in the Old South.* Baltimore: J. H. Furst Company, 1931.

Baptist, Edward E. "'My Mind Is to Drown You and Leave You Behind': 'Omie Wise,' Intimate Violence, and Masculinity." In *Over the Threshold: Domestic Violence in Early America*, edited by Christine Daniels and Michael V. Kennedy, 94–110. New York: Routledge, 1999.

Bardaglio, Peter W. *Reconstructing the Household: Families, Sex, and the Law in the Nineteenth-Century South.* Chapel Hill: University of North Carolina Press, 1995.

———. "'Shamefull Matches': The Regulation of Interracial Sex and Marriage in the South before 1900." In *Sex, Love, Race: Crossing Boundaries in North American History*, edited by Martha Hodes, 112–38. New York: New York University Press, 1999.

Basch, Norma. *Framing American Divorce: From the Revolutionary Generation to the Victorians.* Berkeley: University of California Press, 1999.

———. *In the Eyes of the Law: Women, Marriage, and Property in Nineteenth-Century New York*. Ithaca: Cornell University Press, 1982.

———. "Marriage and Domestic Relations." In *The Cambridge History of Law in America*. Vol. 2, *The Long Nineteenth Century, 1789–1920*, edited by Michael Grossberg and Christopher Tomlins, 245–79. Cambridge: Cambridge University Press, 2008.

Berkin, Carol. "Clio's Daughters: Southern Colonial Women and Their Historians." In *The Devil's Lane: Sex and Race in the Early South*, edited by Catherine Clinton and Michele Gillespie, 15–23. New York: Oxford University Press, 1997.

Berlin, Ira. *Slaves without Masters: The Free Negro in the Antebellum South*. New York: Pantheon, 1974.

Bernard, Joel. "The American Drinking Tradition." *Reviews in American History* 8 (June 1980): 206–14.

Binder, Guyora, and Robert Weisberg. *Literary Criticisms of Law*. Princeton: Princeton University Press, 2000.

Bishir, Catherine W. *North Carolina Architecture*. Chapel Hill: University of North Carolina Press, 2005.

Blake, Nelson Manfred. *The Road to Reno: A History of Divorce in the United States*. New York: Macmillan, 1962.

Block, Sharon. "Lines of Color, Sex, and Service: Comparative Sexual Coercion in Early America." In *Sex, Love, Race: Crossing Boundaries in North American History*, edited by Martha Hodes, 141–63. New York: New York University Press, 1999.

———. *Rape and Sexual Power in Early America*. Chapel Hill: University of North Carolina Press, 2006.

Blume, William Wirt, and Elizabeth Gaspar Brown. "Territorial Courts and Law: Unifying Factors in the Development of American Legal Institutions." *Michigan Law Review* 61 (November 1962): 39–106.

Boatwright, Eleanor Miot. *Status of Women in Georgia, 1783–1860*. Brooklyn, N.Y.: Carlson Publishing, 1994.

Boswell, Angela. "Married Women's Property Rights and the Challenge to the Patriarchal Order: Colorado County, Texas." In *Negotiating Boundaries of Southern Womanhood: Dealing with the Powers That Be*, edited by Janet L. Coryell, Thomas H. Appleton Jr., Anastatia Sims, and Sandra Gioia Treadway, 89–109. Columbia: University of Missouri Press, 2000.

Botham, Fay. *Almighty God Created the Races: Christianity, Interracial Marriage, and American Law*. Chapel Hill: University of North Carolina Press, 2009.

Brearley, H. C. "The Pattern of Violence." In *Culture in the South*, edited by W. T. Couch, 678–92. Chapel Hill: University of North Carolina Press, 1934.

Brewer, Holly. *By Birth or Consent: Children, Law, and the Anglo-American Revolution in Authority*. Chapel Hill: University of North Carolina Press, 2005.

———. "The Transformation of Domestic Law." In *The Cambridge History of Law in America*. Vol. 1, *Early America (1580–1815)*, edited by Michael Grossberg and Christopher Tomlins, 288–323. Cambridge: Cambridge University Press, 2008.

Brown, Kathleen M. *Good Wives, Nasty Wenches, and Anxious Patriarchs: Gender, Race, and Power in Colonial Virginia*. Chapel Hill: University of North Carolina Press, 1996.

Buckley, Thomas E. *The Great Catastrophe of My Life: Divorce in the Old Dominion*. Chapel Hill: University of North Carolina Press, 2002.

———. "'Placed in the Power of Violence': The Divorce Petition of Evelina Gregory Roane, 1824." *Virginia Magazine of History and Biography* 100 (January 1992): 29–78.

———. "Unfixing Race: Class, Power, and Identity in an Interracial Family." *Virginia Magazine of History and Biography* 102 (July 1994): 349–80.

Burr, Virginia Ingraham, ed. *The Secret Eye: The Journal of Ella Gertrude Clanton Thomas, 1848–1889*. Chapel Hill: University of North Carolina press, 1990.

Bynum, Victoria E. *Unruly Women: The Politics of Social and Sexual Control in the Old South*. Chapel Hill: University of North Carolina Press, 1992.

Cahow, Clark R. *People, Patients, and Politics: The History of the North Carolina Mental Hospitals, 1848–1960*. New York: Arno Press, 1980.

Camp, Stephanie M. H. *Closer to Freedom: Enslaved Women and Everyday Resistance in the Plantation South*. Chapel Hill: University of North Carolina Press, 2004.

———. "The Pleasures of Resistance: Enslaved Women and Body Politics in the Plantation South, 1830–1861." *Journal of Southern History* 68 (August 2002): 533–72.

Cashin, Joan E. *Our Common Affairs: Texts from Women in the Old South*. Baltimore: Johns Hopkins University Press, 1996.

Catterall, Helen, ed. *Judicial Cases Concerning American Slavery and the Negro*. 5 vols. Washington, D.C.: Carnegie Institution, 1932. Reprint, New York: Octagon Books, 1968.

Censer, Jane Turner. *North Carolina Planters and Their Children, 1800–1860*. Baton Rouge: Louisiana State University Press, 1984.

———. "'Smiling through Her Tears': Ante-bellum Southern Women and Divorce." *American Journal of Legal History* 25 (January 1981): 24–47.

Chroust, Anton-Hermann. *The Rise of the Legal Profession in America*. Vol. 2, *The Revolution and the Post-Revolutionary Era*. Norman: University of Oklahoma Press, 1965.

Chused, Richard H. "Married Women's Property Law: 1800–1850." *Georgetown Law Journal* 71 (June 1983): 1359–1426.

———. *Private Acts in Public Places: A Social History of Divorce in the Formative Era of American Family Law*. Philadelphia: University of Pennsylvania Press, 1994.

Clark, Elizabeth B. "Matrimonial Bonds: Slavery and Divorce in Nineteenth-Century America." *Law and History Review* 8 (Spring 1990): 25–54.

Clinton, Catherine. "Caught in the Web of the Big House: Women and Slavery." In *The Web of Southern Social Relations: Women, Family, and Education*, edited by Walter J. Fraser Jr., R. Frank Saunders Jr., and Jon L. Wakelyn, 19–34. Athens: University of Georgia Press, 1985.

———. *Fanny Kemble's Civil Wars*. New York: Simon and Schuster, 2000.
———. *The Plantation Mistress: Woman's World in the Old South*. New York: Pantheon, 1982.
Cooledge, Harold N., Jr. "A [Samuel] Sloan Check List, 1849-1884." *Journal of the Society of Architectural Historians* 19 (March 1960): 34-38.
Cott, Nancy. "Divorce and the Changing Status of Women in Eighteenth-Century Massachusetts." *William and Mary Quarterly* 33 (October 1976): 586-614.
———. "Eighteenth-Century Family and Social Life Revealed in Massachusetts Divorce Records." *Journal of Social History* 10 (Fall 1976): 20-43.
Dabney, Joseph Earl. *Mountain Spirits: A Chronicle of Corn Whiskey from King James' Ulster Plantation to America's Appalachians and the Moonshine Life*. New York: Charles Scribner's Sons, 1974.
Davis, Natalie Zemon. *Fiction in the Archives: Pardon Tales and Their Tellers in Sixteenth-Century France*. Stanford: Stanford University Press, 1987.
Deyle, Steven. *Carry Me Back: The Domestic Slave Trade in American Life*. New York: Oxford University Press, 2005.
Dougan, Michael B. "The Arkansas Married Woman's Property Law." *Arkansas Historical Quarterly* 46 (Spring 1987): 3-26.
Drake, W. Magruder, ed. "Notes and Documents. A Discourse on Divorce: Orleans Territorial Legislature, 1806." *Louisiana History* 22 (Fall 1981): 434-37.
Durrill, Wayne K. "A Tale of Two Courthouses: Civic Space, Political Power, and Capitalist Development in a New South Community, 1843-1940." *Journal of Social History* 35 (Spring 2002): 659-81.
Edwards, Laura F. "Law, Domestic Violence, and the Limits of Patriarchal Authority in the Antebellum South." *Journal of Southern History* 65 (November 1999): 733-70.
———. *The People and Their Peace: Legal Culture and the Transformation of Inequality in the Post-Revolutionary South*. Chapel Hill: University of North Carolina Press, 2009.
Escott, Paul D. *Many Excellent People: Power and Privilege in North Carolina, 1850-1900*. Chapel Hill: University of North Carolina Press, 1985.
Evans, Robert, Jr. "The Economics of American Negro Slavery, 1830-1860." In *Aspects of Labor Economics: A Conference of the Universities-National Bureau Committee for Economic Research*, 185-256. Princeton: Princeton University Press, 1962.
Farnam, Henry W. *Chapters in the History of Social Legislation in the United States to 1860*. Washington, D.C.: Carnegie Institution, 1938.
Faust, Drew Gilpin. *Mothers of Invention: Women of the Slaveholding South in the American Civil War*. Chapel Hill: University of North Carolina Press, 1996.
Feigenson, Neal R. "Extraterritorial Recognition of Divorce Decrees in the Nineteenth Century." *American Journal of Legal History* 34 (April 1990): 119-67.
Fernandez, Mark. *From Chaos to Continuity: The Evolution of Louisiana's Judicial System, 1712-1862*. Baton Rouge: Louisiana State University Press, 2001.
Ferrell, Joseph S. "Early Statutory and Common Law of Divorce in North Carolina." *North Carolina Law Review* 41 (1962-63): 604-16.

Fisher, William W., III. "Ideology and Imagery in the Law of Slavery." In *Slavery and the Law*, edited by Paul Finkelman, 43–86. Boston: Rowman and Littlefield, 2002.

Forret, Jeff. "Conflict and the 'Slave Community': Violence among Slaves in Upcountry South Carolina." *Journal of Southern History* 76 (August 2008): 551–88.

———. *Race Relations at the Margins: Slaves and Poor Whites in the Antebellum Southern Countryside*. Baton Rouge: Louisiana State University Press, 2006.

Fox-Genovese, Elizabeth. "Family and Female Identity in the Antebellum South: Sarah Gayle and Her Family." In *In Joy and in Sorrow: Women, Family, and Marriage in the Victorian South, 1830–1900*, edited by Carol Bleser, 15–31. New York: Oxford University Press, 1991.

———. *Within the Plantation Household: Black and White Women of the Old South*. Chapel Hill: University of North Carolina Press, 1988.

Franklin, John Hope. *The Militant South, 1800–1861*. Cambridge: Harvard University Press, 1956.

Franklin, John Hope, and Loren Schweninger. *In Search of the Promised Land: A Slave Family in the Old South*. New York: Oxford University Press, 2006.

———. *Runaway Slaves: Rebels on the Plantation*. New York: Oxford University Press, 1999.

Friedman, Jean E. *The Enclosed Garden: Women and Community in the Evangelical South, 1830–1900*. Chapel Hill: University of North Carolina Press, 1985.

Friedman, Lawrence M. *A History of American Law*. New York: Simon and Schuster, 1973.

Frierson, J. Nelson. "Divorce in South Carolina." *North Carolina Law Review* 9 (April 1931): 265–82.

Getman, Karen A. "Sexual Control in the Slaveholding South: The Implementation and Maintenance of a Racial Caste System." *Harvard Women's Law Journal* 7 (Spring 1984): 115–52.

Glymph, Thavolia. *Out of the House of Bondage: The Transformation of the Plantation Household*. Cambridge: Cambridge University Press, 2008.

Goodheart, Lawrence B., Neil Hanks, and Elizabeth Johnson. "'An Act for the Relief of Females . . .': Divorce and the Changing Legal Status of Women in Tennessee, 1796–1860," pt. 1. *Tennessee Historical Quarterly* 44 (Fall 1985): 318–39.

———. "'An Act for the Relief of Females . . .': Divorce and the Changing Legal Status of Women in Tennessee," pt. 2. *Tennessee Historical Quarterly* 44 (Winter 1985): 402–16.

Greene, Sally. "*State v. Mann* Exhumed." *North Carolina Law Review* 87 (2009): 701–55.

Griswold, Robert L. "The Evolution of the Doctrine of Mental Cruelty in Victorian American Divorce, 1790–1900." *Journal of Social History* 20 (Autumn 1986): 127–48.

———. "Law, Sex, Cruelty, and Divorce in Victorian America, 1840–1900." *American Quarterly* 38 (Winter 1986): 721–45.

Grob, Gerald N. *The Mad among Us: A History of the Care of America's Mentally Ill.* New York: Free Press, 1994.
Gross, Ariela J. *Double Character: Slavery and Mastery in the Antebellum Southern Courtroom.* Princeton: Princeton University Press, 2000. Paperback ed., Athens: University of Georgia Press, 2006.
———. *What Blood Won't Tell: A History of Race on Trial in America.* Cambridge: Harvard University Press, 2008.
Grossberg, Michael. *Governing the Hearth: Law and the Family in Nineteenth-Century America.* Chapel Hill: University of North Carolina Press, 1985.
———. "Guarding the Altar: Physiological Restrictions on Marriage and the Rise of State Intervention in Matrimony." *American Journal of Legal History* 26 (July 1982): 197–288.
———. *A Judgment for Solomon: The d'Hauteville Case and Legal Experience in Antebellum America.* Cambridge: Cambridge University Press, 1996.
Grossberg, Michael, and Christopher Tomlins, eds. *The Cambridge History of Law in America.* Vol. 2, *The Long Nineteenth Century, 1789–1920.* Cambridge: Cambridge University Press, 2008.
Gundersen, Joan R., and Gwen Victor Gampel. "Married Women's Legal Status in Eighteenth-Century New York and Virginia." *William and Mary Quarterly* 39 (January 1982): 113–34.
Gutman, Herbert. *The Black Family in Slavery and Freedom, 1750–1925.* New York: Pantheon, 1976.
Hadden, Sally. "The Fragmented Laws of Slavery in the Colonial and Revolutionary Eras." In *The Cambridge History of Law in America.* Vol. 1, *Early America (1580–1815)*, edited by Michael Grossberg and Christopher Tomlins, 253–87. Cambridge: Cambridge University Press, 2008.
———. "Judging Slavery: Thomas Ruffin and *State v. Mann.*" In *Local Matters: Race, Crime, and Justice in the Nineteenth-Century South*, edited by Christopher Waldrep and Donald G. Nieman, 1–28. Athens: University of Georgia Press, 2001.
Hall, Kermit L., ed. *Law, Society, and Domestic Relations: Major Historical Interpretations.* New York: Garland Publishing, 1987.
Hall, Kermit L., Paul Finkelman, and James W. Ely Jr., eds. *American Legal History: Cases and Material.* New York: Oxford University Press, 2005.
Hartog, Hendrik. *Man and Wife in America: A History.* Cambridge: Harvard University Press, 2000.
———. "Marital Exits and Marital Expectations in Nineteenth Century America." *Georgetown Law Journal* 80 (October 1991): 95–130.
Higginbotham, A. Leon, Jr. *In the Matter of Color: Race and the American Legal Process: The Colonial Period.* New York: Oxford University Press, 1978.
Higginbotham, A. Leon, Jr., and Barbara K. Kopytoff. "Racial Purity and Interracial Sex in the Law of Colonial and Antebellum Virginia." In *Interracialism: Black-White Intermarriage in American History, Literature, and Law*, edited by Werner Sollors, 81–139. New York: Oxford University Press, 2000.

Hodes, Martha. *White Women, Black Men: Illicit Sex in the Nineteenth-Century South*. New Haven: Yale University Press, 1997.
Hollinger, David A. "Amalgamation and Hypodescent: The Question of Ethnoracial Mixture in the History of the United States." *American Historical Review* 108 (December 2003): 1363–90.
Howard, George Elliott. *A History of Matrimonial Institutions: Chiefly in England and the United States with an Introductory Analysis of the Literature and the Theories of Primitive Marriage and the Family*. 3 vols. Chicago: University of Chicago Press, 1904.
Isaac, Rhys. *The Transformation of Virginia, 1740–1790*. Chapel Hill: University of North Carolina Press, 1982.
Isenberg, Nancy. *Sex and Citizenship in Antebellum America*. Chapel Hill: University of North Carolina Press, 1998.
Jabour, Anya. *Scarlett's Sisters: Young Women in the Old South*. Chapel Hill: University of North Carolina Press, 2007.
Jacobson, Paul H. *American Marriage and Divorce*. New York: Rinehart and Company, 1959.
Jensen, Joan M. *Loosening the Bonds: Mid-Atlantic Farm Women, 1750–1850*. New Haven: Yale University Press, 1986.
Johnson, Albert L., Jr. *Probate Genealogy of Williamson County, Tennessee, 1833–1852*. Franklin, Tenn.: Genealogy Pubs, 2002.
Johnson, Guion Griffis. *Ante-Bellum North Carolina: A Social History*. Chapel Hill: University of North Carolina Press, 1937.
Johnson, Michael P., and James L. Roark. *Black Masters: A Free Family of Color in the Old South*. New York: Norton, 1984.
Johnson, Walter. *Soul by Soul: Life inside the Antebellum Slave Market*. Cambridge: Harvard University Press, 1999.
Johnston, James Hugo. *Race Relations in Virginia and Miscegenation in the South, 1776–1860*. Amherst: University of Massachusetts Press, 1970.
Katz, Stanley N. "The Politics of Law in Colonial America: Controversies over Chancery Courts and Equity Law in the Eighteenth Century." *Perspectives in American History* 5 (1971): 485–518.
Kaye, Anthony E. *Joining Places: Slave Neighborhoods in the Old South*. Chapel Hill: University of North Carolina Press, 2007.
Kemble, Frances Anne. *Journal of a Residence on a Georgian Plantation in 1838–1839*. Edited by John A. Scott. Athens: University of Georgia Press, 1984.
Kennedy, Randall. *Interracial Intimacies: Sex, Marriage, Identity, and Adoption*. New York: Pantheon, 2002.
Kennedy-Haflett, Cynthia. "'Moral Marriage': A Mixed Race Relationship in Nineteenth-Century Charleston, South Carolina." *South Carolina Historical Magazine* 97 (July 1996): 206–26.
Kerber, Linda K. *Women of the Republic: Intellect and Ideology in Revolutionary America*. Chapel Hill: University of North Carolina Press, 1980.
Kierner, Cynthia A. *Beyond the Household: Women's Place in the Early South, 1700–1835*. Ithaca: Cornell University Press, 1998.

———. *Southern Women in Revolution, 1776–1800: Personal and Political Narratives.* Columbia: University of South Carolina Press, 1998.

Kleinberg, S. J. *Women in the United States, 1830–1945.* New Brunswick, N.J.: Rutgers University Press, 1999.

Konig, David Thomas. "Regionalism in Early American Law." In *The Cambridge History of Law in America.* Vol. 1, *Early America (1580–1815)*, edited by Michael Grossberg and Christopher Tomlins, 144–77. Cambridge: Cambridge University Press, 2008.

Lazarou, Kathleen Elizabeth. *Concealed under Petticoats: Married Women's Property and the Law of Texas, 1840–1913.* New York: Garland Publishing, 1986.

Lebsock, Suzanne. *The Free Women of Petersburg: Status and Culture in a Southern Town, 1784–1860.* New York: Norton, 1984.

Lender, Mark Edward, and James Kirby Martin. *Drinking in America: A History.* New York: Free Press, 1982.

Mann, Bruce H. *Republic of Debtors: Bankruptcy in the Age of American Independence.* Cambridge: Harvard University Press, 2002.

McBride, Janet, and Ransom McBride. "Divorces and Separations from Petitions to the North Carolina General Assembly from 1779," pt. 7. *North Carolina Genealogical Society Journal* 17 (November 1991): 201–8.

McBride, Ransom. "Divorces, Separations, and Security of Property Granted by Act of the NC Assembly from 1809 through 1830." *North Carolina Genealogical Society Journal* 9 (February 1983): 43–46.

McCandless, Peter. *Moonlight, Magnolias, and Madness: Insanity in South Carolina from the Colonial Period to the Progressive Era.* Chapel Hill: University of North Carolina Press, 1996.

McCurry, Stephanie. *Masters of Small Worlds: Yeoman Households, Gender Relations, and the Political Culture of the Antebellum South Carolina Low Country.* New York: Oxford University Press, 1995.

McMillen, Sally G. *Motherhood in the Old South: Pregnancy, Childbirth, and Infant Rearing.* Baton Rouge: Louisiana State University Press, 1990.

———. *Southern Women: Black and White in the Old South.* Arlington Heights, Ill.: Harlan Davidson, 1992.

Moncrief, Sandra. "The Mississippi Married Women's Property Act of 1839." *Journal of Mississippi History* 47 (1985): 110–25.

Morris, Thomas D. *Southern Slavery and the Law, 1619–1860.* Chapel Hill: University of North Carolina Press, 1996.

Munroe, John A. *History of Delaware.* Newark: University of Delaware Press, 1993.

Oakes, James. *The Ruling Race: A History of American Slaveholders.* New York: Vintage, 1982.

O'Hear, Michael M. "'Some of the Most Embarrassing Questions': Extraterritorial Divorces and the Problem of Jurisdiction before *Pennoyer* [1877]." *Yale Law Journal* 104 (March 1995): 1507–37.

Oldham, James. *English Common Law in the Age of Mansfield.* Chapel Hill: University of North Carolina Press, 2004.

Owsley, Frank. *Plain Folk of the Old South*. Baton Rouge: Louisiana State University Press, 1949.

Painter, Nell Irvin. "Soul Murder and Slavery: Towards a Fully Loaded Cost Accounting." In *Southern History Across the Color Line*, by Nell Irvin Painter, 15–39. Chapel Hill: University of North Carolina Press, 2002.

Pargas, Damian Allen. *The Quarters and the Fields: Slave Families in the Non-Cotton South*. Gainesville: University of Florida Press, 2010.

Pascal, Robert A. "The Sources of Order According to the Revised Civil Code's Preliminary Title." *Tulane Law Review* 54 (1980): 916–41.

Pascoe, Peggy. *What Comes Naturally: Miscegenation Law and the Making of Race in America*. New York: Oxford University Press, 2009.

Penningroth, Dylan. "African American Divorce in Virginia and Washington, D.C., 1865–1930." *Journal of Family History* 33 (January 2008): 21–33.

Phillips, Roderick. *Putting Asunder: A History of Divorce in Western Society*. Cambridge: Cambridge University Press, 1988.

———. *Untying the Knot: A Short History of Divorce*. Cambridge: Cambridge University Press, 1991.

Phillips, Ulrich Bonnell. *The Slave Economy of the Old South: Selected Essays in Economic and Social History*. Edited by Eugene D. Genovese. Baton Rouge: Louisiana State University Press, 1968.

Pippenger, Wesley E. *Connections and Separations: Divorce, Name Change, and Other Genealogical Tidbits from the ACTS of the Virginia General Assembly*. Westminster, Md.: Heritage Books, 2007.

Popkin, William D. *Statutes in Court: The History and Theory of Statutory Interpretation*. Durham: Duke University Press, 1999.

Ransom, Roger L. *Conflict and Compromise: The Political Economy of Slavery, Emancipation, and the Civil War*. Cambridge: Cambridge University Press, 1989.

Ransom, Roger L., and Richard Sutch, "Capitalists without Capital: The Burden of Slavery and the Impact of Emancipation." *Agricultural History* 62 (Fall 1988): 133–60.

Riddell, William. "Legislative Divorce in Colonial Pennsylvania." *Pennsylvania Magazine of History and Biography* 57 (1933): 175–80.

Riley, Glenda. *Divorce: An American Tradition*. New York: Oxford University Press, 1991.

———. "Legislative Divorce in Virginia, 1803–1850." *Journal of the Early Republic* 11 (Spring 1991): 51–67.

Robinson, Charles F. *Dangerous Liaisons: Sex and Love in the Segregated South*. Fayetteville: University of Arkansas Press, 2003.

Rorabaugh, W. J. *The Alcoholic Republic: An American Tradition*. New York: Oxford University Press, 1971.

Rothman, Joshua D. "'Notorious in the Neighborhood': An Interracial Family in Early National and Antebellum Virginia." *Journal of Southern History* 67 (February 2001): 73–114.

———. *Notorious in the Neighborhood: Sex and Families across the Color Line in Virginia, 1787–1861*. Chapel Hill: University of North Carolina Press, 2003.
———. "'To be Freed from Thate Curs and Let at Liberty': Interracial Adultery and Divorce in Antebellum Virginia." *Virginia Magazine of History and Biography* 106 (Autumn 1998): 443–81.
Salmon, Marylynn. "Women and Property in South Carolina: The Evidence from Marriage Settlements, 1730 to 1830." *William and Mary Quarterly* 39 (October 1982): 655–85.
———. *Women and the Law of Property in Early America*. Chapel Hill: University of North Carolina Press, 1986.
Savitt, Todd L. *Medicine and Slavery: The Diseases and Health Care of Blacks in Antebellum Virginia*. Urbana: University of Illinois Press, 1978.
Scarborough, William. *The Overseer: Plantation Management in the Old South*. Baton Rouge: Louisiana State University Press, 1966.
Schafer, Judith Kelleher. *Slavery, the Civil Law, and the Supreme Court of Louisiana*. Baton Rouge: Louisiana State University Press, 1994.
Schwarz, Philip J. *Slave Laws in Virginia*. Athens: University of Georgia Press, 1996.
Schweninger, Loren. "Slavery and Southern Violence: County Court Petitions and the South's Peculiar Institution." *Journal of Negro History* 85 (Winter–Spring 2000): 33–35.
———. "'To the Honorable': Divorce, Alimony, Slavery, and the Law in Antebellum North Carolina." *North Carolina Historical Review* 86 (April 2009): 127–79.
———. "The Vass Slaves: County Courts, State Laws, and Slavery in Virginia, 1831–1861." *Virginia Magazine of History and Biography* 114 (Winter 2006): 464–97.
———, ed. *The Southern Debate over Slavery*. Vol. 1, *Petitions to Southern Legislatures, 1778–1864*. Urbana: University of Illinois Press, 2001.
Schweninger, Loren, ed., and Marguerite Howell and Nicole Mazgaj, asst. eds. *The Southern Debate over Slavery*. Vol. 2, *Petitions to Southern County Courts, 1775–1867*. Urbana: University of Illinois Press, 2008.
Shammas, Carole. "Early American Women and Control over Capital." In *Women in the Age of the American Revolution*, edited by Ronald Hoffman and Peter J. Albert, 134–54. Charlottesville: University of Virginia Press, 1989.
———. "Re-assessing the Married Women's Property Acts." *Journal of Women's History* 6 (Spring 1994): 9–30.
Silkenat, David. *Moments of Despair: Suicide, Divorce, and Debt in Civil War Era North Carolina*. Chapel Hill: University of North Carolina Press, 2011.
Soltow, Lee. *Distribution of Wealth and Income in the United States in 1798*. Pittsburgh: University of Pittsburgh Press, 1989
———. *Men and Wealth in the United States, 1850–1870*. New Haven: Yale University Press, 1975.
Sommerville, Diane Miller. "'I Was Very Much Wounded': Rape Law, Children, and the Antebellum South." In *Sex Without Consent: Rape and Sexual Coercion*

in America, edited by Merril D. Smith, 136–77. New York: New York University Press, 2001.

———. *Rape and Race in the Nineteenth-Century South*. Chapel Hill: University of North Carolina Press, 2004.

Spalletta, Matteo. "Divorce in Colonial New York." *New York Historical Society Quarterly* 39 (October 1955): 422–40.

Stampp, Kenneth. *The Peculiar Institution: Slavery in the Ante-Bellum South*. New York: Vintage, 1956.

Stevenson, Brenda. "Distress and Discord in Virginia Slave Families, 1830–1860." In *In Joy and in Sorrow: Women, Family, and Marriage in the Victorian South, 1830–1900*, edited by Carol Bleser, 103–24. New York: Oxford University Press, 1991.

Stone, Lawrence. *Broken Lives: Separation and Divorce in England, 1660–1857*. New York: Oxford University Press, 1993.

———. *Road to Divorce: England, 1530–1987*. New York: Oxford University Press, 1990.

Stowe, Steven M. *Doctoring the South: Southern Physicians and Everyday Medicine in the Mid-Nineteenth Century*. Chapel Hill: University of North Carolina Press, 2004.

Sturtz, Linda L. *Within Her Power: Propertied Women in Colonial Virginia*. London: Routledge, 2002.

Tadman, Michael. *Speculators and Slaves: Masters, Traders, and Slaves in the Old South*. Madison: University of Wisconsin Press, 1989.

Tushnet, Mark. *The American Law of Slavery, 1810–1860: Considerations of Humanity and Interest*. Princeton: Princeton University Press, 1981.

Tyrrell, Ian. "Drink and Temperance in the Antebellum South: An Overview and Interpretation." *Journal of Southern History* 48 (November 1982): 485–510.

Van Ness, James S. "On Untieing the Knot: The Maryland Legislature and Divorce Petitions." *Maryland Historical Magazine* 67 (Summer 1972): 171–75.

Van Riemsdijk, Tatiana. "His Slaves or Hers?: Customary Claims, a Planter Marriage, and a Community Verdict in Lancaster County, 1793." *Virginia Magazine of History and Biography* 113 (December 2005): 46–79.

Varon, Elizabeth R. *We Mean to Be Counted: White Women and Politics in Antebellum Virginia*. Chapel Hill: University of North Carolina Press, 1998.

Waldrep, Christopher, and Donald G. Nieman, eds. *Local Matters: Race, Crime, and Justice in the Nineteenth-Century South*. Athens: University of Georgia Press, 2001.

Wallenstein, Peter. *Tell the Court I Love My Wife: Race, Marriage, and Law—An American History*. New York: Palgrave Macmillan, 2002.

Warbasse, Elizabeth. *The Changing Legal Rights of Married Women, 1800–1861*. New York: Garland Publishing, 1987.

Wates, Wylma. "Precursor to the Victorian Age: The Concept of Marriage and Family as Revealed in the Correspondence of the Izard Family of South Carolina." In *In Joy and in Sorrow: Women, Family, and Marriage in the Victorian South, 1830–1900*, edited by Carol Bleser, 3–14. New York: Oxford University Press, 1991.

Weiner, Marli F. *Mistresses and Slaves: Plantation Women in South Carolina, 1830–80*. Urbana: University of Illinois Press, 1998.

Weisberg, D. Kelly. "Under Great Temptations Here: Women and Divorce Law in Puritan Massachusetts." In *Women and the Law: The Social Historical Perspective*. Vol. 2, *Property, Family, and the Legal Profession*, edited by D. Kelly Weisberg, 117–32. Cambridge, Mass.: Schenkman Publishing, 1982.

Welke, Barbara Young. *Law and the Borders of Belonging in the Long Nineteenth Century United States*. Cambridge: Cambridge University Press, 2010.

Werthheimer, John W. *Law and Society in the South: A History of North Carolina Court Cases*. Lexington: University of Kentucky Press, 2009.

Whitman, T. Stephen. "'I have Got the Gun and Will Do As I Please with Her': African-Americans and Violence in Maryland, 1782–1830." In *Over the Threshold: Domestic Violence in Early America*, edited by Christine Daniels and Michael V. Kennedy, 254–67. New York: Routledge, 1999.

Wiethoff, William E. *Crafting the Overseer's Image*. Columbia: University of South Carolina Press, 2006.

Wikramanayake, Marina. *A World in Shadow: The Free Black in Antebellum South Carolina*. Columbia: University of South Carolina Press, 1973.

Wood, Kirsten E. *Masterful Women: Slaveholding Widows from the American Revolution through the Civil War*. Chapel Hill: University of North Carolina Press, 2004.

———. "'The Strongest Ties That Bind Poor Mortals Together': Slaveholding Widows and Family in the Old Southeast." In *Negotiating Boundaries of Southern Womanhood: Dealing with the Powers That Be*, edited by Janet L. Coryell, Thomas H. Appleton Jr., Anastatia Sims, and Sandra Gioia Treadway, 61–82. Columbia: University of Missouri Press, 2000.

Wyatt-Brown, Bertram. *Honor and Violence in the Old South*. New York: Oxford University Press, 1986.

———. *Southern Honor: Ethics and Behavior in the Old South*. New York: Oxford University Press, 1982.

Yanni, Carla. "The Linear Plan for Insane Asylums in the United States before 1866." *Journal of the Society of Architectural Historians* 62 (March 2003): 24–49.

Zaher, Claudia. "When a Woman's Marital Status Determined Her Legal Status: A Research Guide on the Common Law Doctrine of Coverture." *Law Library Journal* 94 (Summer 2002): 459–86.

Zainaldin, Jamil. *Law in Antebellum Society: Legal Change and Economic Expansion*. New York: Knopf, 1983.

INDEX

Abandonment. *See* Desertion

Abram (slave held by unnamed owner), 24

Absolute divorce, 2–4, 8, 11, 37, 58–59, 68, 75, 77, 121

Abuse: in Arkansas, 54; attitudes toward, 51–52; as cause for divorce, 4, 38, 47, 50, 52, 56, 63, 65, 67, 70–71, 79, 98–99; cruelty without violence, 54–55; definition of cruelty, 47; descriptions of physical abuse, 47–50, 63; and divorce law, 8–9, 33, 47, 63, 70; husbands' justification for, 52; in Louisiana, 54–55; mental abuse, as cause for divorce, 33, 52, 54–56; in Missouri, 79; in North Carolina, 54; prevalence of, 48, 52, 115; in South Carolina, 64; in Tennessee, 54; in Texas, 54; as threat to wife's life, 2, 48–50, 63; threat of bodily harm to wife, 1, 37, 58, 94; use of weapons, 48–49, 58. *See also* Cruelty; Defamation of character; Extreme cruelty; Violence

Adultery: in Alabama, 69; attitudes toward, 70; as cause for divorce, 4, 17–19, 21, 23–28, 31, 52, 54, 65, 67, 69–71, 79, 83–84, 101, 106; and divorce law, 2–3, 6–9, 11, 33, 69, 79; in Missouri, 79. *See also* Interracial sex; Sexual relations, of white men; Sexual relations, of white women

Alcoholic husbands, 40–42, 48, 85, 94, 119

Alcoholism: in Arkansas, 42; as cause for divorce, 38–42, 52, 56, 64, 67, 71, 79, 94; consumption of alcohol, 39–40; as contributor to violence, 46, 48, 71; and divorce law, 8, 11, 33, 42, 64, 79; effect of on community, 40; effect of on family, 41–42; in Florida, 42; in Georgia, 42; in Louisiana, 42; in Mississippi, 42; in Missouri, 42, 79

Alimony: award of, 2, 31, 36, 42, 45, 59, 89; deprivation of, 85; and divorce law, 3, 6–7; impact of on slaves, 103; petitioned for, 17, 31, 33, 36, 45–46, 50, 59, 84–85, 87, 89–90, 94; in South Carolina, 4, 46

Allen (slave held by Richard Moore), 45

Allen, John, 21

A mensa et thoro. *See* Separation of bed and board

Ann (slave held by James E. Black), 17

Ann (slave held by unnamed owner), 106

Asylums, 32–33, 37, 39, 56

A vinculo matrimonii. *See* Absolute divorce

Ayer, Cornelius K., 114

Ayer, Mrs. Cornelius K., 98

Bainbridge, Eliza, 63

Baker, James, 70

Banks, Elizabeth, 97

Banks, James M., 80, 96

Banks, Louisiana, xiii, 80–81, 94, 97. *See also* Reid, Louisiana

Banks, Thomas, 97

Beard, Harriett Anne, 94

Betts, Maria, 88

Bigamy: as cause for divorce, 79, 52, 54; and divorce law, 3, 6, 8–9, 33, 54, 79; in lieu of divorce, x, 26

Black, James E., 17, 28, 30 (ill.), 31

Black, Joseph Alonzo, 17, 31

Black, Sarah H., xiii, 17–18, 28, 30 (ill.), 31, 124

Black, William, 17, 31

Blackstone, William, 3

Bob (slave held by Richard Moore), 45

Brannock, Martha, 108
Brannock, Wright, 108
Breckinridge, James D., 63
Brewer, Jane, 67
Brewer, William, 67
Brown, Susan A., 103
Bryan, John H., 66
Bryan, Jonathan, 101–2
Byrnes, Eliza, 54

Campbell, David, 81
Campbell, G. W., 62
Caroline (slave held by Edward Coleman), 111
Caroline (slave held by unnamed owner), 101
Cash, Thomas, 80, 96
Chancery, or equity, courts: compared with common law, xiii, 2–4, 61, 87; as final arbitrator in divorce and separation cases, 9; process of, 6–7, 59, 72, 76, 116; with regard to female petitioners, 75
Chaney (slave held by unnamed person), 105
Child custody: award of, 41, 64; entrusted to husband in Louisiana, 8; petitioned for, 17, 51
Children, slave: as go-betweens for owners, 102; punishment of, 102. *See also* Slaves
Chiles, Celia, 24
Chiles, Robert, 24
Clark, James, 67
Clarke, Mary M., 89
Class structure: adultery within non-slaveholding families, 26; adultery within slaveholding families, 19, 23, 26–28; divorce among slaveholding women, xi; divorce within lower-class families, x; divorce within non-slaveholding families, 71–73, 77–78; divorce within slaveholding families, 59, 71–73, 77, 90–92, 122; divorce within wealthiest slaveholding families, 17, 28, 72, 78; domestic violence among wealthy slaveholders, 49 (ill.), 50; insanity among wealthy slaveholders, 38; interracial sex within slaveholding families, 28; sex between lower-class white women and black men, 22, 26; sex between white women from respectable families and black men, 23; wealthy landowners, 97; wealthy slaveholders, 80
Cobb, Thomas R. R., 22
Coleman, Edward, 111
Collins, Celeste, 55
Concubinage, and Louisiana law, 8, 19
Consanguinity: as cause for divorce, 65; and divorce law, 3, 9
Covey, Mr., 106
Cruelty, and divorce law, 8–9, 11, 79. *See also* Abuse
Cyrus (slave held by William Duncan), 59

David (slave held by William Duncan), 59
Davis, Mary, 48
DeBow, J. D. B., 91–92
Defamation of character: as cause for divorce, 52–55, 98; and divorce law, 8, 33. *See also* Abuse
DeSaussure, Henry William, 64
Desertion: in Alabama, 44; in Arkansas, 44; as cause for divorce, 44–46, 52, 54, 64–65, 67–68, 71, 79, 84, 89; and divorce law, 3, 6–9, 11, 33, 44, 50, 64, 79; effect of on abandoned wife, 44–46; in Florida, 44; husband abandons wife, 43–46, 64, 103–6; husband abandons wife to live with female slave, 1, 20; husband forces wife to leave, 20, 25; husbands' justifications for, 43–44; in Kentucky, 44; in Maryland, 44; in Mississippi, 44, 64; in Missouri, 44, 79; in Virginia, 44; wife abandons husband, 26, 58–59, 67–68, 70, 115; wife abandons

husband to live with free people of color, 25; wife flees husband, 6–7, 41, 48, 50–51, 63, 94, 107, 114, 116; wife pursues deserting husband, 45–46
De Tocqueville, Alexis, 52
Dick (slave held by Elizabeth Hamilton), 83
Dinah (slave held by Matilda Payne), 104
Dinah (slave held by unnamed owner), 105
Divorce: adversarial process of, x–xi; among free persons of color, 77–78; attitudes toward, ix–x, 76–77, 116, 120; impact of on skilled slaves, 103; impact of on slave families, 102–5; impact of on slaves, 100, 102–5, 112, 117, 121; impact of on wives, 85; rate of increase of, x. *See also* Separation of bed and board
Domestic violence. *See* Abuse
Douglass, Frederick, 106
Dower, 3, 14, 80, 82, 94, 96. *See also* Married women's property; Widows
Dowry, 83
Doyle, John, 102
Duncan, Sarah Ratliff, xiii, 58–59, 60 (ill.), 78–79
Duncan, William, 58–59, 60 (ill.), 78–79

Eliza (slave held by Isaac and Lydia Rawdon), 36
Elsey (slave held by Margaret Vause), 88
Emeline (slave held by Louisiana Banks), 97
Emily (slave held by James Whitehead), 113
Ester (slave held by Matilda Payne), 104
Everton, Matilda, 95 (ill.)
Extra-dotal property. *See* Married women's property
Extreme cruelty: as cause for divorce, 58; and divorce law, 2–3, 6, 8, 11. *See also* Abuse

Family: attitudes toward, 93; importance of, ix
Fanna (slave held by Lydia Rawdon), 57
Felony conviction: in Arkansas, 56; as cause for divorce, 53, 56, 65; and divorce law, 6, 8; in Georgia, 56; in Kentucky, 56; in Louisiana, 56; in Mississippi, 56; in Missouri, 56; in Tennessee, 56; in Virginia, 56
Feme covert. *See* Marriage
Feme sole, xiii, 16, 45, 82, 88–89. *See also* Married women's property
Fleming, Leonard, 70
Fletcher, Thomas H., 62
Flowers, Temperance, 25
Flowers, Thomas, 25

Gallee, Eliza (free woman of color), 27
Gardenhire, Vories & Routt, law office of, 58
Garner, Margaret (of Alabama), 85
Garner, Margaret (of Florida), 69
Garner, Thomas, 111
George (slave held by Elizabeth Hamilton), 83
Gibson, Edmund D., 121
Gibson, Eliza, 121

Hager (slave held by unnamed owner), 106
Hamilton, Elizabeth, 83
Harvey, Rebecca, 55
Haskell, Nathan, 2
Henry (slave held by Elizabeth Hamilton), 83
Henry, Misella Ann, 45
Historiography: of circuit court verdicts, 73; general, xi–xii; of interracial sexual relations, 18, 22; of southern violence, 46; of southern women, 82
Holly, Joshua, 104

Houston, Cassandra, 53
Huskey, Martha, 106

Impotence: as cause for divorce, 52, 54, 65; and divorce law, 3, 6, 8–9, 33, 79. *See also* Sexual relations, of white men
Imprisonment. *See* Jail
Incest, as cause for divorce, 52, 54
Infidelity. *See* Adultery
Insanity: attitudes toward, 37–38; as cause for divorce, 35–38, 52, 65, 67; as contributor to violence, 32–35, 38, 70; declaration of, 32, 36, 39; descriptions of, 33–37, 39; and divorce law, 3, 11, 33; effect of on family, 33, 38; legal definition of, 35; treatment of, 37
Intemperance. *See* Alcoholism
Interracial cohabitation: as cause for divorce, 20; and the law, 11, 14; with slave mistresses, 19–20, 25, 43. *See also* Interracial sex
Interracial marriage: in Alabama, 14; in Florida, 14; in Georgia, 14; and the law, 11, 14, 18–20, 22, 54; in Louisiana, 11; in Maryland, 11; in Mississippi, 14; in North Carolina, 14; in South Carolina, 14; in Tennessee, 14; in Texas, 14; in Virginia, 11
Interracial mixing, as cause for divorce, 54
Interracial sex: attitudes toward, 22, 69; birth of mixed-race children, 4, 14, 20–21, 23–25, 99, 105, 108–9, 112, 119; as cause for divorce, 17–19, 21, 23–28, 62, 65, 77; as criminal offense, 11; criminal penalties of for white men, 22; and the law, 26, 69; in Maryland, 9, 54; mixed-race ancestor as cause for divorce, 52. *See also* Adultery; Concubinage; Interracial cohabitation; Sexual relations, of white men; Sexual relations, of white women

Isaac (slave held by Elizabeth Hamilton), 83
Isadore (slave held by Richard Moore), 45

Jail, 11, 14, 32, 36–37, 51, 69, 102, 105–6
Jenny (slave held by William Duncan), 59
Jeter, Augusta, 50
Jim (slave held by Lydia Rawdon), 57
John (slave held by Richard Moore), 45
Johnson, Sarah, 46
Jones, Marmaduke, 23
Josh (slave held by Lydia Rawdon), 57
Julia (slave held by Richard Moore), 45

Kent, James, 69
King, Austin A., 59
Kornegay, Margaret, 66

Lacy, Dorcas, 55
Laspeyre, Bernard, 1, 16
Laspeyre, Harriet, xiii, 1, 16
Laspeyre, William H., 16
Last will and testament of husbands, as conveyance of property to wives, 80–81, 84, 96
Laws, and divorce: 66; in Alabama, 9, 11, 118; in Arkansas, 9, 11; in colonial America, 2–4, 11, 20; in Connecticut, 2; in Delaware, 5, 8; in District of Columbia, 11; expansion of grounds for divorce through laws, 11, 33, 56, 62, 115; in Florida, 9; in Georgia, 5, 7, 9; in Kentucky, 6; in Louisiana, 7–9, 14, 118; in Maryland, 4–5, 9; in Massachusetts, 2; in Missouri, 9, 58, 79; in North Carolina, 5–9; in South Carolina, 4, 11, 46, 118; in Tennessee, 5–7, 9, 118; in Texas, 7, 9; in Virginia, 3–7, 9
Laws, and prohibition of alcohol: in Arkansas, 40; in Mississippi, 40; in North Carolina, 40; in Tennessee, 40; in Virginia, 40

Lawyers: fashioning arguments in petitions, 15, 25, 28, 31, 47, 61–66, 70–71, 73, 78; responsibilities of, 62, 64; verdicts obtained for husbands, 68, 70–71, 117; verdicts obtained for wives, 62–63, 65–67, 73, 75–76, 115, 117

Lee, Stephen L., 105–6

Legislatures: in Alabama, 126; and divorce, 4–5, 9; and divorce acts, 5–6, 73–74, 76, 116, 121, 126; in Maryland, 37, 74–75, 126; problems of in judging divorces, 5–6; prohibited from granting divorces by constitutional amendments, 9; in Tennessee, 74–75; in Virginia, 74–75

Lenora (slave held by Richard Moore), 45

Lesesne, Joseph, 69

Letitia (slave held by Elizabeth Hamilton), 83

Lewis (slave held by Matilda Payne), 104

Lewis, Robert, 68

Littleton, Susan, 55

Lucien (slave held by Richard Moore), 45

Lucy (slave held by unnamed person), 105

Luke (slave held by Richard Moore), 45

Mackall, Jane, 104

Macnamarra, Margaret, 2

Margaret (slave held by Thomas Ransom), 98

Maria (slave held by Matilda Payne), 104

Maria (slave held by unnamed person), 109

Marital community property: petition for separation of, 17, 31, 33; right to, 117; separation of, 8–9, 82

Marriage: attitudes toward, ix, 77; legal entity of wife, x, xii, 4, 66, 82, 87; to preserve aristocracy, 81; prevalence of, ix; to procure property from wife, 81, 94

Marriage contracts, 4, 81, 83–84, 86–88, 92, 98. *See also* Prenuptial agreements

Married men's property: placed in trust due to insanity, 33, 36, 38, 56; protected from sale due to insanity, 36

Married women's property: in Arkansas, 14; confiscated by husband's creditors, 88; constraints on, xiii; in Delaware, 83; in Florida, 14; in Georgia, 83; inherited property, 68, 80, 84, 94, 96, 103, 117; joint property with husband, 84; and the law, 14–15, 61, 86, 88, 115; in Louisiana, 14, 82–83; in Mississippi, 14, 83; in Missouri, 58; in North Carolina, 83; owned before marriage, 14, 58, 84–85, 89, 103; protection of, 1, 5, 14–15, 45, 46; protection of from husband's creditors, 14, 88, 117; as separate property, 83–84; separate trust estates, 81, 84, 86–88, 94, 96, 103, 117; sole and separate designation, 15, 86–88, 92, 103, 117; in South Carolina, 83; in Tennessee, 84; in Texas, 82; in Virginia, 3–4, 83. *See also* Dower; *Feme sole*; Women, married

Mattison, Leroy, 51

McClure, Rebecca, 101

McClure, William, 100–101

McPherson, William, 34 (ill.)

Medley, Isaac, 50

Men, white: sense of honor of, 88, 96; sense of honor and manhood of, x, 23–26, 28, 53, 77; patriarchal role of, x, 52, 93

Mental illness. *See* Insanity

Miller, Mary, 84

Miller, Rachel, 94

Milly (slave held by unnamed owner), 85

Moore, Mary, 45
Moore, Richard, 45
Morgan, Eleanor, 41
Mourning (slave held by Elizabeth Hamilton), 83
Mulattoes, 11, 17, 19–21, 23–24, 54, 105–6, 109, 111
Murder, 32

Nance (slave held by Lydia Rawdon), 57
Next friend: xiii, 4, 6, 17, 66–67, 72, 82, 84, 87, 115; female, 72
Non compos mentis. *See* Insanity

Overbay, Elizabeth, 55

Paraphernal property. *See* Married women's property
Payne, Matilda, 104
Peter (slave held by unnamed owner), 25
Peters, John, 87
Petitions for divorce: as historical records, xv, 122; influence of on existing laws, 33–34; as narratives of domestic violence, 46–48, 50, 115; as narratives of household dissolution, 15–16, 18, 42, 115–16, 119–21
Phillips, Isaiah, 67
Polly (slave held by Braddock Richmond), 62
Pope, Tabitha, 69
Population migration, 17, 43–44, 54, 116
Poston, Melinda, 64
Premarital sex, and divorce law, 9–10
Prenuptial agreements, 1, 4, 81, 83, 86–89, 92, 94, 103, 117; in wealthy families, 87. *See also* Marriage contracts
Prochein ami. *See* Next friend
Profligacy: as cause for divorce, 41, 46, 65, 85; and divorce law, 33

Prostitution: white women with white men, 26; white women with black men, 25–27. *See also* Sexual relations, of white women
Puckett, Elizabeth, 26
Puckett, James, 26
Punishment, of female slaves: for assault, 102; for insubordination, 17, 108; for resisting sexual advances, 22; for running away, 105; for siding with mistress, 101. *See also* Whipping
Punishment, of male slaves: for having sexual relations with white women, 22; for protecting white women, 106; for running away, 105
Pyles, Abner, 101
Pyles, Frances, 101

Ransom, Eliza Taylor, xiii, 98–99, 108, 114
Ransom, Thomas S., 98–99, 114
Rape, 21–22
Rawdon, Isaac, 32–33, 56
Rawdon, John, 32–33
Rawdon, Lydia, xiii, 32–33, 34 (ill.) 39, 56–57
Reed, John, 58–59, 79
Reid, Louisiana, 81, 92, 96–97. *See also* Banks, Louisiana
Reid, Thomas McDaniel, 81, 96
Religion: as related to alcohol, 39–40; as related to bigamy, 54; as related to divorce, ix, 2; as related to domestic violence, 49, 51; as related to insanity, 32, 37–38; religious opposition to divorce, 5
Richmond (slave held by unnamed owner), 105
Richmond, Bradford, 62
Richmond, Winnefrid, 62
Roane, Evelina, 49 (ill.)
Robinson, William D., 21
Rose (slave held by Jane Mackall), 104

Rose, Nancy, 55
Rowe, Thomas, 35

Sally (slave held by Thomas Ransom), 98–99, 108, 114
Sally (slave held by unnamed owner), 105
Scott, David, 62
Separation of bed and board: and the law, 2–3, 6–8, 11; petitioned for, 1–2, 75, 105. *See also* Divorce
Sexual relations, of white men: attempted incest, 42; homosexuality, 54; impotence, 23, 52–53; incest, 52–53; within marriage, 19; with neighbors' slaves, 21, 27; with own slaves, xiii, 1, 17–21, 27–28, 43, 62–63, 98, 108–9, 112, 113, 116, 119; with slave mistresses, 19–20, 110; with white women outside marriage, xiii, 18–19, 27–28, 43, 106, 116. *See also* Adultery; Concubinage; Impotence; Interracial sex; Sexual relations, of white women
Sexual relations, of white women: with black men, 18, 23–25, 101, 105, 116; with white men outside marriage, 26, 101, 106. *See also* Adultery; Interracial sex; Prostitution; Sexual relations, of white men
Shouse, Henry, 24
Silvia (slave held by unnamed owner), 109
Simon (slave held by Matilda Payne), 104
Slaves: enlisted to assist owner, 101; as insubordinate to white women, 112; and intervention to protect white women, 107; monetary value of, 36, 84, 89–91, 97, 103, 123; reactions of to divorcing families, 100, 121; runaways, 105–6; testimony of in court inadmissible, 62; viewed as property, xiii, 20–22, 90, 113, 116–17, 120; viewed in economic terms, 57, 89–91, 113, 123; as witnesses to marital discord, 99, 101–2. *See also* Children, slave; Women, black
Smith, John, 20
Smith, Penelope, 40
Smith, Sarah, 112
Stephen (slave held by Elizabeth Hamilton), 83
Sterrett, Alphonso A., 67
Story, Joseph, 61
Summers, Nancy, 19
Sumter, Natalie DeLage, 92
Susan (slave held by James E. Black), 17

Taff (slave once held by William McClure), 101
Tatham, Ayres, 24
Taylor, Charles, 114
Taylor, Nancy, 35
Thomas (slave held by Martha Huskey), 106
Thomas, Ella Gertrude Clanton, 119
Tinges, Elizabeth, 54
Tinges, William, 54
Tom (slave held by Matilda Payne), 104
Tudor, Winni, 19
Turner (slave held by Matilda Payne), 104

Underage marriage partners, and divorce law, 3, 11

Vause, Margaret, 87
Violence: as accepted culture of discipline, 33, 38–39, 46, 52, 63, 70; and threat of bodily harm to slaves, 38. *See also* Abuse

Watkins, William, 94
Watson, Henry, 43
Watts, David, 7 (ill.)
Watts, Elizabeth [Betsy], 7 (ill.)

Index | 235

West, Ann, 41
Whipping: of slaves, 17, 33, 98, 106, 108, 114; of wives, 48–52, 98, 107, 110; of wife by slave, 112. *See also* Punishment, of female slaves
Whitehead, James, 113
Widows: 80, 92–94; attitudes toward, 92–93. *See also* Dower
Wilkinson, Elizabeth, 49–50
Winn, Alexander, 101
Womack, Sarah, 50
Women, black: and consequences of siding with mistresses in domestic conflicts, 101–2; contempt of for white women, 110; as de facto heads of household, 108–11, 113, 113 (ill.), 116–17; as de facto wives, 1, 20, 108, 111; insubordination of to white women, 17, 55, 111–13; purchased for sexual pleasure, 20; resistance of to sexual advances, 21–22; as seducers of white men, 109. *See also* Slaves
Women, married: defrauded of property by husband, 81, 87; petition to retain property, 81, 83–85, 88, 96; petition to prevent sale of property, 59, 85, 87, 96; as property owners, 82, 85–86. *See also* Married women's property
Women, white: compare their plight to that of slaves, 48, 50, 52; intervene to protect female slave, 98, 104, 108; as property owners, xii–xiii, 16, 31, 57, 97
Word, Judith, 41
Wright, B. D., 69

www.ingramcontent.com/pod-product-compliance
Lightning Source LLC
Chambersburg PA
CBHW020648230426
43665CB00008B/348